D1231592

Poetic Transformations

HARVARD EAST ASIAN MONOGRAPHS 419

Poetic Transformations

Eighteenth-Century Cultural Projects
on the Mekong Plains

Claudine Ang

Published by the Harvard University Asia Center
Distributed by Harvard University Press
Cambridge (Massachusetts) and London 2019

The Harvard University Asia Center publishes a monograph series and, in coordination with the Fairbank Center for Chinese Studies, the Korea Institute, the Reischauer Institute of Japanese Studies, and other facilities and institutes, administers research projects designed to further scholarly understanding of China, Japan, Vietnam, Korea, and other Asian countries. The Center also sponsors projects addressing multidisciplinary and regional issues in Asia.

Library of Congress Cataloging-in-Publication Data

Names: Ang, Claudine, 1976– author.
Title: Poetic transformations : eighteenth-century cultural projects on the Mekong plains / Claudine Ang.
Other titles: Harvard East Asian monographs ; 419.
Description: Cambridge, Massachusetts : Published by the Harvard University Asia Center, 2019. | Series: Harvard East Asian monographs ; 419 | Based on the author's thesis, issued under the title: Statecraft on the margins : drama, poetry, and the civilizing mission in eighteenth-century southern Vietnam (Ph. D.—Cornell University, 2012). | Includes bibliographical references and index.
Identifiers: LCCN 2018034045 | ISBN 9780674237230 (hardcover : alk. paper)
Subjects: LCSH: Politics and literature—Mekong River Watershed—History—18th century. | Nguyễn Cư Trinh, 1716–1767. | Mạc, Thiên Tích, 1706–1780. | Mekong River Watershed—History—18th century.
Classification: LCC DS556.7 .A54 2019 | DDC 959.7/802—dc23 LC record available at https://lccn.loc.gov/2018034045

Index by Alex Trotter

Printed on acid-free paper

Last figure below indicates year of this printing
28 27 26 25 24 23 22 21 20 19

For Taran

Contents

Maps and Figures

Maps

Acknowledgments

In the course of completing this book, I benefited greatly from the encouragement of family, friends, and teachers, and I am grateful for the opportunity to acknowledge them here. Keith Taylor supported my exploration into the world of frontier literature and offered me his intellectual guidance and wisdom throughout my years in graduate school and beyond; this project would not have been possible without him. Ding Xiang Warner, whose generosity knows no bounds, illuminated my path to understanding Chinese poetry and taught me to appreciate its interpretative depths, thereby igniting an enduring fascination in me. Sherman Cochran has been a source of inspiration with his thoughtful reflections on life and scholarship, and I cherish the ongoing series of lunches we share in the summer. I seek to emulate Eric Tagliacozzo's kindness and graciousness as I navigate the academic profession. I thank all of them for holding my scholarship to their high standards and encouraging me when I fell short.

I was fortunate to have met many people who offered me opportunities to present my work and contributed in important ways to this project in its various stages: Kathleen Baldanza, Alexander Cannon, Chang Yufen, Haydon Cherry, Jack Chia, Nola Cooke, Scott Cook, Pamela Corey, Kenneth Dean, Olga Dror, Prasenjit Duara, Daena Funahashi, Tim Gorman, Erik Harms, Jessica Hanser, Derek Heng, T. J. Hinrichs, Naoko Iioka, Andrew Johnson, Liam Kelley, Ada Kuskowski, Peter Lavelle, Alvin Lim, Samson Lim, Cathay Liu, Liu Oi-Yan, Tamara Loos, Lauren Meeker, Michael Montesano, Marie Muschalek, Nguyen Thi Tu Linh,

Nguyen To Lan, Lorraine Paterson, Rajeev Patke, Tom Patton, Trais Pearson, John Duong Phan, Joe Pittayaporn, Bruce Rusk, Mira Seo, Ivan Small, Althea Tan, Natalie Tan, Tan Tai Yong, Risa Toha, Jason Hoai Tran, Nhung Tuyet Tran, Nu-Anh Tran, Eileen Vo, Geoff Wade, and Nurfadzilah Yahaya. I am especially grateful to Andrew Hardy and Hue Tam Ho Tai for their comments on chapters of my book.

This book was published with the assistance of a Yale-NUS College subvention grant. The research for this project was made possible through the financial support of Yale-NUS College, Cornell University's History Department, Southeast Asia Program, East Asia Program, Graduate School, the Judith Reppy Institute of Peace and Conflict Studies, and the Mario Einaudi Center for International Studies. I would like to acknowledge the support of Robert Graham and the editorial team of Harvard University Asia Center Publications and offer my thanks to the two anonymous reviewers of my manuscript for their thoughtful comments. Chapter 4 appeared previously in *T'oung Pao* 104 (2018): 626–71, ©2018 Koninklijke Brill NV, Leiden, The Netherlands; it has benefitted from the insightful comments of the journal editors.

Finally, I thank my parents, my sisters, and my niece for their belief in the importance of my work, and my husband, who read and commented on every chapter, for his incisive insights and unfailing support.

Note on Translation

Bringing a concept or an idea from one language to another seems akin to shining a weak candlelight to illuminate an object immersed in the dark, an act that sometimes successfully convinces the object to give up its secrets and reveal its form but at other times renders it only partially visible to the viewer. Even when the translator succeeds in making the object perceptible, the surrounding context is still lost to the darkness, for the flickering candlelight is never sufficient to fully illuminate the original contextual world. But this translator doggedly presses on. The limits of translation are particularly acute when I am faced with the task of translating into English words that are used in the plural senses of their meaning in the original Vietnamese or Chinese text. Unable to find a single word to capture the layers of meanings, I am left with the unsatisfying task of choosing one of several and identifying the others in a note. In such cases, I have chosen to translate, in the main body of the text, the one of most immediate relevance and consigned the others to the notes. I imagine this act of relegation of alternative meanings to the notes as a kind of whisper in a friend's ear, behind a cupped hand for discretion, to bring her up to date with an inside joke. Moreover, the *Sãi Vãi* and the *Ten Songs of Hà Tiên* are rich in historical and literary allusions. Because these texts are not embedded in established commentarial traditions, and because the work of translation is intimately intertwined with the act of interpretation, I have devoted my energies to elucidating the origins of these references, knowledge about which determines interpretive strategies and translation choices. I offer explanatory notes on the historical and literary allusions found in the *Sãi Vãi* and the *Ten Songs of Hà Tiên*, citing the original sources of the references and drawing readers' attention to English translations where they are available. Whether they pertain to the landscape poems or the satirical play, these little notes, which link the present-day reader to the classical text from which the allusion derives, represent lonely musings that attest to the separation of the contemporary reader from the riches of the classical world.

The texts that form the basis of my analysis in this book are composed in the vernacular Vietnamese demotic script, *chữ Nôm*, and in classical Chinese. In undertaking to transliterate names and places from the character to a romanized script, I had several options to choose from, one of which was to transliterate all terms that appear in the vernacular Vietnamese and the classical Chinese texts into *quốc ngữ* and Pinyin, respectively. The advantage of such a transliteration practice is that it distinguishes, in the translation, the scripts in which the works were originally composed. In this way, references to classical and historical figures in the *Sãi Vãi* would be transliterated into *quốc ngữ*, and those appearing in Nguyễn Cư Trinh's letters to Mạc Thiên Tứ, as well as those in Mạc Thiên Tứ's and Nguyễn Cư Trinh's landscape poems, would be transliterated using Pinyin. I stumbled, however, when it came to translating the Vietnamese chronicles, for although they were composed in classical Chinese, the Vietnamese personal and place names would have been rendered unrecognizable had I transliterated them using Pinyin. Furthermore, this transliteration practice, though consistent with the script of the works' original composition, creates a false impression that the classical Chinese texts are foreign to the Vietnamese literary heritage.

I eventually decided to transliterate the terms in the *Sãi Vãi* and the Vietnamese chronicles using *quốc ngữ*. In the bilingual appendix, place names and historical figures appear only in Vietnamese; however, when quoting lines of the *Sãi Vãi* in the chapters of the book, I provide Pinyin transliterations in parentheses so that the reader who is unfamiliar with the Vietnamese names does not have to constantly refer to the notes to follow along. Because Mạc Thiên Tứ's poems about Hà Tiên were intended for a southern Chinese and diasporic Chinese audience, I adopted Pinyin transliterations where necessary in my translations of the poems; it should be noted, however, that Mạc Thiên Tứ's poems were probably read aloud in Cantonese, rather than Mandarin, from which the Pinyin pronunciation derives. I transliterated the terms in Nguyễn Cư Trinh's landscape poems using Pinyin, because his poetic contributions were intended for the same literary project, the *Ten Songs of Hà Tiên*, to which poets from the southern Chinese provinces of Guangdong and Fujian contributed. Doing so allowed me to maintain a level of consistency within the whole project. For simplicity's sake, I similarly chose to transliterate the terms in Nguyễn Cư Trinh's letters to Mạc Thiên Tứ using Pinyin.

In my discussion of the various texts, I typically refer to historical figures and classical references using Pinyin, for they are more easily recognizable in this form to a greater number of readers. Thus, for example, the sage-kings are identified as Yao and Shun instead of Nghiêu and Thuấn, and the cruel founder of the Qin dynasty is Qin Shihuang instead of Tần Thủy Hoàng. At the first mention of a historical figure or a translated term, *quốc ngữ* and/or Pinyin romanizations are provided in parentheses, marked by "v" and "p," respectively. These are followed by the Chinese characters and, where appropriate, an English translation.

A note on specific terms: throughout my translation of the *Sãi Vãi*, I used the word *cultivate* in its various forms (*cultivating, cultivation*) to render into English the word *tu* (p: *xiu* 修). I do this even when other words, such as *practice*, might give the passage more fluidity in translation, so as to keep constant a word that is used repeatedly in the original text. I use "way" or "Way" to translate the word *đạo* (p: *dao* 道), which is ubiquitous throughout the text. When referring to it as a "way," I mean it in the sense of a path; occasionally, when it signifies a manner of doing something, I translate it using the word *technique*. In those cases where it seems to be referring to the religious Way, I capitalize it. Sometimes, it refers to both at the same time; in these instances, I do not capitalize it.

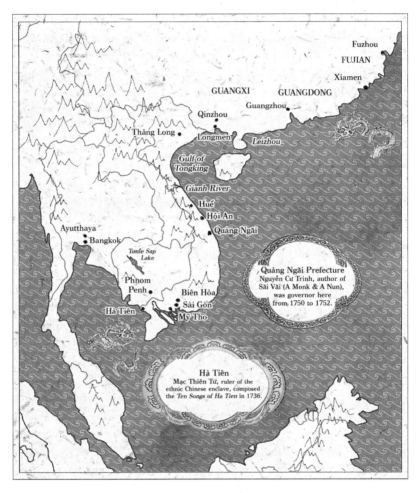

MAP I: Quảng Ngãi and Hà Tiên, home of Nguyễn Cư Trinh's and Mạc Thiên Tứ's literary projects, respectively. Illustrated by Natalie Christian Tan, 2018.

INTRODUCTION

Cultural Projects on the Southern Vietnamese Frontier

In the late seventeenth century, an unprecedented series of migrations toward the Mekong delta led to a reconfiguration of the power dynamics between the existing polities in the region. Here the path of a territorially expanding Vietnamese state overlapped with a network of diasporic Chinese Ming loyalists who had left the Chinese mainland, sailed the seas, and settled on the Mekong delta. Arriving primarily in two waves, the Ming loyalists formed two distinct settlements, one on the western part of the delta and the other on the east. At this historical juncture, the Vietnamese kingdom was divided into two polities. Home to the traditional seat of Vietnamese power and situated close to the Chinese mainland, the northern realm, Đàng Ngoài, was attuned to the politics of its neighbor and attentive to the interests of the newly established Qing dynasty; conversely, the southern realm, Đàng Trong, had its capital in Phú Xuân (present-day Huế) and its political sights set on the south, where it was one of several important players in the regional politics of the Mekong delta and the Gulf of Siam. When the Ming loyalist migrants arrived in the late seventeenth century, it was with the southern Vietnamese realm that they principally engaged.

Perhaps they perceived a closer cultural affinity, or perhaps they carefully evaluated the various players' relative political strengths; whatever the case, both groups of Ming loyalists, after settling down in their respective territories on the Mekong delta, came to ally themselves with the southern Vietnamese instead of the Khmer or the Siamese. The settlers' physical presence in key regions of the delta gave the Nguyễn lords of the southern Vietnamese state the support that they needed to lay claims on the delta lands. In the mid-eighteenth century, the Nguyễn lords began to aggressively extend their domain's borders southward. However, the territories to which the southern Vietnamese and the Ming loyalists migrated were far from unclaimed, let alone uninhabited. The lands of the Mekong delta constituted the eastern edge of the Cambodian kingdom, and the Khmer kings did not take Vietnamese designs on their borders lightly. The Siamese of the Kingdom of Ayutthaya also joined in the fray and fought to assert political influence over the lucrative ports in the delta region. The antagonisms between these different peoples and polities continued and intensified in the course of the eighteenth century.

During this time of upheaval and displacement, the Mekong plains witnessed the ascent of two shrewd political actors who initiated cultural projects that decisively shaped the subsequent development of the region. Well suited to frontier living, these men were able military leaders with successful records of both winning battles and avoiding them to protect the fragile peace of the frontier world. More distinctive, perhaps, was the fact that they were also highly educated men of letters. As scholars and officials living on the frontier, they were not content with carrying out the work of annexing territories, building settlements, and relocating soldiers and their families on the new lands. On top of the physical work of establishing settlements and encouraging immigration, they sought to fully inhabit the worlds in which they lived by infusing the frontier lands with culture and literature. To this end, they composed drama and poetry in their quest to elevate the civilizational status of the frontier lands and its inhabitants. These two men's lives and their literary works provide us with insight into eighteenth-century cultural projects on the southern Vietnamese frontier. This book explores the intertwining lives and works of Nguyễn Cư Trinh (p: Ruan Juzhen 阮居貞, 1716–67) and Mạc Thiên Tứ (p: Mo Tianci 鄭天賜, 1710–80)[1] and investigates their undertakings in Quảng Ngãi and Hà Tiên (see map 1).[2] Through a careful engagement

---

1.   See Gaspardone, "Un chinois des mers du sud," 384, for the problems associated with determining Mạc Thiên Tứ's birth year.

2.   The region under study in this book extends from the territory south of Huế, the south-central region of what is now Vietnam, to the western extremities of the Mekong delta, the area that separates Cambodia and Vietnam today. In the eighteenth century, the region constituted the frontier of the southern Vietnamese kingdom, Đàng Trong.

with and analysis of their literary productions, it uncovers how these men intellectually and culturally appropriated and transformed the new lands. For them, literature was no mere ornament, no charming supplement to adorn the high culture of the region; it was crucial to their project of bringing the lands out of the realm of chaos and into the domain of civility. Disrupting the opposition between high and low culture, their writings simultaneously aimed to transform the unlettered frontier inhabitants' moral sensibility and sought to enter into the cultivated discourse of classical literature. An exploration of the political dimensions of their literary endeavors deepens our understanding of cultural projects pursued on the southern Vietnamese frontier in the eighteenth century; beyond that, it discloses how different literary genres reconfigure social relations and geographical space.

In the case of Nguyễn Cư Trinh, a high-ranking official of the southern Vietnamese state, we see how his employment of satirical drama composed in the Vietnamese vernacular inculcated in the Việt migrants a sense of their civilizational distinctiveness from the local communities and thereby strengthened the porous borders of the expanding Vietnamese state. As for Mạc Thiên Tứ, the son of a Ming loyalist migrant to the Mekong delta, he took the scenic sites of his domain as the subject of ten landscape poems written in the Chinese script, which he then distributed via the coastal trading network to thirty-one other poets scattered along the Vietnamese and southern Chinese coast; these poets composed matching poems and returned them with the next sailing season. In undertaking this literary endeavor, Mạc Thiên Tứ brought his domain into civilized discourse and circumscribed his realm as a political haven for the Chinese diaspora.

My inquiry draws out the complexities of these men's cultural projects through a close reading of four major literary works—Nguyễn Cư Trinh's vernacular Vietnamese play, the *Sãi Vãi* (A Monk and a Nun), which was composed in Quảng Ngãi in 1750; Mạc Thiên Tứ's ten-poem suite dedicated to the landscape of Hà Tiên, written in 1736 and published the following year; a ten-poem suite of responses to Mạc Thiên Tứ's original poems of Hà Tiên, which Nguyễn Cư Trinh composed sometime between 1754 and 1765; and two letters that Nguyễn Cư Trinh sent to Mạc Thiên Tứ, in which he expounded on issues related to frontier governance and the political uses of literature. As their writings attest, the cultural projects they carried out diverged in method, scope, and intent. A defining factor in the eventual shape of the two projects, one that helps account for some of the differences between them, was the fact that the two men came to inhabit the southern regions of Vietnam following two divergent paths of migration, namely, contiguous territorial expansion and noncontiguous diasporic settlement.[3]

In the eighteenth century, Vietnamese territorial expansion into the southern regions was fueled by the efforts of the Nguyễn family, who had ruled the southern Vietnamese polity of Đàng Trong since the mid-sixteenth century. Prior to this, the Nguyễn had been an important family in the political scene of Đại Việt, the Vietnamese kingdom that had its capital in Thăng Long (present-day Hà Nội). They were initially allied with another important family, the Trịnh, and together sought to defend the Lê dynasty from the threat of usurpation by the Mạc 莫 clan.[4] In 1545, the Nguyễn patriarch, Nguyễn Kim (p: Ruan Gan 阮淦, 1476–1545), was assassinated, and Trịnh Kiểm (p: Zheng Jian 鄭檢, 1503–70) took effective control of Đại Việt. For reasons that are recorded differently in the Trịnh and the Nguyễn historical records, Nguyễn Kim's son, Nguyễn Hoàng (p: Ruan Huang 阮潢, 1525–1613), moved south to Thuận Hoá with his followers in 1558.[5] In 1620, the Nguyễn stopped sending taxes

3.   In his study of twentieth-century Chinese migration, Adam McKeown argues for the importance of placing migration in global perspective to adequately understand and articulate the local experiences of migrants. See McKeown, *Chinese Migrant Networks*, particularly his first chapter, "Chinese Migration in Global Perspective." I am similarly attentive to the divergent global (in this case more accurately called "regional") processes that led to the migration of Việt and Chinese peoples to the Mekong delta, which I believe influenced their interactions with the delta lands and its inhabitants.

4.   The Mạc 莫 clan usurped the Lê throne in 1527. Mạc Thiên Tứ, whose literary works are studied here, is unrelated to them.

5.   Keith Taylor has studied two narratives of Nguyễn Hoàng's departure to Thuận Hoá, one from the *Đại Việt Sử Ký Toàn Thư* (p: *Da Yue shiji quanshu* 大越史記全書), which he calls the Northern Annal, and the other from the *Đại Nam Thực Lục* (p: *Da Nan shilu* 大南定錄), which he calls the Southern Annal. He notes that the former records Nguyễn Hoàng's departure for the south as a simple administrative affair—he was sent there by the Trịnh to ensure that the southern provinces did not fall into the hands of the Mạc clan. The latter source, however, accords greater significance to Nguyễn Hoàng's departure from the north and casts it as a momentuous event that marks or at least foreshadows a break from the north and the begining of an administratively separate Vietnamese domain. See Taylor, "Nguyễn Hoàng."

to the north, thus signaling their separatist intentions; unsurprisingly, this act ushered in a period of wars and skirmishes along the border of the Vietnamese polities. By the time of the mid-seventeenth century, however, Nguyễn Phúc Tần (p: Ruan Fubin 阮福瀕, r. 1648–87), the fourth Nguyễn lord of Đàng Trong, was directing his expansionist energies toward the southern part of his kingdom. Although he was vigilant in protecting his northern border and took care to build walls and fortifications to keep the Trịnh armies out of Đàng Trong, Nguyễn Phúc Tần also kept a keen eye on developments in the southern regions. Under his rule 3,000 Chinese migrants, together with their families, came to be settled in the Gia Định area in 1682; the chronicles record that one of his reasons for settling the migrants in the southernmost provinces was to ensure that the Nguyễn would be better able to wrest the area away from Cambodian control.[6] By the mid-eighteenth century, the Nguyễn family claimed nominal control over most of the Mekong delta. Nguyễn Cư Trinh's presence on the southern Vietnamese frontier in the eighteenth century was a result of Đàng Trong's contiguous territorial expansion toward the south and his cultural project in Quảng Ngãi reflected his political connection with the southern Vietnamese center of power in Phú Xuân.[7]

A different path of migration led the Mạc 鄚 family to settle on the Mekong plains.[8] In the seventeenth century, the dynastic transition from the Ming to the Qing resulted in the dispersal of many Chinese who continued to profess loyalty to the fallen dynasty. Following trading routes that were familiar to them, these Chinese migrants fled to various East

6. *Đại Nam Thực Lục Tiền Biên* [p: *Da Nan shilu qianbian* 大南寔錄前編; Veritable Records of the Great South, Premier Period], 5.22–23. I discuss the significance of this resettlement of Chinese migrants further in chapter 4. The *Đại Nam Thực Lục* dates this event to 1679, but the scholarly consensus is that the event occurred in 1682 instead. See, for example, Nola Cooke, "Later-Seventeenth-Century Cham-Viet Interactions," 13–52; Niu Junkai and Li Qingxin, "Chinese 'Political Pirates'," 139; and Li Tana, "Epidemics, Trade, and Local Worship," 198. Chen Jinghe proposes that Yang's troops came in two groups in 1682 and 1683. See Chen Jinghe, "Qingchu Zheng Chenggong canbu," part 1, 433–59.

7. For a detailed account of this period of Vietnamese history, see Taylor, *A History of the Vietnamese*, chaps. 5–7.

8. The Mạc family in Hà Tiên changed their name from 莫 to 鄚, perhaps in an attempt to better differentiate themselves from the Mạc clan that usurped the Lê throne in sixteenth-century Đại Việt.

and Southeast Asian kingdoms, including Japan, Korea, Siam, Vietnam, Java, and the Philippines.[9] Unlike the case of the Vietnamese expansion to the south, seventeenth-century Chinese migration to the region reflected the pattern of noncontiguous diasporic settlement, in which the Chinese settlers found themselves to be without the support of a strong imperial center. The migrants adapted to the changed conditions in different ways. While some joined the ranks of local society, others maintained independent enclaves for as long as possible. The Chinese settlement at Hà Tiên is an example of an independent enclave. Even though its leader and founder, Mạc Cửu (p: Mo Jiu 鄚玖, d. 1735), initially styled himself as an *okña*, an official of Cambodia, when he arrived in 1671 and later acknowledged Vietnamese suzerainty in 1708, he ran Hà Tiên autonomously until his death in 1735. His son, Mạc Thiên Tứ, continued his legacy thereafter. Other Chinese migrants and their descendants came to play integral roles in the politics of the countries in which they settled. Taksin (1734–82), a son of a Chinese migrant and a local Siamese woman, famously wrested control of the Siamese kingdom in 1767. His ambition to extend the Siamese empire eastward toward Cambodia and Vietnam was a defining factor in the political tumult of the Mekong region in the 1770s. These Chinese migrants played prominent roles in the politics of the Southeast Asian region in the mid-eighteenth century.[10]

Lives of Two Political Actors

To apprehend the nature of the two cultural projects in eighteenth-century Đàng Trong and the personal and political relationships that connected their two proponents, an examination of the literary works by Nguyễn

9.   See Kuhn, *Chinese among Others*, for a systematic account of Chinese migration to Southeast Asia from the fifteenth century to the present. See also Salmon, *Ming Loyalists in Southeast Asia*, for a study of the migratory waves of Ming loyalists into Southeast Asia in the immediate aftermath of the demise of the Ming.

10.   For more information about overseas Chinese politics in the Mekong region in the eighteenth century, see Chen Jinghe, "Kasen Tei shi no bungaku katsudō," 149–54; see also Chen Jinghe, "Mac Thien Tu and Phrayataksin"; see also Sakurai, "Eighteenth-Century Chinese Pioneers," 39–46.

Cư Trinh and Mạc Thiên Tứ proves indispensable. My interpretation foregrounds the hopes, ideals, and ambitions of the frontier officials as they were expressed in their often deeply personal compositions. It builds on scholars' rich accounts of diverse aspects of southern Vietnamese society in the seventeenth and eighteenth centuries; these accounts have drawn on a wide range of sources such as Vietnamese chronicles and imperial biographies, village and family historical records, privately written histories, land tenure and other economic records, missionary letters, and foreign traveler reports.[11] The addition of a study of frontier literary texts to this body of scholarship contributes to our understanding of the intellectual lives and the lived experiences in the dynamic frontier world. The literary works give us a glimpse into the cultural and political connections that existed between the southern Vietnamese coastal cities and other communities of the coastal trading world.[12] Before we enter into an analysis of the literary works, however, it is necessary to become acquainted with the lives of these political actors and the world they inhabited. As we will see, the meaning and the significance of their compositions cannot be separated from their political activities and their role in the transformation of the frontier.

NGUYỄN CƯ TRINH IN QUẢNG NGÃI

Nguyễn Cư Trinh was born in 1716 to a prominent family from the southern Vietnamese kingdom. His family, originally from Thiên Lộc in Nghệ An, was among the first to move to Thuận Hóa in the sixteenth century, during which time they fought alongside the Nguyễn family against the

---

11. See, for example, the works of Li Tana, *Nguyễn Cochinchina*; Taylor, "Nguyễn Hoàng" and "Surface Orientations"; Choi Byung Wook, *Southern Vietnam under the Reign of Minh Mạng*; Dutton, *The Tây Sơn Uprising*; and Cooke, "Regionalism and the Nature of Nguyen Rule" and "Strange Brew."

12. There has been a push to study water bodies and their regional ports as integrated social and economic worlds. See, for example, the essays in the two collections: Cooke and Li (eds.), *Water Frontier*, and Cooke, Li, and Anderson (eds.), *The Tongking Gulf through History*. In addition, see the older but still very relevant work by Dian H. Murray, *Pirates of the South China Coast*.

Mạc usurpers.[13] By the time that Nguyễn Cư Trinh's father, Nguyễn
Đăng Đệ (p: Ruan Dengdi 阮登第, 1669–1727), was born, the family had
moved further southward and settled in An Hòa village in Hương Trà,
which was located near Phú Xuân, the Nguyễn family's capital city.
Nguyễn Cư Trinh belonged to the eighth generation to have settled in
Đàng Trong. As is to be expected of a family that tied its personal for-
tunes so closely to the successes of the emerging southern Vietnamese
polity, many of its male members actively participated in Đàng Trong's
administrative governance.[14] Nguyễn Đăng Đệ was in charge of all the
prefectures in Quảng Nam and at the height of his career was appointed
to the elevated position of Principal Secretary of the Garrisons (v: *chính
doanh ký lục*, p: *zhengying jilu* 正營記錄).[15] Nguyễn Cư Trinh's own career
trajectory was not so different from his father's. He was first appointed
to office in 1740 as a county chief, and from there he moved swiftly up the
bureaucratic ladder until he was eventually made controller of all the
regions the Nguyễn claimed in the Mekong delta. So close was Nguyễn
Cư Trinh to the Nguyễn lord, Nguyễn Phúc Khoát (p: Ruan Fukuo 阮福濶,
r. 1738–65), that his biography records that when the lord declared the
Nguyễn family a ruling house in 1744, credit for the elegance of the de-
cree's wording was ascribed to Nguyễn Cư Trinh.[16]

In 1750, Nguyễn Cư Trinh was promoted to the position of Provin-
cial Governor (v: *tuần phủ*, p: *xunfu* 巡撫) of Quảng Ngãi. Quảng Ngãi
first appears in the Nguyễn dynasty imperial records in the entry for 1570
as Tư Ngãi, a small prefecture (v: *phủ*, p: *fu* 府) subsumed under Quảng

13.   It is recorded in the biography of Nguyễn Đăng Đệ, Nguyễn Cư Trinh's
father, that the family traced their ancestry to a person named Trịnh Cam, an official
of the Lê dynasty, who had moved to Thuận Hóa in the sixteenth century to organize a
resistance movement against the Mạc. Nguyễn Đăng Đệ's biography can be found in
Đại Nam Liệt Truyện Tiền Biên [p: *Da Nan liezhuan qianbian* 大南列傳前編; Biographies of the Great South, Premier Period], 5.2–3.

14.   Five family members have individual entries in the *Đại Nam Liệt Truyện Tiền
Biên*: Nguyễn Cư Trinh, Nguyễn Đăng Đệ (Nguyễn Cư Trinh's father), Nguyễn Đăng
Thịnh (Nguyễn Cư Trinh's cousin), Nguyễn Đăng Tiến (Nguyễn Đăng Thịnh's
younger brother), and Nguyễn Đăng Cẩn (Nguyễn Cư Trinh's elder brother). Two of
Nguyễn Cư Trinh's sons, Nguyễn Cư Dật and Nguyễn Cư Tuấn, and his grandson
Nguyễn Cư Sĩ are mentioned as well.

15.   *Đại Nam Liệt Truyện Tiền Biên*, 5.3.

16.   *Đại Nam Liệt Truyện Tiền Biên*, 5.5.

Nam.[17] The prefecture grew quickly in size and significance, and in 1604 it underwent administrative restructuring and a name change to Quảng Ngãi.[18] Quảng Ngãi was well integrated into the Đàng Trong civil and military apparatus; it contributed soldiers to the Nguyễn army and supplied officials to support its bureaucracy. The record for 1632 indicates that the Nguyễn set up a drafting and selection station in Quảng Ngãi itself.[19] Quảng Ngãi was, moreover, well connected to the other prefectures of the southern Vietnamese state through its six harbors at Chu Ố, Sa Kỳ, Tiểu, Đại Nham, Mỹ Á, and Sa Hùynh.[20] In the early eighteenth century, Quảng Ngãi's boat owners played an indispensable role in the smooth functioning of the Nguyễn state as they supplied the labor for transporting rice from the southern territories on the Mekong delta to the northern province of Thuận Hóa, where the Nguyễn stationed the bulk of their army in defense against the Trịnh. As demands for rice grew in Thuận Hóa, boat owners found the Nguyễn system of conscription increasingly burdensome and less lucrative in comparison to the profits to be made in private business. In 1714, the Nguyễn monetized their economy and paid for the services they required in exchange for establishing a taxation system on private shipping.[21] Quảng Ngãi, which lay on the route along which rice was transported, began to receive payment for the human and horse labor used between the relay stations.[22] The region in which Quảng Ngãi was ensconced was home to both Việt and non-Việt settlements; in 1726, Nguyễn Cư Trinh's father conducted an inspection tour of all the prefectures in Quảng Nam to determine the number of "dependent settlements" (v: *thuộc*, p: *shu* 屬) there and bring them into Nguyễn administrative supervision.[23] He found that Quảng

17. Tư Ngãi itself comprised three counties: Bình Sơn, Mộ Hoa, and Nghiã Giang. Refer to *Đại Nam Thực Lục Tiền Biên*, 1.8.

18. *Đại Nam Thực Lục Tiền Biên*, 1.22.

19. *Đại Nam Thực Lục Tiền Biên*, 2.22–23.

20. The port in Chu Ố was classified as "medium-deep," while the others were classified as "shallow." See Li and Reid (eds.), *Southern Vietnam under the Nguyễn*, 51.

21. Monetization of the economy created disastrous fiscal problems for Đàng Trong in a few decades, since the supply of coins from China and Japan was shrinking. See Li Tana, *Nguyễn Cochinchina*, 94–98.

22. *Đại Nam Thực Lục Tiền Biên*, 8.19.

23. *Đại Nam Thực Lục Tiền Biên*, 9.4. "Dependent settlements" refer to non-Việt settlements.

Ngãi had four such non-Việt settlements, which was far fewer than the thirty-eight in another province, Phú Yên. Even so, it is possible that the Nguyễn decided that Quảng Ngãi needed additional administrative oversight, for in 1744, when Đàng Trong's expanding territory was reorganized into twelve garrisons, Quảng Ngãi, subsumed under the Quảng Nam garrison, was nonetheless assigned its own governor so the Nguyễn could better govern and control it.[24]

As it does today, in the eighteenth century, Quảng Ngãi comprised a fairly slim strip of land wedged between the coast and the mountains. It was home to a variety of indigenous peoples, most notably the Đá Vách (Stone Wall) people who inhabited the mountains (see map 2). The lowlanders and the uplanders in the mountainous terrain of Quảng Ngãi traded with each other, and they exchanged upland goods, such as precious woods, rattan, wax, honey, oxen, cinnamon, areca, and gold for lowland ones such as salt, fish sauce, dried fish, iron wares, and copper pots.[25] Because of the importance of upland–lowland trade in Đàng Trong, early Nguyễn policies toward the uplanders had been ones of peaceful coexistence.[26] From the late 1740s, however, possibly because of Nguyễn Phúc Khoát's lax policies, which did not punish Vietnamese officials who harassed the uplanders, the Đá Vách began to raid the lowland Vietnamese villages in Quảng Ngãi.[27] Quảng Ngãi occupied the narrow lands that strategically linked the northern and southern territories of Đàng Trong; consequently, it required a stable Việt population to maintain the security of the coastal area and the smooth integration of the polity. Compared to its surrounding areas, it was home to a fairly small Việt population, and it was losing some of its Việt inhabitants

24. *Đại Nam Thực Lục Tiền Biên*, 10.12. The only other prefecture with additional administration is Quy Nhơn, which suggests that they might have been the two prefectures with the most problems on the ground. Quy Nhơn was where the Tây Sơn uprising emerged.

25. Li Tana, *Nguyễn Cochinchina*, 122.

26. See Hickey, *Sons of the Mountains*, 144–89 for an account of pre-twentieth-century Vietnamese–highlander relations.

27. Li Tana suggests that the deteriorating fiscal situation in mid-eighteenth-century Đàng Trong might have affected the Nguyễn's ability to pay their officials. Vietnamese officials might have begun extracting revenues from the uplanders to make up for the shortfall, which could explain why the Nguyễn lord made no attempt to stop this practice.

MAP 2: Map of Quảng Ngãi showing the Đá Vách people and mountain range. From *Bản Quốc dư Đồ* 本國輿圖, ca. 1800.

to the mountains, where settlers could escape the extractive policies of the Nguyễn government in the mid-eighteenth century.[28] It was probably this issue of a shrinking Việt population that prompted Nguyễn Cư Trinh's cultural project in Quảng Ngãi. To encourage the Việt migrants to band together against the uplanders, Nguyễn Cư Trinh wrote the *Sãi Vãi*, a play in the vernacular Vietnamese script (*chữ Nôm*), and staged it for the inhabitants of Quảng Ngãi.[29] His play served as both entertainment and edification, and it successfully exhorted the Việt lowlanders to rise up against the Đá Vách uplanders, securing a temporary peace between the peoples. As my reading of the *Sãi Vãi* will show, this political victory was contingent on the play's cultural workings on the people of Quảng Ngãi.

MẠC THIÊN TỨ IN HÀ TIÊN

The Mạc family first settled in the western regions of the Mekong delta in 1671, after Mạc Thiên Tứ's father, Mạc Cửu, fled the Manchu regime in China during the transition from the Ming to the Qing dynasty.[30]

28.   Nguyễn Cư Trinh suggests this in his 1751 petition to Nguyễn Phúc Khoát, which I discuss in greater detail in chapters 1 and 3. For a theorization of the political appeal of mountainous regions, see Scott, *The Art of Not Being Governed*. For studies on the issue of ethnic differentiation at border regions, see Shin, *The Making of the Chinese State*; Hostetler, *Qing Colonial Enterprise*; Crossley, Siu, and Sutton (eds.), *Empire at the Margins*; and Harrell (ed.), *Cultural Encounters on China's Ethnic Frontiers*. For a study of the Sino-Vietnamese borderland in the nineteenth century, see Bradley Davis, *Imperial Bandits*.

29.   Nguyễn Cư Trinh had suggested advancing against the Đá Vách and sought the men to do so, but "many used the [border's] dangerous distance and miasmic environment [as an excuse] to thwart his suggestion" 多以險遠嵐瘴撓阻其議. *Đại Nam Liệt Truyện Tiền Biên*, 5.5.

30.   The location of Mạc Cửu's first settlement has been the subject of much inquiry. Hà Tiên, the settlement most closely associated with the Mạc family, is often conflated with Banteay Meas (also Pontiamas, Pontay Mas, and other variants of the same). Vietnamese imperial records from the nineteenth century, for example, state that Mạc Cửu settled in Phương Thành 芳城 (i.e., Hà Tiên) after seeing that Sài Mạt 柴末 (i.e., Banteay Meas) played host to traders from near and far, suggesting that Phương Thành was, if not the same place as Sài Mạt, then a city within it. See Mạc Cửu's biography in *Đại Nam Liệt Truyện Tiền Biên*, 6.1. Trịnh Hoài Đức, writing the Gia Định Gazetteer in the 1820s, confirms that Phương Thành was the name by which the Chinese called Hà Tiên; more-

Originally from Leizhou in Guangdong, southern China, Mạc Cửu submitted to Khmer authority when he arrived in the region. He moved to Hà Tiên after he saw that there was a lively trading community composed of Chinese, Khmer, and Malay peoples there, and upon this mercantile foundation he built a port city that grew daily in strength. Newly ensconced in a region located far from Manchu-controlled China, Mạc Cửu soon discovered that he had fled the political chaos of his homeland only to be caught up in political circumstances that were no less volatile. The success of the port in Hà Tiên drew the unwanted attention of the expanding Siamese state, and Mạc Cửu realized that his Cambodian overlords were too weak to protect him from Siamese advances. In 1708, he sought the protection of the Nguyễn lords of Đàng Trong and subordinated his ethnic Chinese enclave to Vietnamese control.[31] Vietnamese suzerainty was not difficult to bear, however, and Mạc Cửu continued to run his domain fairly autonomously. It is unclear if, in his initial foray into the Mekong delta, he had expected to reside there permanently, but his intention to make it his home was apparent when he sent for his aged mother, who abandoned their ancestral place and relocated to her son's distant domain, where she lived out her last years.[32]

Mạc Cửu died in 1735, leaving control of Hà Tiên to Mạc Thiên Tứ. Like the father, the son was a versatile political actor. With the

---

over, he conflates Banteay Meas (here referred to as Mang Khảm 茫坎) with Phương Thành (河仙乃真臘故地。俗稱茫坎。華言芳城也). See Trịnh Hoài Đức, *Gia Định Thành Thông Chí*, 159, 320 (the latter page number refers to the hand-copied Chinese character manuscript appended to the back of the volume). Émile Gaspardone suggested in 1952 that Hà Tiên and Banteay Meas were two different cities. See Gaspardone, "Un chinois des mers du sud," 363–85. Claudine Salmon, using carthographic evidence, has corroborated Gaspardone's assertion and identified the location of Mạc Cửu's first settlement as Banteay Meas, which she locates further inland on the western side of a river by the name of Hà Tiên; Hà Tiên, a coastal city, is situated at the same river's estuary. For an account of Mạc Cửu's early settlement in the region and the subsequent establishment of Hà Tiên, see Salmon, *Ming Loyalists in Southeast Asia*, 41–46.

31. For more information about the consequences of Hà Tiên's subordination to the Nguyễn for Siamese–Vietnamese relations, see Li Tana, *Nguyễn Cochinchina*, 141–44. On Chinese settlement aiding Nguyễn control of the Mekong delta, see Boudet, "La conquête de la Cochinchine."

32. *Đại Nam Liệt Truyện Tiền Biên*, 6.2–3.

Cambodians, Mạc Thiên Tứ backed and shielded factions of the royal family and even represented himself as the king of Cambodia in his interactions with the Japanese. With the Vietnamese, he took on the part of a loyal subject and styled himself as a guardian of Vietnamese interests on the western extremities of the delta.[33] He traveled to Phú Xuân to report his father's passing to the Nguyễn lord, who in turn granted him the title of Commander-in-Chief (v: *đô đốc*, p: *dudu* 都督) of Hà Tiên and bestowed on him three ships that bore the Nguyễn insignia, which were not subject to taxation. To facilitate trade in Hà Tiên, the Nguyễn lord established a facility there to mint coins.[34] Mạc Thiên Tứ continued his father's work of building citadel walls, recruiting soldiers, widening roads, and expanding markets. He ensured, moreover, the cultural eminence of his domain. A Qing envoy traveling through the region in the 1740s marveled at the level of educational advancement that Hà Tiên had attained. He recorded that

> they value literature and are fond of the Classics. The kingdom has a Confucian temple and the king and the people all respectfully pay obeisance to it. There is also a public school where the brightest of the country's children are taught, even those who are too poor to pay. Han people who sojourn there and understand the meaning of sentences are invited to teach. The students are all refined.[35]

33. Evidence of Mạc Thiên Tứ's social and political standing among the various players in the region can be found in his official biography in *Đại Nam Liệt Truyện Tiền Biên*, 6.3–14. There exists a letter written in 1742 in the Khmer language by Mạc Thiên Tứ, addressed to Japanese authorities on behalf of the king of Cambodia, to request the continuation of junk trade between the two polities. The letter is reproduced in *Bulletin de l'École Française d'Extrême-Orient* 23 (1923), pl. IX and X; transcription and French translation on 131 and 132. For more on the range of roles that Mạc Thiên Tứ played as a political actor, see Chen Jinghe, "Mac Thien Tu and Phrayataksin," 1534–75, and Sakurai, "Eighteenth-Century Chinese Pioneers," 44–45.

34. *Đại Nam Liệt Truyện Tiền Biên*, 6.3–4. "Imperial insignia" (v: *long bài*, p: *long-pai* 龍牌) is exuberance on the part of nineteenth-century Nguyễn scribes. The Nguyễn lords only declared themselves kings in 1744 and their house a dynasty in 1802. Previous Nguyễn lords were all given posthumous titles.

35. These observations were recorded in the Qing dynasty's *Qingchao wenxian tongkao*, 297.7463. The text has been reprinted in Gaspardone, "Un chinois des mers du sud," 363–64. The section above is reproduced from Liam Kelley's translation of the text. See Kelley, "Thoughts on a Chinese Diaspora," 80–82.

The Chinese official's glowing report corroborates the Vietnamese records of Mạc Cửu's and Mạc Thiên Tứ's labors there. The high level of education and culture was undoubtedly due to Mạc Thiên Tứ's efforts, as he was greatly concerned with elevating the civility of his newly inherited domain. Just a year after taking control of Hà Tiên, Mạc Thiên Tứ launched an ambitious literary project. In 1736, together with a guest, Chen Zhikai, who traveled to Hà Tiên from Guangzhou, he composed ten poems in praise of its ten scenic sites. Chen Zhikai distributed copies of the poems to poets living along the Vietnamese and southern Chinese coastline on his way back to Guangzhou and solicited response poems from them. In all, thirty-two poets composed poems in praise of Hà Tiên's ten scenic sites. Although many of the poets had probably never set foot in Hà Tiên, they nonetheless sent their poems back to Mạc Thiên Tứ when the boats sailed again the next season. Mạc Thiên Tứ compiled the 320 poems as a collection that he claimed added to the "airs and odes" (v: *phong nhã*, p: *fengya* 風雅) of Hà Tiên. Mạc Thiên Tứ's literary undertaking was aimed at civilizing his domain in a way that was perhaps even more ambitious than his father's project of building markets, roads, and citadel walls. Whereas the building plans had an eminently practical end in mind, the poetry project could be considered a superfluous luxury indulged in for the sole purpose of self-aggrandizement. As my decoding of his poems will demonstrate, however, Mạc Thiên Tứ's literary endeavors sought to ennoble not the author but his domain, and they are tied to a larger political project to orient his land toward the remnant Ming loyalists scattered across the seas.

Language and Cultural Projects

Both Nguyễn Cư Trinh's and Mạc Thiên Tứ's cultural projects sought to transform the peripheral regions under their charge. At the foundations of these projects was a belief in the transformative power of language; the two authors deploy language and, more specifically, writing to effect change in the people and the landscape. The mutually constitutive relationship between language and refinement is integral to the Chinese and Vietnamese intellectual worldview; within this framework, literature, a form of ornamentation that language makes possible, not only confers aesthetic value on an object under description but is itself constitutive of civility and civilization.[36] In the *Selections of Refined Literature* (v: *Văn Tuyển*, p: *Wen xuan* 文選), the oldest surviving anthology of Chinese literature, its compiler, Xiao Tong (v: Tiêu Thống 蕭統, 501–31), begins his preface with a discussion of *wen* (v: *văn* 文) as encapsulating both culture and writing:

> Let us examine the primordial origins of civilization,
> And distantly observe the customs of the remote past—
> Times when men dwelled in caves in winter, nests in summer,
> Eras when people consumed raw meat and drank blood.
> It was a pristine age of simple people,
> And writing had not yet been invented.
> Then when Fu Xi ruled the empire,
> He first
> > Drew the Eight Trigrams,
> > Created writing
> To replace government by knotted ropes.
> From this time written records came into existence.
> The *Changes* says, "Observe the patterns [*wen*] of the sky
> To ascertain the seasonal changes.
> Observe the patterns [*wen*] of man
> To transform the world."
> The temporal significance of writing [*wen*] is far-reaching indeed![37]

Xiao Tong's preface identifies the invention of writing as the turning point in the civilization of humankind. During an age in which people ate uncooked food and lived in dwellings undifferentiated from those of

36. For scholarship representing various views on the cultural relationship between Vietnam and China in the premodern era, see Baldanza, *Ming China and Vietnam*; Kelley, "Vietnam as a 'Domain of Manifest Civility'" and *Beyond the Bronze Pillars*; Wolters, "Assertions of Cultural Well-Being in Fourteenth Century Vietnam"; Woodside, "Conceptions of Change"; and Yu Insun, "Lê Văn Hưu and Ngô Sĩ Liên."

37. *Wen xuan*, preface, 1; the translation above is taken from Knechtges, *Wen xuan* 1:73. For another translation of the preface, see Hightower, "The Wen Hsüan and Genre Theory," 518. Here, Xiao Tong identifies Fu Xi (v: Phục Hy 伏羲) as the creator of writing, but it is more commonly attributed to Cangjie (v: Thương Hiệt 倉頡), minister of Huangdi (v: Hoàng Đế 黃帝).

the animals, the discovery of writing brought humans out of their primordial state and into a patterned realm. In this narrative of emergent culture, what is prized is not the pristine or the unmolested; rather, the world that has been ordered by the regulating effect of patterns is eulogized. Instead of a story of a fall from nature into artifice, we are given a tale of luminous beginnings, in which the inception of a new technology enables the realization of humanity. What accounts for writing's pivotal role in this transformation? The written word is the site in which the patterns inherent in the world are captured in a script invented by humans. It is not only an instrument that facilitates communication between people; the written word has a special, almost mystical affinity with the larger world that it expresses and mirrors. With the inception of this vehicle of representation—at once, natural and manmade—humankind triumphs over the forces of disorder, to which it had previously been in thrall, and is empowered to bring order to itself and the surrounding environment. Drawing from the wisdom of the *Book of Changes* (v: *Kinh Dịch*, p: Yijing 易經), Xiao Tong identifies the presence of *wen* in both the heavens and humankind. Celestial patterns inform us of seasonal changes, but "the patterns of man" have the ability to transform the world. Taking "patterns" to mean both culture and writing, we can understand this statement to be saying that through writing, humans are able to refashion and give structure to the unpatterned parts of the world.

Nguyễn Cư Trinh's and Mạc Thiên Tứ's cultural projects bring writing to bear on the people and the landscape of the peripheral regions in their care. Through the mobilization of literature, these men sought to pattern their domains and thereby mark them as different from their surrounding environs. The literary projects differ, however, in their modes of articulation. In a series of landscape poems, which are written in the Chinese script and closely follow Tang classical convention, Mạc Thiên Tứ reimagines his territory as a place where culture can find a home and flourish. He makes use of a rather conservative literary genre in the service of a cultural project that creatively and subversively resituates Hà Tiên, a domain that lies outside of the Middle Kingdom and that mainlainders would have consigned to the fringes of barbarism. Nguyễn Cư Trinh's *Sãi Vãi*, composed in the Vietnamese vernacular, is recorded in the *Nôm* script. This system of writing makes use of existing Chinese characters to create new *Nôm* characters, which are used for their symbolic and phonetic values; deployed with Chinese characters, the two scripts in conjunction successfully transpose the Vietnamese language into writing. In the composition and the performance of the *Sãi Vãi*, Nguyễn Cư Trinh used language that was intelligible to village people living on the frontier, and he also drew on a rich tradition of classical allusions, some of which would have been fully understandable only to an erudite elect. The success of Nguyễn Cư Trinh's and Mạc Thiên Tứ's cultural projects was dependent on their authors' skillful deployment of language, operative in multiple registers. For both, language functioned as an instrument of designation and a means of expression.

The designative aspect of language is evident in its power to differentiate, to make distinctions, and, once identified, to invest these distinctions with significance. In the *Sãi Vãi*, the line drawn between those on the inside and those on the outside, the civilized peoples within and the barbarians without, strengthens social bounds by defining the civilized group in opposition to the undifferentiated mass that stands against it. The moment of othering is important because it contributes to the cohesion of the in-group and solidifies its sense of identity; the importance of this linguistic operation is brought home when we recall that at the time of the *Sãi Vãi*'s composition, some of the inhabitants of Quảng Ngãi were actually fleeing into the uplands and joining the Đá Vách "barbarians." The *Sãi Vãi* is not simply a rallying cry but an exhortation to prevent people from abandoning their lands and changing their identity—an option at a place and in a time in which ethnic identity markers were remarkably fluid. Precisely because the distinction between groups was so porous and labile on the frontier, using correct designations was of fundamental importance. In such liminal spaces, at once nebulous and chaotic, naming acquires an even greater importance than usual on account of its power to make things orderly and intelligible.

Designation allows us to think through and imagine differences between groups of people. Beyond that, it plays a vital role in how we order, conceptualize, and make sense of the natural world and our place in it. Through the selection of the right word or character, the essence of a thing is captured; when the world is described in adequate terms, that which lies latent is made manifest. In his poems on the landscape of Hà Tiên, Mạc Thiên Tứ seeks to draw out those aspects of his domain's character that are hidden and to bring them to light, to show that the frontier region, ostensibly a land of barbarism, is in fact a site of structuring patterns that make it a fit place for the flourishing of culture. Put in these terms, the process of designating, the finding and naming of concealed patterns, appears to be akin to a kind of discovery. It is also, however, an exercise in invention. Mạc Thiên Tứ's description of the landscape, with its recourse to a wealth of classical allusions that reconfigure how we see Hà Tiên and its place in cultured discourse, is a creative intervention, the deliberate refashioning of a terrain to suit it better to the author's political vision and aspirations. This becomes even more evident when we look at Nguyễn Cư Trinh's suite of response poems, in which Mạc Thiên Tứ's characterization of Hà Tiên is contested and re-patterned in such a way as to align the frontier enclave with a contrary political vision and a rival cultural project. The importance accorded to *wen*, with its dual meanings of pattern and writing, is crucial in understanding the significance of language to both men's cultural projects. The act of designating a place is a transformative act, one through which a thing is ordered and structured. And the furtherance of a cultural project, its ultimate success, is intimately linked to the endurance of the designations that undergird it.

In an epistle to Mạc Thiên Tứ, Nguyễn Cư Trinh puts forth his thoughts on the relationship between interior and exterior, the intent of the poet and the poem in which intention achieves articulacy. This pithy meditation on poetic composition is intended not as a theoretical discourse removed from practical concerns or an apolitical reflection on aesthetics; it is intimately tied to his thoughts on the uses of poetry and its function as a medium of expression. In the depiction of the scenic sites of Hà Tiên, Mạc Thiên Tứ's and Nguyễn Cư Trinh's lyric verse gives voice to what would otherwise remain voiceless. Nature speaks through the poet. In addition, the language of poetry allows the poet to express his inmost sentiments and aspirations. In the *Sãi Vãi*, Nguyễn Cư Trinh shares his thoughts and feelings on life on the frontier, the ideals he wishes to see realized, and the corrupt practices he wants to extirpate. He also aims to join his voice to the voice of the people, giving expression to their hopes and fears, most notably their hope for security and fear of the barbarians. This is especially evident in the concluding sections of the play, where the monk and the nun speak of the dangers of frontier life. The fear of the Đá Vách, and courage in the face of it, binds the actors and the spectators together. The *Sãi Vãi* holds up a mirror to the audience, showing it how it is and how it should be. In the act of performance, the audience can see itself in the stories of virtue and vice narrated before them. The play acts on the people, appealing to their reason and to their emotion, hoping to sweep them up in defense of the frontier and in the struggle against external enemies.

The use of language here is manipulative—taking that term not in a pejorative sense, but simply a descriptive one. Nguyễn Cư Trinh's drama seeks to shape the audience, inculcate certain virtues in the spectators, and encourage them to act in accordance with them. Although less immediately obvious, this same manipulative tendency is at work in the act of designating, as present in the portrayals of Hà Tiên in Mạc Thiên Tứ's and Nguyễn Cư Trinh's landscape poetry. The first type of manipulation, which is perhaps the more familiar one, targets the people; it aims to transform their mode of comportment, their values, and their practice. The second type works on the landscape. This reworking of the landscape does not physically alter the terrain in the fashion of a large-scale building project; the alteration that occurs comes about through a discursive procedure whereby the meaning of objects is altered and the world around them is reframed. By virtue of this procedure, the domain itself, inclusive of its land and its people, is raised to a higher civilizational level. Indeed, the fact that the frontier region was able to produce works of such high literary quality as the *Sãi Vãi* and the *Ten Songs of Hà Tiên* was taken to demonstrate its character and worth. The poet not only re-creates and elevates, through language, the space in which he lives; his very existence is ennobling, bestowing on the land that produced him a mark and a proof of cultural superiority. Nguyễn Cư Trinh and Mạc Thiên Tứ are agents and initiators of cultural projects, but they are also testaments to the viability of the projects they aim to advance; they are proof of the high status of the lands they inhabit and their cultural fecundity.

PART I

Drama on the Frontier

CHAPTER I

Frontier Humor and the
Inadequacies of Orthodoxy

The people of Đàng Trong's expanding frontier were no strangers to the use of humor in public entertainment in politically sensitive situations. Christoforo Borri, a Jesuit priest who lived in Đàng Trong from 1618 to 1622, published an account in 1631 of the kingdom of Cochinchina in which he recounted a revealing anecdote that he dubbed "Mistaken Conversions." Borri's colleague, Father Francis Buzome, who had arrived in Cochinchina before Borri, knew that the interpreters for the ship chaplains who had been there before him had converted several Cochinchinese to Christianity; the problem, according to Buzome, was that the converts might not actually have been aware of what they were agreeing to convert to. Buzome discovered this fact when he chanced upon a skit that was acted out in a public marketplace in Đà Nẵng that featured an actor, in

> the habit of a *Portuguese*, brought in by way of ridicule, with a belly so artificially made, that a boy was hid in it; the player, before the audience, turn'd him out of his belly, and ask'd him, Whether he would go into the belly of the *Portuguese*? Using these words, *Con gnoo muon bau tlom laom Hoalaom chiam?* [*Con nhỏ muốn vào trong lòng Hoa Long chăng?*] That is, *Little boy, will you go into the belly of the* Portuguese, *or not?* The boy answer'd, *He would*: and then he put him in again, often repeating the same thing to divert the spectators.[1]

1. Borri, *An Account of Cochin-China*, 139. In the quotation, the modern transcription in brackets is that of Olga Dror. Originally written in Italian, the English

Father Buzome realized that this was the same phrase the interpreters had used whenever they asked someone if they would like to be a Christian. He came to the conclusion that the Cochinchinese had mistakenly thought that they were being asked whether they would "cease being *Cochin-Chinese*, and become a *Portuguese*," and thus were making fun of the conversion process by making a child go into the belly of the actor playing a Portuguese man. Borri recorded that Buzome rectified this problem by instructing the newly converted on the significance of baptism and being a Christian and making sure that the interpreters changed their question to "*Muon bau dau Christiam Chiam*? [*Muốn vào đạo Christian chăng*?] That is, *Will you enter into the Christian law, or no*?" Borri assured his readers that "within a few days," Father Buzome was successful in converting more people and bringing about "the reformation of those who before were Christians only in name."[2]

From this anecdote, it appears that both Borri and Buzome thought the Việt inhabitants of Đàng Trong made fun of the conversion process only because they did not understand what they were being asked to do; the Jesuit fathers assumed that the public performance mocking the Portuguese priest made fun not of the act of conversion to Christianity but of the ridiculousness of asking a person to switch from being Cochinchinese to being Portuguese. The interpreters that Buzome referred to were probably using the word *lòng* in the context of the compound word *lòng tin*, meaning "faith"; the question asked of potential converts was probably, "Will you enter into the Portuguese faith [*lòng tin*]?" The Cochinchinese, in their publicly staged mockery, had the stage character contract the word *lòng tin* so that it became only *lòng*; taken literally, the Portuguese character on stage would be asking the Cochinchinese person if he would like to enter the Portuguese gut (*lòng*), hence the act with the child repeatedly entering the actor's fake belly. Even though Borri and Buzome understood the literal meaning of the sentence, they appear to have reached the wrong conclusion that the Cochinchinese had misunderstood the question that was asked of potential converts.

translation of Borri's account dates to 1704. For more information about the translation of this text into various languages, see the introduction in Dror and Taylor, *Views of Seventeenth-Century Vietnam*, 64–66.

2. Borri, *An Account of Cochin-China*, 139–40. The modern Vietnamese transcription is Dror's.

Borri's account of the episode presents the object of ridicule as the heavily caricatured Portuguese man, with whom Borri and Buzome identified. Even though his account leads one to suspect that the Jesuits did not identify the malapropism at that time, the creators of the little skit were indeed making a joke at the expense of an outsider's poor mastery of the local language. Moreover, Borri and Buzome did not seem to adequately consider that the Cochinchinese convert might have been under as much, if not more, ridicule than the Portuguese man. The local convert was represented using a small child, while the Portuguese man had a very large presence on stage. The imbalance in the visual representation of the actors accentuated the paternalistic relationship the foreign priest had with the infantilized new convert. The child did not have much of a role to play in the performance except to agree readily and repeatedly to an absurd request, creating an exaggerated impression of simple-mindedness. Much more than ridiculing the Portuguese priest, the play can be understood as a mockery of newly converted Christians in Đàng Trong.

The details of how this skit came to be staged, whether it was commissioned, and who the actors were remain unknown to us. Borri's fortuitous inclusion of this anecdote in his account of Cochinchina, however, gives us a glimpse of what some people of Đàng Trong in the early seventeenth century thought of Portuguese priests and newly converted Việt Christians. The skit parodying the conversion process represents one way of dealing with the intrusion of the foreign: Việt inhabitants of Đàng Trong, in theatrically performing the foreign role, familiarized the foreign and gave themselves the means of expression to incorporate the foreign experience of religious conversion into their daily lives. Even more powerful than that, the fact that the skit was humorous at the expense of the foreigner presumably gave the unconverted Việt inhabitant of Đàng Trong a sense of superiority and control over the foreigner; "foreigner" in this case came in the guise of both the priest from another land and the newly converted local inhabitant.

Borri's anecdote suggests that humorous dramatic performances in Đàng Trong were a fairly elaborate affair: the aforementioned skit was performed in a public marketplace, and the actors were armed with costumes imitating Portuguese dress, complete with a huge fake belly. It was in all likelihood a small-scale production made for mass consumption. Performances of this kind were probably one form of entertainment regularly available to the population of Đàng Trong. Jean Koffler, a missionary who lived in Vietnam from 1740 to 1755, wrote an account of Cochinchina in 1766 that was edited and published in 1803.[3] Because he was a royal doctor in the court of Nguyễn Phúc Khoát from 1747 to 1753, his account of Đàng Trong comes from a different vantage point from Borri's.[4] In the chapter "Of the Court and Royal Entertainment," Koffler related the importance of staged performances:

> There is no lack of actors; they are divided into four troupes and on fixed days each year or whenever it pleases His Majesty, they act out dramas in which the subject is drawn from the most remarkable stories and they strive to imitate the stage acting of our best actors in Europe.[5]

It is not clear from Koffler's description whether the dramatic performances contained only spoken dialogue or if they were accompanied by music; however, he discussed music, feasts, and acting in the same section on royal entertainment, which suggests a close association between musical and dramatic forms of entertainment. The performances were, in all likelihood, an early form of *hát bội*. Also known as *hát tuồng* or simply *tuồng*, and often translated as "Vietnamese opera," these performances are believed to have been introduced into Đàng Trong by Đào Duy Từ (p: Tao Weici 陶維慈, 1572–1634), an educated man who was nonetheless unable to participate in politics in Đàng Ngoài because he hailed from a lowly family of professional actors; in search of better opportunities, he migrated to the southern Vietnamese polity in 1627.[6]

3. Koffler wrote his account of Cochinchina while he was in prison in Lisbon. It was later abridged by Anselme d'Eckart and further edited by Christophore Théophile de Murr before its publication in 1803.

4. Koffler remained in Cochinchina in the capacity of royal doctor after most of the other missionaries were ejected from the kingdom in 1750.

5. Koffler, "Description historique de la Cochinchine," 277; English translation mine. The text in French: "Les comédiens ne manquent pas; ils sont divisés en quarte troupes et aux jours fixés chaque année ou quand il plaît à S.M. [Sa Majesté], ils jouent des drames dont le sujet est tiré des histoires les plus remarquables et s'efforcent d'imiter le jeu scénique de nos meilleurs acteurs d'Europe." I translate both "comédiens" and "acteurs" as "actors."

6. See, for example, the entry on Đào Duy Từ in Nguyễn Lộc, *Từ Điển Nghệ Thuật Hát Bội Việt Nam*, 112–13. For a discussion of the problems associated with crediting

A performance genre that blended musical accompaniment with sung renditions of stories from the Chinese literary tradition such as the *Romance of the Three Kingdoms, hát bội* was popular in southern Vietnam during the eighteenth and nineteenth centuries.[7] Taking Borri's account from the seventeenth century and Koffler's account from the eighteenth century together, we can surmise that staged performances constituted an important part of royal and public entertainment in Đàng Trong.

An Introduction to the Sãi Vãi

Most transcripts or notes from these plays, if they ever existed, are not extant in surviving historical records, and we know little about the subjects that were treated and the details of performance. One important play from the mid-eighteenth century, however, has survived in its entirety. Nguyễn Cư Trinh's *Sãi Vãi* (A Monk and a Nun) was written in 1750 while he was governor of Quảng Ngãi prefecture. The *Đại Nam Thực Lục* records that in the second month of 1750, during the spring season, the Nguyễn lord Nguyễn Phúc Khoát appointed Nguyễn Cư Trinh to be the governor of Quảng Ngãi. The edict states:

> [If] minor officials are covetous, verily, you are to investigate and put [them] straight; [if] the rich and powerful trespass and rob, verily, you are to judge and restrain [them]; [if] prison terms are undecided, verily, you must extend reason; [if] the number of inhabitants is insufficient, verily, you must populate [the place]; [if] the people are impertinent, verily, you must spread education; [if] degenerates thieve and pilfer, verily, you must impose limits. All the sentiments of the soldiers and the sorrows of the people, [I] hand to you to take appropriate action. Want only success; do not fear exhaustion.[8]

Đạo Duy Từ with this feat, see Nguyễn Tô Lan, *Khảo luận về tuồng Quần Phương Tập Khánh*, 260–61.

7. For more information on *hát bội*, see Huỳnh Khắc Dụng, *Hát bội, théâtre traditionnel du Việt Nam.*

8. See entry for 1750 in *Đại Nam Thực Lục Tiền Biên*, 10.16.

胥吏貪墨惟汝究治；豪右侵漁惟汝裁抑；奸獄不決惟汝伸理，戶口不登惟汝繁殖，人民不遜惟汝數教，姦宄偷竊惟汝式度。一切軍情民瘼，聽隨宜從事。惟期底績，毋或憚勞。

The edict reads as a generic court order exhorting an official to do his utmost at his duty. The pertinence of the statements to the situation in Quảng Ngãi, however, suggests that the commands given were specific in nature. The document states that in Quảng Ngãi, minor officials were covetous, the rich and powerful abused their positions, appropriate punishments were not meted out, the province suffered from a lack of inhabitants, the inhabitants it did have were in need of education, and degenerates stole and pilfered. Notably, the *Sãi Vãi* addresses all but the third of these commands, which Nguyễn Cư Trinh leaves to a memorial he later submits to the court. Moreover, the play intimates who these offending minor officials and wealthy abusers of power were; it allows us to identify the former as low-level literati officials the court had sent to administer the province, and it suggests that the latter were the religious men, specifically Buddhist clergymen, who held sway over the inhabitants of the province. Left unstated is that Quảng Ngãi was plagued with conflict between the Đá Vách and the Việt peoples; it is unclear whether the court was aware of the conflict, but Nguyễn Cư Trinh was quickly confronted with the situation upon his arrival.

While Nguyễn Cư Trinh was in Quảng Ngãi, he realized that the Đá Vách uplanders frequently raided the Việt lowlanders of the region. Nguyễn Cư Trinh's biography in the *Đại Nam Liệt Truyện* states that he tried to reason with the Đá Vách to no avail; he suggested advancing against them and sought men among the Việt to join him, but many feared the dangers and refused. Nguyễn Cư Trinh "thereupon composed a story about a monk and a nun in the language of the country's speech; [he] arranged it as a verse-poem in the mode of a dialogue, and used it to criticize [the Việt people] indirectly and to instruct them" 居貞乃作僧尼傳，語用國音，設爲問答辭，以諷示之。[9]

The story alluded to here, which had the effect of rallying the people of Quảng Ngãi to brave the dangers of the mountains and to fight the

---

9. *Đại Nam Liệt Truyện Tiền Biên*, 5.5.

Đá Vách, was the *Sãi Vãi*. This satirical play, which comprises 270 lines of rhyming couplets, depicts a humorous conversation between a monk and a nun about religion, good governance, and civilizational hierarchy. In 1951, two Vietnamese scholars, Lê Ngọc Trụ and Phạm Văn Luật, compiled a standardized transliteration of the *Sãi Vãi* out of six existing ones that had been produced in the romanized Vietnamese alphabet, *quốc ngữ*, between 1886 and 1932.[10] Lê Ngọc Trụ and Phạm Văn Luật proposed a systematic rhyme scheme for the work that follows two main rules, the first concerning the syllabic count of the couplets, and the second concerning the rhyming pattern.[11] The structure of the syllabic count works such that the first part of the couplet has the same number of syllables as the second part. The couplets, however, do not have a constant number of syllables, nor do they follow any consistent sequential structure in terms of syllable count. In terms of a rhyming pattern, the last syllable of the second part of a couplet rhymes with the last syllable of the first part of the next couplet. See, for example, the following lines:

Mới tụng kinh vừa xuống, nghe tiếng khánh gióng *lên*.
Ngớ là chuông vua Hạ Võ chiêu *hiền*; ngớ là đạc đức Trọng Nhi thiết *giao*.
Sãi yêu vì *đạo*, sãi dấu vì *duơn*.
Thấy mụ vãi nhan sắc có *hơn*; sãi theo với tu hành kẻo thiệt.[12]

The first couplet has five syllables in each part, the second has eight, the third has four, and the fourth has seven. The rhyming pattern works such that *lên* rhymes with *hiền*, *giao* rhymes with *đạo*, and *duơn* rhymes with *hơn*. None of the six transcriptions from which they worked were a perfect match for their proposed rhyme scheme.

10. The six transliterations that they use are the works of A. Chéon (1886); Lương Khắc Ninh, Nguyễn Khắc Huề, and Nguyễn Dư Hoài (1901); Cao Hải Để (1923); Trần Trọng Huề (1920); Trần Trung Viên (1932); and Dương Mạnh Huy (1932). See Lê Ngọc Trụ and Phạm Văn Luật, *Nguyễn Cư Trinh với Quyển Sãi Vãi*. There is at least one *quốc ngữ* version that Lê Ngọc Trụ and Phạm Văn Luật did not take into consideration. This is *Sãi vải luận đàm*, trans. Lê Duy Thiện.
11. Lê Ngọc Trụ and Phạm Văn Luật, *Nguyễn Cư Trinh với Quyển Sãi Vãi*, 60–62.
12. I take these four lines from the transcription compiled by Lê Ngọc Trụ and Phạm Văn Luật, *Nguyễn Cư Trinh với Quyển Sãi Vãi*, 69.

Four copies of the *Sãi Vãi* recorded in the *Nôm* script are extant. Two can be found in the Viện Nghiên Cứu Nôm và Hán Việt (Institute for Research on Nôm and Sino-Vietnamese, also known as the Viện Hán Nôm). They are undated, hand-copied versions of the character text that are parts of larger compilations.[13] The third is a hand-copied version published as an appendix in Nguyễn Văn Sâm's *Văn học Nam Hà: Văn học Đường Trong thời phân tranh (Literature of the Southern Region: Literature of Đàng Trong in the Period of Separation).*[14] The author notes that it is a copy from his personal library. The final *chữ Nôm* version of the *Sãi Vãi* is housed in the Bibliothèque Interuniversitaire des Langues Orientales in Paris.[15] It is a woodblock print publication dating to 1874, edited by Duy Minh Thị, which I hereafter refer to as the Duy Minh Thị manuscript. Because of the presence of dating and publication information and the internal coherence of its contents, this final version is the text on which I base my translation and analysis of the *Sãi Vãi.*

None of the manuscripts, whether they be the *Nôm* character versions or the *quốc ngữ* ones that Lê Ngọc Trụ and Phạm Văn Luật examined for their standardized transcription, are exactly the same. Besides insignificant variations throughout, the main difference among the various manuscripts is that some of them include an additional thirty-four lines at the beginning of the play; these lines are found in two of the six *quốc ngữ* transcriptions of the *Sãi Vãi.*[16] Of the four *Nôm* character texts,

13.   One compilation is the *Quốc văn tùng kí*. It is a collection of literary works by various authors including Trần Hưng Đạo, Chu Mạnh Trinh, and Hồ Xuân Hương, together in one volume as they are all written in *chữ Nôm*. Yale University's Maurice Durand collection, part of the holdings of the Sterling Library, includes a hand-written copy of the version of the *Sãi Vãi* that was originally from this particular compilation; the copy in the Durand collection contains both the *chữ Nôm* text and a *quốc ngữ* transcription. For the purpose of textual comparison, I use the *chữ Nôm* version found in the Viện Hán Nôm; hereafter, I refer to it as AB.383 manuscript. The other compilation is *Ca văn thi phú thư truyện tạp biên*. This is a collection of miscellaneous works on diverse topics such as an exhortation to study, a letter from a wife to her husband, and a dispute among domestic animals regarding the services they render. The version of the *Sãi Vãi* compiled in this collection is truncated.

14.   Hereafter, I refer to this copy of the *Sãi Vãi* as the Nguyễn Văn Sâm manuscript.

15.   Their holdings have since been integrated into those of the Bibliothèque Universitaire des Langues et Civilisations, also in Paris.

16.   These are the transcriptions produced by Lương Khắc Ninh et al. and Cao Hải Để.

the additional lines appear in only Nguyễn Văn Sâm's personal copy. Of interest is the title of his copy of the manuscript, which reads *Sãi Vãi tân lục quốc âm diễn ca* (A New Record of the *Sãi Vãi*, a Ballad in Our Country's Tones); the title suggests that this "new" version of the *Sãi Vãi* is modified from its original form. Indeed, the first thirty-four lines introduce an element of Buddhist religious worship that is incongruous with the rest of the text that begins on line 35, which raises suspicions that they were later inclusions. I do not include these lines in my study of the text.

While remaining conscious of the textual variations between the manuscripts, many of which occur at the level of script or of alternative expressions within particular lines, I yet rely mainly on one manuscript version. For contemporary scholars interested in the range of variations, Lê Ngọc Trụ and Phạm Văn Luật's standardized version exists for consultation. To address some of the problems associated with interpreting a work with discrepancies among the various extant manuscripts, I use two strategies in my reading practice. First, in my interpretation of the work, I am led by specific lines that I identify as turning points or significant markers. These lines, though present in the Duy Minh Thị manuscript, are not consistently present in all the others. Second, to augment my line-based interpretation, I pay close attention to the work's textual structure, by which I mean the situation or positioning of particular passages within the text. The *Sãi Vãi*'s textual structure is consistent across the various extant manuscripts, and reading the work at its structural level reveals strategies of representation central to the play's agenda.

Through the use of literary devices such as parody, double entendre, hyperbole, parallelism, and catachresis, the *Sãi Vãi* engaged with important topics relevant to the prefecture and the larger political world in Đàng Trong. Like the performance that Father Buzome witnessed, in which the actor dressed as a Portuguese man played a dominant role while the small Cochinchinese child performed the part of an important accessory, the *Sãi Vãi* dramatizes the interactions of two characters, a monk and a nun, where the former acts as the principal protagonist and the latter serves a subordinate function as his foil. In its dyadic structure, there is a striking similarity between the *Sãi Vãi* and the nonmusical entertainments that Stephen West and Wilt Idema describe as Song dynasty "variety show" (v: *tạp kịch*, p: *zaju* 雜劇) and Jin dynasty "performers' texts" (v: *viện bản*, p: *yuanben* 院本). The "farces and comical skits" associated with these genres feature two main role types—the butt and the jester—and were known for their "jokes, cleverly rhymed poetry, and slapstick comedy."[17] Although the *Sãi Vãi* was produced in the eighteenth century, it fits this description well. It was composed in poetic meter, has slapstick elements, and makes use of jokes and clever puns; the monk performs the role of the jester while the nun takes on the role of the butt. It is plausible that Vietnam partici- pated in the development of the Song *zaju* and Jin *yuanben*.[18] This genre merged with others in northern China to form new modes of performance in the mid-thirteenth century, but it could have survived in a different form in Vietnam, vestiges of which might have influenced the composi- tion of the *Sãi Vãi*.[19] It is difficult to pin down with any specificity the genre to which the *Sãi Vãi* belongs because it does not fit neatly into any of the literary or performative forms that have since been identified as stan- dard in the Vietnamese cultural realm. On the one hand, the rhyme scheme in the play does not follow the "six-eight" (*lục-bát*) pattern that was popular with vernacular Vietnamese works composed in the nine- teenth century, such as *Truyện Kiều* (The Tale of Kiều) by Nguyễn Du (1766–1820) and *Truyện Lục Vân Tiên* (The Tale of Lục Vân Tiên) by Nguyễn Đình Chiểu (1822–88). On the other hand, while it has been re- corded that the *Sãi Vãi* was performed before an audience, the surviving scripts do not give any indication that it was staged with musical accompa- niment. *Hát bội*, which included both music and spoken dialogue, was one of the most popular forms of entertainment in nineteenth-century Đàng Trong; an important part of the *hát bội* scripts is the performance directives, such as *nói lối* (rhythmic sung or spoken dialogue), *hát nam* (sung in the southern style, which drags out as in a lament), and *hát khách* (sung in the "guest" style, which is hectic and rousing), that accom- pany each section of the work. None of the *Sãi Vãi* manuscripts include such directions, which suggests that it was not composed in the style of

17. West and Idema, *Monks, Bandits, Lovers, and Immortals*, x.

18. Sino-Vietnamese interactions in this time period include an episode where several hundred Song dynasty officials chose to seek refuge in Annam rather than serve the Mongols. Refer to Chan Hok-Lam, "Chinese Refugees in Annam," 1–10.

19. West and Idema discussed how Song *zaju* and Jin *yuanben* merged with "all keys and modes" (v: *chư cung điệu*, p: *zhugongdiao* 諸宮調) in mid-thirteenth-century north- ern China to create new genres that retained parts of the original ones. Refer to West and Idema, *Monks, Bandits, Lovers, and Immortals*, x.

nineteenth-century *hát bội*.[20] In fact, its chronological position in Vietnamese literary history suggests that the *Sãi Vãi* occupies a rather unique place. It appears to be a mid-eighteenth century precursor to the literary and performative genres described above, which became standard forms in late eighteenth- and early nineteenth-century Vietnam. The rhyme scheme of the *Sãi Vãi*, for instance, in which the last syllable of the first part of a couplet rhymes with the last syllable of the second part of the previous couplet, is similar to that of the *nói lối* sections in a *hát bội* script.[21] Regardless of its particular creative genealogy and legacy, it participates in the general tradition of humorous responses to politically sensitive situations in Vietnam, a tradition to which the public entertainment that Father Buzome witnessed also belonged.

The *Sãi Vãi* was performed in front of a village audience, and the vernacular allowed the author to communicate most directly with the people of Quảng Ngãi. The transcript of the play was probably circulated among the author's contemporaries, and given what we know of the nature of the author's relationship with the Nguyễn lord, it would not be surprising if it was also staged for a royal audience. In educated circles, the activities of reading the transcript and watching the performance sometimes took place simultaneously; in this way, puns that are found in the written script could be better appreciated. For a less learned audience, the performance—complete with crass jokes and slapstick elements—could be appreciated on its own. Although the play was ostensibly created for the people of Quảng Ngãi, it refers specifically to their problems with the Đá Vách people only in its final section. Much of the social commentary in the *Sãi Vãi* thus applied to mid-eighteenth-century Đàng Trong more generally.

Nguyễn Cư Trinh's choice of a monk as the protagonist of his play shines a spotlight on Buddhism and is suggestive of the religion's hold on the Đàng Trong community.[22] The religious men, also known as *ông*

---

20. For a brief description of some *hát bội* song styles, see Brandon, *Cambridge Guide to Asian Theatre*, 249.

21. Refer to the entry on *nói lối* in Nguyễn Lộc, *Từ Điển Nghệ Thuật Hát Bội Việt Nam*, 440. For an overview of the research done on southern Vietnamese literary history, in particular on the place of plays composed in the vernacular *Nôm* script, see Nguyễn Tô Lan, *Khảo luận về tuồng Quần Phương Tập Khánh*, 143–52.

22. On the history of Buddhism in Vietnam, see Nguyễn Tài Thư et al., *History of Buddhism in Vietnam*; Wheeler, "Buddhism in the Re-ordering of an Early Modern

sãi, were the first group to come under attack in the *Sãi Vãi*. The first two out of a total of eight sections in the play are dedicated to a commentary on the excesses of Buddhist monks; in these two sections, Nguyễn Cư Trinh puts forward a critique of the hypocritical worldliness of the *ông sãi*, but this critique culminated not in the indictment of those who are immersed in the world but of the orthodoxy that taught the people to disregard this world in favor of one to come. In the third section, the monk extols the virtues of the Confucian gentleman and juxtaposes these with the vices of the petty man; like the section that precedes it, it brings together two contrasting categories and leaves the reader wondering if the similarities between them are of more consequence than their differences. Advancing a critique of religious men to comment on the faults of minor government officials serves to draw attention to the two groups' dependence on each other; indeed, it is hardly a stretch to imagine them colluding for personal gain.[23]

Pivotal to the staging of this satire is the character of the monk. Dressed in Buddhist robes, the monk first depicts the moral wantonness of religious men and, in the next breath and in the same garb, preaches Confucian values that are contrary to the practice of Buddhism. In fact, he moves, in the course of the play, from an errant religious figure, to a dubious Confucian gentleman, to a reluctant village bard, to a perfected Confucian official, and finally to a terrified villager. These rapid and abrupt shifts in character prevent the audience from drawing a simple identification between the protagonist and any particular group of people in Đàng Trong. A chameleon figure, the monk continually dons new masks and adopts new voices, a procedure that is at once amusing, disconcerting, and thought provoking. The nun contributes much less to the dialogue and often appears only as a foil against which the monk vents his spleen. Her words, however, drive the play; they determine the monk's responses and raise the topic of conversation for the section that follows. In his myriad personalities, the monk functions both as a caricature and as a mimic. Nguyễn Cư Trinh uses the monk to caricature figures and prac-

---

World"; Nguyen Tu Cuong, *Zen in Medieval Vietnam*; and Thich Thien-An, *Buddhism and Zen in Vietnam*.

23.   Such collusion is explicitly referred to in vernacular Chinese fiction. See Hegel (ed.), *Idle Talk under the Bean Arbor*, 153.

tices that he finds objectionable; in his role as a caricature, the monk speaks naively and invites the audience to laugh at his foibles. There are also times when the monk appears to possess far more self-consciousness and self-reflexivity; in these moments, the naive mode yields to an ironic one, wherein the monk, in his gestures of self-mockery, knowingly mimics and thereby undermines the social and religious group to which he belongs. As the play advances, this mimicry extends to encompass not only Buddhist monks but also Confucian officials. The fact that the monk remains dressed in religious costume underscores his roles as caricature and mimic: in the first instance, the errant monk, in the attire of a religious man, conveys an exaggerated, even grotesque image of a misbehaving monk and discloses his veiled misdeeds for the world to see. In the second instance, the cultivated manners of a literati official, most ably performed by an actor dressed as a monk, shows the audience the ease with which a monk—and not just any monk but one who has proven himself to be less than righteous—is able to imitate the affected airs of a Confucian gentleman. The *Sãi Vãi* is not a simplistic satire in which its characters are reduced to caricature, nor is it solely a vehicle for the author to sound his voice through the figure of a single character. The play operates on diverse, often intersecting levels and an attentiveness to these is necessary to understand its humor and its didacticism.

Misbehaving Monks and the Inherent Worldliness of Buddhism

Right from the start, the *Sãi Vãi* invites the audience's participation in the monk's thought world. It opens with a scene in which a monk emerges from his daily meditation on the sutras; he is just descending from the temple steps when he espies an especially attractive nun, whose beauty prompts his heart to beat with a desperate desire for her. He tells the audience:

1   I had just recited sutras and was descending,
     When I heard the sound of a stone gong beating.
2   I mistook it for Hạ Vũ's [Xia Yu's] bell summoning the sages;
     Thought it was Confucius's clapper announcing his teaching.

3   I love the Way;
      I also love beauty.
4   Seeing that this nun has beauty beyond measure,
      I'll follow after and cultivate with her, lest I lose out.

He calls out after the nun to slow down and proceeds to utilize his powers
of persuasion on her in the hopes that she might consent to a daytime
excursion to his room:

5   Wait up! I do not yet know
      Which temple you are residing in.
6   Pure and fresh are your willowy eyelashes and peachy cheeks;
      How beautiful are your starry eyes and snowy skin!
7   The human heart might be desirous,
      But the time for the Way is also near.
8   The passage to Western Paradise remains blocked by sprite-filled mountains;
      But behind, in the monk's room, a Buddhist altar stands at the ready.
9   Outside, thick blinds conceal us;
      Inside, thin curtains hang low.
10   If it is cold, there is brocade of eight silks;
      If it is hot, I have a fan of reed leaves.
11   A sleeping mat glossy and smooth as grease;
      Tobacco scented with aromatic *ngâu* blossoms.[24]
12   Wine the color of red chrysanthemum, oh so red;
      Tea of everlasting perfume, oh so fragrant!
13   There are things, there are fittings;
      There is you, there is me.
14   The small back room is so near here;
      Enter with me to cultivate to depletion, cultivate to destruction.

In this section, the spiritual and the worldly realms are deliberately conflated at the levels of word and imagery. The "sound of a stone gong beating" is, of course, the monk's heart pounding with desire for the nun,
but rather piously, he first mistakes it for the sound of the sage king Yu's

---

24.   *Ngâu* is a pun for *ngẫu*, which means (among other things) to mate.

bell as he summons the sages, and then wonders if it might be the steady rhythm of Confucius's clapper as it announces the master's teaching. Just as the sound is at once that of a man's heart beating with lustful desire for a woman and one that inspires religious sentiment, the monk finds it possible to simultaneously love both the Way and physical beauty (*duyên*). Read as a *Nôm* character, *duyên* means charm or beauty, that is, *có duyên* or *vô duyên*; as a *Hán* character, *duyên* (p: *yuan* 緣) carries Buddhist connotations of karmic cause and effect. The author's use of this character—and the reader is unsure to which meaning the monk primarily refers—effectively conveys the monk's conflation of the religious and the worldly.

An exceptionally skillful use of double entendre is found in line 8. *Phương trượng* (p: *fangzhang* 方丈) is a monk's room in a temple; it also refers to the "isle of bliss," which, according to Daoist mythology, is one of three fabled islands—Bồng Lai (p: Penglai 蓬萊), Doanh Châu (p: Yingzhou 瀛洲), and Phương Trượng—in the Eastern Sea that the immortals inhabit and that pilgrims seek out in their quest for the elixir of youth.[25] Here, Phương Trượng forms a pair with the Western Paradise referred to in the first part of the couplet, which is the realm of enlightenment for Pure Land Buddhists; in coaxing the nun to return with him to his *phương trượng*, the monk audaciously refers to his earthly chamber as a place of everlasting bliss and he likens his humble room to the lofty realm of Buddhist enlightenment. The message the monk has for the nun is that striving to journey to the Western Paradise is too difficult; it would be easier and more profitable for her to cultivate religion in his personal chamber since there is a Buddhist altar there! Fittingly, the indecorous passage ends with imagery of destruction, a condition for rebirth.

The opening scene of the *Sãi Vãi* in fact anticipates a topic that will prove to be central to the play, namely the import of one's place in the physical world. The first of two framing bookends, this passage pits two rival impulses—staying put in one's place and journeying in search of a

---

25. *Shiji*, 6.313; Nienhauser, *The Grand Scribe's Records*, 1:142. These islands found their way into the historical record when Qin Shihuang's spiritual advisers wrote to tell the emperor of their existence and ask for permission to purify themselves, recruit young children, and embark on a journey in search of the immortals. Qin Shihuang sent them on their way with thousands of young boys and girls.

better one—against each other. Here the issue is cast as a religious di-
lemma, and in this passage the nun appears as the one who seeks to
physically relocate, whereas the monk rejects this form of religious cultivation and advocates instead one that can be practiced *in situ*. Of course,
his counsel proves to be an ill-disguised attempt to lure the nun to his
chamber, and, for the moment, the author puts aside the topic of the
importance of one's devotion to the physical land to focus his attention
on the more immediate problem of the religious man who conflates
spiritual aspirations with carnal desires. The success of this passage lies
in the use of religious terminology to refer to indulgence in sensual
pleasures, as if the words were a thin veil thrown carelessly over the monk's
immodest proposal in a feeble attempt to cover up his audacity. In
impiously deploying religious terminology in a way that plays up their
dual meanings, the author of the *Sãi Vãi* satirizes the corrupt practitioners of Buddhism in Đàng Trong who hide beneath the cover of religiosity
to conceal and perhaps justify their misdeeds.[26]

Quite predictably, and most understandably, the nun rejects the
monk's advances. Making it clear that she finds his argument for com-
bining religious cultivation and sexual gratification to be unacceptable,
she questions his cultivation, which appears to be based on his desire for
worldly possessions and pleasures:

15   Why do you speak such falsehoods;
      You must not be true in character.
16   Why is your cultivation concerned with loss and gain?
      Why is your cultivation greedy for worldly riches and sensual pleasure?
17   That certainly does not foster virtue;
      Do not cultivate those things!

In contrast to the monk, the nun draws a sharp distinction between
cultivating virtue and indulging in one's desire for worldly possessions.
After she chides him for his opening speech, the monk gives the impression of being chastened and tries to explain why he is unable to undertake religious cultivation in the correct fashion. He claims that he, "too,
would like to cultivate properly; unfortunately [he] lack[s] the necessary

26.   A third meaning of the word *phương trượng* is "Buddhist elder."

implements."[27] He goes on to recite a long list of things he lacks. These items include "a bell," "a drum," "prayer books," "sutras," "castanets," "clackers," "a flute," "cymbals," "a jar," "a bowl," "beans," "soy sauce," "an incense burner," "a tablecloth of lotus leaf," "shoes," "a hat," "a tunic," "a robe," "a front hall enclosed within a bamboo fence," "an ornamental hall decorated with parallel scrolls," "a vermilion stick," "a sprinkling vase," "a sounding staff," "a Buddhist cassock," "incense," "flowers," and "a wooden fish."[28] This list consists of implements used in a Buddhist temple or parts of a temple building, the place within which religious cultivation is performed. In responding to the nun's accusation that he was too interested in things of this world, the monk highlights Buddhism's reliance on a wide range of instruments and accessories, a dependency that seems rather incongruous with the faith's purported goal of worldly renunciation.

If the nun develops any sympathy for the materially bereft monk, she is quickly disabused of the sentiment. The monk no sooner speaks the words than he sweeps them aside in favor of another list of items he creates that consists of "things of greater importance" to which he gives priority:

29   Shanghai fabric! I will buy a pair of trousers for good occasion;
Ko-hemp cloth! I will buy a shirt to look nice and pretty.[29]

30   A hat adorned with wintry landscapes! I will buy one to look good
    and handsome;
A fan bearing images of spotted bamboo! I will buy one to treasure and
    display.

31   A pair of red shoes! I will buy to tread on;
An emerald headwrap! I will buy to cover my head.

32   I will also train a young novice, quite small,
to carry my pipe under his arm, oh marvelous!

33   Whichever market has many damsel customers;
Whichever hamlet is crowded with maiden laypersons;

---

27. *Sāi Vāi*, line 18.

28. *Sāi Vāi*, lines 19–26. A sounding staff is a *khakkhara*, which is a staff with tin rings attached. A monk carries it to warn sentient beings that he is approaching, so that they may move out of his way and not be trodden upon.

29. Ko-hemp is fiber derived from the kudzu plant, which can be used to make cloth.

34   I'll definitely cultivate here and there;
        I'll certainly cultivate up and down!

35   I will, on the one hand, prepare a monk's room,[30]
        So I have a deserted back room for myself.

36   On the face of it, it is open and reputable,
        But underfoot, there is a secret space.[31]

37   For when I am enjoying a meal of meat,
        And see a layperson about to arrive,

38   I'll hear that small child calling softly,
        And the plates of meat I'll toss in there.

39   I will, on the other hand, prepare a villa, quite small,
        That is situated away from the hamlet, quite far,

40   As shelter for when a layperson becomes pregnant,
        Then it shall be easy for me to fold my arms, sitting thus.

The monk scandalizes the nun and the audience with his list of priorities. This "naughty" list, consisting of, among other things, wardrobe items and fashion accessories to enhance one's physical appearance, forms a contrast with those implements on the previous "nice" list. Viewed one after the other, the two lists appear to be complete opposites of each other. However, the juxtaposition of the two lists invites the audience, or the reader, to view the "naughty" list as a warped reflection of the "nice" one; functioning as a mirror held up against the "nice" list, the "naughty" list reveals the possibility that the assiduous cultivation of religion is not dissimilar to the vain cultivation of one's physical image, with its attendant pleasure-seeking and deceitfulness.

Of note is the dominating presence of religious space in the *Sãi Vãi*. When the monk begins his flirtations with the nun, he has just completed his recitations and descended from the temple steps. The monastery looms large behind him, even if only in the audience's imagination. In this

30. Nguyễn Cư Trinh uses the word *phương trượng* to refer to the monk's chamber, the same word he used in the first section of the play.

31. In the AB.383 manuscript, after lines 36, 39, and 42, the nun interjects with the phrase "And why would you do that?" (*sắm để làm gì*), which maintains the dialogical nature of the satire in the monk's lengthy monologue. The monk scandalizes the nun by revealing what he intends to do with what he buys, prepares, and trains.

passage, the monk describes his two abodes: one that lies within the confines of orthodox religious space and the other located far away from the village. The monk, who is expected to be vegetarian, hides the meat in his private chamber within the temple to conceal his misdeed from visiting laypersons; in the opening section of the play, the monk tries to convince the nun to return with him to a room that is also within the temple. The fact that unorthodox activities, imagined or otherwise, are carried out in the temple sullies religious space and effectively erases the distinction between the sacred and the profane. It is only when the transgression becomes too visible to be hidden that the monk is obliged to move the pregnant layperson away from it. In drawing out the different functions of the two abodes the misbehaving monk wishes to keep, Nguyễn Cư Trinh directs attention to the complicity of the orthodox religious order in regard to the behavior of its errant monks; the author levels his accusation of hypocrisy not only at misbehaving monks but also at the formal religious order for enabling their actions.

This section of the play is clearly humorous. The monk, who is supposed to have austere tastes and live an ascetic life, decks himself out in the finery of the moment; the colorful attire that he dreams up contrasts with the typical clothing in which a monk is dressed.[32] This extravagant image leaves a lot of room for exaggerated gestures and slapstick humor and thus has immense comic potential in performance. The audience is moreover invited to invert conventional hierarchies and take a position of moral superiority vis-à-vis religious men. In featuring the misbehaving monk prominently in his satire, using him to caricature Buddhist clergymen in general, Nguyễn Cư Trinh advanced his criticism of a group of powerful men in Đàng Trong society. Moreover, he dismantled orthodox Buddhism by pointing out the worldliness inherent in the cultivation of it, both in terms of the implements required for proper practice and the tolerance of orthodox members toward the misbehavior of its errant clergymen. Nguyễn Cư Trinh's message was not a call for the reform of errant monks or a recommendation of the path of orthodoxy—it was an attack on orthodox Buddhism itself. The next targets of his

---

32. Koffler reported that the monks wore "ash-colored" robes. Koffler, "Description historique de la Cochinchine," 595. Borri noted that some monks were "clad in white, others in black, others in blue." Borri, *An Account of Cochin-China*, 169.

critique were the literati officials of the region. The author here employed a different set of literary devices, namely, hyperbole and catachresis, to discredit these errant gentlemen.

The Gentleman, the Petty Man, and the Ways of Cultivation

Whereas the nun previously attacked the monk for blurring the boundaries between the sacred and the profane in his practice of cultivation, she now criticizes him for not cultivating the Way at all. Again, we see that the nun's speech facilitates a transition to the next topic that the satire will take up, which is to question the practice of cultivation itself.

49   Although you remain hidden in your chamber,
      You are not making a way of cultivation!
50   The distant heaven sees clearly and is not blind;
      The vast [heavenly] net is sparsely woven but nothing falls through.

51   For one word that falls short of the law,
      Ten thousand lifetimes cannot compensate for it.
52   To the heavenly places, you, sir, alas have yet to ascend;
      To the hellish places, you, sir, are about to quickly descend.

Originally an image and metaphor from the *Dao De jing* (v: *Đạo Đức Kinh* 道德經), here the vast heavenly net is used to refer both to the law of heaven and to the law of the state, which would let no evil man escape.[33] The nun accuses the monk of being false and "not making a way of cultivation" (*nào phải đạo tu*); in so doing, she assumes that there exists a correct way to cultivate. The monk responds to her accusation with a discussion of not one but several different forms of cultivation. He launches into a comparison of two kinds of men—the gentleman and the petty man—and he shows the nun that both kinds engage in the practice of cultivation, even if that cultivation leads to different ends. This section's

---

33.   Section 73 of the *Dao De jing* states: "Heaven's net is vast. Though its mesh is sparsely woven, nothing falls through" 天網恢恢，疏而不失. *Laozi Dao De jing*, 1B.21b.

textual structure, in which two contrasting categories are set against each other, is a repetition of what we have just seen in the previous section, where the "nice" and the "naughty" lists of items are positioned to illuminate the underlying and unflattering similarities between the two; here, the gentleman's and the petty man's cultivations are held up to scrutiny with similar results. This section begins with a description of the cultivation of a model Confucian gentleman. The monk explains:

53   Whoever is a gentleman,
      His virtue exceeds his talent.
54   When venerating his king, he is completely upright;
      When venerating his father, he is completely filial.
55   A single word spoken for humaneness and for the Way, that is cultivating
         speech.
      A single deed done that is not harmful or greedy, that is cultivating action.
56   Taking up humaneness, he cultivates his personality;
      Taking up virtue, he cultivates his physical self.
57   He cultivates luminous virtue so as to renew the common people;
      Cultivates running a household so as to govern a country.
58   That is a worthy and virtuous person;
      A person who correctly cultivates techniques of cultivation.
59   Externally, he cultivates gentleness and generosity;
      Internally, he cultivates peacefulness and uprightness.
60   He cultivates reverence, cultivates respectfulness;
      Cultivates trustworthiness, cultivates sincerity.
61   If he masters the techniques of cultivating his actions,
      He will increasingly embody good fortune and fine form.
62   Arising from this, he will get official status, get position;
      Get a long life, get a reputation.
63   Get wealth and honor and glory and splendor;
      That is heaven indeed.
64   Whoever is a worthy man,
      He cultivates ascending to heaven.

In extolling the virtues of the Confucian gentleman, this passage relies on the authority of classical primers and their definition of such a man. Line 53 derives its inspiration from Sima Guang's (v: Tư Mã Quang 司馬光, 1019–86) *Comprehensive Mirror to Aid the Government* (v: *Tư Trị Thông Giám*, p: *Zizhi tongjian* 资治通鉴), which states: "Therefore, [if his] talent and virtue are complete and to the utmost, call him a sage; [if his] talent and virtue have both perished, call him a fool; [if his] virtue exceeds his talent, call him a gentleman; [if his] talent exceeds his virtue, call him a petty man" 是故才德全尽谓之圣人，才德兼亡谓之愚人，德胜才谓之君子，才胜德谓之小人.[34] Line 57 borrows from the famous opening of the *Great Learning* (v: Đại Học, p: *Da Xue* 大學), one of the four books in the canon of Confucian classics, which says: "The Way of the Great Learning is to illuminate luminous virtue, to renew the people, and to rest in the utmost excellence" 大學之道，在明明德，在親民，在止於至善.[35] In his cultivation, the model gentleman of the *Sãi Vãi* conforms to what is expected of him, and his cultivation is based on nothing less than the forms prescribed by the classics.

The unproblematic description of the virtuous gentleman is complicated, however, when one considers its position beside the passage on the cultivations of a petty man, which immediately follows it. The main technique on which Nguyễn Cư Trinh relied in this part of the play is catachresis, whereby a word is used in a manner that departs from its conventional usage. In particular, he expanded his creativity on the usage of the word *cultivate* (v: *tu*, p: *xiu* 修), and employed *tu* as his verb of choice to discuss the bad habits of petty men:

66   Petty men's vulgar manners,
     cultivate worldly natures.

67   They *cultivate* hearts that are ungrateful, cruel, treacherous, and greedy;
     Cultivate minds that are stubborn, ferocious, tyrannical, and wicked.

68   Having been nurtured to adulthood, they yet *cultivate* hearts that are unfilial;
     Having eaten to fullness, they yet *cultivate* stomachs that are disloyal.

69   They *cultivate* attractive looks to flatter others and ingratiate themselves;
     They *cultivate* clever speech to gloss over wrongdoings and faults.

---

34. *Zizhi tongjian*, 1.14.

35. *Liji*, 19.9a. The *Da Xue* was originally one of the chapters of the *Book of Rites* (v: Lễ Kí, p: Liji 禮記); Zhu Xi (v: Chu Hi 朱熹, 1130–1200) later selected the *Da Xue* for inclusion as one of the four books of the Confucian canon. Note that the *Sãi Vãi* follows the neo-Confucian commentarial tradition and interprets 親 ("familiar") as 新 ("renew").

70 Of worthy men, they are jealous and hold back their welcome;
    But guilty men, they seek out ever so eagerly.

71 They *cultivate* slick tongues to take property and gratify their desire;
    Cultivate wicked schemes to harm people and satisfy their anger.

72 Petty men are like lice,
    They *cultivate* sucking the blood of people.

    The more they *cultivate* the more they humiliate their grandfathers and
73   fathers;
    The more they *cultivate* the more they harm their children and grandchildren.

74 They *cultivate* recklessness and thoughtlessness,
    Cultivate promiscuity and wantonness.

75 Whoever is a petty man,
    He *cultivates* unrighteousness paths.

76 In this way, in darkness he is one whom sprites and ghosts harm,
    In daylight he is one whom the king's laws punish.

77 That is the cultivation of a petty man,
    and so he *cultivates* entering hell.

This is not a typical usage of the verb *cultivate*; in fact, the word is not used to refer to the cultivation of bad habits except perhaps in jest, as is the case here. Here the petty man sincerely pours the entirety of his energies into cultivation, but unfortunately his cultivation is directed toward unsavory ends. Besides the cultivation of wicked attributes, such as a tyrannical mind and an ungrateful heart, the petty man in the *Sāi Vāi* abuses what ought to be external manifestations of virtue, such as an attractive appearance and clever speech, for the sake of flattering others and ingratiating himself. In blatantly misusing the word *cultivation* and in treating it so carelessly, the author forces the reader to question the concept on which the orthodox practice of religion is dependent. The issue of cultivation, moreover, links the passage describing the actions of the petty man with the previous one on the gentleman, and the parallelism of the two gives the reader reason to reevaluate the *Sāi Vāi*'s earlier depiction of the paradigm of virtue.

That passage, read with an eye to the distorted image of the gentleman's faulty double, leads to an alternative interpretation of the cultivation of virtue. The reader wonders if the gentleman performs seemingly virtuous actions to profit himself, just as the petty man does, and a seed of doubt about his sincerity takes root. Apparently innocuous and even favorable words now present themselves as instances of overstatement. In the line: "When venerating his king, he is completely (*hết*) upright; when venerating his father, he is completely (*hết*) filial," the reader divines, in the word *hết*, the exaggerated degree of the gentleman's uprightness and piety in his veneration of king and father.[36] Line 54 might thus be read as follows: "When venerating his king, he *completely exhausts* his uprightness; when venerating his father, he *completely exhausts* his piety." The emphatic terms extend the possibility that the "virtuous" gentleman's cultivation was really a conspicuous performance of goodness. Emphatic words likewise animate line 55. Speech and action are typically paired to describe a "trustworthy" (v: *tín*, p: *xin* 信) person—one whose actions matched his speech.[37] Speech and action can also be understood as outward manifestations of a person's virtue, so a model gentleman cultivates his speech through speaking for humanity and the Way, just as he cultivates his actions through deeds that are neither harmful nor selfish. In itself, *một*, which signifies the number one, appearing before the characters for "word" and "deed," does not imply anything negative; in fact it suggests that every action or word would accumulate toward a person's cultivation of virtue. It does, however, tempt the reader into constructing a less generous interpretation of this gentleman. The gentleman in question could think that he is cultivating speech and action just by speaking a single word for humanity and performing a single action that does not cause harm, suggesting a shallow form of cultivation instead of a deeper process of refinement. Line 55 can in fact be understood as the monk's direct response to the nun's charge that a person would not be able, in 10,000 lifetimes, to compensate "for one (*một*) word that falls short of the law."[38] Here, he demonstrates to the nun the folly of her statement by showing how the single word (or deed) done for the sake of the good can fall quite far from the spirit of the law.

In a staged performance, emphatic terms are easily acted out to direct the audience to deduce the second level of meaning. The actor could,

---

36. *Hết* is a *Nôm* reading of the character 歇. Its function is similar to that of the *Hán* character 盡.

37. Lau, *Confucius: The Analects*, 25.

38. *Sãi Vãi*, line 51.

for example, make a show of the *single* word and *single* deed the gentleman counted as the only actions necessary in cultivating speech and action, and act out preening when speaking the lines, indicating that the gentleman used humaneness and virtue to cultivate his personality and physical self. The performed version in fact benefits from the divergence of speech and action to show not only the two levels of meaning but also the untrustworthiness of a person whose speech does not match his actions! The fact that the performance of empty goodness was literally done on a stage, and the same actor who was the misbehaving monk now made a performance of performing virtue, powerfully brings to light the hypocrisy of real-life "performers of virtue." This section of the play, which contrasts the actions of a gentleman with those of a petty man, operates on a subtler level than the previous section, in which Buddhist monks were made the butt of Nguyễn Cư Trinh's slapstick jokes. One imagines that the message the audience derives from watching the performance will be different, depending on its level of literary sophistication. On the one hand, a less educated audience might understand this to be a didactic lesson, where the gentleman's cultivation is contrasted with the petty man's misdeeds; on the other hand, a more astute audience could understand the juxtaposition less as a contrast between the two kinds of men and more as a procedure to draw out the similarity between them. It is worth recalling that here and throughout the play, the monk is dressed in religious costume; his words, which preach adherence to Confucian behaviors, contrast starkly with his outward appearance as a Buddhist religious figure, and the incongruity between form and function allows the character to better portray a mimic who self-consciously mocks the real mimics of virtuous action.

In pairing the gentleman, who cultivates his speech and action for his personal advancement, and the petty man, who assiduously cultivates his physical appearance and speech to gain more than he deserves, Nguyễn Cư Trinh diminishes the moral distance between the "virtuous" gentleman and the petty man. Perhaps, if the "virtuous" gentleman cultivates in a shallow manner and only for the show of it, beneath this pretense lies the "true" nature of his cultivation as depicted in the section on the petty man. In this way, "a person who correctly cultivates techniques (ways) of cultivation" (*người tu phải dạo tu*) is also one who "cultivates unrighteous paths (ways)" (*tu những lộ bất ngãi*).[39] In responding to the nun's initial assessment that he was not bound for heaven but descending straight to hell, the monk shows the nun the faulty logic behind her assumption that heaven was reserved for those who engaged in cultivation and hell for those who did not.

But why is Nguyễn Cư Trinh intent on blurring the distinction between the gentleman and the petty man? Here it is important to note the social standing of the two figures. In terms of social hierarchy, the gentleman rules over the petty men, who are those who hold low-ranking office; petty men, in turn, can be distinguished from "the people" (v: *dân*, p: *min* 民), who hold no office.[40] The *Sãi Vãi*'s depiction of the petty man can thus be read as a condemnation of lower-ranking officials in the Vietnamese imperial bureaucracy, and the association the play draws between the gentleman and the petty man suggests that there were officials at every level of the bureaucracy who did not live up to the standard of a virtuous official. Significantly, Nguyễn Cư Trinh's polemic against the cultivation of literati officials leaves one wondering what he was arguing for. As with the case of the misbehaving monk, the reader suspects that the author was not promoting a return to orthodox practices as a corrective for errant power holders in Đàng Trong society. Instead, as we will see, he attempted to modify traditionally accepted practices to render them suitable to the frontier world.

The 1751 Memorial

The *Sãi Vãi* portrays southern Vietnamese frontier society as one that was plagued with errant religious men and bureaucrats; a critical study of the first three sections further reveals the extent to which Nguyễn Cư Trinh viewed orthodox religious ideals and administrative models as inadequate to the situation on the frontier. His assessment of the failures of literati officials is in fact contained in another document composed

39. *Sãi Vãi*, lines 58 and 75.
40. Lau, *Confucius: The Analects*, 14.

shortly after the *Sãi Vãi*.[41] In the winter of 1751, Nguyễn Cư Trinh submitted a memorial to the Nguyễn lord, Nguyễn Phúc Khóat, in which he openly condemned the local officials of Quảng Ngãi. Two of four sections of his memorial were dedicated to detailing the dishonesty and incompetence of the local officials:

> First, in the prefectures and districts, [those in] office to govern the people have of late been irresponsible in their jobs and only instigate investigations and lawsuits. I request that from now on all shortfalls and surpluses from land rents and various other taxes be routinely given to the county magistrate to consolidate, and handed over to Quảng Nam to manage the transfer [to the court]; mending [the process of collecting rents] in this way will reduce annoyances.
>
> Second, [those in] the prefectures and districts, ever since arriving, have taken to arresting and investigating [the people] in order to have a regular salary. The more the people's riches are exhausted, the more their manners and customs are weakened. I request that [the court] regularly give out fixed salaries and use their honesty or corruption, diligence or laziness, as the basis for promotions and demotions.[42]
>
> 一言府縣乃治民之職比來不責以事，只令勘問詞訟。請嗣後差餘田租、諸稅、例一切付知縣編收，交廣南營遞，納以省煩擾。二言府縣從來以拘查爲常祿。民財愈耗民俗愈薄。請定給常俸，以廉貪勤怠爲黜陟。

The memorial provides us with information about the quality of the local officials in Quảng Ngãi and the dubious activities in which they were engaged. In the first article of the memorial, Nguyễn Cư Trinh charged that local officials were mismanaging the taxes collected from the people of the province. His recommendation that tax collection be simplified and handed over to the administration of the Quảng Nam garrison suggests that he perceived a systemic problem arising from the

41. Given the paucity of sources for a detailed study of any prefecture in eighteenth-century Vietnam, Quảng Ngãi is notable for having several documents that address issues pertaining to it. They are, however, penned by one person: Nguyễn Cư Trinh.

42. The memorial is included in Nguyễn Cư Trinh's biography in *Đại Nam Liệt Truyện Tiền Biên*, 5.6–7. A transcript of the memorial can also be found in *Đại Nam Thực Lục Tiền Biên*, 10.18–19.

fact that too many local officials were involved in the process, which created opportunities for abuse. His proposal called for the court to decrease the number of local officials in the region to "reduce annoyances." The second article of the memorial directs the king's attention to the fact that his officials were poorly paid, which Nguyễn Cư Trinh identified as a reason for their predatory behavior. Moreover, he hinted that promotions and demotions were carried out with criteria other than the officials' performance in mind, and they were neither judged poorly for their laziness and corruption nor rewarded for their diligence and honesty. For this reason, the prefecture was facing difficulties.

Nguyễn Cư Trinh identified problems and presented solutions in his memorial, which included limiting the power of the prefectural and subprefectural officials and giving appropriate salaries and promotions to competent ones. When his memorial received no reply from the Nguyễn lord, Nguyễn Cư Trinh tried to resign from his position, but the lord assigned him a different appointment, which he accepted.[43] His description of the problem of corrupt officials in his memorial was intended for a small audience—Nguyễn Phúc Khóat and his closest advisers; in the Sãi Vãi, he displayed his contempt for errant monks and incompetent officials to a larger audience. The memorial was written about a year after the Sãi Vãi was composed, and it suggests that Nguyễn Cư Trinh identified a pressing problem on the frontier and tried, through satire and a formal petition, to correct the problem by addressing the villagers, the errant power holders, and the Nguyễn lord himself. That a memorial from such an esteemed member of the Nguyễn bureaucracy did not receive a reply suggests the magnitude of the problems facing the Nguyễn court, which was unable to put in place the solutions Nguyễn Cư Trinh recommended. The remaining sections of the Sãi Vãi and his petition provide further elaboration on these problems and the solutions he devised to address them.

43. *Đại Nam Liệt Truyện Tiền Biên*, 5.7.

CHAPTER 2

The Classical in the Vernacular

The *Sāi Vāi* is a work that exists simultaneously in both the classical and the vernacular worlds. In invoking the opposition between the classical and the vernacular, I draw out the distinction between the Han realm, a world that revolves around the literary Chinese language and the classical Confucian texts from which the elite of the various East Asian domains derived their learning, and the local world, a particular one embedded in the language of everyday use. The *Sāi Vāi* is composed in the vernacular *Nôm* script, although it is heavily indebted to the Han world for its allusions and references. But the vernacular is not merely a vehicle for disseminating classical stories and promoting classical ideals; it plays a pivotal role in the reshaping, reimagining, and even distorting of classical elements. Just as the work operates simultaneously in two registers, its author moves concurrently in two worlds; Nguyễn Cư Trinh is a member of the Đàng Trong literary circle and a scholar belonging to a larger educated elite that extends beyond the confines of the southern Vietnamese domain. Similarly, the *Sāi Vāi* transcends the site of its production, reaching out into a larger cultural world, even as it remains embedded in Đàng Trong politics.

This chapter presents an analysis of sections 4, 5, and 6 of the *Sāi Vāi*, sections that form the crux of Nguyễn Cư Trinh's thought relating to good governance. In terms of literary technique, there is a significant difference between these sections and the preceding ones. Whereas the first part of the play relies heavily on double entendre, hyperbole, and catachresis, the momentum of sections 4, 5, and 6 is generated through the use of examples from history. In a similar manner, this chapter is devoted to a discussion of historical personalities. Historical exemplars derived from the classical world act as a kind of shorthand in the contemporary one; the audience of the play understands each abbreviated reference to have a particular meaning, or even a plurality of meanings, as established by the classical tradition. The context helps us determine which associations are primary in making sense of the signification of polyvalent figures. Classical allusions in the *Sãi Vãi* not only lend the author's views the weight of ancient authority but also convey, in a highly condensed form, the substance of his political theory. A notable aspect of the play is that all the historical examples cited in it come from what we would now categorize as Chinese history; no Vietnamese leaders or dynasties are mentioned. However, a member of the early modern Vietnamese literati would not have considered these "Chinese" personages extraneous to his own cultural heritage; instead, he would have regarded them as part of the shared Han tradition. The use of such classical characters and historical examples in a vernacular play intended for a broad village audience suggests the presence of some level, however rudimentary, of classical literacy among the people in Đàng Trong.[1]

A question remains: why did Nguyễn Cư Trinh not feel the need to include any historical examples from Vietnamese history? It is possible

1. Alexander Woodside discusses an instance in which nineteenth-century villagers of the Red River delta region (in the northern part of Vietnam) exhibited a high degree of comprehension of the classics. In 1854, during the uprising led by Cao Bá Quát (1809–1855) against the Nguyễn dynasty, he succinctly explained his revolt in a slogan written in classical Chinese characters, which translates as: "Bình Dương (p: Pingyang) and Bồ Bản (p: Puban) lack their Nghiêu (p: Yao) and Thuấn (p: Shun); Mục Dã (p: Muye) and Minh Điều (p: Mingtiao) have their Vũ (p: Wu) and Thang (p: Tang)" 平陽蒲阪無堯舜・牧野鳴條有武湯. Without further explication, the villagers understood the reference to mean that the relationship between their polity and the Nguyễn emperor Tự Đức (p: Si De 嗣德, r. 1847–83) was like that of Pingyang and Puban, capitals of the mythical sage emperors Yao and Shun, without Yao and Shun. As a consequence of such bad governance, Muye and Mingtiao, sites where King Wu of Zhou and King Tang of Shang had defeated bad rulers respectively, had the right to throw off their bad rulers. Cao Bá Quát positioned himself as the Wu or Tang that Vietnam needed, and the Nguyễn ruler Tự Đức as the bad ruler who deserved to be deposed. See Woodside, "Conceptions of Change," 112–13. Scholars have typically understood the inhabitants of the northern Vietnamese polity to be more conversant with classical allusions than those of the southern Vietnamese polity, but the *Sãi Vãi* suggests otherwise.

that in filling his play with historical figures from the larger Han cultural tradition, he sought to demonstrate the civility of his domain and establish the Vietnamese people as participants in that tradition. Alternatively, his decision not to include any Vietnamese historical exemplars might suggest an unfamiliarity among his southern audience with the Vietnamese historical tradition or that, unlike the more established Han stories, those from the Vietnamese tradition had yet to enter into the literary language and become transformed into recognizable cultural expressions. But perhaps the most probable reason for his choice of references is that citing examples from Vietnamese history would simply not convey his intended sentiment or thought as effectively as would the examples from the Han tradition. Although the Vietnamese particular remained at the level of the particular, the classical Han particular was raised to the status of the universal. Citing the mythical sages as examples of good governance, for instance, conjured forth paradigms that in their potency far surpassed anything that later history, Vietnamese or Chinese, could offer. The full extent of the treachery of bad leaders and traitorous officials could be most dramatically displayed when the dynasties they destroyed were the glorious ones of old.

The historical personalities invoked in the *Sãi Vãi* give form and force to Nguyễn Cư Trinh's discourse on good governance. To harness them for his use, the author removes them from their indigenous classical contexts and replants them in the vernacular soil. At times, classical figures undergo noteworthy transformations even as they remain recognizable as historical figures from the classical world. Yet on account of their changed countenances and novel characteristics, the contemporary reader appraises them with new eyes and, sometimes, raised eyebrows. In the three sections of the *Sãi Vãi* that this chapter examines, the author creatively pairs historical exemplars, and in so doing makes clever use of the couplings to illuminate the commonalities between them. In the first two sections discussed here, the commonalities between the pairs of historical figures undergird didactic stories; in the third section, the curious couplings prevent the narrator (the monk) from completing the didactic stories he wishes to tell. Taken together, the sections deliver the author's critique of conventional governance and his suggestions on ways to modify it for southern Vietnamese frontier society.

To Be Free from the Mundane

In drawing out the practical similarities between the cultivation of the gentleman and that of the petty man (as in section 3), Nguyễn Cư Trinh presents the reader with a problem. A possible solution lay in reforming the gentleman, so that his cultivation accords better with Confucian orthodoxy; the reader recalls, however, that the author had borrowed from classical primers such as the *Zizhi tongjian* and the *Da Xue* for his definition of the gentleman depicted in the passage and suspects that reform is not the author's intended solution. Instead of promoting a correction of the gentleman's cultivation to widen the moral distance between him and the petty man, Nguyễn Cư Trinh advocates transcending the dichotomy itself. He presents an alternative form of cultivation that is "free from the mundane," which hints to the reader that his objection to the classical Confucian gentleman's cultivation lies in the fact that he believes it to be either forced or formulaic. He ascribes this transcendent form of cultivation to the people of superior wisdom:

78   As for cultivation that is free from the mundane;
       There remain those with the cultivation of superior wisdom.

79   Recall the ancient times of Đường [Tang] and Ngu [Yu],
       When sages were proclaimed the Two Thearchs.

80   The Two Thearchs were people who cultivated themselves;
       Consequently all under heaven was stable.

81   The Three Sovereigns were people who cultivated humaneness;
       Consequently the entire population was in order.

82   Be it in the rise and fall of the Hán [Han] and the Đường [Tang] dynasties,
       Or the successions and transitions of the Minh [Ming] and
          the Tống [Song] dynasties,

83   [It holds true that] when there was the cultivation of virtue,
          then all under heaven was stable;
       When there was the cultivation of humaneness,
          then foundations were created.

84   As for cultivating civil administration and cultivating military might,
       People cultivated these according to the times.

85   In times of great peace,
          they abandoned the military to cultivate civil administration;
      In times of rebellion and suppressing chaos,
          they abandoned civil administration to cultivate military might.

86   When just one person cultivated himself sufficiently,
      Then all under heaven was victorious and peaceful.

87   Hale and hearty in the region of longevity and the palace of springtime;
      To cultivate in this way, is it not the cultivation of superior wisdom?

On a fundamental level, to be "free from the mundane" (v: *thoát tục*, p: *tuosu* 脱俗) is to be free from prescribed forms of behavior, the implication being that this freedom elevates one to greater refinement in manner and taste. In a Buddhist context, *thoát tục* is understood as "renouncing the world" by freeing oneself from the conventions of this world and retreating into the life of a religious recluse. As the play will show, Nguyễn Cư Trinh did not prescribe religious reclusiveness but adaptive engagement with the world. In employing the phrase *thoát tục* in a sense that is completely different from its meaning in the Buddhist context, he proposes a form of cultivation liberated from the two concepts that he finds objectionable: first, the rigidly formulaic cultivation of the gentlemen, and second, Buddhist renunciation of the world.

Nguyễn Cư Trinh takes transcendent cultivation to refer to the way of the sage kings. Because he names the realms over which they ruled, the identities of the Two Thearchs the monk invokes are most certainly Yao (v: Nghiêu 堯) and Shun (v: Thuấn 舜). The identities of the Three Sovereigns are less obvious, but because of their placement after Yao and Shun and before the monk's list of ethnic Han dynasties (Han, Tang, Song, Ming), I believe they refer to the most famous rulers of the Xia, Shang, and Zhou dynasties, which would be their respective founding rulers, Yu (v: Vũ 禹), Tang (v: Thang 湯), and either Wen (v: Văn 文) or Wu (v: Võ 武) for the Zhou dynasty.[2] This aspect of the sage kings' rule, their successful establishment of dynasties, was especially relevant to Đàng Trong politics at the historical moment in which the *Sãi Vãi* was

2.   The sequence of Yao, Shun, Yu, and Tang appears elsewhere as a list of rulers who yielded the throne to worthy men when they considered it appropriate to do so, although Tang was succeeded by his son. Idema and West, *Battles, Betrayals, and Brotherhood*, 56.

composed. Previously governing under the mandate of lordship over the southern Vietnamese realm, Nguyễn Phúc Khoát declared himself Võ Vương (p: Wu Wang 武王) in 1744, just six years before the *Sãi Vãi* was written. Although Võ Vương's change in status was in many ways more symbolic than real, some in his court opposed such a bold act of self-elevation. Nguyễn Cư Trinh's choice of historical exemplars for the cultivation of superior wisdom might have hinted to his audience that he, in his praise of foundational heroes, supported the king's assertion of independence.[3]

As the king's official sent to govern a chaotic frontier region, Nguyễn Cư Trinh was naturally concerned with issues of stability and order, and he invoked the classical sage kings who brought peace to the realms they governed. Through these historical borrowings, he lent weight to his argument that good governance rests on the cultivation of the polity's talents according to the needs of the times. "Military might" and "civil administration" represent two ends of a spectrum, and this passage can be understood more broadly as a call for leaders to embrace a form of cultivation that took into account the pressing demands of the moment. After all, the classical sage kings did not adhere stubbornly to one method of governance but proved themselves to be adaptive.

Lest the reader be misled into thinking that the cultivation that was "free from the mundane" to which the monk referred was religious in nature, the subsequent sections quickly disabused one of that notion. The monk elaborates on his governing philosophy by contrasting the cultivation of those in the category of "superior wisdom" with those of "middling wisdom" and "inferior wisdom"; in so doing, he demonstrates the folly of allowing the pursuit of religious cultivation to interfere with good Confucian governance:

88   There are still those with the cultivation of middling wisdom.
89   [Such were] Mạc Địch [Mo Di] and Dương Chu [Yang Zhu];
     Who cultivated either for the people or for the self.

3. The Nguyễn family had effectively been ruling Đàng Trong autonomously since the early seventeenth century and had not remitted taxes to the Lê kings in the northern Vietnamese realm for more than a century. Symbolically, however, Võ Vương's elevation marked a deliberate break away from the Lê dynasty, which was then completely under the control of the Trịnh family, and signified the political independence of his domain.

90 Even if by plucking one tiny hair he could benefit all of humanity,
    Dương Chu would not be happy to do it.

91 To exhaust all of his strength to benefit just one person,
    Mạc Địch would wholeheartedly give and not flinch.

92 As for those who cultivate like *Thích Ca* on the one hand,
    Đạt Ma on the other;[4]

93 Kumarajiva cultivated assiduously,
    Manjusri cultivated with agonizing effort.

94 This is how it all started, foreigners came
    Discoursing according to the customs of the Central Hoa civilization.

95 Spurning wealth, honor, glory, and splendor,
    Seeking pleasure in quietness, idleness, reclusivity, and happiness.

96 Calling themselves by the name of Buddha,
    [Written with] the characters "not" and "human";

97 Just as their logic in the truest form
    Is to be unconcerned with human affairs.

98 And so it goes: whoever suffers infelicity is left to his adversity,
    Whoever meets serendipity is left to his good fortune.

99 Then households may prosper or die out: fathers and sons need
        not defend them!
    Countries may be in order or in chaos: lords and officials need not care!

100 Nevertheless, they speak of humaneness and speak of propriety,
     Speak of human nature and speak of human affections.

101 A worldly person who is greedy for Heaven will do good;
     If he is afraid of Hell he gets rid of bad habits.

102 Ten thousand generations making offerings;
     That is the cultivation of middling wisdom.

In the category of the cultivation of middling wisdom, the monk brings to the audience's attention two pairs of historical figures whose teachings illustrate ideologies that he considers to be unsuitable for governance. The first pairing comprises Mo Di (v: Mạc Địch 墨翟, ca. 470–391 BCE) and Yang Zhu (v: Dương Chu 楊朱, ca. 440–360 BCE), classical examples of philosophers whom the Confucianists considered heterodox. Mozi

---

4. *Thích Ca* refers to the historical Buddha, Sakyamuni. *Đạt Ma* refers to Bodhidharma, a semi-legendary sixth-century figure that came from India to China.

preached "love without discrimination," something the Confucianists found unacceptable because it stood opposed to one of their central teachings; against Mohist impartiality, they insisted that love should be greatest toward one's parents, then in lesser degrees toward other members of one's family, and finally, as an extension of this principle, toward the whole of humanity. Yang Zhu, conversely, stood for hedonism and extreme egotism since he would not part with "one tiny hair" to "benefit all of humanity." It is likely that this characterization misrepresents Yangism, which maintained that life was so precious that one should not even sacrifice a strand of hair in exchange for possession of the whole empire.[5] Regardless of the accuracy of the portrayal, Mozi and Yang Zhu have come to represent a rigid adherence to a position that is characterized by a disregard for situational nuance.

The second pairing in the category of middling wisdom consists of Kumarajiva, a translator of sacred Sanskrit texts who traveled to China in the fourth century, and Manjusri, a Bodhisattva associated with wisdom whom some believe lived on the Wutai Mountain (v: Ngũ Đài Sơn 五臺山). The monk undermines their teachings in two ways: first, he highlights the fact that they were foreigners, thus emphasizing his point that their philosophies were inherently unsuitable for the people of his own culture, which he does not differentiate from that of the "Central Hoa civilization." Second, he claims that Buddhist philosophy is fundamentally irrelevant to governance because the aim of Buddhism, as exhibited in the Han character for Buddha (佛 combines the characters 弗, which means "not," and 人, which means "human"), is to escape from human affairs. This denial of one's own humanity leads to the neglect of crucial tasks necessary for maintaining stability within the polity and among the population.

The monk's ambivalence toward the historical figures in the category of middling wisdom is apparent, but these philosophers and religious men fare rather well when compared with the inhabitants of the category of "inferior wisdom"; there, the monk demonstrates how an obsession with

5. Both Mencius (ca. 372–289 BCE) and Xunzi (ca. 312–230 BCE) found reason to criticize them. D. C. Lau conjectures that Mencius was possibly right in giving Yang Zhu's school of thought this much attention, even though it lost its influence relatively quickly, because it might actually have become the precursor of Daoist philosophies. Lau, *Mencius*, 29–31.

religious philosophies has historically caused great harm to the practitioner
and to the people:

103   As for cultivation that is very stupid,
      There are many people of inferior wisdom.

104   Yonder like Hán Võ Đế [Han Wudi],[6]
      Who was a highly illustrious man;
105   Here like Tần Thủy Hoàng [Qin Shihuang],
      Who was a ferocious and cruel fellow.

106   One was greedy to cultivate the Way,
      The other dived and forded to cultivate immortality.
107   They exhausted the strength of the people—all under heaven suffered worry
      and cares;
      They spent the resources of a country—ten thousand peoples shouted
      in hardship.

108   A hundred strategies to cultivate religion, there were,
      But even a tiny hair of benevolence or sympathy, there was not.
      In the land of Luân Đài [Luntai], did Hán [Han] not have to repent his
109   heart?
      [Only when the enemy was] at the Hàm Cốc [Hangu] pass
      did Tần [Qin] realize there were rebellious intentions.

110   Alas! Many resemble Hán [Han];
      Many are unreasonable like Tần [Qin]!
111   In what age has anyone cultivated to keep up with Tống Đạo
      Quân [Song Daojun],
      in what age is anyone esteemed to be the equal of Lương Võ Đế
      [Liang Wudi]?

112   Nevertheless, why did immortals not appear to give [Tống] urgent assistance?
      [When Lương] starved in Đài Thành [Taicheng], why did Buddha himself
      not avert the disaster?
113   A pity about the foundational labors of establishing rivers and mountains;[7]
      They destroyed the work that their virtuous ancestors created.

114   The army of Chu [Zhou] had let loose their arrows and cannons;
      Why did the ruler of Tề [Qi][8] rely on preaching the Way endlessly?

---

6.   This version of the *Sãi Vãi* mistakenly records his name as Liang instead Han.
7.   Rivers and mountains refer to a dynasty.
8.   Qi Yuan 齊元, which I translated as ruler of Qi, to match 周師, the armies of Zhou.

115   The Khitan had already encircled them inside and outside;
    Why did Vương Khâm [Wang Qin] still advocate closing the door to
        cultivate?

116   [Dynasties] decayed: their time was up;
    [Leaders] died: nobody mourned them.

For the first pairing, Nguyễn Cư Trinh groups together Qin Shihuang
(v: Tần Thỉ Hoàng 秦始皇, 259–210 BCE), the first emperor of the short-
lived Qin dynasty, and Han Wudi (v: Hán Võ Đế 漢武帝, 156–87 BCE),
the sixth emperor of the illustrious Han dynasty. Both emperors made
extensive use of the people's labor, and the constant demands on their
subjects led to widespread suffering in the empire. Qin Shihuang undertook a series of large-scale construction projects, which included building the great wall to the north and constructing a canal to connect the
northern and the southern parts of his domain.[9] Han Wudi sought to
expand his territory at great cost to his people and without regard to the
immense cruelty he inflicted on others; in one instance, in the midst of
a four-year campaign against the Central Asian state of Dayuan, the
people of Luntai failed to provide material support for the imperial army
and were consequently butchered.[10] Perhaps more germane to the issue

---

9. The *Sāi Vāi* notes that Qin Shihuang realized, quite belatedly, that a revolt was
brewing only when the enemy was at the Hangu Pass, which was a strategic point for
the Qin empire; the events at the pass brought the Qin dynasty to collapse, but it was Qin
Shihuang's son who bore witness to that, rather than his father. When the first emperor
died, his youngest son, Qin Er Shi (v: Tần Nhị Thế 秦二世, 229–207 BCE), ascended
the throne, thanks to the machinations of the eunuch Zhao Gao (v: Triệu Cao 趙高, d.
207 BCE); unfortunately, the son proved himself to be as cruel as his father. In 207 BCE,
revolts broke out east of the Hangu Pass and Zhao Gao, afraid that the emperor would
hold him responsible, decided to launch a palace coup to replace Qin Er Shi with his
nephew, who was in fact the son of the original heir. Qin Er Shi was left with no choice
but to take his own life. Zhao Gao was assassinated by the new ruler, and the short-
lived Qin dynasty collapsed soon after. *Shiji*, 6.332–44; Nienhauser, *The Grand Scribe's
Records*, 1:55–63.

10. *Han shu*, 61.2701; Hulsewe, *China in Central Asia*, 231. Toward the end of his
life, Han Wudi admitted his guilt in what became known as the Edict of Luntai. See *Han
shu*, 96B.3912–14; Hulsewe, *China in Central Asia*, 168–74. For more information on Han
Wudi's campaigns into the Central Asian region, see the "Traditions of the Western Regions" in *Han shu*, 96.3871–932.

this section of the *Sāi Vāi* treats is that the two emperors were desperate to overcome their mortality, and they spared no efforts in their search for ways to attain eternal life. Obsessed with finding the elixir of youth, the first emperor of Qin sent several thousand young boys and girls to seek out the immortals in the seas; to recover one of the nine tripods of the Zhou that had allegedly escaped his father's possession, Qin Shihuang ordered a thousand men to dive into the rivers in search of it.[11] Likewise, Han Wudi sought to live forever and desired to reach the immortals who purportedly had knowledge of the drug of longevity; like Qin Shihuang, he sent expeditions to the Eastern Sea in his quest for them. Persuaded by the magicians and alchemists who flocked to him, he propitiated the hearth spirits, hoping to receive instructions for turning cinnabar into gold.[12] The search was for naught, and, like the emperors' construction and military projects, the quest for immortality led to great hardships for the people.

The second pairing consists of Song Daojun (v: Tống Đạo Quân 宋道君), the "Emperor Patriarch and Sovereign of the Way" 教主道君皇帝, who is better known as Emperor Huizong (v: Tống Huy Tông 宋徽宗, 1082–1135) of the Northern Song dynasty, and Liang Wudi (v: Lương Võ Đế 梁武帝, 464–549), the founder of the Liang dynasty. Emperor Huizong rejected Buddhism and elevated Daoism's position during his reign. A fervent follower of the Way, he was unfortunately unprepared in military affairs, and his negligence resulted in the Jurchens' capture of the Song capital Kaifeng in 1127. The Jurchens held Emperor Huizong prisoner and marched him to the northern steppes, where they subjected him to all manner of degradations until his death in 1135.[13] A similarly humiliating

11. *Shiji*, 6.313–14; Nienhauser, *The Grand Scribe's Records*, 1:142.
12. On Han Wudi's quest to turn cinnabar into gold and on his search for immortality, see *Han shu*, 25A.1216–37.
13. For a comprehensive study of Emperor Huizong, see Ebrey, *Emperor Huizong*, esp. 421–505 on the Jurchen attack and fall of the emperor, and 131–58 on his cultivation of Daoism. The line in the *Sāi Vāi* questioning where the immortals were when Emperor Huizong needed help possibly derives from the *Dijian tushuo* (v: Đế Giám Đồ Thuyết 帝鑒圖說; The Emperor's Mirror, Illustrated and Discussed), a Ming dynasty text composed for the education of the young Wanli emperor, in which the good and bad rulers of earlier dynasties are discussed. About Emperor Huizong's fate, it states: "Of the three Pure Ones, why did not one save him?" 三清天尊者，何不一救之. See *Dijian tushuo*, postface (*hou*), 88–89. For more on the *Dijian tushuo*, see J. K. Murray,

fate befell Emperor Wu of Liang, who was a devout Buddhist.[14] Because his religious pursuits left him little time for governance, his inattentiveness gave the general Hou Jing (v: Hầu Cảnh 侯景, d. 552) the chance to usurp the throne and take the imperial city. The emperor died while in captivity in his own palace, where his food supply was restricted. It is recorded that at the moment of his death, he asked for some honey to alleviate the bitterness in his mouth, but none was brought to him; he thereupon cried out in resentment and died with a curse on his lips.[15] In the pairing of these two historical figures, one a fervent Daoist and the other a devout Buddhist, the *Sãi Vãi* issues a dire warning to the rulers who would prioritize religious cultivation over affairs of governance.

The third pairing brings together Qi Yuan (v: Tề Nguyên 齊元) and Wang Qin (v: Vương Khâm 王欽). It is likely that Qi Yuan refers to Gao Wei (v: Cao Vĩ 高緯, 557–77, r. 565–77) of Northern Qi, and that Wang Qin refers to Wang Qinruo (v: Vương Khâm Nhược 王欽若, 962–1025), a chancellor of the Song. Gao Wei led a profligate lifestyle, loved play-acting, and had his palace women adorned in the finest silks; moreover, he tired of his palaces so quickly that construction never ceased. In times of calamity, where there were strange omens, invasions, or raids, Gao Wei would not examine himself for faults but merely set out vegetarian meals for Buddhist monks as a means of cultivating virtue.[16] The defeat, in 577, of the Northern Qi at the hands of the Northern Zhou, whose rulers were members of the Tuoba clan of the Xianbei, a proto-Mongolian nomadic group, is typically attributed to Gao Wei's incompetence.[17] Similarly, Wang Qinruo has been held responsible for the Song's diplomatic loss to

---

"From Textbook to Testimonial"; see also J. K. Murray, "Didactic Illustration in Printed Books."

14.   *Wei shu*, 98.2187.

15.   *Zizhi tongjian*, 162.5016–17. This historical record does not explicitly state that he died of starvation. For a discussion of the range of opinions in historical texts regarding Liang Wudi, his devotion to Buddhism, and the cause of the dynasty's destruction, see Strange, "Representations of the Liang Emperor Wu."

16.   *Zizhi tongjian*, 172.5339.

17.   Although there is nothing in the historical record to suggest that Gao Wei remained in a state of religious cultivation while the Zhou troops were laying seige to Ping-yang, the *Sãi Vãi* probably refers to his alleged habit of ignoring state affairs and relying instead on minimally engaging in religious cultivation as a solution to grave problems.

the Khitan Liao in 1005. Although not himself a ruler, Wang Qinruo, a devotee of Daoism, sought to assert his pacifist influence on the emperor and urged the emperor to abandon the city and move capitals; as a result of his reluctance to engage the Khitan, he conceded both territory and prestige to them. The conflict ended with the Treaty of Shanyuan in January 1005, which was a diplomatic loss for the Song, who had to recognize the Khitan Liao as equals and pay them indemnities for years.[18]

The pairings of the historical figures in the category of inferior wisdom reveal three harmful effects of religion on governance: in the first case, the emperors' ardent quest for Daoist elixirs caused immense hardships for the people; in the second, the pious emperors lost their kingdoms and suffered unspeakable humiliations in the process; and in the third, even the superficial cultivation of religion, in the hands of influential men, put the kingdom at risk of being taken over by nonethnic Han peoples. The monk closes this section on the three categories of wisdom with some well-chosen words on the dangers of being obsessed with the Way:

117   As for the way to be an emperor or a king,
       Cultivate humaneness and cultivate administration;
118   Cultivate power and cultivate influence,
       Cultivate laws and cultivate principles

119   First cultivate to be like Nghiêu [Yao] and Thuấn [Shun]
           and Vũ [Yu] and Thang [Tang];
       Then cultivate the classic books, moral laws, tactics, and strategy.
120   Where does anyone imitate masters and monks in order to cultivate?

121   Consider the matter of cultivation to hone magic and obtain miracles;
       Ponder that way of governing, what benefit has it for the country?
122   How many people have really received blessings?
       Know that all [those ways] brought disaster.

---

18.   Kou Zhun (v: Khấu Chuẩn 寇準, 961–1023), Wang Qinrou's political opponent, made the timorous emperor march on the Khitan, and his actions probably stemmed the Khitan's advance. On Wang Qinruo's influence on Emperor Zhenzong, see *Song shi*, 283.9559–62. For more on the Treaty of Shanyuan, see Mote, *Imperial China*, 68–71. The line in the *Sãi Vãi* on "closing the door to cultivate" probably refers to Wang Qinruo's advice to the emperor to avoid, rather than to engage, the Khitan.

123   Always mesmerized with the way endlessly;
     How is that practicing correct techniques of cultivation?

Line 123 wraps up Nguyễn Cư Trinh's discussion of "cultivation that is free from the mundane." The phrase translated as "mesmerized with the way" (v: *mê đạo*, p: *midao* 迷道) can also be understood to mean "losing the way." The standard phrase used to describe the phenomenon of losing one's sense of orientation is *mê lộ* (p: *milu* 迷路), literally "losing the road," as in *mê thất đạo lộ* (p: *mishi daolu* 迷失道路). Since *đạo* can refer to "a path" as well as "the way" in a philosophical sense, and Nguyễn Cư Trinh had been using these various meanings for *đạo* in his satire, taking *mê đạo* to encompass the meaning of *mê lộ* would be in character with the rest of the play. Using the phrase *mê đạo* combines the layered meanings so that being "mesmerized with the way" results in "losing the way," both in terms of neglecting the Way and losing one's sense of direction. Line 123 has to be understood as a response to lines 47–52, where the nun condemned the monk to hell for not "making a way of cultivation." Nguyễn Cư Trinh's monk shows her how leaders in history who had been obsessed with cultivating the way (*đạo*) had in fact all lost their way (*đạo*) on account of being too mesmerized with it. Through the three categories of wisdom, the author, via the monk, lays out the foundation of what he considers to be good governance. Good governance is characterized by its adaptability to the times; conversely, leaders who adhere stubbornly to rigid philosophies do so to the detriment of the dynasties under their charge.

In these pairings of historical figures, the author of the *Sãi Vãi* brings to the reader's attention particular traits that link them. It is interesting that the lessons on governance are largely those that are relevant to a ruler or a king, which makes one suspect that the king was the author's intended audience, at least for this part of the play. Nguyễn Phúc Khoát was not known to be susceptible to religious teachings or divine omens; in 1744, when he elevated himself from a lord (v: *chúa*, p: *zhu* 主) to a king (v: *vương*, p: *wang* 王) and declared the Nguyễn family a ruling house, he did so to stem the rampant spread of a prophecy that the Nguyễn would lose its lordship over the southern Vietnamese polity in its eighth generation. Nguyễn Phúc Khoát attempted to fulfill the prophecy through rhetoric and in doing so defuse a tense religious situation in his realm, where Buddhist monks and Catholic priests vied for influence in the Nguyễn court. The sixth lord, Nguyễn Phúc Chu (p: Ruan Fuzhou 阮福淍, r. 1691–1725), had supported the Buddhist faction, whereas the seventh lord, Nguyễn Phúc Trú (p: Ruan Fushu 阮福澍, r. 1725–38), threw his weight behind the Catholic one; eschewing both camps, Nguyễn Phúc Khoát chastised the Buddhist monks and banned Catholic priests from Đàng Trong in 1750.[19] Nguyễn Cư Trinh's indictment of rulers who were mesmerized by religion can be read as indirect praise of Nguyễn Phúc Khoát, who did not allow himself to be misled by religious teachers. It is noteworthy that the monk's and the author's voices are conflated at this point, which adds to the sense that this section is didactic. It is all the more significant, then, when the next section inverts the positions of the monk and the nun, and the nun takes her turn to teach the monk some historical lessons.

Don't Forget about the Women

In response to the monk's discussion of the gentleman, the petty man, and those of superior, middling, and inferior wisdom, the nun admits that he has surprised her. She had initially thought that he knew of only one way of cultivation, the corrupted one that combines religious practice with indulgence in the pleasures of the flesh; she now realizes that he knows much and is not the fool she had thought him to be. This particular section transition enacts a reversal that allows the nun to lead the section that follows:

The nun says:

124 I had mistakenly thought that you, sir,
Knew to cultivate in only one way.

19. The Đại Nam chronicles make no mention of such an event, but some scholars describe a "religious crisis" (*cuộc khủng hoảng tôn giáo*) in Đàng Trong under the reign of Nguyễn Phúc Khoát. See Lê Ngọc Trụ and Phạm Văn Luật, *Nguyễn Cư Trinh với quyển Sãi Vãi*, 24–35; Cadière, "Le changement de costume sous Vo-Vuong," 419–20; Maybon, "Koffler, auteur de Historica Cochinchinae Descriptio," 542–44.

125   Who could have known that this foolish fellow
Was really a smart and polite person.

126   You are sagacious and uncontaminated,
You care about knowledge and love harmony.

127   Certainly, there is gold here that is not yet alloyed;
Truly, there is jade there that is still hidden.

128   You are not arrogant and not deceitful;
You know reverence and know deference.

129   You know that a petty man is like weed or rubbish so you throw him out;
You know that a gentleman is like jade and gold so you cherish him.

130   You know what to despise and what to respect;
You know what is one's own and what belongs to others.

131   If, by chance, you know stories of the times,
Speak and I will listen, it is enjoyable and also good.

The monk says:

132   This nun is somewhat strange;
Don't speak, you make me miserable.

133   To waste a five-stringed instrument on the ear of a buffalo;
To waste ten thousand measures of water washing the head of a duck.[20]

134   I know nothing, I discern nothing.

135   Lean in, but avoid my arm,
Or else I might inadvertently touch your breasts.

The nun, realizing that good governance is intimately tied to a responsiveness to the specific problems of the age, wants to know "stories of the times" (v: *chuyện đời*) and invites the monk to educate her. To her surprise, the capricious monk refuses to tell her such stories and instead rebuffs her with a series of insults. Faced with the charge of ignorance, the nun refutes the monk's claim that leading a religious life is necessarily accompanied by an ignorance of the world. In her reply, she adopts the method he had used in the previous section, where he evoked historical figures to elucidate his point. In what follows, she lists examples of superior women

20. A "measure" here is a described as a *hộc*, a unit equivalent to five pecks.

in history to demonstrate her own erudition and facility in the classics and the significance of women who had proven themselves to be the equals of or superior to their male counterparts:

136   This mister lacks manners,
       And moreover is unfeeling.

137   You see that I have chosen a religious life,
       And you think that I do not understand the affairs of the times.

138   We already know that men
       Have the ambition for administration.

139   However, illustrious women
       Also have many talents to assist the world.

140   Yonder like Chu Thái Tự [Zhou Tai Si],
       Whom the classics still praise for her virtue that shone beyond
           the women's quarters.

141   There like Tống Tuyên Nhân [Song Xuanren],
       Whom history still praises as a woman who attained the level of
           Nghiêu [Yao] and Thuấn [Shun].

142   A woman like Tạ Đạo Uẩn [Xie Daoyun],
       A woman who could chant about snow to make poetry.

143   A woman like Thái Văn Cơ [Cai Wenji],[21]
       A woman who could sing with her lute to make airs.

---

21. There appears to be some ambiguity regarding this name. The Duy Minh Thị manuscript records it as Song Banji (v: Tống Ban Cơ 宋班姬). There is a mistake here because Banji 班姬, also known as Ban Zhao, did not live in the Song dynasty but in the time of the Han dynasty. Banji helped finish the *Han shu* (*History of the Han Dynasty*), which her father, Ban Biao, had started, and her brothers Ban Chao and Ban Gu continued but died before its completion. She also wrote the *Admonitions for Women*. Other *Nôm* versions of the *Sãi Vãi* record this name as Thái Văn Cơ or Cai Wenji 蔡文姬, a woman who also lived in the time of the Han dynasty. She lost her first husband early, was captured by the Xiongnu, and bore the Xiongnu leader two children while she was in captivity. She was later ransomed by Cao Cao and returned without her two children. Qing dynasty portrayals of her typically show her playing an *erhu* (a string instrument). A modern Vietnamese (*quốc ngữ*) transcription of the *Sãi Vãi* by Lê Phước Thành even records the name as Thái Ban Cơ, a combination of the two names. See Lê Phước Thành, *Sãi Vãi Luận Đàm*. I adopt the name Thái Văn Cơ because she is a better fit for the couplet, which refers to the woman's understanding of her lot in life and her talent for expressing her feelings through musical composition.

144   As for the scheme to help her lord abandon idleness and desire,
       It is attributed to no one but Đường Huệ [Tang Hui],
            the second-rank consort.[22]

145   As for the plan to help her father escape danger,
       It is attributed to no one but Hán Đề Oánh [Han Tiying], the young girl.

146   Among men, there are many who are heroic men;
       Among women, there are many who are heroic women.

147   A cypress boat drifts for a thousand miles and still goes on;
       Hán books left aside for ten thousand years still remain bright.

148   There are women who have talent and who have beauty,
       Women who have virtue and who have merit.

149   Beautiful women are not inferior to heroic men;
       How could you, Mr. Monk, have the heart to bully me, a nun!

This section addresses a topic that the monk, in his previous elucidation
of the suitability of Confucian philosophy to governance, had failed to
consider. The nun introduces six women who used their talents to "assist
the world"; grouped into three pairs, the exemplars are carefully chosen
to represent particular virtues, and the pairings help illuminate the traits
in these women that the nun prizes. The first grouping consists of two
women who received the approval of history and whose names are recorded in classical texts. Tai Si of Zhou (v: Chu Thái Tự 周太姒) was
the wife of King Wen of Zhou (v: Chu Văn Vương 周文王), the first
king of the Zhou dynasty (1046–221 BCE), and the mother of ten sons,
including King Wu (v: Chu Vũ Vương 周武王) and the Duke of Zhou
(v: Chu Công 周公). Her virtue merited her an entry in the *Biography of
Exemplary Women* (*Lienü zhuan* 列女傳, c. 18 BCE), which quotes lines
devoted to her in two poems in the *Book of Songs* (v: *Kinh Thi*, p: *Shijing*
詩經).[23] Tai Si is paired with Xuanren of Song (v: Tống Tuyên Nhân 宋宣仁,

---

22.   The Duy Minh Thị edition of the *Sãi Vãi* records her name as Hui of Tang
唐惠, whereas the other *Nôm* texts record it as 唐慈惠. I believe this is a reference to Xu
Hui of Tang 唐徐惠, consort of Emperor Taizong of the Tang dynasty.

23.   See *Shiji*, 35.1881; Nienhauser, *The Grand Scribe's Records*, 5(1): 191–93. *Lienü
zhuan*, 1.4b–5a. The lines of poetry cited in her entry in the *Lienü Zhuan* are from "Major
Bright" (v: Đại minh, p: Da ming 大明; *Maoshi*, no. 236) and "Great Dignity" (v: Tư tề, p:
Si zhai 思齊; *Maoshi*, no. 240). *Shijing* (*Maoshi zhengyi*), 16B.238–41 and 16C.248–49. For
English translations of these poems, see Waley, *Book of Songs*, 229–30 and 235–36.

1032–93), who was consort to the Song Emperor Yingzong (v: Tống Anh Tông 宋英宗, r. 1063–67) and the Empress Dowager when her son ascended the throne as Emperor Shenzong (v: Tống Thần Tông 宋神宗, r. 1067–85). Against her wishes, her son supported Wang Anshi (v: Vương An Thạch 王安石, 1021–86) and his plans to introduce wide-ranging reforms to all aspects of Chinese society, including its economy, military, and governance. Upon his death, her grandson, Emperor Zhezong (v: Tống Triết Tông 宋哲宗, r. 1085–1100), ascended the throne, and she, as Grand Empress Dowager Gao, was finally able to put into effect her ideas for governance. She recalled the historian Sima Guang, Wang Anshi's political opponent, who had previously withdrawn from courtly life, to the capital to head the new government. Perhaps unsurprisingly, in light of her alliance with Sima Guang, she found favor with later historians, who compared her to Yao and Shun for the way she employed good officials and curbed the power of imperial relatives.[24]

The second pair of women, Xie Daoyun (v: Tạ Đạo Uẩn 謝道韞) and Cai Wenji (v: Thái Văn Cơ 蔡文姬), were famous for their excellence in poetry and music. While still a child, Xie Daoyun's uncle, an Eastern Jin statesman and poet Xie An (v: Tạ An 謝安, 320–385), convened a competition for the children at a family gathering, challenging them to come up with a couplet describing the snow falling outside. Xie Daoyun's unconventional comparison of snow and willow catkins surpassed her elder male cousin's comparatively trite contribution. In her adulthood, she helped defend her uncle against the slanderous attacks of Huan Xuan (v: Hoàn Huyền 桓玄, 369–404), who eventually usurped the Jin dynasty.[25] Cai Wenji, conversely, features in a story of an erudite and literarily talented woman whose sad lot during the time of the Xiongnu invasion of the Han—forced marriage and then forced separation from

---

24. *Song shi*, 242.8625–27; the comparison to Yao and Shun can be found in *Song shi*, 242.8627. Sima Guang is now identified as a political conservative and Wang Anshi a reformist whose ideas are considered either measured or misguided. Depending on one's perspective, Song Xuanren could be someone who saved the empire from the ruin or held the empire back from reform. Upon Emperor Zhezong's death, he was succeeded by his half-brother Emperor Huizong, earlier referred to in the category of the practitioners of inferior wisdom and on whom the blame for the collapse of the Song dynasty is placed.

25. For Xie Daoyun's biography, see *Jin shu*, 96.2516–17; see also Mann, *Precious Records*, 83.

the two children that she had borne in captivity in order to return to her homeland—was channeled into her beautifully sorrowful poetry and music. She later remarried, and history records that she saved her new husband, the local official Dong Si (v: Đổng Tự 董祀), who had been sentenced to death for a committing a crime, with an impassioned plea that moved Cao Cao (v: Tào Tháo 曹操, 155–220) to retract the death sentence in the nick of time.[26] Unlike Xie Daoyun, who symbolizes innate talent and inborn excellence, Cai Wenji represents women who have risen above their lot to realize the full extent of their talent. Both women used their quick wits to save men's reputations and even their lives.

The third pair of women, Concubine Xu Hui of Tang (v: Đường Từ Huệ 唐徐惠) and the young Tiying of Han (v: Hán Đề Oánh 漢緹縈), are grouped together for their powers of persuasion, which prevented wrongdoing from being committed. Xu Hui of Tang, consort of Emperor Taizong (v: Đường Thái Tông 唐太宗, r. 626–649) of the Tang dynasty, represents the perfect concubine who entreats the emperor to do right. Concerned that her lord was exhausting the people with his numerous military campaigns and his palace-building activities, specifically the

---

26. *Hou Han shu*, 84.2801–3 contains the two long poems she composed in which she expressed her hurt and grief. That she managed to move Cao Cao's hand in regard to Dong Si's death penalty is truly remarkable, and I reproduce the story from the *Hou Han shu* below:

Si was functioning in the capacity of the colonel of a *tuntian* [a military-plantation system] when he violated the law to the level that matched the death penalty. Wenji went to see Cao Cao to plead on behalf of Si. At that time, those present, including high-ranking officials, reputable members of the gentry class who were not in service, and ambassadors from distant regions, filled the reception hall. Cao said to the guests, "Cai Bojie's daughter is outside now, on behalf of you various lords, I present her to you." When Wenji entered, unkempt, disheveled, and barefooted, she prostrated herself and begged for mercy; her voice and words were clear and well-spoken, the expression of her words were grief-stricken and moving. As for those present, all altered their countenance on her behalf. Cao said, "Truly, I pity you, yet the official paper has already been sent, what can I do?" Wenji said, "Your eminence, you have ten thousand horses in your stable, your ferocious fighters are as numerous as the trees in the forest, why are you stingy about one quick-footed horse and rider to save a life that is on the verge of death!" Cao felt moved by her words; only then did he chase back his sent-out official paper and forgive Si's sins. (*Hou Han shu* 84.2800–2801, my translation.)

Palace of Halcyon-blue Haze and the Jade Splendor Palace, she wrote a letter urging him to prudence, explaining that "a sovereign in possession of the Way exploits his own ease to bring ease to his people while a sovereign who is devoid of the Way takes pleasure in pleasing himself."[27] She succeeded in keeping the emperor in check. Tiying of Han was the youngest daughter of Chunyu Yi (v: Thuần Vu Ý 淳于意, 216–150 BCE), a physician sentenced to bodily mutilation for having offended a powerful patient. As he was carried away, her father cried out in desperation that daughters were of no help in times of need. Tiying thereupon memorialized the emperor, asking to be a slave in his court in exchange for her father's freedom. She argued that "one who is dead cannot return to life, and one who is corporally punished cannot be made whole again; even if he committed an offense and wished to turn over a new leaf, there is no path for him to follow and in the end he would not be able to fulfill this." The emperor was so affected by her petition that he not only released her father but also abolished corporal punishment.[28] Xu Hui of Tang and Tiying of Han both submitted memorials to their emperors and put forward cogent arguments in favor of their positions; their skill in logical persuasion bind them together in this third pairing.

The nun in the *Sãi Vãi* celebrates women who contributed to the betterment of the societies they lived in through their assistance in governance, their ability to persuade with moving speech, and their artful writing in which they promoted insightful plans that righted potential wrongs. Significantly, the nun omits examples of chaste widows who resisted remarriage to remain faithful to their dead husbands. The widow chastity cult had reached a high point during Qing rule in China.[29] In

27.   有道之君，以逸逸人；無道之君，以樂樂身. *Xin Tang shu*, 76.3472 and *Jiu Tang shu*, 51.2168. Translated by Paul Kroll. For the full letter, see *Xin Tang shu*, 76.3472–73 and *Jiu Tang shu*, 51.2167–69. Xu Hui's efforts to reign in her emperor's excesses are also recognized in *Zizhi tongjian*, 198.6254, where her letter is largely reproduced. For more on Xu Hui's poetic and political writings, see Kroll, "The Life and Writings of Xu Hui."

28.   死者不可復生而刑者不可復續，雖欲改過自新，其道莫由，終不可得. My translation. Tiying's story is recorded as part of her father's biography in the *Shiji*, 105.3362; Nienhauser, *The Grand Scribe's Records*, 9:27–28. It should be noted that Tiying is more often praised for her filial piety than for her skills at argumentation.

29.   For more information on Qing government campaigns to promote widow chastity, see Mann, *Precious Records*, 24.

the Ming dynasty, widow suicides were honored because young widows who followed their husbands to their deaths or died resisting forced remarriages were seen as exemplars of faithfulness and chastity; during the Qing, such suicides took on the dangerous undertone of loyalty to the preceding dynasty. The Qing thus frowned on the practice of widow suicide, considering it "a cowardly way to escape Confucian family duties," and honored chaste widows instead.[30] Not only does the nun in the *Sāi Vāi* not celebrate any widow suicides, she does not even acknowledge chastity as a virtue worthy of inclusion in her list. An even more striking omission is the absence of any treatment of the domestic sphere and its attendant feminine virtues. The nun's concern was not with defining the moral boundaries within which the woman should operate but with demonstrating how women in history have shown great aptitude even in domains traditionally associated with men.

The inclusion of a section dedicated to remarkable women in the *Sāi Vāi* was in keeping with the literary fashion of the times. In Qing China, one of the outcomes of the drive to return to the classics was the unearthing of stories of exemplary women who had been neglected in favor of chaste widows. For some male scholars, educated women from the past embodied "pure erudition untainted by the competition for degrees and office"; in the Qing, this imagery was put to use to criticize the corruption and competition of the contemporary moment.[31] For others, the debate was about the role of educated women in the Qing dynasty. Contrasting images of the "moral instructor" and the "brilliant prodigy" emerged as opposing symbols of a woman's erudition.[32] The female literary voice was also used at this time to level important political and social criticisms that would otherwise have been considered dangerous; examples include "Song of a Soldier's Wife" (v: "Chinh Phụ Ngâm" 征婦吟), composed by a male Đàng Ngoài scholar Đặng Trần Côn (1710–45), and "Complaint of a Palace Maid" (v: "Cung Oán Ngâm Khúc" 宮怨吟曲), a vernacular Vietnamese work com-

---

30. Mann, *Precious Records*, 25. This view was captured in an edict issued by the Yongzheng emperor in 1728.

31. Mann, *Precious Records*, 31.

32. Mann identifies Zhang Xuecheng and Yuan Mei, respectively, as the chief proponents of these two views. Mann, *Precious Records*, 83–94.

posed by Nguyễn Gia Thiều (1741–98).[33] Moreover, women's real participation in the production of literature during this period expanded exponentially. The famous poet Yuan Mei (v: Viên Mai 袁枚, 1716–97) boasted of his numerous lady pupils, and poetry clubs made up solely of women appeared during this time.[34] This section of the *Sãi Vãi*, in which a nun gets her turn in the limelight, captured some of the spirit of its time.[35]

The double feminine voice in this section of the *Sãi Vãi*—first the voice of the nun and then the voice of the historical women she invokes—emphasizes the agency of the female. This section in itself functions as an indication of "the times" to which a good leader should adapt. In the context of the expanding frontier, women's labor and participation in building frontier society were crucial. The new Vietnamese polity required the total mobilization of its people and needed to enlist its women inhabitants as cobuilders. Consequently, the play does not call for women to "know their place" in the domestic sphere but exhorts them to contribute to building the nascent state. The nun's speech reminded both male and female members of the audience of the worth of women to society; it also reminded the monk—and the king—that the issue of female participation was not one that could be neglected in any proposal for best governance of the southern Vietnamese realm.

Stories that Cannot Be Told

The monk is delighted by the nun's response to his provocation. He mollifies her by saying he was merely testing her and he is now willing to reveal his stories to her:

33. Several poets have translated the "Chinh Phụ Ngâm," originally composed in classical Chinese, into the vernacular Vietnamese; one such translation is attributed to the female poet Đoàn Thị Điểm (1705–48). Some scholars refute this attribution and believe it to be the work of Phan Huy Ích instead. See Hoàng Xuân Hãn, *Chinh Phụ Ngâm bị khảo*, and Huỳnh Sanh Thông, *The Song of a Soldier's Wife*.

34. Waley, *Yuan Mei*, 179–80 and 183.

35. Keith Taylor identifies the eighteenth century as a time when Vietnamese literature gained an appreciation for women and their point of view. Taylor, *A History of the Vietnamese*, 327. For a study of women in early modern Vietnam, see Nhung Tuyết Tran, *Familial Properties*.

150   Very true, very true!
       How wonderful, how wonderful!
151   It's like seeing clouds when one is thirsty in a drought;
       Or like meeting an audience while one is holding a lute!

152   If the tree is not hard, how does one know the axe is sharp?
       One knows a good horse by means of a long road.
153   Therefore I will roll away clouds and fog, clear away the spikes
          and thorns;
       So that you can see a blue sky and find the main road.[36]

154   I do not lack strange tales,
       All the unusual things.
155   Bring your ear close so as to listen,
       But do move your breasts apart in case I bump against them.

He tells the nun that he will help her "find the main road," perhaps a reference to line 123 where he implies that being "mesmerized with the way" means in fact "losing the way." The fact that the monk does not to use the word *đạo* to refer to the road in line 153 and uses instead the vernacular Vietnamese word *đường* prevents the audience from misunderstanding his intentions; the monk is not interested in showing the nun a new way (*đạo*). He reveals that he would like to tell her stories about four topics. The first is about the relationship between a lord and his officials, the second the relationship between a father and his son, the third the relationship between wealth and human-heartedness, and the fourth the relationship between wealth and population stability.

160   I want to tell a story: "The lord employs his officials according to rituals";
       But I am afraid that Tần [Qin] and Hán [Han] would be irritated.
161   I want to tell a story: "An official devotes himself to his lord with loyalty";
       But I am afraid that Mãng [Mang] and Tào [Cao] would be resentful.

162   I want to tell a story: "To be a father is to be compassionate" so you learn;
       But I am afraid that Mr Cổ Tẩu [Gu Sou] would decry this idea as naive.
163   I want to tell a story: "To be a son is to have filial piety" so you know;
       But I am afraid that Tùy Dương [Sui Yang] would criticize it as doltish.

36. The word Nguyễn Cư Trinh uses for "road" here is *đường* (*Nôm* character: 唐).

164   I want to tell a story: "To be humane is to be without wealth";
        But I am afraid Mr Nhan Tử [Yanzi] would scold, saying:
            "Anyone who opens his mouth is just currying favor."
165   I want to tell a story: "To be wealthy is to lack human-heartedness";
        But I am afraid Thạch Sùng [Shi Chong] would heap reproach, saying:
            "Why be so clever at splitting hairs to find fault?"
166   I want to tell a story: "When wealth accumulates, the population scatters"
            for you to know;
        Then the reason the Thương [Shang] dynasty was lost must be revealed.
167   I want to tell a story: "When wealth scatters, the population gathers"
            for you to grasp;
        Then the reason the Chu [Zhou] dynasty arose must be declared.

The first two themes spell out two central relationships in Confucian philosophy that are essential to the smooth running of the state and the stability of all under heaven.[37] On the topic of relations between a lord and his officials, the monk recycles two examples he previously raised: Qin Shihuang and Han Wudi, who were included in the category of people of inferior wisdom. Their bad examples are matched with two cases, that of Wang Mang (v: Vương Mãng 王莽, 45 BCE–23 CE) and Cao Cao, neither of whom was a model official. Wang Mang, a Han dynasty scholar-official who rose through the ranks, seized power for himself and founded the Xin dynasty (9–23 CE), a "new dynasty" 新朝 that lasted for the length of a single reign.[38] The Xin dynasty marks the break between the Western Han and the Eastern Han dynasties. Whereas Wang Mang is blamed for the downfall of the Western Han, Cao Cao is held responsible for the collapse of the Eastern Han some 200 years later.

37.   Although it is now conventional to refer to three, rather than two, fundamental relationships, the *Analects* records only the two discussed in the *Sãi Vãi*. The relationship between husband and wife is absent, both in the *Analects* and in the *Sãi Vãi*. See *Lun yu*, 12.11.

38.   He lived during the time of the Western Han dynasty and was related to the imperial family by virtue of the fact that his father, Wang Man (v: Vương Mạn 王曼), was the brother of Empress Wang Zhengjun (v: Vương Chính Quân 王政君, 71 BCE–13 CE). For a discussion of whether the name of Wang Mang's dynasty should be translated as "New" or left transliterated as "Xin" to indicate its connection to Wang Mang's fief, Xindu, see Goodrich, "The Reign of Wang Mang."

Cao Cao, a crafty statesman who rose to immense power, did not seize the throne himself, but left that work to his son.[39]

Both Wang Mang and Cao Cao were, in fact, infatuated with model exemplars from the past and, in their quest to emulate them, committed all manner of atrocities. Wang Mang was obsessed with the Duke of Zhou and sought to act, as the duke did, as regent to the emperor; unlike the Duke of Zhou, however, he wielded his power cruelly and eventually committed regicide.[40] Cao Cao was enamored of the Zhou dynasty and compared himself to King Wen of Zhou, who had refused to depose the last king of Shang, to whom he was subordinate; it was Wen's son, King Wu, who destroyed the Shang and posthumously named his father king.[41] Similarly, although Cao Cao all but destroyed the Eastern Han dynasty, he refrained from declaring himself king. Instead, his son, Cao Pi (v: Tào Phi, 187–226 CE), deposed the Han emperor, ascended the throne as Emperor Wen of the Wei dynasty, and awarded Cao Cao the posthumous title of Emperor Wu of Wei. The examples of Wang Mang and Cao Cao, both of whom, in emulating model exemplars from antiquity, corrupted

39.   He was an extremely powerful statesman and general in the Eastern Han. Known for his military prowess and craftiness, he effectively controlled the last Han emperor but ultimately failed to unify the fragmented Chinese empire. See de Crespigny, *Imperial Warlord*.

40.   Wang Mang started out as a loyal scholar-official of the Han dynasty and was initially well regarded by all. Obsessed with the Zhou dynasty, in particular the Duke of Zhou, he sought to replace various Han emperors who he felt had lost the mandate of heaven. Not entirely wrong in his perception of the declining quality of the Han emperors, he received the support of the people and other officials. Soon, however, he proved himself to be violent and self-serving. When the young Emperor Ping (v: Bình 平, r. 1 BCE–6 CE) ascended the throne, Wang Mang became his regent and was finally able to fulfill his desire to be the contemporary equivalent of the Duke of Zhou. Wang Mang's son, Wang Yu (v: Vương Vũ 王宇, d. 3 CE), fearing that the emperor would grow up resenting the Wang family for Wang Mang's sins, conspired with the emperor's uncles of the Wei clan to remove his father but was discovered. Wang Mang killed his own son and the entire Wei clan. *Han shu*, 99A.4065–66. In 6 CE, Emperor Ping died; Wang Mang himself chose the next emperor, an infant who never had the chance to ascend the throne because Wang Mang ruled first under a new reign period, "The Regency," then staged a coup and established the Xin dynasty in 9 CE. *Han shu* 99A.4078–81 (the regency) and 4095–96 (the coup). For an annotated translation of Chapter 99 of the *Han shu*, see Sargent, *Wang Mang*.

41.   *Sanguo zhi*, 1.52.

them, gave Nguyễn Cư Trinh's monk pause; on one hand, in his imagined conversations with the historical figures, the monk believes the two men would resent him, and so he holds his tongue. On the other hand, their corrupted use of model exemplars, a didactic technique the monk was presently employing, holds him back from completing his story.

As for the relationship between fathers and sons, the monk brings up two negative exemplars: Gu Sou (v: Cổ Tẩu 瞽瞍), the sage king Shun's wicked father, and Emperor Yang of Sui (v: Tùy Dương 隋煬, 569–618), the second emperor of the short-lived Sui dynasty, who murdered his father to become the emperor. Gu Sou loved Shun's half-brother Xiang 象 but hated Shun with a ferocious intensity; he tried to kill Shun on several occasions, once ordering him up a granary before setting it on fire, and another time commanding him to dig a well that he subsequently filled with dirt while Shun was still inside.[42] Each time, Shun planned ahead and managed to escape with his life and his love for his father intact. Conversely, Emperor Yang of Sui was his father's favorite son and, even though he was second-born, was made crown prince after his father deposed his elder brother in favor of him. Historians suspect that while he was tending to his ill father, he made advances toward his father's favorite consort, who rejected him and reported him. Fearful that he would lose his position as crown prince, he murdered his father in the night.[43]

The two cases of Gu Sou and Emperor Yang are, in a sense, mirror opposites. On the one hand, Gu Sou was as terrible a father as could be to Shun, but it made no difference to Shun's sageliness. On the other hand, Emperor Yang's father favored him, but the imperial favor did not

42. *Shiji*, 1.40; Nienhauser, *The Grand Scribe's Records*, 1:12–13. The story is typically told to demonstrate the extent of Shun's filial piety, which was so great that with each attempt on his life he merely loved his father more; here, the story focuses instead on Gu Sou as an example of a terrible father.

43. The consort, Lady Chen (v: Trần 陳), reportedly told the emperor of his son's advances, and, incensed, the dying Emperor Wen summoned his eldest son to the capital. Worried that his father was about to leave the empire to his older brother, Sui Yang took over care of his father and sent his lackey, Zhang Heng (v: Trương Hành 張衡), to the emperor's chamber to tend to him. The emperor died that evening, and historians believe that Yang of Sui murdered his father through Zhang Heng. Account of the patricide is recorded in *Zizhi tongjian*, 180.5601–4. For a study of the life and legacy of Emperor Yang of Sui, see Xiong, *Emperor Yang of Sui*.

prevent the father from dying at his son's hands. Nguyễn Cư Trinh's monk falters, having barely begun to tell his story, since he fears the two historical figures, who behaved in a fashion contrary to the model behavior he espouses, would laugh at his naiveté. The historical men proved the Confucian maxim to be impotent. Shun's father was not fatherly, but Shun remained a model son; Emperor Yang's father loved him dearly but was killed by his favorite son. Prescribed behaviors, followed or unfollowed, ultimately make no difference to historical outcomes.

The third relationship concerns that between "human-heartedness" (v: *nhân*, p: *ren* 仁) and "wealth" (v: *phú*, p: *fu* 富). The monk claims to be unable to tell the story not because such stories do not exist but because Yan Hui (v: Nhan Hồ 顏回, c. 521–481 BCE), a favorite disciple of Confucius, would find fault with the monk for trying to flatter him; the monk, moreover, is unable to discuss "wealth without human-heartedness" on account of Shi Chong (v: Thạch Sùng 石崇, 249–300), who lived during the Jin dynasty and was possibly the wealthiest man of his time. Yan Hui lived a life of near destitution and was often seen with only "a single bamboo bowl of food and a gourd cup of drink in a shabby alley"; able to tolerate penury and even remain unaffected by it, he never hankered after riches.[44] As someone reputed for both his virtue and his voluntary poverty, he is a likely candidate for the subject of a moral story on humaneness without wealth; however, he loathed talking about his virtues and deeds. Once, while conversing with Confucius and a fellow disciple, Zhong You (v: Trọng Do 仲由, 542–480 BCE), he pondered the question of what he most wanted. Unlike Zhong You, who desired carriages and fine clothes to share with his friends, Yan Hui wished only that he would not boast of his moral goodness or flaunt his meritorious deeds.[45]

Conversely, Shi Chong was not only prosperous but also unafraid to make a show of his riches. Once, when he was visiting the Imperial Academy together with the Jin general Wang Dun (v: Vương Đôn 王敦, 266–324), he encountered the statues of two disciples of Confucius, Yan Hui and Yuan Xian (v: Nguyên Hiến 原憲, b. 515 BCE), who were admired for their scruples and abject poverty. Looking at them, Shi Chong

44. *Lun yu*, 6.11.
45. *Lun yu*, 5.26.

sighed and wondered aloud why, if he were able to ascend into Confucius's Hall together with them, there should still be a separation between them. His companion Wang Dun observed that Shi Chong was perhaps more similar to Duanmu Ci (v: Đoan Mộc Tứ 端木賜, 520–456 BCE), courtesy name Zigong (v: Tử Cống 子貢), a wealthy man who was one of Confucius's most prominent disciples and whom the master himself had once declared inferior to Yan Hui.[46] In response to a question posed by Zigong about a practice worth cultivating for life, Confucius replied that "empathetic feeling" (v: *thứ*, p: *shu* 恕) was the answer, for a man should always strive not to do unto others what he would not want done to him.[47] In another passage, when Zigong claimed to have achieved the realization of that practice, Confucius countered that he had not, in fact, attained it.[48] Set apart by his wealth, Zigong was incapable of attaining the level of empathetic feeling or human-heartedness that would allow him to accurately perceive what others, who did not have his riches, wanted or did not want. Perceiving the slight in Wang Dun's response, Shi Chong asked him what living in poverty had to do with attaining eminence in moral quality and reputation. He accused Wang Dun of engaging in pedantic fault-finding on account of his wealth, which he considered irrelevant to the matter at hand.[49]

Yan Hui and Shi Chong, though living in different historical eras, are connected by the latter's physical encounter with the statue of the former in the Temple of Confucius. Desiring to join the ranks of the virtuous elect, Shi Chong accuses his interlocutor of fault-finding, which is in fact what Yan Hui engages in when he accuses others of flattery when they speak of his virtue. The historical figures are bound together in the monk's story not only because they exemplify two opposing ends of the spectrum in terms of their wealth but also because of their association with fault-finding. The monk does not continue his story because he imagines that the historical figures would either find fault with him or accuse him of finding fault with them. He also ceases his account of the

46. *Lun yu*, 5.9.
47. *Lun yu*, 15.24.
48. *Lun yu*, 5.12.
49. *Jin shu*, 33.1007. For an English translation of Shi Chong's official biography, see Wilhelm, "Shih Ch'ung and His Chin-Ku-Yüan."

didactic tale because the stories, when taken together, are obstructive and self-defeating. They place disproportionate emphasis on minor points of detail and ultimately prevent the lesson from being conveyed.

In regard to the theme of wealth accumulation and population stability, the monk's inability to speak about the fall of the Shang alludes to a passage from the Basic Annals of Zhou in Sima Qian's (v: Tư Mã Thiên 司馬遷, d. 86 BCE) *Records of the Historian* (v: *Sử Ký*, p: *Shiji* 史記). There it is recorded that two years after King Wu of Zhou had defeated the Shang, he asked the Viscount of Ji why he had been able to do so. The question discomfited the viscount because a truthful answer would require him to recount the Shang prince's avarice and sexual deviance; the viscount's reticence, in turn, caused King Wu to become embarrassed, and the two men ended up discussing Heaven's Way.[50] Drawing attention to the Shang prince's avarice, the story of the Zhou victory over the Shang shows how wealth accumulation leads to the scattering of the population; it cannot be told, however, because telling it would upset the norms of propriety.

The counterpart to the story of the fall of the Shang, the story about the rise of the Zhou, probably refers to the episode where Gugong Danfu (v: Cổ Công Đản Phủ 古公亶父), the father of King Wen of Zhou, gave away his wealth and goods to the people of the Rong (v: Nhung 戎) and the Di (v: Địch 狄) tribes, who had attacked him for his treasure. When they attacked again, this time with the intention of annexing his lands and subjugating his people, he decided that it made no difference to the people whether they were ruled by him or by the tribesmen; consequently, he voluntarily abandoned his territory to forestall further bloodshed. His actions had the contrary effect; the people followed him and multitudes sought him out to be their ruler.[51] Unlike the monk's prior tales, this appears as if it can be told, but its place in this section of the play gives us

---

50. *Shiji*, 4.168. The passage reads: 武王已克殷，後二年，問箕子殷所以亡。箕子不忍言 殷惡，以存亡國宜告。武王亦醜，故問以天道. Translation: Two years after King Wu had overcome Yin [Ân], he asked the Viscount of Ji [Cơ Tử] the reason why Yin was destroyed. The Viscount of Ji could not bear to speak of the evils of Yin, so he told the king the conditions under which a state would be preserved or destroyed. King Wu was also embarrassed [by his question] and so he purposely asked about the Way of Heaven. See Nienhauser, *The Grand Scribe's Records*, 1:64.

51. *Shiji*, 4.148; Nienhauser, *The Grand Scribe's Records*, 1: 56–57.

reason to be suspicious. The case of King Wen of Zhou tells a story about a monarch who worried about wasting the lives of the men under his care and willingly gave them up to non-Han peoples; seen from this perspective, the story becomes one about a king who was excessively flippant with respect to maintaining civilizational boundaries. A story warning against "civilized" people being ruled by "barbarians," moreover, was particularly relevant to the situation in Quảng Ngãi, where Việt–Đá Vách relations were especially tense. Not telling the story of King Wen of Zhou reverses its conventionally accepted moral, and, with its new message, was potentially a rallying call for the Việt inhabitants to rise up and fight the Đá Vách.

In transposing stories and historical actors from the classical to the vernacular, the author resituates them without consideration for where they reside in the historical chronology. Gu Sou of mythical times rests quite comfortably alongside Yangdi of the Sui dynasty, and Yan Hui sits, though perhaps also scowls and complains about his seat, beside Shi Chong. In a way, Shi Chong's wish is fulfilled; he is finally permitted into Yan Hui's company. The vernacular—and here I mean the form of the vernacular story—removes the classical allusions from their original sites of meaning. In the process of transposition, historical figures are violently torn from their sites of origin in the classics and grafted onto the frame of the vernacular story. But here they are given new room to grow. Yan Hui, still Confucius's favorite disciple, is transformed into a fault-finding and nitpicky man. Wang Mang and Cao Cao, originally usurpers and traitors, now give the audience reason to reconsider the roots of their infamy, as they ponder how the two men tried their utmost to emulate historical exemplars. The vernacular perverts the original meaning of the allusions but also expands upon them and gives them a new lease on life.

It is noteworthy that these redeployments appear to be in contradiction to the historical figures' values as classical exemplars. Here we have to consider the role that the vernacular form plays and the moment when that particular incarnation of the vernacular is the most popular. Transformed into the vernacular, classical figures undergo surprising and humorous mutations. The popular appeal of this type of distortion suggests a political climate conducive to the subversion of the classics and an audience that seeks to break free of the strictures of the classical even as they remain conversant in it. This section is targeted less at villagers and more at the play's literati audience. The soldier or villager watching this performance saw only a monk on stage trying to tell didactic stories and failing to do so; that the monk would fear Wang Mang's or Cao Cao's scorn, or that he would be afraid of Gu Sou's disapproval, is funny in itself. But for the literati audience, this section demonstrates the extent of both their and the author's facility in the classics; it establishes the author's, and by extension Đàng Trong's, position in a wider world of high culture, for it participates in the contemporary trend of vernacular stories that cleverly upset classical paradigms.[52] Moreover, it establishes the vernacular in Vietnam as being on par with those of the Middle Kingdom. The people of Đàng Trong were not merely participants in the Han tradition; they were also participants in an emergent vernacular one.

In addition to its unmistakable comedic element, the monk's speech—which teases the nun and the audience and holds their attention with a promise of a good yarn that is never fulfilled—has a deeper, subtler ideological dimension. In identifying those who would be upset with him for proceeding in his narration, he tellingly includes both heroes and villains; it is not only that the wicked are upset with these stories since they recall their infamous deeds, the virtuous are also impatient. While intimating that these stories cannot be told, the monk simultaneously discloses to the audience what is most essential in these stories, namely, the moral precept they should take away from them. At the same time, in breaking off these stories before beginning their narration, he points to the problem of their transmissibility. In this context, the presence of the voice of Yan Hui, who appears in the company of despots and usurpers, is particularly startling. The most beloved of Confucius's disciples, he appears in the monk's account as a fastidious stickler, whose adherence to virtue is so rigid that it actually prevents speaking about it and, by implication, instruction in it. Although his reasons to desist from the telling of stories differ from those that the other more villanous characters give, his advice resembles theirs in that, by silencing the teller of stories, it invites moral and intellectual paralysis. It appears here as if the tradition itself has closed off the principal means through which it can continue

---

52. Around the same time that the *Sãi Vãi* was composed, *The Scholars* (v: *Nho lâm ngoại sử*, p: *Rulin waishi* 儒林外史), a satirical novel composed in the Chinese vernacular, was completed in Qing China. Its author, Wu Jingzhi (v: Ngô Kính Tử 吳敬梓, 1701–54), had worked on it for about ten years.

and survive—the transmission of stories that enshrine its moral principles. Nguyễn Cư Trinh hints that this tradition, in its rigidity and
conservatism, suffers from a type of self-stultification. What is required,
however, is not the discarding of tradition but its prudent reappropriation
and a redeployment sensitive to the pressing concerns of the moment and
the immediate needs of the living.

Nguyễn Cư Trinh was not alone in questioning the classical canon.
There existed a trend among intellectuals active in mid-eighteenth-century
China toward a light-hearted treatment of classical themes and figures.[53]
Yuan Mei, for example, irreverently titled his book of "strange stories,"
which included ghost stories, *What the Master Did Not Speak Of* (v: *Tử
Bất Ngữ*, p: *zibuyu* 子不語), a reference to a passage in the seventh book
of Confucius's *Analects*: "The Master never talked of wonders, feats of
strength, disorders of nature or spirits."[54] Not confined to the literature
of the eighteenth century, a set of vernacular short stories from the 1660s,
published under the pseudonym of Aina the Layman, poked fun at the
classics with wicked inversions of classical tales and themes.[55] The literati
world in which Nguyễn Cư Trinh lived, connected to the Chinese intellectuals through the circulation of literature, was similarly one where
the classics and conventional modes of literary expression were challenged
and sometimes subjected to ridicule.

These sections of the *Sãi Vãi* demonstrate the extent to which the Han
classical world was a part of the consciousness of the people of Đàng
Trong, be they villagers, soldiers, or literati. The text also speaks to the reach
of Confucian ideas in the southern Vietnamese realm. Contemporary
scholars do not believe that Confucianism had much of a foothold in
Vietnam in general and Đàng Trong in particular.[56] The *Sãi Vãi*, a text

53.   In his biography of Yuan Mei, who retired at the age of thirty-two and thereafter lived extravagantly as a well-known poet in the Middle Kingdom, Arthur Waley
observes that "the men of the early eighteenth century were on the whole stern and
puritanical, those of the mid-century pleasure-loving and tolerant, those of its closing
years and the early nineteenth century once more straightlaced and censorious." See
Waley, *Yuan Mei*, 131.

54.   Waley, *Yuan Mei*, 120.

55.   The collection is titled *Doupeng xianhua* (v: *Đậu bằng nhàn thoại* 豆棚閒話).
For a translation and introduction, see Hegel (ed.), *Idle Talk under the Bean Arbor*.

56.   Olga Dror, evaluating the state of Confucianism in northern Vietnam in the
eighteenth century, believes that "Confucianism in Vietnam never gained the status it

that captures a Vietnamese scholar-official's thoughts about Confucianism's relevance to frontier governance, gives us reason to pause and reconsider this characterization of the southern Vietnamese realm. On the one hand, the prominent place that Nguyễn Cư Trinh accords to Buddhism in his critical assessment of it gives us an indication of Buddhism's dominance in Đàng Trong society. On the other hand, the *Sãi Vãi* leads us to suspect that Confucianism had made considerable inroads into southern Vietnamese society. Given that the *Sãi Vãi* was a well-known work performed for audiences ranging from the common villager to the king and his advisers in court, the reach of Nguyễn Cư Trinh's thought was considerable. Beyond that, the play's apparent success in mobilizing the soldiers is indicative of the relevance of its form and content to the frontier settlers.

---

acquired in China but has largely remained an artificial 'superstructure' amidst a Vietnamese reality permeated with Buddhist and other religious practices." See the translator's introduction to Di St. Thecla, *Opusculum de Sectis apud Sinenses et Tunkinenses*, 40. Li Tana explains that "Confucianism in Đàng Trong played a political and social role that was relatively minor compared to its role in the north, where the Chinese-style examination system ensured neo-Confucianism never lost its grip on the literati elite." See Li Tana, *Nguyễn Cochinchina*, 103.

CHAPTER 3

The Illness of Human Emotions

The import of Nguyễn Cư Trinh's cultural project is most apparent in the final sections of the *Sãi Vãi*, where he directs the Việt inhabitants of the frontier to embrace Confucian humanistic morality. In patterning the Việt people's sense of morality in a culturally specific way, the non-Việt peoples of the region are left unpatterned and therefore uncivilized. This inculcation of a sense of civilizational distinctiveness and cultural superiority discouraged the Việt frontier settlers from abandoning the newly inhabited lands for more peaceful parts of the Đàng Trong polity or, worse, moving up the hills in sympathy with the indigenous uplanders. But moral precepts alone were insufficient to fully convince the Việt settlers to stay, much less fight; Nguyễn Cư Trinh therefore integrated his Confucian teachings with a form of this-worldly Buddhism to fully capture the imagination of his audience. Sections 7 and 8 of the *Sãi Vãi* deliver the author's framework for a moral-religious worldview and his call to action. The play seems to have ground to a halt at the conclusion of section 6, where the monk's creative coupling of historical figures leads him to a dead end in which further speech is impossible. This moment of textual rupture and inaction in fact marks the start of the real action, where the Việt people are incited to rise up against the Đá Vách "barbarians." As usual, the nun's words hurry the play along. She responds to the monk's uncompleted stories with an expression of admiration for his knowledge of the classics and the authenticity of his religious transmission. She notes, however, that he is still sitting around, being useless, instead of going out to make a name for himself:

170   You, mister, cultivate and train;
      You have the ambition to be a hero!
171   As a reader of history and classics, you retain them until your heart is filled;
      As a bearer of the robe and bowl, the true transmission has surely surfaced.
172   If you are not to be "The living Buddha of the ten thousand households,"
      Then surely you will be the "One in Lộ [Lu] who seeks the fortune star."
173   Your fate is yet to be realized; why are you just waiting around for a title?
      Your destiny is yet to be fulfilled; why are you still boasting of your fame?

Here, drawing attention to his Confucian learning ("history and classics") and his Buddhist cultivation ("robe and bowl"), the nun identifies the dual provenance of the monk's knowledge and practice. Not content to leave the two philosophies separate, however, she deploys two allusions, one derived from the Buddhist tradition ("the living Buddha") and the other Confucian ("one in Lu"), to refer to the same thing, which is an upright and incorrupt official.[1] These lines address and resolve a tension between Buddhism and Confucianism; she teaches the audience that both are acceptable and compatible, as long as their practice is directed toward perfecting the official. Indeed, they have the potential to inspire and transform the coarse into the cultured, the unlettered into the learned. The nun wonders why the monk's talent remains untapped and, perhaps intending to be provocative, pointedly asks him why he does not make himself more useful. In keeping with his character, the monk scoffs at the nun and defends his inaction with examples of men in history who patiently awaited their

---

1. The phrase "The living Buddha of the ten thousand households" is succinctly rendered in Sino-Vietnamese through a mere four characters: vạn gia sinh phật (p: wanjia shenfo 萬家生佛). It is used in praise of a good and incorrupt official. Similarly, the phrase "One in Lộ who seeks the fortune star" (v: nhất lộ phước tinh, p: yilu fuxing 一路福星) refers to a well-loved senior official who seeks good fortune for the people of Lu (v: Lộ 路), an administrative region in the Song dynasty. Both phrases can be deployed together; see, for example, Deng Zhiyuan and Deng Gang, Youxue qionglin, 32. For more information on the content and significance of the Youxue qionglin, see Brokaw, "Reading the Best-Sellers of the Nineteenth Century," 210–11.

turn for official glory. However, the nun's words have a rousing effect on him, and in the speech that follows, he confesses to an excess of emotions. The monk says:

174   It has been written, "Women are hard to teach";
        What, oh nun, do you really know?
175   With a hook beside the river, Lã [Lü] waited for the nobles;[2]
        Plowing in the plains, Doãn [Yin] dreamt of Nghiêu [Yao] and Thuấn [Shun].[3]

176   I may not be known but I'm not indignant;
        For those with virtue will surely have neighbors.[4]

---

   2.   Lü refers to Lü Shang (v: Lã Thượng 呂尚, 1046–1015 BCE), also known as Jiang Ziya (v: Khương Tử Nha 姜子牙), a sagely man who lived during the reign of the last king of the Shang, who, finding the king unbearable, concealed himself, appearing again only in an encounter with King Wen of Zhou. *Shiji*, 32.1781–83; Nienhauser, *The Grand Scribe's Records*, 5(1): 31–41. There are several accounts of Jiang Ziya's life and his meeting with King Wen; the *Shiji* states that he was destitute, old, and fishing as he waited for King Zhou. In the *Zhuangzi*, the old man's fishing line was without a hook, the implication being that only those who really wished to be caught would be captured by him; the wise ruler who would seek him out for his assistance was King Wen. See Wang Shumin, *Zhuangzi jiaoquan*, 21.789–90. For English translations of this passage, see Mair, *Wandering on the Way*, 205–6, and Watson, *Complete Works of Chuang Tzu*, 228–30. For an account of the various early stories of Jiang Ziya, see Allen, "The Identities of Taigong Wang."
   3.   Yin refers to Yi Yin (v: Y Doãn 伊尹, 1648–1549 BCE). The *Shiji* records two stories about his entry into official service with Cheng Tang (v: Thành Thang 成湯, c. 1675–1646 BCE), founder of the Shang dynasty. In one, he desired to seek Tang out but lacked a way to do so; consequently, he made himself a servant and, because he was skilled in gastronomy, became Tang's chef. Having gained proximity to Tang, he helped him become a righteous king to found the Shang dynasty. In another story, Yi Yin is at home, either retired or yet to be employed, and Tang sent men to seek him out five times before Yi Yin agreed to serve him. Yi Yin rose to high positions, and at one point he administered the government of the Shang on behalf of an incapable king. *Shiji*, 1.122–23, 128–29; Nienhauser, *The Grand Scribe's Records*, 1:43–46. The *Sãi Vãi* probably alludes to the latter of the two stories, where Yi Yin waited patiently for Tang to seek him out. In pairing Lü Shang and Yi Yin, Nguyễn Cư Trinh draws attention not only to those who waited to be employed but also to the founding of dynasties, for the former helped King Wen found the Zhou and the latter helped King Tang found the Shang.
   4.   *Lun yu*, 4.25.

177   In youth, Cam La [Gan Luo] wore an official's headwrap;[5]
       Late in life, Khương Tử [Jiang Zi] time and again sought generalship.[6]

178   Because I am skilled at talking in a round-about fashion,
       I carry an illness of seven emotions.

179   When true feelings within are not yet tempered and calm,
       Its manifestation without cannot be centered and moderate.

Section 7 of the *Sãi Vãi* is devoted to a protracted discussion of the "seven emotions" (v: *thất tình*, p: *qiqing* 七情). One of the earliest references to the seven emotions is the Confucian classic, the *Book of Rites*, which states: "What are human emotions? Happiness, anger, sadness, fear, love, hate, and desire; of these seven, there is no need to study in order to acquire them" 何謂人情? 喜怒哀懼愛惡欲, 七者, 弗學而能.[7] In the *Book of Rites*, these seven emotions encompass the full range of feelings that are natural to humankind. Innately neither good nor evil, they are to be regulated in accordance with the rules of propriety. In the *Sãi Vãi*, however, the seven emotions are dubbed "an illness" (v: *một bình thất tình*), a characterization that gives them a Buddhist slant. In Buddhist doctrine, emotions were seen as an impediment to the attainment of enlightenment, a position well captured in the following lines from Nguyễn Gia Thiều's "Cung oán ngâm khúc":

5.   Gan Luo (v: Cam La 甘羅, b. 256 BCE) is a young prodigy of the Qin and a strategist of the Warring States period. Upon hearing that Lü Buwei (v: Lã Bất Vi 呂不韋, 291–235 BCE), prime minister of Qin, was unhappy because Zhang Tang 張唐 refused to serve as prime minister of Yan and use his new position to attack Zhao with Qin, Gan Luo successfully convinced the latter that it would be in his best interest to accede to the former's request on account of the former's powerful influence. Not content with this small victory, Gan Luo convinced the Zhao to seek an alliance with the Qin with an offer of land so as to fend off the joint attack. Zhao then attacked Yan and won even more territory for Qin. Thereafter, Gan Luo was enfeoffed as a Senior Excellency at the tender age of twelve. *Shiji*, 71.2802–4; Nienhauser, *The Grand Scribe's Records*, 7:153–55; see also Watson's translation of *Shiji, Records of the Grand Historian*, 110–12.

6.   Jiang Zi, or Jiang Ziya (v: Khương Tử Nha), is another name for Lü Shang 呂尚. See note 2 in this chapter.

7.   This passage is found in the *Liyun* (v: Lễ Vận 禮運; Conveyance of Rites) chapter of the *Liji*, 7.7a. A more popularly known list, shortened from this set of seven emotions, has only four emotions: happiness, anger, sorrow, and joy.

[I] would rather be like a quadruped, strolling easily through Buddha's gate;
Decisively terminate the seven [human] emotions to the point of their extinction.

Thà mượn thú tiêu dao của Phật,
Mối thất tình quyết diệt cho xong.[8]

The seven emotions are deemed to be impediments in Buddhist philosophical thought because their presence in devotees prevents them from crossing the threshold into the Buddhist paradise. But far from being distressed about the "illness of seven emotions," the monk in the *Sãi Vãi* cheerfully embraces it—he delights in having this ostensible shortcoming. The monk's response to his illness suggests that he rejects the Buddhist doctrine of self-negation; instead, he rejoices in the fact that he continues to feel the elemental impulses that make him human. His inflamed passions act as the impetus to tell rousing stories, which are based on Confucian humanistic principles and illustrate the particular ends to which he channels each emotion. In so doing, the monk makes a performance of emotional outbursts that are simultaneously orderly and regulated. Using the nun's lines as a guide, I interpret the monk's performance not as a repudiation of Buddhism but as a demonstration of how the practice of Buddhism can coexist with Confucian humanism. Through the monk's performance, the author of the *Sãi Vãi* proposes a form of this-worldly Buddhism that conforms to Confucian moral principles, and the monk, dressed in Buddhist garb yet preaching Confucian morality, comes to embody this doctrinal synthesis. Whereas the monk previously took on the roles of a mischievous Buddhist clergyman and a hypocritical Confucian gentleman, here he mutates into a perfected official and becomes the author's mouthpiece.

In the penultimate section of the *Sãi Vãi*, the monk takes the audience through the seven emotions in turn, and at each stop on his tour of the human's emotional range, he expounds on his experience.[9] Whereas

8. Lines 109–10. See Nguyễn Gia Thiều, *Cung oán ngâm khúc*, 36.

9. The Duy Minh Thị manuscript records only five emotions. Of the extant *Nôm* manuscripts, the same two emotions—fear and greed—are absent in the Nguyễn Văn Săm manuscript, but the Viện Hán Nôm's AB.383 manuscript contains them at the end of the sequence of emotions; of the six *quốc ngữ* transcriptions that Lê Ngọc Trụ and

the previous sections relied on pairings of historical exemplars, this section uses an eclectic mix of classical allusions and general moralistic statements. Nguyễn Cư Trinh develops a moral-religious framework around which he constructs a worldview suitable to Đàng Trong's frontier society. The framework establishes the importance of the physical environment to Buddhist and Daoist religious beliefs and teaches the members of the audience to direct their human emotions toward Confucian humanistic principles. In this way, the audience is made aware of the necessity of this world to its religious cosmology and is given a moral compass with which to navigate the world. The Việt inhabitants of Đàng Trong are taught to love, to hate, to have compassion, to be indignant, and to delight in Confucian moral principles and all that springs from them.

A Moral Compass: Happiness, Compassion, Hatred, Love, and Anger

The monk begins his speech on the illness of human emotions with a preamble on happiness, which establishes the importance of the physical world to religious thought and practice:

180   Though I cultivate with an ardent heart,
      I have the illness of excessive happiness.
181   I am happy because, below, there is the broad ground;
      I am happy because, above, there are the expansive heavens.

Phạm Văn Luật included in their study, only two of them, by Trần Trung Viên (1932) and Dương Mạnh Huy (1932), contain the two emotions. See Lê Ngọc Trụ and Phạm Văn Luật, *Nguyễn Cư Trinh với quyển Sãi Vãi*, 102–5. In all the versions, the sequence of the emotions is different. The absence of the same two emotions might indicate that most of the remaining copies stem from the same textual record or oral tradition. It is possible that the parts associated with these emotions were not dropped accidentally. This section of the play, on the illness of the seven emotions, is the longest; it could have been intentionally shortened to five emotions, which would still be substantial enough to sustain the message of the section but would reduce the overall drag. Moreover, fear (*sợ*) and greed (*muốn*) were the dominant emotions in the previous section, where the monk "wanted" (*muốn*) to tell the stories but was "afraid" (*sợ*) to do so. In this way, in the shortened version, the two emotions are accounted for.

182   Happy with blue waters and green mountains, splendid, splendid;
       Happy with the clear and radiant moon, dazzling, dazzling.

183   Internally, [as for the] three thousand, I keep them in a gourd;[10]
       Externally, [as for the] six ways, I penetrate and understand the three worlds.[11]

184   Toward Bồng Lai [Penglai] Mountain, I step forward;
       I am happy together with the eight immortals.

185   For the scenery of Sơn Nhạc [Shanyue], I go up in search;
       I am happy together with the four hoary heads.

186   Happy with humaneness and with the way;
       Happy with sages, happy with worthies.

187   Happy with the bell's ringing, urging pilgrims as they depart
         in their boats;
       Happy with the sandal, spreading out its sail against the wind.

188   For blocking out vulgar customs, I am happy with the course of Prajña;
       For washing away the dust, I am happy with the waters of Ma Ha.

189   For its way of compassion for people, I am happy with the teachings of the
         Buddha;
       For his humaneness to save mankind, I am happy to call on the
         Bodhisattva.

190   I am happy with one bottle and one bowl;
       I am happy with one Way and one servant.

191   Discussing happy matters for a splendid time;
       Why don't I be happy together with you?

The monk's ruminations on happiness invite the frontier audience to delight in the surrounding physical environment—securely bounded by

---

10. "Three thousand" refers to the 3,000 realms of existence that are thought to exist in a single moment. The gourd is a container with a narrow entrance but spacious interior; a secluded and perfect site, comprising a mountain and a stretch of water, is referred to as a "gourd-heaven." For more information on the gourd-heaven, see Stein, *The World in Miniature*, 58–77.

11. "Six ways" refers to the six paths of metempsychosis: *devas* (v: *thiên*, p: *tian* 天), man (v: *nhân*, p: *ren* 人), *asuras* (v: *tu la*, p: *xiuluo* 修羅), beasts (v: *súc sinh*, p: *chusheng* 畜生), hungry ghosts (v: *ngạ quỷ*, p: *ergui* 餓鬼), and hell (v: *địa ngục*, p: *diyu* 地獄). These are the six realms of karmic existences. "Three worlds" (v: *Tam giới*, p: *sanjie* 三界) are the regions associated with the threefold division of the universe: desire, form, and formlessness.

the "broad ground" below and the "expansive heavens" above. Rather than striving to transcend it, he revels in the beauty of the environment with its "blue waters," "green mountains," and "radiant moon." Furthermore, he shows how his relationship to the physical world is congruent with Buddhist and Daoist thought and practice.[12] The gourd refers to a "gourd-heaven," a bounded space that contains a mountain and a stretch of water; considered a perfect site, the reference to it highlights the importance of mountains and rivers to classical notions of paradise. Moreover, Penglai (v: Bồng Lai 蓬萊), one of three fabled islands on which a mountain stands, is believed to be the home of the eight immortals of Daoist mythology.[13] And Shanyue (v: Sơn Nhạc 山岳), literally "Lofty Mountain," refers to Shang Mountain, the peak to which the four famous white-haired recluses, who had witnessed the decline of the Qin dynasty, retired to avoid being advisors to Liu Bang (v: Lưu Bang 劉邦, 256–195 BCE), the founder of the Han dynasty.[14] These mountains, recognized as important elements of the religious and classical tradition, are very much a part of the physical environment of the present world.

The sacred mountains are presented in conjunction with another aspect of the physical world integral to the Buddhist tradition—waterways. The monk describes pilgrimages that the natural waterways make possible, and he delights in the echoes of the pilgrims' bells as they depart from the sacred sites. He finds happiness in the thought of the Bodhidharma's sandal, on which pilgrims meditate as they journey home in sailing boats.[15] In the next couplet, Prajña, which means wisdom or understanding, is imagined as a coursing river separating the vulgar from the enlightened life. It is not completely clear to which river Ma Ha (p: Mohe 摩訶), a transliteration of the Sanskrit term Mahā, meaning great,

12. The correct identification of a sacred mountain's physical location was believed to be essential for the efficacy of religious practice. See Robson, *Power of Place*.

13. The other islands are Fangzhang and Yingzhou. For more information on these islands, see note 25 in chapter 1.

14. The four hoary heads appear in the historical record in *Han shu*, 40.2033–36. For a discussion of the legend of the four recluses, see Berkowitz, *Patterns of Disengagement*, 64–80.

15. Legend has it that when the Bodhidharma died, he left China for India barefooted, swinging a sandal on his staff. When his coffin was opened, his body was missing and there was only one sandal buried in it.

refers; given the allusion to washing off the dust of the world, it could mean the Ganges, which is sacred in Buddhist cosmology.[16] In highlighting mountains and waterways important to Buddhist beliefs, Nguyễn Cư Trinh brings the importance of the physical world to Buddhist metaphysical thought into sharp relief.

From an excess of happiness, the monk moves on to his illness of having compassion, about which he says:

193   I have compassion for the period of the Three Sovereigns;
           I have compassion for the age of the Five Rulers.

194   I have compassion for humaneness and for righteousness,
           Compassion for virtue and for talent.

195   I have compassion for King Nghiêu [Yao], who wore a coarse shirt and
           hemp trousers;[17]
           I have compassion for King Thuấn [Shun], who plowed in the clouds and
           hoed by moonlight.

196   For eating mean fare, I have compassion for King Võ [Wu]—my
           compassion is increasingly intense;
           For suffering imprisonment, I have utmost compassion for King Văn [Wen]—
           my compassion is burningly painful.

197   I have compassion for the Duke of Chu [Zhou], whose loyalty was the ideal
           of loyalty yet was trapped by slanderous talk;

---

16.   Ma Ha is listed as one of eight large rivers in India of importance to Buddhism. See entry for Eight Rivers (八水) in *Từ điển Phật học Hán Việt*, 1:127.

17.   The sage king Yao is known for his many achievements; however, I have not been able to locate a reference to him wearing rough clothing. The most significant passage on Yao's attire is probably from the *Mencius*. There, Mengzi tells Cao Jiao (v: Tào Giao 曹交) that he should "wear the clothes of Yao, intone the words of Yao, and perform the actions of Yao, as this is to be Yao" 子服堯之服，誦堯之言，行堯之行，是堯而已矣. *Mengzi*, 6B.2. In the sixteenth century, a disciple of Wang Yangming (v: Vương Dương Minh 王陽明, 1472–1529), Wang Gen (v: Vương Cấn 王艮, 1483–1541), interpreted this statement to mean that he should fashion for himself clothes such as those that Yao wore: "How can I speak the words of [the sage] Yao, and perform the actions of Yao, and not wear the clothing of Yao?" 言堯之言，行堯之行，而不服堯之服可乎. So saying, he had a long cotton gown and other accessories made after some prescriptions from the *Liji*. See *Mingru xue'an*, 32.6a; see also Huang Tsung-hsi, *Records of Ming Scholars*, 174. On Wang Gen, see de Bary, *Sources of East Asian Tradition*, 442–45. See also Handler-Spitz, *Symptoms of an Unruly Age*, 75.

I have compassion for Confucius, a sage who had already become a sage, yet
time and again faced adversity.

198   Compassion for the strategizing advisers of Hán [Han], who, for no good
reason, died unjustly;
Compassion for the scholars of Tần [Qin], who did nothing wrong but were
buried alive.

199   I have compassion for Gia Cát [Zhuge], who was a pillar of the state
but met his lord at an inopportune time.[18]

200   I have compassion for Nhạc Phi [Yue Fei], who was an imposing general
but was imperiled and suffered harm.[19]

201   I have compassion here and compassion there;
My compassion knows no end.

202   Because he sat out in the winter night, I have compassion for the person
who lay on ice, crying for bamboo;
For being on the northern pass, I have compassion for the fellow who herded
rams and drank snow.

203   My compassion is increasingly intense;
My compassion is very sentimental.

204   I have compassion for all the four quarters;
And I have compassion for you.

Included under the category of those who excite compassion are historical
figures who suffered precisely because they acted in ways that upheld high
moral standards in the domains of loyalty, filial piety, and humility. King
Shun endured hardship on Mount Li out of a sense of filial piety to a father
who wished to kill him;[20] the Duke of Zhou suffered slanderous gossip from

18.   Zhuge Liang (v: Gia Cát Lượng 諸葛亮, 181–234). He served Liu Bei loyally and
assisted the latter's son, but he did so while the Cao clan was in power. *Sanguo zhi*,
35.911–31.

19.   Yue Fei (v: Nhạc Phi 岳飛, 1103–1142). His biography is recorded in *Song shi*,
124. For more on Yue Fei's life and legacy, see Wilhelm, "From Myth to Myth," and
James C. Liu, "Yueh Fei and China's Heritage of Loyalty."

20.   To escape his father who wanted to kill him, the sage king Shun moved to
Mount Li 歷山, where he tilled the ground. The *Shiji*, 1.38, only notes that Shun farmed
at Mount Li, but other stories note that the creatures of the Earth were so moved by his
actions that elephants came to plow for him and birds helped him weed. The story of
Shun's piety is the first story of the *Twenty-Four Filial Exemplars* (v: *Nhị Thập Tứ Hiếu*,
p: *Ershisi xiao* 二十四孝), a compilation of twenty-four historical stories on extreme cases

those who believed that he intended to wrest the throne from his nephew, on whose behalf he governed loyally until the young man came of age;[21] and King Yu, founder of the Xia dynasty, satisfied himself with meager rations on account of his humility, even when he had become king.[22] The people for whom the monk feels compassion extends to those who, although not themselves sages or kings, nevertheless demonstrated consummate filial piety and fidelity. These include Meng Zong (v: Mạnh Tôn 孟宗), a filial son who lived in the period of the Three Kingdoms, whose ill mother craved bamboo shoots in the winter and whose tears of despair as he lay on the ice caused bamboo to sprout from the snowy ground.[23] They also include Su Wu (v: Tô Võ 蘇武, d. 60 BCE), the Han envoy who was captured by the Xiongnu and refused to renounce his loyalty to the Han for nineteen long years. He persisted in his loyalty even when the Xiongnu confined him to a storage pit, where he ate the felt of his garments and drank the snow that rained down from the heavens; they moved him to the desolate shores of the Northern Sea with a herd of rams, where he was told that he would be able to return only when the rams gave milk, yet his resolve remained unbroken.[24]

---

of filial piety; it is commonly attributed to Guo Jujing (v: Quách Cư Kinh 郭居敬) of the Yuan dynasty, but there exist earlier precedents of such compilations. The *Ershisi xiao*, a useful morality guide for children, is often accompanied by illustrations. For examples of such illustrated stories, many dating to the period before the Yuan dynasty, see Yang Jun, *Ershisi xiao tushuo*. For more on the *Ershisi xiao*, see Kutcher, *Mourning in Late Imperial China*, 45–46. On some of the different versions of the tale of the sage king Shun and Mount Li, see Knapp, *Selfless Offspring*, 49–51.

21. The Duke of Zhou made himself regent when his king was young; suspicious of his motives, several feudal lords rebelled. The duke quelled the rebellion and maintained his position as regent for seven years, until his king had grown up, whereupon he returned administration to the king and took a ministerial position. *Shiji*, 4.169; Nienhauser, *The Grand Scribe's Records*, 1:64–65.

22. *Lun yu*, 8.21.

23. See Pei Songzhi's (v: Bùi Tùng Chi 裴松之, 372–451) commentary in *Sanguo zhi*, 48.1169. Meng Zong's story is one of the twenty-four cases of filial piety celebrated in the *Ershisi xiao*; see Yang Jun, *Ershisi xiao tushuo*, 102–8. For a short discussion of divine aid in filial acts such as Meng Zong's, see Knapp, *Selfless Offspring*, 94–96.

24. Su Wu's courtesy name was Ziqing (v: Tử Khanh 子卿). His biography is found in *Han shu*, 54.2459–69; on drinking snow and herding rams, see *Han shu*, 54.2462–63. See also Watson, *Courtier and Commoner in Ancient China*, 34–45. Happily for him, he was eventually released. He lived a long life and died when he was over eighty years of age.

The people for whom the monk has compassion also comprise the hapless, who suffered wrong despite themselves having committed no wrongdoing. For instance, King Wen, the benevolent founder of the Zhou dynasty, was imprisoned in Youli (v: Dū Lí 羑里) by King Zhou (v: Trụ Vương 紂王) of the Shang dynasty, who took advantage of a false rumor to reduce the influence of his political rival.[25] The advisers of Han, Han Xin (v: Hàn Tín 韓信, d. 196 BCE) and Peng Yue (v: Bành Việt 彭越, d. 196 BCE), assisted Liu Bang, the future Emperor Gaozu of Han, to defeat the Chu, but in spite of their service, they suffered cruel deaths after the emperor came to fear they were fomenting rebellion.[26] Qin Shihuang buried more than 460 Confucian scholars alive at Xianyang for having failed in the impossible task of bringing him the elixir of immortality.[27] Through these exemplars, the filial, the loyal, the humble, and even the hapless sufferers who were harmed because their virtue and their talent put them in others' crosshairs, Nguyễn Cư Trinh guided his audience to direct their compassionate outflows toward those who suffered while upholding moral principles. In so doing, he instilled in the people of Đàng Trong admiration for those very principles on whose account men of virtue were punished.

On his illness of harboring hatred, the monk says:

205   I, furthermore, have an illness of knowing hate.
206   I hate King Kiệt [Jie] and King Trụ [Zhou];
        I really hate King Lê [Li] and King U [You].

25. King Wen's allies brought a beautiful girl, teams of horses, and other unusual things to King Zhou to secure his release. *Shiji*, 4.151–52; Nienhauser, *The Grand Scribe's Records*, 1:57–58.

26. Han Xin's biography can be found in the *Han shu*, 34.1861–78; on the rumors of his rebellious intent, which led eventually to his death at the hands of Empress Lü, see *Han shu* 34.1875–78. Peng Yue's biography can be found in the *Han shu*, 34.1878–81; on his death, also at the hands of Empress Lü, see *Han shu*, 34.1880–81. Whatever their intentions, neither man had launched any rebellions, but the Han emperor feared the rumors around these militarily powerful men.

27. *Shiji*, 6.324–25; Nienhauser, *The Grand Scribe's Records*, 1:149–50. This event is typically told together with another, in which Qin Shihuang burned all the books that were not of the Qin, as he did not want to be compared with previous rulers. Some scholars do not believe that the emperor buried the Confucian scholars alive, reading the passage instead as him entrapping and executing them. See Neininger, "Burying the Scholars Alive," 121–36.

207 I hate when humane governance is not practiced,
Causing all dynasties to perish.

208 Pushing my hatred to its extreme—
I hate a fellow who betrays his father, betrays his lord.

209 I frequently hate in excess of ten parts;
I hate those who are very wicked and very cruel.

210 I hate the crude and hate the oppressive;
I hate the peculiar and hate the odd.

211 Reading about Ngu [Yu], I hate the four brutish clans;[28]
Perusing Tống [Song] histories, I hate the band of five devils.[29]

212 I hate carnage and hate destruction;
I hate the cloying and the saccharine.

213 I hate the wicked fellow so ready to fawn he killed his son,
Hate the flatterer so greedy for wealth he harmed his wife.

214 For curled tongues bent crooked, I hate the people of the state of Sở [Chu];
For stomachs greedy to be filled, I hate the people of the state of Tề [Qi].

215 I hate a dishonest fellow who presumes upon power and opportunity;
I hate a violent fellow who harms his household and stirs up his country.

216 I hate a fellow who, seeing [a chance for] benefit, races upstream
and downstream;
I hate a fellow who sees [a chance for] righteousness but worries about
loss and gain.

217 I hate people who are selfish and harm others;
I hate adulterers and adulteresses;

218 I hate fellows who are querulous and quarrelsome;[30]
I hate people who are untruthful and dishonest.

28. The four evil clans date to the time of Yao and Shun. They are Emperor Hong's
(v: Hồng 鴻) clan, which was called "The Chaotic"; the Shaohao (v: Thiếu Hạo 少皞) clan,
which was called "The Eccentrics"; the Zhuanxu (v: Chuyên Húc 顓頊) clan, which was
called "The Blockheads"; and the Jinyun (v: Tấn Vân 縉雲) clan, which was called "The
Rapacious." Yao was unable to get rid of them, but Shun succeeding in banishing them
from his domain. *Shiji* 1.43; Nienhauser, *The Grand Scribe's Records*, 1:13.

29. The five devils of the Song are Wang Qinruo, Ding Wei, Lin Te (v: Lâm Đặc
林特), Chen Pengnian (v: Trần Bành Niên 陳彭年), and Liu Chenggui (v: Lưu Thừa
Khuê 劉承珪).

30. The line reads: *Ghét đứa hay co hay cú*; although no longer in use today, *co-cú*
can be found in Taberd's 1838 *Vietnamese-Latin Dictionary* as a compound word meaning "quarrelsome." See Taberd, *Dictonarium Anamtico-Latinum*, 80.

219   That is to hate everyone,
       and then furthermore to hate you, that you should have no feelings for me.

Under the category of hatred, the monk switches from providing examples of extreme virtue to those of extreme wickedness and thus guides the audience's outbursts of rage into orderly expressions of righteous indignation. His hatred is directed especially toward the repugnant and the grotesque. In the realm of governance, he singles out King Jie (v: Kiệt 桀, 1728–1675 BCE) and King Zhou (v: Trụ 紂, r. 1075–1046 BCE), the last kings of the Xia and the Shang dynasties, respectively, and King Li (v: Lệ 厲, r. 857–842 BCE) and King You (v: U 幽, r. 781–771 BCE), the tenth and twelfth kings of the Zhou dynasty, as worthy of his audience's hatred.[31] All of these monarchs were cruel, and their actions contributed to the downfall of their kingdoms, but King Zhou was especially debauched. He was a man of strength but also a man of many vices, and he filled his palace with luxuries, showed contempt to gods and spirits, and indulged his penchant for licentiousness. For his amusement, he had naked men and women chase one another by a pool filled with wine and in a forest of hanging meat, and he made mincemeat of people with whom he was displeased. Not sparing members of his own family, he had his wise uncle, who had attempted to counsel him, cut open so he could examine if his heart truly had the seven apertures of a sage.[32] His actions were so unspeakable that they were not even considered suitable as negative examples for future moral instruction.[33]

In terms of familial relationships, the monk introduces two shocking stories of murder. The first is about Yiya (v: Dịch Nha 易牙), who was

31. King Jie was warlike and not virtuous, and he brought great suffering to the people. *Shiji*, 2.108; Nienhauser, *The Grand Scribe's Records*, 1:38. King Li was extractive and monopolized the profits of the Earth for himself. To stop the people's criticism, he killed anyone who dared speak against him. *Shiji*, 4.179–81; Nienhauser, *The Grand Scribe's Records*, 1:70–72. King You was flippant with the kingdom's defenses for the sake of humoring a woman, and his actions cost him his kingdom. *Shiji*, 4.184–88; Nienhauser, *The Grand Scribe's Records*, 1:72–74. On King You and the Lady Si, who did not like to laugh, see note 41 in this chapter.

32. *Shiji*, 3.135–39; Nienhauser, *The Grand Scribe's Records*, 1:49–52.

33. Refer to note 50 in chapter 2.

the chef of Duke Huan of the state of Qi (d. 643 BCE) during the Spring and Autumn Period (771–476 BCE). Yiya sought to please the duke, who had tried all foods except for human flesh, and so he killed and cooked his own firstborn son and served him as an exotic dish; in so doing, he not only committed murder, he also caused the duke to inadvertently engage in cannibalism.[34] The second story is about Wu Qi (v: Ngô Khởi 吳起), a military strategist originally from the state of Wei 衛, who served the Lu and the Wei before eventually becoming the prime minister of the state of Chu. When he first tried to enter into the service of the Lord of Lu, the latter distrusted him because Wu Qi's wife was from the rival state of Qi; eager to prove his loyalty to the state of Lu, he willingly murdered his wife.[35] Together the cases of Yiya and Wu Qi are horror stories showing the extremes to which people have gone for the sake of political advancement; these moralistic shockers, intended to make the audience sick to their stomachs, simultaneously defend the sanctity of family relations and caution against unreasonable political ambition.

In the domain of culture, the monk expressed his distaste for the peoples of the states of Qi and Chu. On the people of Qi, the *Guanzi* states that they are "greedy, uncouth, and warlike" on account of the state's "forceful, swift, and twisting" waters. Unlike the *Sãi Vãi*, however, the *Guanzi* notes the wholesome nature of the people of Chu: "The water of Chu is gentle, yielding, and pure. Therefore its people are lighthearted,

---

34. The story of Yiya's cannibalism is recorded in several places, including *Han Feizi*, 2.7b–8a and 3.8a–8b; *Guanzi*, 11.11a–11b (for an English translation, see Rickett, *Guanzi*, 1:428); *Huainanzi*, 7.13a and 9.16a; and *Shiji*, 32.1798 (for an English translation, see Nienhauser, *The Grand Scribe's Records*, 5(1):77). On the two opposing portrayals of Yiya, one as a paragon of good taste and the other associating him with cannibalism, see Sterckx, *Food, Sacrifice, and Sagehood*, 74–76.

35. *Shiji*, 65.2621–22; Nienhauser, *The Grand Scribe's Records*, 7:41–42. See also Chauncey S. Goodrich, "Ssu-Ma Ch'ien's Biography of Wu Ch'i," for a translation and discussion of the biography. Wu Qi is typically mentioned together with Sunzi; see Sawyer, *Seven Military Classics of Ancient China*, 187–224, for a translation of the *Wuzi*, a text on military strategy attributed to Wu Qi. Nguyễn Cư Trinh's inclusion of this legalist philosopher as an example of a person who deserved the enmity of his audience could have stemmed from his Confucianist disdain for the governing methods of the legalists.

resolute, and sure of themselves."[36] The people of Chu, from whom the *Chuci* derives, are, however, associated with shamanistic rituals, which include dancing and singing to summon the spirits and which Confucians consider to be vulgar and barbaric. The *Sãi Vãi* probably refers to their singing, which includes trills produced with curled tongues.[37] The habits of the people of the states of Qi and Chu represent practices that fall outside the bounds of properly patterned behavior; raising them as examples of repugnant habits worthy of their hatred suggests to the Việt audience of Đàng Trong that they should nurture and cultivate the converse of those practices.

These examples of grotesque, malformed behaviors help delineate and define the field of the orderly and the morally acceptable. Although some of these lessons are presented to the audience by referencing specific historical examples, many of the bad behaviors, such as a calculating spirit, selfishness, adultery, nastiness, and deceitfulness, are simply stated, which give a sense of their widespread prevalence. The *Sãi Vãi* teaches its audience to ground its righteous indignation in classical stories of wickedness, and it encourages them to observe and reflect on the immoral actions around them.

On the emotion of love and the act of loving, the monk says:

220   I, moreover, have an illness of excessive love.

221   I do not love the wicked;
        I love to love the upright.

222   In considering one's heaven-given disposition,
        What is equal to loving one's family?

223   Taking [Buddhist] logic in its truest form,
        The last priority is to love physical substance.

224   I love profoundly—love the person who is wise and worthy;
        I love intensely—love the fellow who is loyal and steadfast.

225   I love the man who is expansively open and generous,
        Love the gentleman whose disinterested heart is never troubled.

36. For stereotypes of the characters of people from the various warring states arising from the relationship between the people and the water of their land, see *Guanzi*, 14.3b–4a; Rickett, *Guanzi*, 2:106–7.

37. On the people of Chu and the *Chuci*, see Wu Fusheng, "Sao Poetry."

226 I love strong courage that is not worn down when ground,
     Love a vermilion heart that does not turn black when dyed.

227 I love ears that are familiar with hearing loyal and upright words,
     Love eyes that see clearly the affairs of past and present times.

228 In the wintry years, I love the imposing cypresses and pines;[38]
     From a great distance, I love the experienced *ki* [*qi*] and *ki* [*ji*] horses.[39]

229 If a son is devoted to his father, I love him like jade or gold;
     If a subject is upright with his lord, I love him like pearls or treasure.

230 When it comes to loving the Way—I love the doctrine of the mean;
     When it comes to loving the heart—I love a heart that is humane and proper.

231 As for love that benefits the household, country, and entire realm,
     What can compare with loving the sages?

232 As for love that brings talent, virtue, riches, and honor,
     What can compare with loving an official?

233 I love people of wisdom and intelligence,
     Love fellows of talent and ability.

234 As for loving the various things,
     What is equal to loving you?

In directing the audience's love, the monk does not cite specific historical examples but makes general statements about qualities worthy of admiration. Rather than exhort the audience to model themselves after historical figures who embodied the good, he appeals to man's innate nature, his "heaven-given disposition," which naturally leads him to love the upright and reject the wicked. Not content to leave this natural disposition to find its own way, the monk engages in shaping the domain of virtue. Foremost is man's love for his family, as compared with the love of material things, which he ranks as having the lowest priority. The monk tells the audience that he loves sons and subjects who observe proper relationships with their fathers and lords, and kings who love the sages as well as their officials. Beyond holding the relational bonds in high esteem, he encourages the audience to love generosity, equanimity,

38. Unlike other plants that fade, cypresses and pines are able to survive the winter weather.

39. *Qi* (v: *ki* 騏) is a breed of piebald horse and *ji* (v: *ki* 驥) is a thoroughbred horse. They run very fast and cover a lot of ground in a day.

courage, faithfulness, steadfastness, humaneness, wisdom, and talent. The monk's general statements on behaviors that merit the love of his audience indicate the ideal form of those qualities.

When he comes to speak of anger, the monk says:

235   I, moreover, have an illness of frequent anger.
236   I know true anger; I do not know false anger.

237   I am angry that I am often wrong and make many mistakes;
       When wrong and mistaken, I have destructive anger.
238   I am angry that I have little virtue and little talent;
       In thinking about talent and virtue, my anger increases to its utmost.

239   I am angry that I do not know about administration;
       I am angry that I do not know about military strategy;
240   I am angry that I am far from my lord and king and waste a loyal heart;
       I am angry that in honoring my parents I do not illuminate the way
           of filial piety.

241   In thinking about the humane way,
       I have a bitter anger.
242   When considering the past and present,
       I am increasingly angry.

243   Seeing Đồng Trác [Dong Zhuo] ravage the Hán dynasty,
       I am angry that Hà Tiến [He Jin] did not anticipate it.
244   Seeing Khuyển Nhung [Quan Rong] plunder the Chu [Zhou] dynasty,
       I am angry that the Marquis of Thân [Shen] erred in his scheming.

245   Blood is boiling—bubbling down the waters of Vị [Wei];
       Bones are overflowing—filling up the city of Trường [Chang].
246   I am angry that Thương Quân [Shang Jun] was tyrannical and not
           gentle;
       I am angry that Bạch Khởi [Bai Qi] was incompetent and very cruel.

247   Hán was imperiled, why did [Empress] Lữ [Lü] plot and covet?
       Đường was weakened, how dare [Empress] Võ [Wu] be saucy!
248   In this case, [Empress] Võ's crime against Đường resounds like that of
           Sơn [Shan].
       [Empress] Lữ's guilt toward Hán reverberates like that of Mãng [Mang].

249   I am angry at the many offensive matters;
       My anger knows no end.

250   Seeing that I am old, you abandon me and go;
       Don't blame me for being frequently angry.

The monk's expressions of anger are aimed in two directions: at himself and at historical figures. He turns his wrath onto himself—for lacking the skills for administration and military strategy that he could have used to serve his lord and country, and for being too far away to perform the roles of a loyal official and a filial son—and in so doing encourages the audience toward similar introspection and self-examination. Whereas his hatred was directed at the grotesque, his anger is channeled toward those whose hubris upset the moral and the political order. The monk uses the by-now-familiar method of deploying historical figures to illustrate a point, and he vents his spleen at those whose schemes to secure political advantage for themselves backfired and resulted in delivering power to outsiders. He Jin (v: Hà Tiến 何進, d. 189), an ambitious military general who lived at the end of the Eastern Han dynasty, was involved in a power struggle with the eunuch faction after the death of the emperor; he called in Dong Zhuo (v: Đồng Trác 董卓, d. 192), a frontier warlord, to help him take care of the eunuchs but was beheaded by the eunuchs before Dong Zhuo arrived. Seizing the opportunity, Dong Zhuo invited himself into the capital, wrested control of the court, and deposed the new emperor.[40] The Marquis of Shen (v: Thân Hầu 申侯, d. 771 BCE), angry that King You of Zhou had abandoned his daughter, who had been queen, allied himself with the Quan Rong (v: Khuyển Nhung 犬戎), an ethnic group from the west, against the king. The Quan Rong killed King You and ran amok, plundering the country.[41] In both cases, these figures' poorly calculated schemes caused dynasties to come to harm.

40.   On Dong Zhuo, see *Hou Han shu*, 72.2319–32, and *Sanguo zhi*, 6.171–79. On He Jin, see *Hou Han shu*, 69.2246–52. See also de Crespigny, *A Biographical Dictionary*, 157–58 and 311–12.

41.   *Shiji*, 4.186–88; Nienhauser, *The Grand Scribe's Records*, 1:73–74. King You abandoned his heir and his queen, who was the daughter of the Marquis of Shen, in favor of Lady Si of Bao (v: Bao Tự 褒姒, d. 771 BCE). Bao Si did not like to laugh, and King You tried his best to make her smile. One day, he lit the beacons, a messaging system to bring word out to his feudal lords if his state was threatened, when there was no threat; the lords arrived and Bao Si burst out laughing. King You thereupon did it a few more times, and the feudal lords ceased responding to the lit beacons. When the Marquis of Shen

The monk's anger reaches new heights as he recounts episodes of extreme cruelty. It was on the banks of the Wei River (v: Vị Thủy 渭水) that Shang Yang (v: Thương Dương 商鞅), the legalist reformer of the state of Qin, oversaw the beheading of more than 700 criminals in one day.[42] The city of Changping (v: Trường Bình 長平) is the site of a famous battle between the Qin and the Zhao, in which the army of the Qin was led by Bai Qi (v: Bạch Khởi 白起, d. 258 BCE), a fearsome military commander. In 260 BCE, the Qin forces laid siege to Changping, where the Zhao troops were barricaded; after being deprived of food for forty-six days, Zhao soldiers attacked Qin fortifications in an attempt to end the siege. Eventually 400,000 soldiers surrendered to Bai Qi; convinced that the soldiers would never be loyal to the Qin, he massacred all but 240 of the youngest, which he returned to the Zhao. In all, it is believed that he killed 450,000 men.[43]

The monk inveighs against hubristic empresses who coveted power for themselves or their families. He is furious with Empress Lü (v: Lữ 呂, 241–180 BCE), the wife of Liu Bang, the first emperor of the Han dynasty, for plotting to gain power for her clan in the wake of the emperor's death.[44] The monk is outraged at the infamous Empress Wu (v: Võ 武)

---

plotted with the Quanrong and attacked King You, the king lit the beacons but no one came. He was killed and Lady Si taken prisoner. Thereafter, the former heir, the Marquis of Shen's grandson, was enthroned.

42. Shang Yang is referred to in the *Sāi Vāi* as Shang Jun (v: Thương Quân 商均). His biography is recorded in *Shiji*, 68.2693–2708; Nienhauser, *The Grand Scribe's Records*, 7:87–95. On his political philosophy, see Hsiao Kung-chuan, *A History of Chinese Political Thought*, 368–424. The episode of the beheading of the 700 criminals by the Wei River is recorded in Liu Xiang's (v: Lưu Hướng 劉向, 77–6 BCE) "new preface" (v: *tân tự*, p: *xinxu* 新序), which is preserved in Pei Yin's (v: Bùi Nhân 裴駰, fl. 465–72, during the Liu-Song period) commentary on the *Shiji*; see *Shiji jijie*, 68.9–10; see also Duyvendak, *The Book of Lord Shang*, 3–7.

43. The battle of Changping and Bai Qi's decision to kill the men is recorded in *Shiji*, 73.2819–22; Nienhauser, *The Grand Scribe's Records*, 7:169–71. Bai Qi eventually incurred the wrath of the King of Qin and was asked to slit his own throat; on his own reflection at what he might have done to offend Heaven (and not the king), he thought of the massacre of the Zhao soldiers who had surrendered, and thereupon believed that he deserved death and killed himself. *Shiji*, 73.2824; Nienhauser, *The Grand Scribe's Records*, 7:173.

44. We have seen that Empress Lü ensured the deaths of Han Xin and Peng Yue, generals who helped her husband, Liu Bang, come to power; her biography in the *Shiji* is devoted not to these assassinations but to the events after the death of Liu Bang.

of the Tang dynasty, also known as Wu Zetian (v: Võ Tắc Thiên 武則天, 624–705; regency 684–90, r. 690–705), who ruled the empire through her husband and sons, and then became the first female monarch in the Middle Kingdom when she took the throne and founded her own short-lived Zhou dynasty in 690.[45] In comparing Empress Lü and Wu Zetian to Wang Mang and An Lushan (v: An Lộc Sơn 安祿山, 703–57), respectively, two men who usurped the thrones they served, the monk singles out the empresses' crimes of usurpation as being the most egregious. One suspects that the monk was angry that these women had the audacity to trespass on an institution of male authority and trample on its political and moralistic order.[46]

This section of the *Sãi Vãi* demonstrates Nguyễn Cư Trinh's mission to exhort the frontier audience to embrace Confucian moral ideals such as filial piety, loyalty, and uprightness. Like the Thearch Yu who tamed the primordial floods and guided its waters through the mountains, Nguyễn Cư Trinh regulated his audience's untamed feelings and channeled them through appropriate avenues. The audience was encouraged to love and have compassion for those who upheld those principles and to hate and harbor anger toward those who flouted them. He offered the audience a moral compass by which they could calibrate their behaviors; he articulated a set of qualities to which they should aspire, and he clearly laid out patterns of behavior that were considered

---

Empress Lü seemed to have been particularly cruel to Beauty Qi (v: Thích Cơ 戚姬), Liu Bang's favorite consort, and the latter's son, Ruyi (v: Như Ý 如意), for she perceived them as threats to her political authority. After Liu Bang's death, Empress Lü killed Ruyi and maimed Beauty Qi; her extreme cruelty caused her son, Emperor Hui, to fall into illness and despair. The statement in the *Sãi Vãi* on the Han warding off peril refers to the events immediately following the death of Emperor Hui, who died without an heir. Empress Lü enthroned Emperor Hui's son from a consort, governed as ruler in his stead, and plotted for the Lü clan to take power over from the Lius. Her machinations weakened the house of the Liu and caused the death of many members of the clan; after her death, the feudal lords enthroned one of Liu Bang's surviving sons as emperor and killed many of the Lü clan. *Shiji*, 9.497–518; Nienhauser, *The Grand Scribe's Records*, 2:105–38.

45. On Wu Zetian, see *Jiu Tang shu*, 6.115–34; *Xin Tang shu*, 4.81–105 and 76.3474–85.

46. Wang Mang and An Lushan are referred to in the *Sãi Vãi* as Mang and Shan, respectively. An Lushan was a Tang general who rebelled and proclaimed himself ruler of a new dynasty, Yan 燕, in 756. On An Lushan and the rebellion, see Pulleyblank, *The Background of the Rebellion of An Lushan*. On Wang Mang, see notes 38 and 40 in chapter 2.

either desirable or despicable. Even though the monk declares, at the start of this section on the "illness of human emotions," that he speaks in a "round-about fashion," his manner is relatively direct when compared with the "straightforward" manner with which he claimed to speak in the previous section on "stories that cannot be told." This section of the *Sãi Vãi* serves as a lesson in moral education for the Việt frontier population. Through education, Nguyễn Cư Trinh sought to induct them into a cultural world ordered by Confucian moral principles; the implication, moreover, was that those who remained unpatterned by these principles occupied the lower levels of the civilizational hierarchy.

"Smite the Barbarians"

In the course of the play, the nature of the monk and nun's relationship changes. In the beginning, the nun exhibits an aversion to her mischievous interlocutor, admonishes him, and engages in verbal battles with him. By the end, however, she marvels at the monk's erudition and invites him, with his expansive knowledge, to show her the way out of the frontier lands and to the Pure Land paradise. She says:

255   At Thunderclap Temple, if one has merit one becomes a Buddha;[47]
       On reaching Thiên Thai, if one is fortunate one becomes an immortal.[48]

----

47.   In the Duy Minh Thị manuscript, the temple name is Lôi Am Tự (Lei'an si 雷庵寺); in the AB.383 and the Nguyễn Văn Sâm manuscripts, the temple name is recorded as Lôi Âm Tự (Leiyin si 雷音寺). I believe the latter manuscripts are correct, and that this is a reference to the Thunderclap Temple where the four pilgrims in the *Journey to the West* (v: *Tây Du Ký*, p: *Xiyou ji* 西遊記) received the scriptures from the Buddha. There, Xuanzhang (v: Huyền Trang 玄奘) and Sun Wukong (v: Tôn Ngộ Không 孫悟空) were found worthy and themselves became Buddhas; Zhu Bajie (v: Trư Bát Giới 豬八戒) and Sha Wujing (v: Sa Ngộ Tịnh 沙悟淨) received lesser appointments. Wu Cheng'en, *Xiyou ji*, 100.1349–50.

48.   Thiên Thai (p: Tiantai 天台) refers to a sacred mountain inhabited by immortals. The earliest known reference to Mount Tiantai as a place where sages roamed and transformed themselves into immortals is "Rhapsody on Roaming the Celestial Terrace Mountains" (v: Du Thiên Thai Sơn phú, p: You Tiantai shan fu 游天台山賦) by Sun Chuo (v: Tôn Xước 孫綽, 314–371). The rhapsody is recorded in *Wen xuan*, 11.3–10. For an English translation, see Knechtges, *Wen xuan*, 2:243–53.

256   If you know of any road to penetrate the Western Heaven,
        Please instruct me and cultivate with me all night and day.

With this, the start of the final section of the *Sãi Vãi*, there is an inversion
of the positions with which the monk and the nun began the play. Whereas
the monk had been the one to make outrageous requests of the nun, it is
now the nun who places outlandish demands on the monk. The monk has
so far taught the Việt frontier inhabitants to focus on being Buddhists in
this world. Instead of seeking to transcend their human desires, he urges
the members of his audience to embrace their human emotions and direct
the expression of those feelings toward a Confucian morality. The nun's
request provides the monk with an opportunity to bring his teachings to
their intended conclusion. By embracing their humanity, the Việt frontier
inhabitants are to engage more deeply with human affairs, and, in so
doing, forgo any attempts to escape from the physical world. Instead, they
are incited to defend their newly annexed lands against invading uplanders. To the nun's invitation, the monk retorts:

257   Moderate the crazy talk;
        Diminish this monster within!
258   The heavenly region is still so far beyond—it's very dim;
        The sacred temple is yet so far away—so very distant.

259   As for the western direction, there is no road to reach it;
        As for the northern direction, the way is very hard;
260   As for the southern direction, it is not very far;
        It's nothing but for the fear of the many bands of Đá Vách.

The monk puts a stop to the nun's thoughts of religious escape and encourages her to drop the idea of journeying in search of paradise. He
tells her in no uncertain terms that the heavenly region, home of the Buddha's sacred abode, is located at an insurmountable distance. Taking the
lead from the nun's request that he accompany her to the Western
Heaven, he states that there is no road to travel in the direction of the
west. This line serves as a point of departure in the monk's speech, where
he ceases to discuss the impracticality of seeking religious escape and
switches to a consideration of the possible routes of migration that the

Việt frontier inhabitants of Quảng Ngãi might follow. It is noteworthy that even though the chronicles record that this play was written for the edification of the people of Quảng Ngãi, the lines in this section represent the first time Nguyễn Cư Trinh referred directly to their particular circumstances.

Given the geographical realities of Đàng Trong, where a long and lofty mountain range stretched across its western flank, travel in that direction was indeed not feasible. The lands to its north were occupied by the northern Vietnamese kingdom, Đàng Ngoài, and beyond that lay the vast and imposing Chinese kingdom. Even though the political north typically indicates the Middle Kingdom, the memory of internecine fighting between the Vietnamese kingdoms was probably still fresh in the minds of Nguyễn Cư Trinh and his southern Vietnamese audience, and it would not have been surprising if Nguyễn Cư Trinh had Đàng Trong's rival Vietnamese kingdom in mind. The monk does not even mention the eastern direction, where the land ends and the sea begins. He brings the audience to the inescapable conclusion that the southern direction is the only one toward which the Vietnamese could plausibly migrate.

The idea of the southern direction as a natural route for Vietnamese territorial expansion gained tremendous force in nineteenth- and twentieth-century Vietnamese historiography. Particularly in the Republic of Vietnam (more commonly known as South Vietnam), the "southern advance" (v: *nam tiến*, p: *nanjin* 南進) became an important event symbolizing the inevitable defeat of indigenous civilizations at the hands of the migrating Vietnamese people. For the southern Vietnamese, recounting Vietnamese history through a narrative of the southward advance demonstrated their disproportionately larger contribution to the work of expanding Vietnamese territory as compared with their northern counterparts.[49] Nguyễn Cư Trinh was one of the earliest Vietnamese on record to articulate this vision of a southward migration. Earlier contenders include a prophecy associated with Nguyễn Bỉnh Khiêm, a sixteenth-century clairvoyant and poet, that has been cited in the Nguyễn dynasty chronicles as the reason Nguyễn Hoàng, the first Nguyễn lord who established Đàng Trong, decided to move southward to Thuận Hoá in 1558.

49. Ang, "Regionalism in Southern Narratives."

In the prophecy, Nguyễn Bỉnh Khiêm told Nguyễn Hoàng to consider the Hoành Sơn mountain area in Thuận Hoá as a base for a new home since it had the capacity to nourish many generations.[50] Interestingly, the prophecy does not mention migrating to the "south" or the "southern direction." Another contender is a passage in the same chronicle containing Nguyễn Hoàng's dying words, spoken to his close associates on his deathbed in 1613. There, Nguyễn Hoàng urged his followers to stay committed to the land of Thuận–Quảng (Thuận Hoá and Quảng Nam), where the Hoành mountain and Linh river flanked its north and the Hải Vân and Bi mountains its south, indicating an auspicious place that would produce great men.[51] Rather than functioning as an exhortation to migrate southwards, the "south" in Nguyễn Hoàng's deathbed speech served to specify the geographical location of the mountains in relation to the Thuận–Quảng region. Compiled in the nineteenth century, the Nguyễn dynasty chronicles record the thoughts and sentiments of the victorious southern Vietnamese dynasty. The *Sãi Vãi*, composed in 1750, is among the earliest—if not the earliest—record of the Vietnamese idea of a natural southward migratory trajectory.

The monk declares that the only thing standing in the way of Vietnamese migration southward is the "many bands of Đá Vách." "Mọi Đá Vách," a vernacular Vietnamese expression, is sometimes also translated as "Thạch Bích Man" (p: *shibi man* 石壁蠻) in Sino-Vietnamese.[52] Both expressions translate as "Stone Wall tribes," a name given to the indigenous uplanders of Quảng Ngãi. Later French scholars have identified these peoples as the Hrê, the Tare, and the Kare, who belong to the Cham and the Jarai families; the Xa Giang and the Ka Giong, of the Sedang family; the Bonom, of the Bahnar family; and the Tava and

---

50. The prophecy states: "In the Hoành Sơn mountain region, a thousand generations can seek shelter" (v: *Hoành Sơn nhất đái, vạn đại dung than*, p: *Hengshan yidai, wandai rongshen* 橫山一帶・萬代容身). See *Đại Nam Thực Lục Tiền Biên*, 1.5.

51. Nguyễn Hoàng's deathbed speech is recorded in the *Đại Nam Thực Lục Tiền Biên*, 1.23–24.

52. Official documents in the Vietnamese kingdoms were recorded in Sino-Vietnamese rather than vernacular Vietnamese. The "Mọi Đá Vách" are referred to as the "Thạch Bích Man" in Nguyễn Cư Trinh's official biography. See *Đại Nam Liệt Truyện Tiền Biên*, 5.5.

the Talieng.[53] Nguyễn Cư Trinh describes the Vietnamese frontier inhabitants' timidity in the face of the Đá Vách peoples; for today's reader,
these lines offer a precious record of the Vietnamese frontier experience.
Rather than an account of inevitable victory one might find in twentieth-
century accounts of Vietnamese annexation of lands belonging to other
ethnic groups encountered on the way to the Mekong delta, the *Sãi Vãi* records a version of these encounters in which the Vietnamese were not confident of successfully defeating the outsiders and in fact suffered losses at their
hands and were plainly terrified at the prospect of further engagement.

261   If I speak of them, I lose my soul;
        When I think of them, my spirit is terrified.
262   They cut down people like they do bananas;
        They ambush us with impunity.
263   Everywhere they go they sweep through thoroughly;
        They capture and kill instantly.
264   They enter villages to loot property and harm people,
        Then descend into fields to chase after buffalos and capture horses.
265   For now let's cultivate here to the point of exhaustion;
        Why should we cross over there?
266   Do not go wandering off or they will capture and take you away,
        Then I'll be left alone, like an orphan.

This description paints a vivid picture of an aggressive outsider encroaching
on Vietnamese lands, looting their property, and harming their people.
The passage positions the Vietnamese as besieged victims and clearly
evinces their reluctance to engage in any form of fighting against the local
population. Expressing fear and cowardice, and delivered in the monk's
frightened voice, this outburst issues an implicit challenge to the audience,
daring them to take steps toward changing the current situation. The
challenge is made by the nun, who calls out to the audience to take action
against these ferocious tribesmen. The nun says:

53. "Les Mois de la Cochinchine et du Sud-Annam," 44. For other works on the
uplanders in the Quảng Ngãi region and its surroundings, see Bernard Bourotte, "Essai
d'histoire"; Lechesne, "Les mois du Centre Indochinois"; "Les mois de Ta-my"; Huguet, "Les provinces d'Annam."

267   In the classics there is a saying:
                "Smite the barbarians."[54]

268   Whoever is willing to respond,
                I'll entrust my life to him.

269   Please repress this ferocious band,
                Or else we'll be abused!

270   Here is poetry.

These lines, cried out by the nun, mark the end of the performance of the *Sāi Vãi*. They correspond to the lines with which the play began, where the monk, espying the beautiful nun, follows after her for fear that he might "lose out." Here the nun urges the monk, and anyone else brave enough to rise to the challenge, to follow her call and go forth, so that they, as a people, will not lose out. The nun relies on a line from the *Book of Songs* to issue this call for action; the classical reference lends historical weight to the contemporary task of fighting back the bands of Đá Vách.[55]

54.   I translated "Smite the barbarians" from the Sino-Vietnamese phrase *Nhung Địch thị ưng* (p: *rong di shi ying* 戎狄是膺). Nhung are tribesmen from the west and Địch are from the north. The locus classicus of this phrase is "The Closed Temple" (v: *bí cung*, p: *bigong* 閟宮; *Maoshi*, no. 300), the last ode of the "Lu Hymns" (v: *Lỗ tung*, p: *Lu song* 魯頌) in the *Book of Songs*. *Shijijng* (*Maoshi zhengyi*), 20B.346–50; Waley, *Book of Songs*, 313–17. See the following note for more explanation of my choice of translation.

55.   Some scholars question the use of the word *barbarian* as a general translation to designate the various ethnic groups that show up in Chinese historical records. Beckwith points out that the word *barbarian* has no equivalent in the Chinese language and argues that the Chinese did not conceive of the ethnic other as a barbarian in the sense that the term's Greek etymology conveys. He argues that a whole host of Chinese words, many of them referring to specific tribes, have been rendered inaccurately in English translation as "barbarian" where words such as "foreigner" or "captive" might have been more appropriate. See Beckwith, *Empires of the Silk Road*, 355–62. Not confined to the issue of translating historically specific labels to a term of ahistorical designation, He Yuming observes a general sensitivity, in the period of the Qing dynasty, to the word *yi* (v: *di* 夷), a historical reference to non-Han peoples to the east of China and one of the terms typically translated in the English language as "barbarian," which some early Qing authors considered to be potentially problematic in the eyes of the new Manchu overlords. See He Yuming, *Home and the World*, 202. The line invoked in this call in the *Sāi Vãi* provides a good case for discussion: *Nhung Địch thị ưng* (p: *Rong Di shi ying* 戎狄是膺) literally translates to "As for the tribes of the Nhung [p: Rong, a tribe from the west of the Chinese territory] and the Địch [p: Di, a tribe from the north of the Chinese territory], [he] smote them." It is clear that Nguyễn Cư Trinh's deployment

Significantly, Nguyễn Cư Trinh mobilizes the nun's feminine voice in the call to action. Instead of a masculine call for war against the uplanders, issued from a position of authority, the author first figuratively emasculates the Vietnamese male by highlighting his fearful and helpless state and then urges him to take action against the belligerents by invoking the feminine voice of persuasion. In this way, Nguyễn Cư Trinh used his literary skills to rally the people to the cause of the Nguyễn court.

Another View of Vietnamese–Đá Vách relations

There exists another record of Vietnamese interactions with the indigenous uplanders in Quảng Ngãi. In Nguyễn Cư Trinh's 1751 memorial to the king, he addressed the problem afflicting the people of Quảng Ngãi in a different manner. From the memorial we can infer another perspective on the conflict. As was noted earlier, the first two articles of the memorial propose dealing with the problem of the corrupt officials of Quảng Ngãi by regulating tax collection and giving the officials proper salaries. Here, we focus on the latter two articles of the same memorial:

> Third, of the people who escape there are two kinds. There are those who dodge the levied taxes and thus become wanderers, and there are those who experience hunger and cold and thus become vagabonds. Presently, [we] do not differentiate between the various kinds; all are entered into the register of criminals to collect the taxes imposed upon them. They are

---

of this phrase from the *Book of Songs* was not intended to elucidate Chinese historical interactions with those specific groups of people. Instead, it was a call to action, made succinctly with just four characters. Not having a word to refer to powerful, nonurban foreigners inclined to violence and cruelty, and instead having many designations for different groups of non-Han peoples with whom the Chinese engaged in specific historical conflicts, I propose that authors such as Nguyễn Cư Trinh relied on literary techniques such as historical allusions to convey the message that a single word, had it existed, could have delivered. I thus translate this phrase simply as "Smite the barbarians."

naturally panic-stricken and scatter, concealing themselves in the thick forests. The people in their community are made to compensate [for the loss in tax revenue]. Why should they suffer this fate? I request that [the court] investigate all the people who have escaped. For those who earn a livelihood, tax them according to regulations; for those who are compelled by hunger and cold, exempt them according to their circumstance; console and nurture [them] so as to revive the poor rustic immigrants.

Fourth, with regard to the people, allow them the freedom to be still but not the freedom to stir. Stirring leads easily to chaos, but stillness leads easily to order. Presently, people are allowed to hunt in the mountains and forests, searching for chickens and rounding up horses; they do not understand your noble intent, and they harass and bother the local people. They falsely use your name, and [they] bustle around and stir up much ado. All the people sigh in resentment. I request that from now on, when [the court] sends someone he should have stamped documentation to present to local officials for their careful examination. If there are those who disturb the people, investigate the cases and punish them, so that the hearts of the people might be stable and calm, and we can avoid bringing about any instability.

三言漏民有二。有規避征稅而遊浪者，有饑寒切身而流移者。今不分等項，一切入簿責收官稅。彼必驚惶流散，潛伏林莽。社民又被賠償。何以堪命。請察諸漏民，猶有生理者收稅如例，饑寒因迫者免之隨方，撫養以蘇窮氓。四言民可使靜，不可使動。動則易亂，靜則易治。今使人畋獵山林，尋鷄索馬，不體德意，騷擾方民。假冒之徒。到處鬧熱，人皆嗟怨。請嗣後差人須有章跡呈地方官審驗。有擾民者糾治，庶民心安靜，免致動搖.[56]

Articles 3 and 4 of Nguyễn Cư Trinh's memorial are particularly interesting for how they categorize the people in Quảng Ngãi. In article 3, which focuses on the issue of tax collection, Nguyễn Cư Trinh divided the Việt people who were dodging taxes into two groups: the poor and the dishonest. In regard to the dishonest, he requested that the court investigate them and tax them according to their livelihoods; as for the poor, he urged the court to take steps toward rehabilitating them so they would once again be able to enter into society. He was concerned with

56. The memorial can be found in Nguyễn Cư Trinh's biography in *Đại Nam Liệt Truyện Tiền Biên*, 5.6–7. A transcript of the memorial can also be found in the *Đại Nam Thực Lục Tiền Biên*, 10.18–19.

the honest villagers who were forced to pay more than their fair share of taxes because they were shouldering the burden of those who were unable or unwilling to pay. In article 4, Nguyễn Cư Trinh drew a distinction between the "people [who] are allowed to hunt in the mountains and forests, searching for chickens and rounding up horses" and the "local people," whom they harassed and bothered. I understand the former group of people as Việt inhabitants of Quảng Ngãi who hunted in the upland areas; they are, first and foremost, officials who misused the king's name for their own material profit. The "local people" refers then to the indigenous uplanders of Quảng Ngãi. The harried and provoked uplanders to whom this petition alluded were most probably the Đá Vách—the same people who were vilified in the *Sãi Vãi*.

The picture of Vietnamese–Đá Vách relations that emerges from this memorial is quite different from the image conveyed in the final lines of the *Sãi Vãi*. Instead of frightened Việt lowlanders suffering at the hands of the ferocious Đá Vách uplanders, Nguyễn Cư Trinh's memorial appears to accuse the Việt inhabitants of Quảng Ngãi of harassing the Đá Vách. Most deplorable were those who impersonated court officials—the people who "falsely used [the king's] name"—and caused anxiety among the uplanders in the name of the Nguyễn court. Nguyễn Cư Trinh implored the king to mete out punishment to the Việt bullies, so the uplanders would be quieted and their animosity against the Việt lowlanders would be quelled. Embedded in the memorial is another issue that was likely a source of concern for the Nguyễn court. In article 3, Nguyễn Cư Trinh reports that there were some among the Việt frontier inhabitants who had taken to "concealing themselves in the thick forests." Instead of a stark line demarcating the societies of the indigenous uplanders and the Việt lowlanders on the Quảng Ngãi frontier, some Việt people were opting for the life of uplanders to escape the control—through taxation or otherwise—of the Nguyễn court. The Nguyễn court was losing population at a time when it needed people to hold on to the frontier lands, and it was in the interests of the court to establish firm lines of division between the Việt lowlanders and the indigenous uplanders to ensure that the Việt people remained lowlanders and under the court's control.

What do we make of the two different accounts that espouse seemingly antithetical positions of Vietnamese–Đá Vách relations? In his memorial, Nguyễn Cư Trinh urged the king to regulate what was under his control—the Vietnamese villagers and officials—to retain the Việt frontier inhabitants in the ranks of the lowlanders and obtain the cooperation of the indigenous uplanders. The nature of this request required Nguyễn Cư Trinh to spell out the faults of the Việt frontier inhabitants so that the king could institute stricter controls on the border. In the *Sãi Vãi*, however, he was persuading the Việt villagers to align themselves with the lowlanders. It was in his interests to present the Đá Vách as pesky and ferocious barbarians in need of discipline and lacking in culture. The two historical records attest to Nguyễn Cư Trinh's ability to use his literary prowess to resolve a problem at a time when an open call for battle against the indigenous peoples might not have been an appropriate course of action.

In staging the performance of the *Sãi Vãi*, Nguyễn Cư Trinh was reportedly successful in persuading the Việt inhabitants of Quảng Ngãi to rally together and fight the Đá Vách. According to his official biography, he advanced an army on Đá Vách territory, upon which the uplanders scattered and fled. Afraid they would return should he withdraw his troops, he orchestrated a show of military strength for the benefit of the Đá Vách people. Nguyễn Cư Trinh occupied their land and made a spectacle of building walls and organizing his people into a "military-plantation system" (v: *đồn điền*, p: *tuntian* 屯田), thus giving the impression that the Việt people intended to make their presence permanent on their newly conquered territory. Allegedly falling for this charade, the Đá Vách came out of hiding to surrender to the Vietnamese. Nguyễn Cư Trinh allowed them to return, withdrawing his troops only when he had secured their guarantees of peace.[57] Just as Nguyễn Cư Trinh depicted two different sides of Vietnamese–Đá Vách relations in the *Sãi Vãi* and his memorial, he staged different performances to gain the cooperation of two groups of people—the Việt inhabitants of Quảng Ngãi and the Đá Vách uplanders. Nguyễn Cư Trinh scored a momentary victory in Quảng Ngãi, but the fight between the Việt people and the Đá Vách was far from concluded with this triumph. Years later, other Vietnamese officials such as Lê Văn Duyệt were once again faced with the task of confronting the feisty and challenging uplanders. Nonetheless, Nguyễn Cư Trinh's success in this particular episode led to him being granted greater responsibilities

57. *Đại Nam Liệt Truyện Tiền Biên*, 5.5–6.

in policing Đàng Trong's porous borders and establishing stability in newly annexed territories.

In Quảng Ngãi province, there exist to this day remains of a wall dividing the uplands from the lowlands. Dubbed the "Long Wall" and initially compared to the Great Wall in China, historians and archeologists have worked under the supposition that it was built by the lowland Việt community in the early nineteenth century to prevent incursions from Hrê uplanders, which they identify as the Đá Vách people. They eventually came to what they describe as a surprising conclusion that the wall was built as a collaborative effort to maintain the distance between Việt lowlanders and Hrê uplanders.[58] Archeological findings provide material corroboration of my interpretation of the *Sãi Vãi*, which makes the literary work the earliest record of conflict between the Việt and the Hrê peoples. Although the *Sãi Vãi* uses language that sought to rouse the Việt people to defensive action against the uplanders, my interpretation of it, after taking into account Nguyễn Cư Trinh's memorial of 1751, is that the author aimed to develop the lowlanders' sense of civilizational superiority over the uplanders and in so doing dissuade them from joining the upland community. The wall, built in the early nineteenth century, supports the claim in Nguyễn Cư Trinh's memorial that the Việt people were moving into the hills and harassing the uplanders. Moreover, it illuminates the uplanders' perspective of the Việt lowlanders. Far from wanting to enter into the society of their eastern neighbors, they collaborated with them to keep their communities separate. The wall, built more than five decades after the *Sãi Vãi* was composed, is a physical reminder of Nguyễn Cư Trinh's cultural project. At the same time, its very presence attests to the fact that the peace that he won for Quảng Ngãi was short-lived.

The *Sãi Vãi* illuminates Nguyễn Cư Trinh's cultural project in Quảng Ngãi, where, faced with the task of keeping the Việt and the Đá Vách communities separated, he exhorted the former to recognize their cultural distinctiveness and implicit civilizational superiority and thus maintain their distance from the latter. In instructing the Việt inhabitants to behave in a way that was patterned by Confucian humanistic morality, Nguyễn Cư Trinh marked the distinction between them and the uplanders in

58.   Hardy and Nguyễn Tiến Đông, "Đá Vách."

political and civilizational terms. The Đá Vách were represented as less civilized outsiders, so that the Việt lowlanders would have greater incentive to band together in opposition against them. The broader implications of this undertaking should now be apparent. In his deft deployment of satirical drama, Nguyễn Cư Trinh not only undermined existing institutions and practices that he felt were objectionable, he also mobilized religious sentiments in the service of a political order that lay at the foundations of his cultural project. Nguyễn Cư Trinh's project, however, was not the only cultural project on the southern Vietnamese frontier. Another project, located on the western flank of the Mekong delta, sought to impose cultural meaning onto the frontier landscape. That project, oriented toward a different group of people, established a competing political vision on the Mekong plains.

PART II

Lyrics and Landscapes

CHAPTER 4

Writing Landscapes into Civilization

Ming Loyalist Ambitions on the Mekong Plains

Upon the death of his father in the summer of 1735, Mạc Thiên Tứ inherited control of the Chinese enclave of Hà Tiên, located on the western extremity of the Mekong delta.[1] Within a year of assuming power, he undertook an ambitious literary project, in which he sought to compose a series of landscape poems about the domain he had recently acquired; he then invited more than thirty poets scattered along the Vietnamese and southern Chinese coastline to provide matching poems in celebration of its scenic sites. This project must be understood not only as a work of art but also as a work of statecraft. It provides a window into the techniques through which the territory of Hà Tiên was "civilized" and sheds light on the obscure political allegiances and machinations of its young ruler. Mạc Thiên Tứ tells the story of the inception of the *Ten Songs of Hà Tiên* in the preface to the work:

In the spring of the *bingchen* year [v: *bính thìn*, 1736], Master Chen [v: Trần] of Guangdong, bearing the courtesy name Huaishui [v: Hoài Thủy], sailed the seas and arrived here. I treated him as an honored guest. Every flowered morning and moonlit night, we recited verses and sang rhymes without ceasing, taking the occasion to compose matching poems of Hà Tiên's ten sceneries. Master Chen, upstanding among our confederate of friends and

1. Recall that Mạc Thiên Tứ was the son of Mạc Cửu, the ethnic Chinese founder of Hà Tiên. This book begins with a narrative of the Mạc family's migration to Hà Tiên in the aftermath of the Ming–Qing dynastic transition in China.

foremost in versifying airs and odes, upon reaching the moment of his return to the Pearl River, disseminated the topics to the literary society. [I am] much obliged to these gentlemen for not dismissing the poems; following each title, [they] composed verses, collecting them together to make one volume. From a distance, they sent [them] to show to me; I took the occasion to commission a printing.[2]

丙辰春，粵東陳子淮水航海至此。予待爲上賓。每花晨月夕，吟咏不輟，因將河僊十景相屬和。陳子樹幟鷄壇，首倡風雅。及其反棹珠江，分題白社。承諸公不棄，如題咏就彙成一册。遙寄示予，因付剞劂。

Accompanied by his guest from Guangdong, Master Chen Zhikai (v: Trần Trí Khải 陳智揩), Mạc Thiên Tứ began to compose landscape poetry about ten of Hà Tiên's scenic sites.[3] As the host, he authored the initial poems, and Chen Zhikai confirmed, in a postface to the project, that he "recited [verses] to match his [Mạc Thiên Tứ's]."[4] The visitor played a vital role in enabling the project to take on the scope that it eventually did. Chen Zhikai stayed with Mạc Thiên Tứ for half a year, and when it came time for him to take his leave, he carried copies of his friend's poems and distributed them to poets along the way as he journeyed home on board a ship. These poets, who resided in various coastal cities of Vietnam and southern China, were members of a literary society called the Summoning Worthies Pavilion (v: Chiêu Anh Các, p: Zhaoying Ge 招英閣), a society that Mạc Thiên Tứ had founded earlier.[5] The gentlemen who received these poems were asked to compose responses and send them back, presumably along the same seafaring network, to Hà Tiên. In all, 310 poems returned, ten from each of the thirty-one poets. Mạc Thiên Tứ compiled those poems with his own—making 320 poems in total—added a preface

2. Mạc Thiên Tứ, preface to *An Nam Hà Tiên thập vịnh*, EFEO microfilm, 1a–1b.

3. Chen Zhikai is referred to by his courtesy name, Huaishui, in the preface to the *Ten Songs of Hà Tiên*, but we know his given name, Zhikai, because he signed off using it in the postface he contributed to the volume. I rendered the names of all the poets residing on the Chinese mainland in Mandarin Pinyin, the standardized romanization of Chinese characters, but the poets were probably communicating in Cantonese.

4. Chen Zhikai, postface to *An Nam Hà Tiên thập vịnh*, EFEO microfilm, 49b.

5. Poetry societies have a long tradition among the Chinese literary elite. However, most of them have regular face-to-face meetings. For a study of a poetry society in Guangdong in its various incarnations from the mid-Ming to the Republican period, see Honey, *The Southern Garden Poetry Society*.

and two postfaces, and sponsored a woodblock print publication of this collection.[6] The project was completed in the summer of 1737, a little more than a year after Chen Zhikai's visit to Hà Tiên.

The fact that Mạc Thiên Tứ initiated this project within a year of taking over the administration of Hà Tiên suggests that this project was of great importance to him. His final thoughts in his preface to the collection of poems are as follows:

> This [i.e., the project of writing landscape poetry about Hà Tiên] is to make known [the fact] that the mountains and rivers have benefited from my late father's action of cultural transformation, which has added to their strength and beauty; [the mountains and rivers] in receiving, in turn, the appraisal of these renowned lords, have been further enhanced in their enchantment. These poems not only contribute to the attractiveness of this sea country; they, for their part, serve as an official gazetteer of Hà Tiên.
>
> 是知山川得先君風化之行，增其壯麗，得復諸名公品題，益滋其靈秀。此詩不獨爲海國生色，亦可作河僊誌乘。

Although there are grounds to be cautious about taking at face value Mạc Thiên Tứ's pronouncements about his reasons for undertaking this project, we can nonetheless identify two of his principal motivations. First, he wished to make known and propagate the fact that his father, Mạc Cửu, founder of the Chinese settlement in Hà Tiên, had affected the "cultural transformation" of the landscape. Second, Mạc Thiên Tứ's act of establishing the scenic sites of Hà Tiên as topics of poetic discourse for a literary community dispersed over southern China and other parts of Vietnam was meant to "further enhance their enchantment."

We find here two means by which cultural transformation takes place. The first, carried out by the father, was a physical form of transformation leading to cultural change. In his official biography, assembled by Nguyễn dynasty scribes, Mạc Cửu is credited with building city walls and defensive fortifications, as well as establishing military and public offices in Hà

---

6. Mạc Thiên Tứ wrote the preface to the collection. One postface was written by Mạc Thiên Tứ's companion in this project, Chen Zhikai; the other was written by an "Old Man from Lingnan [the Guangdong and Guangxi area]" named Yu Xichun (v: Dư Tích Thuần 余錫純).

Tiên. As a result, he was able to attract worthy and talented men to his domain, and a small city developed there.[7] The second form of cultural transformation, which the son carried out, was discursive. In composing verses about Hà Tiên's landscape, Mạc Thiên Tứ subordinated it to a specific cultural genre—Chinese landscape poetry in the style of heptasyllabic regulated verse. He used poetry as a means through which to make his domain culturally congruent with a civilization with which he wished to associate. Through his poems, Mạc Thiên Tứ civilized his peripheral domain by inscribing cultural values on its landscape. *Wen* 文 brings together two concepts integral to the Chinese civilizational discourse: "pattern," the presence of recognizable designs inherent in the warp and woof of nature and, a concept derived from the earlier definition of *wen* as pattern, "literature" or "writing," the manifestation of those natural patterns in script.[8] In saying that Mạc Thiên Tứ civilized his domain, I mean that he brought out the recognizable patterns in the landscape of Hà Tiên through a literary transformation of its scenic sites. This process brought the landscape of Hà Tiên into the realm of *wen*, in terms of patterns and literature, and raised it above the world of pattern-less chaos. Moreover, Mạc Thiên Tứ disseminated his poems and solicited responses in the same genre so that the culturally inscribed landscape would enter into the civilized (*wen*) discourse of intellectuals. Mạc Thiên Tứ's concluding flourish was to commit the collection of poetry to permanence by commissioning its woodblock print publication. The inscriptional character of the woodblock printing technique was particularly fitting for a project concerned with effecting cultural change on the domain.[9]

This chapter focuses on Mạc Thiên Tứ's initial ten poems.[10] The author's preface and Chen Zhikai's postface both note that the poems

---

7. *Đại Nam Liệt Truyện Tiền Biên*, 6.1–3.

8. On using *wen* in the dual senses of "pattern" and "literature," see the introduction to the *Wen xuan* in Knechtges, *Wen xuan*, 1:17; see also Liu Xie, *Wenxin diaolong*, 1.1–16; Shih, *The Literary Mind and the Carving of Dragons*, 8–14.

9. There was also a tradition of engraving poetic compositions directly onto the scenic sites from which the poet derived his inspiration. See Strassberg, *Inscribed Landscapes*, 5–7. There is no evidence that the Hà Tiên poems were ever inscribed onto the physical landscape.

10. Few have studied Mạc Thiên Tứ's ten-poem suite in its entirety. Chen Jinghe drew attention to them in his fine essay "Kasen Tei shi no bungaku katsudō" and repro-

were composed in the spirit of collaborative response, where the poems of the one were matched by the poems of the other. In such instances, two parties typically take turns writing verses, and it is important to study the sets of poetry in relation to each other because the initiating party's poems might in fact have been responding to the second party's preceding poems.[11] It is a curious fact, however, that Chen Zhikai's poetry was not included in the *Ten Songs of Hà Tiên*. Nowhere in the École Française d'Extrême-Orient (EFEO) microfilm copy of the *Ten Songs of Hà Tiên* does it state the total number of poems in the collection; it is possible that Chen Zhikai's poems might have been lost in the process of copying and recopying over the years.[12] However, a nearly contemporary observer,

---

duced them in print, but he did not analyze any of them. Liam Kelley discusses the literary project in "Thoughts on a Chinese Diaspora," but he translates and provides a reading of only the first and third poems. Keith Taylor integrates his interpretation of poems 3 and 6 in "Surface Orientations in Vietnam." In selectively studying only a few of the poems, the authors have left undiscovered the significant motifs and patterns embedded within them that reveal Mạc Thiên Tứ's political ambitions for Hà Tiên. Đông Hồ (Lâm Trắc Chi) made a name for himself in his study of Mạc Thiên Tứ's poems. See Đông Hồ, *Văn Học Hà Tiên*. Incidentally, this book was published a year after the author's death in 1969. He rightly understands them as an important part of the Vietnamese literary heritage, but this same impulse has predisposed him to reading the nation back into history, and in so doing has colored his reading of the poems.

11. See, for example, Warner, "The Two Voices of *Wangchuan Ji*."

12. Mạc Thiên Tứ's official biography in the *Đại Nam Liệt Truyện Tiền Biên* records that the *Ten Songs of Hà Tiên* had been lost because of the chaotic political situation in Hà Tiên in the latter half of the eighteenth century. It notes that it was only in the early nineteenth century that the governor of Gia Định, Trịnh Hoài Đức, managed to find a copy to republish it. See *Đại Nam Liệt Truyện Tiền Biên*, 6.4. Woodblock prints of the *Ten Songs of Hà Tiên* are no longer extant. Mạc Thiên Tứ's poems are, however, recorded in a few texts as described here:

1. Because it has been through the fewest editorial hands, my translation and analysis of Mạc Thiên Tứ's poetry is based on the EFEO microfilm, created in 1955; this version was originally hand-copied and bears no date. Refer to EFEO microfilm A.441, no. 661, n.d., 47a–49b. I refer to this as the EFEO manuscript.

2. Two of his poems (9 and 10), and a small handful of poems by other contributors to the project, were recorded by Lê Quý Đôn in his *Phủ Biên Tạp Lục*, 5.170a–70b. I refer to this as the LQD manuscript.

3. In 1970, the Vietnamese scholar Đông Hồ published a monograph in which he reproduced in print Mạc Thiên Tứ's ten poems. See Đông Hồ, *Văn học Hà Tiên*. Unfortunately, Đông Hồ did not note the source location of the original manuscript. I refer to this as the DH manuscript.

Lê Qúy Đôn, claimed in the 1770s to have received a copy of the volume, and he recorded in his *Frontier Chronicles* that thirty-one other poets contributed to the project besides Mạc Thiên Tứ, of which six were resident in parts of Vietnam and twenty-five in Qing China. Chen Zhikai's name was not on Lê Quý Đôn's list of poets.[13]

I propose that studying Mạc Thiên Tứ's ten poems as a single, independent entity, and not in relation to other poems that might have been composed with them, is in fact closer to the spirit of the *Ten Songs of Hà Tiên* project. The other poets did not receive Mạc Thiên Tứ's poems one at a time but were given the entire suite all at once; this would have affected how they responded to recurring themes, motifs, and sentiments found in his poetry. Mạc Thiên Tứ dedicated his ten poems to an island, a mountain, a temple, a fortress wall, a cave, a cliff, a lake, a bay, a cape, and finally a fishing creek.[14] His poems transformed Hà Tiên by rendering its natural environment regulated instead of chaotic; they illuminate culturally recognizable patterns in Hà Tiên's natural landscape, and they divulge the poet's hidden political agenda. A close textual analysis reveals a repeated motif in his poetry that holds the key to understanding the ultimate aim of this literary project.

4. The poems are reproduced in the appendix to the article by Chen Jinghe, "Kasen Tei shi no bungaku katsudō," 174–75. Chen Jinghe notes that he received a copy of the poems from a colleague in Vietnam. I refer to this as the CJH manuscript.

Where variations exist, I indicate them in the notes to my discussion of each poem. In all cases, I keep each version of a poem as intact as possible, and I select variations from only one manuscript. The exception is where there is a lacuna in the base text, in which case I fill it with a character from another manuscript while preserving the variant of the poem from the base text. Where there is no compelling reason to make a change, I preserve the base text.

13. Lê Qúy Đôn, *Phủ Biên Tạp Lục*, 5.171a. Lê Quý Đôn, an official of the Trịnh-controlled Lê dynasty (which ruled the northern Vietnamese polity), traveled to territories that were previously controlled by the Nguyễn in central and southern Vietnam for about six months in the 1770s during the chaos of the Tây Sơn uprising. The *Phủ Biên Tạp Lục* was published in 1776. For more information about Lê Qúy Đôn and *Phủ Biên Tạp Lục*, see Woodside, "Central Vietnam's Trading World."

14. For a list and description of the geographical features of Hà Tiên, which includes most of the scenic sites that form the topic of Mạc Thiên Tứ's poems, see Trịnh Hoài Đức, *Gia Định Thành Thông Chí*, 95–105 and 170–95. (The latter set of page numbers refer to the hand-copied Chinese character manuscript appended to the back of the volume.) The *Gia Định Thành Thông Chí* was compiled in the 1820s.

Situating Hà Tiên in Verse:
Dangerous Frontier or Distant Sanctuary?

Hà Tiên is located at the intersection of several overlapping political arenas. Khmer royalty regarded it as an integral part of Cambodian territory, but the Nguyễn rulers of Đàng Trong considered it to be their southwestern frontier. Moreover, it housed a busy port that functioned as a node in a larger coastal trading system that connected Hà Tiên to Fujian and Guangdong.[15] Hà Tiên was certainly not the same place in the Vietnamese and the Chinese imagination. From the perspective of the southern Vietnamese political center in Phú Xuân, Hà Tiên was a militarized frontier or a wild peripheral region. Almost fifty years after the *Ten Songs of Hà Tiên* project was initiated, one of the southern Vietnamese princes, Nguyễn Ánh, sought refuge in the wilderness of Vietnam's southwestern terrain in his flight from rebels who had taken control of his family's kingdom.[16] To the Chinese community moving from port to port on the trade route, however, Hà Tiên represented a familiar ethnic Chinese enclave, albeit one situated at a distance from the Chinese mainland. Mạc Thiên Tứ was simultaneously a commander of a Vietnamese garrison and a ruler of a Chinese enclave, and there were, as such, two divergent ways in which he could have chosen to configure Hà Tiên in his poetry: he could treat it as an unknown frontier region in need of being made intelligible to an audience located at the Vietnamese capital, or he could treat it as a far-flung haven for the perpetuation of Chinese cultural tradition. The first two poems of Mạc Thiên Tứ's suite, "Golden Islet Blocking Waves" and "Verdant Folds of Screen Mountain," direct the reader to one of these two possible positionings.

Golden Islet Blocking Waves	金嶼攔濤
An island of rocky peaks settles the emerald waters;	一島崔嵬奠碧漣

15. For a list of the port cities on the trading route and brief descriptions of them, refer to Chin, "Junk Trade between South China and Nguyen Vietnam," 53–66.

16. The rebels were the famous Tây Sơn brothers, who wrested control of southern Vietnam from the Nguyễn family in the early 1770s. For more information about the rebellion, see Dutton, *The Tây Sơn Uprising*.

Flowing waters by a wondrous beauty at mighty
　　Hà Tiên.　　　　　　　　　　　　　　　　横流奇勝壯河僊

Obstructing the power of waves and billows from
　　the southeast seas;　　　　　　　　　　　波濤勢截東南海

Sun's and moon's radiance reflect from the sky and
　　down below.　　　　　　　　　　　　　　日月光迴上下天

Arriving in its waters, fish to dragons will transform;　得水魚龍隨變化

Beside cliffs of trees and rocks, they naturally splash
　　a-flitter.　　　　　　　　　　　　　　　傍崖樹石自聯翩

Wind-sighs and wave-traces see it fit to linger long,　風聲浪跡應長據

In this landscape of shadow and light, an unusual
　　kingdom, distant.　　　　　　　　　　　　濃淡山川異國懸

(Poem 1)

Verdant Folds of Screen Mountain　　　　　　屏山疊翠

Luxuriant vegetation grows naturally on this lofty
　　peak;　　　　　　　　　　　　　　　　　龍葱草木自岧嶢

Folded ridges, fanning open, in graceful purple
　　and verdant.　　　　　　　　　　　　　　疊嶺屏開紫翠嬌

A cloud-filled sky, encircling light, the mountain presses
　　up-close;　　　　　　　　　　　　　　　雲靄匝光山勢近

Just after rain, crisp and pleasant, fauna and flora
　　aplenty.　　　　　　　　　　　　　　　　雨餘爽麗物華饒

Maturing together with heaven and earth, amassing
　　potency through the ages;　　　　　　　　老同天地鐘靈久

Sharing in the splendor of mist and rosy clouds, extending
　　as far as the eye sees.　　　　　　　　　　榮共烟霞屬望遙

I dare say that in Hà Tiên, the scenery is unusual;　敢道河僊風景異

Swelling vapors swirl and trees swish and rustle.　嵐堆鬱鬱樹蕭蕭

(Poem 2)

These poems announce Hà Tiên's natural beauty and its unusual geographical location. In "Golden Islet Blocking Waves," Hà Tiên is presented as a place protected by a rocky island fortuitously positioned in
front of its coast. Mạc Thiên Tứ depicts the "island of rocky peaks"
surrounded by becalmed waters as the legendary Dragon Gate (v: Long
Môn, p: Longmen 龍門), which in Chinese folklore is a mountainous spot
through which the mythical sage Yu, the conqueror of primordial floods,

guided the course of the Yellow River.[17] Dragon Gate is also a mythical place where carp swim against the flow of the water, struggling to jump over the rocks at the top of the stream; the few that succeed would turn into dragons.[18] This image is brought to life in the third couplet of the poem, where the poet describes fish swimming "a-flitter" like birds—creating splashes as they break through the water's surface beside the rocky cliffs of the island—in their quest to arrive at the place beyond and transform into dragons.[19] This imagery, traditionally used to refer to scholars who have successfully undertaken the arduous journey to rise above others in imperial examinations, familiarizes Hà Tiên for the audience.[20] But even as the trope of Dragon Gate familiarizes Hà Tiên, Mạc Thiên Tứ simultaneously defamiliarizes it by declaring it to be a "distant" and "unusual kingdom." Far from presenting these traits as marks of inferiority, however, the final couplet celebrates this distant and unusual kingdom as a place in which even whispers of winds and echoes of waves endure, not suffering to depart after the winds and the waves have subsided. The visitors to Hà Tiên want to remain, and in so doing imbue it with qualities of longevity and changelessness, as if it existed suspended in space and time, an impression that the poem's final character *xuan* (v: *huyền* 懸), in its layered meanings, conveys and reinforces.

The second poem of the suite, "Verdant Folds of Screen Mountain," takes as its subject a mountain with layered ridges. The mountain is depicted as an ornamental screen, fanning open with a pattern traced out

17. The route through which Yu guided the waters is described in the *Book of Documents*, and the water's course past Dragon Gate is mentioned specifically in *Shangshu*, 3.5a and 3.6a. Although the Dragon Gate to which the *Book of Documents* refers is located near modern-day Xi'an, Dragon Gate is in fact the name of several places on the Chinese mainland. For a succinct account of the legend of Yu and Dragon Gate, see Durrant, *The Cloudy Mirror*, xi–xii.

18. *Shui jing zhu*, 4.2a. The idiom "leaping over Dragon Gate" (v: *đăng long môn*, p: *deng longmen* 登龍門) derives from this source.

19. In my reading of this poem, I take "fish" and "dragons" as two separate entities; in subsequent poems, and in my later rereading of this opening poem, I read the two entities as one and understand the term to mean "fish-dragons." "Fish-dragons" is a motif that appears in four of Mạc Thiên Tứ's ten poems; I discuss its significance at the end of this chapter, after I have introduced all of the poems.

20. See, for example, *Hou Han shu*, 67.2195.

by the colors of its natural vegetation and the enlivening radiance of light refracted through the cloud-filled sky. At first glance, the poem appears to be a simple celebration of nature. However, it is more than a memorialization of the "unusual," to be understood in this context as "extraordinary," scenery of Hà Tiên. In the third couplet, the poet describes the extent of Screen Mountain's potency and influence; the phrase "amassing potency" (v: *chung linh*, p: *zhongling* 鐘靈) is particularly apt because it indicates the convergence of the vital spirits of both Heaven and Earth, which implies that Screen Mountain is a fertile place that will bring forth talented men. The first parts of each line of the couplet focus on a conjoint experience, and the poet's choice of the verbs "together with" (v: *đồng*, p: *tong* 同) and "sharing in" (v: *cùng*, p: *gong* 共) hint at the idea of a tie or bond. The suggestion finds its realization in the poem's final couplet, in which the lavish abundance of Hà Tiên's extraordinary scenery is seen in the pregnant clouds swirling in its sky and heard in the rustling of dense leaves on its trees. A poet typically reveals his emotional sentiment in the final couplet, yet Mạc Thiên Tứ here seems to focus the reader's attention solely on the natural environment. But that in itself is the poem's message, for, as is made apparent in the confluence of the poet's "sentiment" (v: *tình*, p: *qing* 情) and Hà Tiên's "scenery" (v: *cảnh*, p: *jing* 景), Mạc Thiên Tứ's emotional state and Hà Tiên's natural state are one and the same. Just as Screen Mountain is teeming with life, so is the poet filled with vitality; his personal fate is tied to that of Hà Tiên's celestial and terrestrial worlds ("maturing together with heaven and earth"), and his personal fame is bound up with that of its natural environment ("sharing in the splendor of mist and rosy clouds").

In the first poems of the suite, the poet embraces the fact that his kingdom is located in a distant place and exults in its unusual scenery. Hà Tiên is different but not dangerous, and the poems do not evoke a sense of longing for the familiar; in this, the poems contrast with those of down-on-their-luck officials sent to border areas, or those of eremitic poets who removed themselves from the capital in protest of political affairs.[21] No lines in the poetry look back directionally to a more familiar location or temporally

---

21. For a good introduction to poetry composed by poets in exile on the geographical fringes of the Chinese empire, see Strassberg, *Inscribed Landscapes*, 33–44; for a study of eremitism in traditional China, see Berkowitz, *Patterns of Disengagement*.

to a better historical time; instead, Mạc Thiên Tứ welcomed the present as a moment of great promise for his kingdom and saw the location of Hà Tiên as fortuitous to the cultural project he had in mind. His poems do not fit easily into the usual categories of frontier poetry. Examples of such literature, which typically seek to make exotic lands on the periphery intelligible to an audience in the capital, abound from the Tang dynasty to the late imperial period. In some, authors offer a guided tour from place to place on the periphery—almost in the fashion of a tourist guidebook for the armchair traveler—and thereby allow readers in the capital to imagine themselves traveling in the peripheral regions. In others, the descriptions serve to entice settlers to exploit the potential of the frontier and transform it through agriculture.[22] As will be clear in his subsequent poems, Mạc Thiên Tứ set a welcoming tone and invited travelers and sojourners to visit Hà Tiên—not to view a curiosity or to work the land but to find respite.

In fact, Mạc Thiên Tứ's first two poems position Hà Tiên as a distant sanctuary. It was not a place to be changed to suit the demands and expectations of those further away; it was suitable precisely because it was different and unusual. This characterization locates Mạc Thiên Tứ's political, social, and cultural orientation. He was not trying to integrate Hà Tiên into a territorially expanding Vietnamese kingdom; instead, he was invested in maintaining it as an "unusual," "distant," and, by extension, separate domain. His first two poems reinforced Hà Tiên's position as a kingdom already endowed with Chinese cultural civilization; it was simultaneously distinct from the Chinese mainland, and Mạc Thiên Tứ betrayed no interest in changing it to cater to mainland tastes.

Patterning Nature

In "Golden Islet Blocking Waves" and "Verdant Folds of Screen Mountain," Mạc Thiên Tứ emphasized the splendor of the natural environment in Hà Tiên. The reader would be mistaken, however, to assume that the

---

22. For an example of the former, see Stephen Owen's discussion of Liu Zongyuan's (v: Liễu Tông Nguyên 柳宗元; 773–819) "An Account of Little Stone Ramparts Mountain" 小石城山記 in Owen, "Reading the Landscape," 48–54. For the latter, see Teng, *Taiwan's Imagined Geography*, 92–99.

poet's main objective was to celebrate the pristine beauty of untouched nature. This poetry does not appear to be concerned with the division between the "pristine" and the "man-made"; in fact, his landscapes encompass both without a sense of contradiction or internal tension. "Rustic Dwellings at Deer Cape" (poem 9), for example, is devoted to both the natural vegetation of the cape and the simple dwelling places of the village people. In another poem, "Clear Waves on South Bay" (poem 8), the poet's attention to the natural beauty of South Bay occurs in conjunction with his interest in the travelers' boats cruising on its waters. Rather than a division between "pristine" and "man-made," I suggest that Mạc Thiên Tứ's landscape poetry established a division between the "chaotic" and the "civilized," the distinguishing feature being that nature was "unpatterned" in the former and "patterned" in the latter. In the very beginning of his preface, Mạc Thiên Tứ writes:

> Hà Tiên town, of Annam, had since ancient times been considered a wild place. From the time that my late father developed it some thirty years ago, the populace began to settle down and gradually mastered plant cultivation.[23]
>
> 安南河僊鎮，古屬荒陬。自先君開創以來，三十餘年，而民始獲安居，稍知栽[24]植。

Thanks to his late father's efforts, Hà Tiên was no longer "a wild place" but one where its inhabitants participated in the rhythms of agricultural activity. Mạc Thiên Tứ undertakes to further pattern the landscape of Hà Tiên with images drawn from the Chinese cultural tradition. In "Golden Islet Blocking Waves," he refashions Golden Islet into Dragon Gate, in the process elevating Hà Tiên's status to that of an important place in classical Chinese mythology. In discursively remaking the landscape in Hà Tiên, he made manifest the patterns that underlay his domain's civility. In what follows, I detail other ways in which Mạc Thiên Tứ poetically represented the unchaotic landscape and, through this very act of representation, thereby civilized it.

---

23. *An Nam Hà Tiên Thập Vịnh*, EFEO microfilm, 1a.

24. The EFEO manuscript records the character as 裁; CJH records it as 栽. Read in the context of the preface, the character was probably mistakenly recorded in the EFEO manuscript.

REGULATING DARKNESS THROUGH
NIGHT WATCHES

In Mạc Thiên Tứ's poetry, the chaotic and potentially dangerous expanse of darkness in Hà Tiên is patterned through the regulating effect of night watches. Through five watches in the night of two hours each, ending with the fifth watch at dawn, the darkness is structured and made orderly. Night watches are present in two poems: "Night Drum at River Wall" (poem 4), which describes the moment of the third watch, and "Dawn Bell at the Temple of Seclusion" (poem 3), which captures the fifth watch.

Night Drum at River Wall	江城夜鼓
Heavenly winds swirl round and around the icy clouds up high;	天風迴繞凍雲高
Fettered and locked upon the long river, its martial air resplendent.	鎖鑰長江將氣豪
A vast stretch of armored ships chills the waters under the moon;	一片樓船寒水月
Drum and horn at night's third watch steady waves and billows.	三更鼓角定波濤
A sojourner remains throughout the night melded with his coat of mail;	客仍竟夜銷金甲[25]
A man presently on the fortress wall is wrapped in brocade robes.	人正干城擁錦袍
Military strategy received from old: a brilliant ruler pays attention;	武略深承英主眷
The whole realm of Rinan, thankfully, is stable and secure.[26]	日南境宇賴安牢
(Poem 4)	

25. In the position of the first character of this line, there is a lacuna in the EFEO manuscript. CJH and DH record the character as 客, which I adopt. The third character of this line is recorded as 警 in the EFEO manuscript; CJH and DH record it as 竟. Here, I adopt the second character because 竟夜 forms a better parallel with its counterpart in the second half of the couplet, 干城, given that both are noun phrases. 警夜, which I would translate as "keeps watch over the night," is a verb-object sequence, which does not offer as neat a parallelism. Given that the Mạc Thiên Tứ was quite conscientious in regard to observing the parallel structure of his poetry, 竟 appears to be the better choice.

26. See Li Tana, "Jiaochi (Giao Chi) in the Han Period Tongking Gulf," 48–49, for a discussion of the nomenclature "Rinan."

"Night Drum at River Wall" is a poem about a fortress, encircled by a river, located to the northwest of Hà Tiên's city center; it is the site of both a military station and a watch post, from which a drum sounds at regular intervals in the night to mark the start and end of each watch. The poem begins, in the first two couplets, with an invocation of the Han dynasty battle of Red Cliff (208–9 CE), where southern warlords Liu Bei (v: Lưu Bị 劉備, 161–223) and Sun Quan (v: Tôn Quyền 孫權, 182–252) joined forces to fight Cao Cao, a northern warlord who attempted to conquer lands south of the Yangtze River. The poem describes a military maneuver in which Cao Cao "fettered and locked" his immense fleet of warships together into "a vast stretch of armored ships" so as to make them more stable on the choppy water's surface.[27] Such an opening, in which a famous historical battle looms large, primes the reader to expect a *huaigu* (v: *hoài cổ* 懷古) poem, a song of nostalgia or lamentation. In this vein, the Song dynasty poet Su Shi (v: Tô Thức 蘇軾, 1037–1101) composed "To the Tune 'The Charm of *Niannu*': Meditation on the Past at Red Cliff" 念奴嬌赤壁懷古 in which he contemplated his fleeting life in the passing of great historical figures,[28] and the Tang poet Liu Yuxi (v: Lưu Vũ Tích 劉禹錫, 772–842) composed "Meditation on the Past at West Fort Mountain" 西塞山懷古, in which he lamented the desolation of what was once significant.[29]

Mạc Thiên Tứ, however, enacts a turn in the third couplet that differentiates his contemplation of an imagined historic battle site from those of the above-mentioned poets; instead of seeking refuge in an idealized past, he sees promise in present circumstances. The shift in the third couplet relies on an allusion to a poem by the Tang dynasty poet

27. Unfortunately, this also gave Cao Cao's ships minimal maneuverability. Liu Bei and Sun Quan sent a small decoy team of "defectors" whose boats, equipped with dried wood, oil, and combustibles, were set on fire once they were near enough to Cao Cao's immobile fleet to set them ablaze. A full account of the battle can be found in the *Zizhi tongjian*, 65.2087–93. This historical episode has also been used to refer to regret that such an impressive naval fleet was wiped out in one battle. In this poem, the allegory does not extend to Cao Cao's defeat, but only to the impressive forces he managed to build up.

28. *Quan Song ci* 1:282. For an English translation and discussion of Su Shi's meditation on the past at Red Cliff, see Lin Shuen-fu, "Ci-Poetry: Long Song Lyrics," 270–73. See also Owen, *An Anthology of Chinese Literature*, 579–80 for another translation of the same poem.

29. *Quan Tang shi*, 359.4058. For an English translation and a short discussion of Liu Yuxi's meditation on the past at West Fort Mountain, see Luo Yuming, *A Concise History of Chinese Literature* 1:357.

made famous by his frontier poetry, Cen Shen (v: Sầm Than 岑參, ca. 715–70), "The Ballad of Running Horse River: Sending Off the Army on a Western Campaign" 走馬川行奉送出師西征:

Have you not seen Running Horse River beside a sea of snow,	君不見走馬川行雪海邊
A vast expanse of level sands stretching yellow to the sky?	平沙莽莽黄入天
At Bugur in November the winds are roaring by night,	輪臺九月風夜吼
With a whole river of shattered stones as large as dippers,	一川碎石大如斗
And along with the wind that fills the Earth the stones run tumultuously.	隨風滿地石亂走
When the Xiongnu grasses turn brown, the horses are at their sleekest,	匈奴草黄馬正肥
West of Golden Mountain we see smoke and dust flying:	金山西見煙塵飛
The House of Han's Grand General is taking the army west.	漢家大將西出師
The general's coat of mail is not removed by night,	將軍金甲夜不脱
As the army moves on at midnight, pikes bump each other,	半夜軍行戈相撥
The edge of the wind is like a knife, faces are as if sliced.	風頭如刀面如割
The coats of horses are streaked with snow, steam rises from their sweat,	馬毛帶雪汗氣蒸
Dappled spots like linked coins instantly turn to ice,	五花連錢旋作冰
Drafting indictments back in camp, the inkstone's water freezes.	幕中草檄硯水凝
When nomad horsemen hear of him, their hearts will surely quail,	虜騎聞之應膽懾
My opinion is that they will never dare cross their swords with ours:	料知短兵不敢接
At the western gate of Junshi we await news of the victory.[30]	軍師西門佇獻捷

---

30. *Quan Tang shi*, 199.2052–53. Translated by Owen in *An Anthology of Chinese Literature*, 467–68. On the Tang general Feng Changqing as the leader of the military campaign commemorated in this poem, see *Cen Shen ji jiaozhu*, 2.178–79.

Cen Shen, a poet with firsthand military experience in the Tang's campaigns to Central Asia, deftly conjures up a scene of the single-minded advance of horses bred for war racing through the harsh barrenness of the northwestern desertscape. Of particular relevance to Mạc Thiên Tứ's poem are the lines depicting the Tang general Feng Changqing (v: Phong Thường Thanh 封常清, d. 756) as a Han general who wears his "coat of mail" (v: *kim giáp*, p: *jinjia* 金甲), a reference to his metal armor, through the night and whose challenge to his "outlander foes" (v: *lỗ kỵ*, p: *luji* 虜騎) frightens them into submission. In the fifth line of "Night Drum at River Wall," Mạc Thiên Tứ describes "a sojourner" dressed for battle; given that the poet was the son of an ethnic Chinese adventurer residing far from his ancestral home on the Chinese mainland, I propose that the figure of the sojourner is self-referential. Like the Han general in Cen Shen's poem, Mạc Thiên Tứ spends the cold night "melded with his coat of mail," his body as though fused as one with his armor, never slackening in his readiness for battle. In the second half of the couplet, the sojourner, represented simply as "a man," is now positioned on Hà Tiên's fortress wall, enveloped in a brocade robe, from which he guards his realm. The parallelism between the two lines of the couplet, and in particular between the characters "remains" (v: *nhưng*, p: *reng* 仍) and "presently" (v: *chính*, p: *zheng* 正), highlights the continuity between the great general of the Han and the sojourner in Hà Tiên. Guarding his domain successfully with "military strategy received from old," Mạc Thiên Tứ continues in the tradition of the Han general. The poet implicitly draws a contrast between the depth of Hà Tiên's inheritance and that of its neighboring domains, which he perceives to be culturally deficient. Unlike the *huaigu* poems, the connection with the past in Mạc Thiên Tứ's poem strengthens, rather than diminishes, the significance of the present.

Like Cen Shen, Mạc Thiên Tứ dramatizes the cold ("icy clouds up high" and "chills the waters") as a means to describe the hostility of the frontier. The portrayal of Hà Tiên as a frontier region seems incongruous with the earlier depiction of it as a civilized realm, even if extraordinary to the point of being unusual. Yet his representation of Hà Tiên as a hostile borderland is tempered in the conclusion of the poem, which describes the security and stability of the region; here the Han general is not merely on an expedition but has made it his business to stay and rule the realm. The allusion to Cen Shen's poem is particularly relevant because of its implication that the threat against which Mạc Thiên Tứ remained vigilant was outlander armies. River Wall military station was located to the northwest of Hà Tiên's city center, on the border with Cambodia. This poem, the only one with a martial tone, provides a stark contrast to the first poem of the suite, where Hà Tiên's coastal frontage was made secure merely because of a rocky islet; in it, strong waves posed the only danger. That poem set a welcoming tone, and its seaward orientation suggests that the welcome was extended to visitors who arrived via the southeast seas—that is, travelers and merchants connected to the coastal trading network. On the contrary, Mạc Thiên Tứ guarded Hà Tiên's northwestern border vigilantly, and his defensive concerns for his realm demonstrate his political orientation away from Cambodia and toward the Chinese traders on the coastline.

Whereas the drum and horn indicating the third watch in "Night Drum at River Wall" reassure the reader that Hà Tiên is protected from harm, a different sound marks the fifth watch in "Dawn Bell at the Temple of Seclusion." Here, a temple bell rings out, indicating the hour of dawn:

Dawn Bell at the Temple of Seclusion	蕭寺曉鐘
Remnant stars, the residual few, toward the heavens are cast;	殘星寥落向天拋
At the fifth watch, a bell tolls, resounding far from the temple.	戊夜鯨音遠寺敲
Purified region and human destiny awaken to the world;	淨境人緣醒世界
A singular sound, clear and distinct, goes out to the river and beyond.	孤聲清越出江郊
Suddenly startled, a crane calls out, soaring on wind around the trees;	忽驚鶴唳繞風樹
Also jolted, a crow caws from a branch that dangled the moon.	又促烏啼倚月梢
At once roused, the thousand households push their pillows back;	頓覺千家欹枕後
Roosters spread the news of dawn, calling out cock-a-doodle-doo.	雞傳曉信亦嘮嘮

(Poem 3)

This poem, perhaps the most beautiful of the suite, conflates two awakenings: the breaking of a new day and the moment of spiritual enlightenment. Its setting is the Temple of Seclusion at the precise moment of dawn, when the bell tolls to mark the fifth watch. This sound, emanating from the temple, causes in rapid succession a chain of events in the natural world, culminating in the awakening of its human and animal inhabitants; at the same time, the sound of the bell effects instantaneous spiritual awakening. The themes of Buddhist enlightenment and physical awakening from slumber occur concurrently in the poem's second couplet. Line 3 describes, on one hand, a purified region, a reference to the Temple of Seclusion and, by metonymic extension, Hà Tiên, which exists on the edge of the human realm, in which people wake up to a new day. On the other hand, it refers to the Pure Land of Sukhāvatī, a blissful place of rebirth for the faithful who hear Amitābha's name. Line 4 diverts the reader's attention back to the tolling of the temple bell, thereby underscoring the causal relationship between the "singular sound" and the two awakenings. This relationship lies at the foundations of the architectural structure of the poem, where notions of cause and effect link each couplet to those that precede and succeed it. The activities that suffuse the third couplet are effects of the sound of the temple bell in the first and the second couplets, which causes the crane to call out and take flight and the crow to caw from its perch on a tree branch, on whose tip the low-lying moon appears to hang. The crow's cry, in turn, is a herald of dawn in advance of the cock's crow, and the fourth and final couplet takes up the subject and concludes the poem with the domesticity of dawn, where people put away their pillows and roosters announce the start of the day. Contained within the final couplet are reminders of spiritual awakening, captured in words borrowed from Buddhist terminology, such as "at once roused" (v: *đốn giác*, p: *dunjue* 頓覺), which is revealing of the poet's conception of enlightenment as instantaneous, and "spread" (v: *truyền*, p: *chuan* 傳), which in this context recalls the transmission of teachings that engender spiritual enlightenment. With these words the concluding couplet brings the poem back to its first lines, where, with the sound of the bell that spreads far away from the temple, the transmission of spiritual teachings disperses from Hà Tiên. At the heart of a poem on the moment of dawn, then, is a song about enlightenment.

Just as the moment of enlightenment is instantaneous, the poem captures time as a succession of instants. The deep tolling of the temple bell at the start of the poem ushers in a chain reaction of noises that awaken the inhabitants of the land even before the bell's reverberations cease. This poem gestures to the spread of religious teachings beyond Hà Tiên, yet it remains strangely isolationist in its message; it expresses Mạc Thiên Tứ's desire to circumscribe his realm as a domain apart from its neighbors in a region not deemed to be part of the classical civilized world. The temple bell strikes a lone sound because the bell sounds but once at the fifth watch; it is also a single sound because there are no other temples in the vicinity sounding the fifth watch. The area around Hà Tiên has yet to become patterned—spiritually and culturally—in the way that Hà Tiên itself has been. Mạc Thiên Tứ accepts that he is ensconced in a wider region that is not yet patterned, yet he also boasts that his domain, unlike its environs, is civilized.

REGULARITY OF DAYS AND SEASONS

In Hà Tiên, where the night is divided into five watches, time progresses along a fixed course, clearly marked by moments of diurnal and nocturnal transition. "Stone Grotto Swallows Clouds," a poem capturing the playfulness of nature in Hà Tiên, delights in the carefree spirit of the place. Nevertheless, like prior poems in the suite, it presents the natural world as highly ordered.

Stone Grotto Swallows Clouds	石洞吞雲
The mountain peak thrusts its verdant crest into the river of stars;	山峰聳翠砥星河[31]
A grotto hides its latticework chambers beneath green jade stones.	洞室玲瓏蘊碧珂[32]

31. The first character of this line is recorded as 有 in the EFEO manuscript, but published as 山 in CJH and DH. Both characters work with the poem's prosody and neither affects my translation; as I will adopt two other variants from the CJH and DH manuscripts, I choose, for the sake of uniformity, to make this change as well.

32. The last character of this line is recorded as 𡼲 in the EFEO manuscript, but published as 珂 in CJH and DH. In terms of prosody, 𡼲 belongs to the 哿 rhyme group, which is of the 上 tone. The poem's rhyme scheme, however, requires that character to have a level tone; the character 珂 belongs to the 歌 rhyme group, which has a level tone. It is thus a better fit for prosody, and I adopt this character instead.

Uninhibited, mists and clouds come and go as they please;	不意烟雲由去住
Unconstrained, grasses and plants dance carelessly together.	無垠草木共婆娑[33]
Wind and Frost, since ages recurring, patterns a-changing;	風霜久歷文章異
Crow and Rabbit, repeatedly swapping, sights aplenty.	烏兔頻移氣色多
At the utmost, the quintessence, heights where few men reach;	最是精華高絕處
I breathe according to the wind, from the lofty peak. (Poem 5)	隨風呼吸自嵯峨

The subject of "Stone Grotto Swallows Clouds" is a cavernous grotto concealed within a rocky mountain. The poet brings its maze-like pattern of interconnected chambers to life with an image borrowed from descriptions of the intricate latticework of windows. In the first half of the poem, nature exhibits a carefree, to the point of careless, existence: the mountain peak, beneath whose moss-green stones the grotto hides, interrupts the celestial river of stars along the Milky Way, mists and clouds insouciantly make a thoroughfare through the imposing mountain's belly, and the vegetation on this verdant mount dance without consideration for its sharp silhouette. In the midst of this ostensibly chaotic natural existence, however, the poet introduces a sense of determined regularity. The third couplet's "Wind and Frost," indicating seasons, years, and months, accentuates the ordered character of recurring seasonal time. Moreover, "Crow and Rabbit," which refer to the sun and the moon, respectively, on account of the black crow in the middle of the sun and the rabbit in the center of the moon, repeatedly swap their positions and thereby create an alternating pattern of day and night. The poet depicts time in Hà Tiên as having occurred in repeated patterns for ages, suggesting that its past is neither nebulous nor chaotic.

That is not to say that order comes at the expense of carefree nature, but that order is inherent in nature. In the poem's final couplet, the poet

---

33.   There is a lacuna in the EFEO manuscript where the second character should be; both CJH and DH recorded it as 垠, which I also adopt.

has roamed the mountain and scaled its heights, and there, at its utmost, he breathes together with the wind. Meditating according to the Daoist practice of nourishing life through breath control techniques, the poet accesses the "purest essence" (another translation of 最是) atop the mountain and undergoes a transcendental experience, where he inhales and exhales the "*yin* and *yang*" (another meaning of 精華) of the universe. Just as the moon (which is associated with aspects of *yin*) and the sun (associated with aspects of *yang*) take their turns in occupying their place in the sky, so does the poet's controlled breathing regulate his own *yin* and *yang*; he draws from the natural order for his vitality. In the swaying motion of the grasses and plants, and in the coming and going of the clouds, the mountain itself, upon which the poet stands, is alive and breathing. Mạc Thiên Tứ's suite of poems, in which he seeks to uncover order and patterns in Hà Tiên, is brought to its pinnacle with this poem on a naturescape that derives its order from within itself. But this uncovering, it should be noted, is itself a creative activity. Patterning is not only about discovering what is already present in nature; it is also an act of poetic invention. Through the literary refashioning of the landscape, Mạc Thiên Tứ draws out those aspects of it that best align with his own cultural ideals and his political vision of Hà Tiên's future. The generative potency of nature mirrors the creative power of the poet.

TAMING NATURE'S FORCES

The poems illustrate the author's hand in regulating the passage of time in Hà Tiên. Another aspect of nature that Mạc Thiên Tứ tamed through his poetry was its tempestuousness, evident in such phenomena as tumultuous waterfalls and breaking waves. In "Golden Islet Blocking Waves," Mạc Thiên Tứ calmed the billows of the southeast seas, just as Yu tamed the primeval floods. The poem reproduced below, "An Egret Descends from Pearl Cliff," shows Mạc Thiên Tứ reining in the chaotic power of a waterfall on Pearl Cliff.

An Egret Descends from Pearl Cliff	珠崖落鷺
Green foliage and dusky clouds mix with the rosy sunset;	綠蔭幽雲缀暮霞

Flying out of the enchanted cliff, a white bird
    emerges, aslant.

靈巘飛出白禽斜[34]

At night, arrayed in heavenly formation, fragrant trees
    spread out.

晚排天陣羅芳樹

At day, falling off the edge of the cliff, jade flowers
    spill forth.

晴落平崖瀉玉花

A waterfall and its shadow, together tumbling, under
    moonlight on the peak;

瀑影共翻明月岫

Clouds and lights, encircling evenly, dusk's glow thrown
    on the sand.

雲光齊匝夕陽沙

Brash sentiments about the course of events, ready to act
    on plans;

狂情世路將施計

In the midst of rushing, I pause, on this rocky shore.
(Poem 6)

碌碌棲遲水石涯

The subject of this poem is a cliff from which a waterfall cascades and out of which a snowy egret flies. Despite being the cliff's most noteworthy feature, the waterfall is surprisingly obscured. In the first half of the poem, the poet refers obliquely to it in the diagonal descent of the bird, which stands in for its plunging waters, and in the milky white jade flowers, which the poet uses to portray its splashes of water droplets. As substitute descriptors, the bird's smooth flight and the sprays of small flowers offer little sense of the awe that waterfalls can inspire. It is only in the third couplet that the poet draws the reader's focus to its tumbling waters, but the water's unruliness is tempered because the waterfall is described as entwined in a dance with its shadow, which contains it in a locked embrace. The waterfall, one of nature's most forceful phenomena, is reined in through description.

    The poem invites the reader to form an association between the scene it depicts and the celestial realm. Its invocation of a "heavenly formation" and "jade flowers," images borrowed from descriptions of the arrangement

34. The last character of this line is 斜 in the EFEO and DH manuscripts, but it is recorded as 斑 in the CJH manuscript. Both characters have the *ping* 平 tone, so both work with the rhyme. 斑, from the compound word 斑白, suggests that the egret has a mottled appearance. I believe the egret here is in fact white to represent the waterfall and invite an association with the Daoist transcendent's white crane, and so I see no reason to deviate from my base text.

of stars in the sky and the jade crumbles of Daoist elixirs, respectively, lifts the reader's thoughts to a higher, spiritual plane. The motif of a solitary and aloof egret is analogous to the Daoist transcendant's white crane. Poems featuring such cranes typically describe fantastical journeys, where, transformed temporarily into a bird, the Daoist sage traverses the celestial world. But in the poem under consideration, the egret does not undertake any fanciful or otherworldly journey. Instead, as a descriptor for the falling water, the egret is so closely associated with the mountain as to meld with it. It emerges from the numinous cliff only to come to rest at the mountain's foot. Similarly, the poet achieves oneness with nature when he, like the bird, lingers on the mountain's rocky shore and ceases to indulge his brash sentiments. Having been poised on the brink of action, he now checks himself and pauses. The pause, however, is poignant. Rather than a timid hesitation, the poet appears to consolidate himself before rushing headlong into the fray.

The foregoing examples of Mạc Thiên Tứ's civilizing hand on Hà Tiên's landscape show how the poet was interested in portraying his domain as a cultured and patterned realm. In expressing how time in Hà Tiên was regulated through man-made devices, such as night watches, and natural mechanisms, such as seasonal changes, and in poetically taming the unrulier aspects of natural phenomena, Mạc Thiên Tứ infused Hà Tiên's landscape with aspects of civilization, separating his kingdom from the chaotic wilderness. The landscape that he portrayed was occasionally pristine and sometimes man-made; his notion of landscape did not seem to draw a line between the two. What appears to have concerned him more was the division between unregulated chaos and regulated civilization. Mạc Thiên Tứ worked repeatedly in his poetry to portray his realm as belonging to the latter category.

Vistas, Movement, and the Poet

A landscape described in a poem often has affinities with its author's inner sentiments; even when these are not mentioned explicitly, they may be discerned in the features of the terrain he chooses to portray and in how they are represented. Stephen Owen points out, for example, that

Wang Bo's (v: Vương Bột 王勃, 649–76) selection of dangerous precipices and steep cliffs "mirrored the perils of his experience."[35] Mạc Thiên Tứ favors scenes of vastness, and he fills his poetry with wide vistas. In "Dawn Bell at the Temple of Seclusion" the poet directs the reader's attention to "the river and beyond" and the stretch of treetops around which a crane soars. The poem neglects to provide a detailed description of the temple building; we know only from the title of the poem, and a line drawing attention to the dawn bell "resounding far from the temple," that the Temple of Seclusion is present. Mạc Thiên Tứ's penchant for meditating on the vastness of the surrounding environment is perhaps unsurprising for a poet who experienced the breadth of the seafaring trade networks that brought different peoples to his port in Hà Tiên.

This inclination is nowhere more pronounced than in the attention he accords to large bodies of water in his poetry; often, the poet even omits details of the scenery around bays, inlets, and lakes. Vastness can evoke different emotional responses: it can accentuate the isolation of a person lost in an immense sea or bring delight at possibilities yet unseen on the horizon. Mạc Thiên Tứ's two poems on East Lake and South Bay are best considered together as illustrative of the connection between his portrayal of the landscape and his inner emotional state.

Moon's Reflection on East Lake	東湖印月
The rain has cleared, mist dissipates into a boundless expanse;	雨霽烟鎖共渺茫[36]
Alongside the water's bend, scenery becomes primeval chaos.	一灣風景接鴻荒
Clear sky and pellucid waves suspend a pair of images;	晴空浪淨懸雙影[37]

---

35. Owen, *The Poetry of the Early Tang*, 117.

36. The EFEO manuscript records the first character of this line as 雨; CJH and DH record it as 雲. Both characters work thematically with the poem. I believe that this poem and the one following it should be read as descriptions of two scenes in similar settings; I thus retain the character from the EFEO manuscript, 雨, as it appears also in the description of the next scene.

37. The EFEO manuscript records the fourth character of this line as 淨; CJH and DH record it as 靜. Both characters are of the *ze* 仄 tone and fit with the poem's prosody. Although 靜 has several other definitions, it shares one with 淨, which is purity. I thus retain the character in the EFEO manuscript.

Cyan Net awash with limpid clouds, purifies the
  myriad directions.   碧落雲澄洗萬方[38]

All-encompassing waters suspend a reflection,
  like a gently rippling sky;   湛澗應涵天蕩漾

Adrift, alone, I do not resent the sea so vast and cold.   漂零不恨海滄凉[39]

Fish-dragons, dreaming in slumber, start, but do not
  break through;   魚龍夢覺衝難破

Now as always, loyal of heart, just as light reflects
  above and below.   依舊冰心上下光

(Poem 7)

In "Moon's Reflection on East Lake," Mạc Thiên Tứ depicts a scene in
which there are two moons; one is the moon in the clear sky, the other is
its reflection on the waters of East Lake. The moon's reflection trans-
forms the lake into a sky, boundless because its edges have melted into
the "primeval chaos," which has a constantly quivering appearance. The
poem's controlled focus on the sky and the water, with nothing to disturb the moon and its reflection, creates an atmosphere of stillness and
tranquility; yet the reader is moved by a feeling of loneliness. This sentiment is at work in the third couplet, where the poet has deftly embedded

38. This line contains the most discrepancy among the three manuscripts. Placing
all three one after the other, we have: 碧落雲澄洗萬方 (EFEO); 碧海月明洗萬方 (CJH); and
碧海光寒洗萬方 (DH). All three versions fit the poem's prosody. The third and fourth
characters are different in all three versions, with the first meaning limpid clouds, the
second bright moon, and the third wintry light; all three are acceptable fits for the thematic content of the poem. The more critical difference lies in the second character.
EFEO records the second character of this line as 落; CJH and DH record it as 海.
Because the poem hints at cosmic beginings ("primeval chaos"), I elect to retain *biluo* 碧落,
a term with Daoist resonances. Here, however, *biluo* and its Daoist scriptural associations
part ways, for it appears that the word refers simply to a cyan-blue sky, though perhaps its
invocation adds celestial luster to the scene at East Lake. See Bokenkamp, "Taoism and
Literature," for a discussion of the varying uses of *biluo* in Tang poetry, ranging from its
domestication into the secular world to its deployment in conveying Daoist doctrinal
concepts. According to the rules of prosody, the second and the third couplets of regulated verse mirror each other, and so 碧落, understood as a reference to the sky, should be
understood as a reflection of 湛澗, indicating the lake. Reading the two lines as mirrors of
each other conveys, in the poem's form, the very image it treats thematically.
39. The EFEO manuscript records the fourth character as 恨; CJH and DH record it as 愧. Both are *ze* tones. I have no reason to reject the character in the EFEO
manuscript and retain it as I have for the other textual variations in this poem.

paired oppositions, with the effect that each half magnifies the other. For example, the "all-encompassing waters" (v: *trạm khoát*, p: *zhankuo* 湛濶), when coupled with "adrift, alone" (v: *phiêu linh*, p: *piaoling* 漂零), amplifies the sense of vastness on the one hand and isolation on the other; "to respond," here translated as "the reflection" (v: *ưng*, p: *ying* 應), and "do not" (v: *bất*, p: *bu* 不) exaggerate the presence of a reply and the lack of one. "Gently rippling" (v: *đãng đạng*, p: *dangteng* 蕩漾) and "vast and cold" (v: *thương lương*, p: *cangliang* 滄涼) heighten, on the one hand, the shivering motion and, on the other, the chill of the sea.

The final couplet discloses the source of the poet's loneliness. Fish-dragons, a motif that was first seen in "Golden Islet Blocking Waves," are absent because they have been unable to "break through" the surface of the water. In the final line of this poem, the poet evokes Wang Chan-gling's (v: Vương Xương Linh 王昌齡, 698–756) "At Lotus Hall: Sending Off Xin Jian" 芙蓉樓送辛漸:

Cold rains stretch to the river, by night entering Wu,	寒雨連江夜入吳
At daybreak bid traveler farewell, loneliness in Chu's mountains.	平明送客楚山孤
If friends and kin in Luoyang should ask you how I am—	洛陽親友如相問
In a vase of whitest jade a heart like a sheet of ice.[40]	一片冰心在玉壺

The poem was composed while Wang Changling occupied an official position in the southern city of Jiangning (Nanjing). At the conclusion of Xin Jian's visit, he sent with his companion word of the purity of his heart, reflective of true understanding, to his literary friends and kin in the northern city of Luoyang, whom he missed. Likewise, Mạc Thiên Tứ invokes the image of the transparent heart to portray the sincerity of his feelings; he directs his loyalty to the fish-dragons, who have not yet shown themselves in the waters of East Lake. In spite of their absence, the poet remains constant of heart, just as the moon is accompanied by its steadfast reflection on the lake.[41] The symmetry of the scene, with the moon high above and its

40. *Quan Tang shi*, 143.1448. English translation by Owen, *The Great Age of Chinese Poetry*, 111–12.

41. The fish-dragon is clearly an important motif that will recur two more times (in poems 8 and 10); I beg the reader's indulgence at this point to await my later discussion of it.

reflection on East Lake below, is mirrored in the structure of the poem, where themes in the first and last couplets resonate. The gradual awakening from dreams in the final couplet finds a counterpart in the lifting of the mists with which the poem begins. Moreover, "now as always" (v: *y cựu*, p: *yijiu* 依舊) harks back to the state of beginnings, the time of the "primeval chaos" (v: *hồng hoang*, p: *honghuang* 鴻荒) prior to the advent of order.

Even though Mạc Thiên Tứ claims not to resent his position as a solitary drifter in the vast and cold seas, "Moon's Reflection on East Lake" hints at his sense of isolation. The poet finds comfort in the hope that his isolation is temporary, soon to be at an end following the arrival of the fish-dragons. In the subsequent poem, "Clear Waves on South Bay," the stillness of the previous poem is broken by the intrusion of motion.

Clear Waves on South Bay	南浦澄波
A stretch of vastness, a stretch so pure;	一片蒼茫一片清
Clarity extending to the mooring bay; familiar autumn feeling!	澄連夾浦老秋情
The heavenly river concludes its rain, radiant mists form;	天河畢雨烟光結[42]
A watery region without any winds, where wave-froth is calm.	澤國無風浪沫平
Approaching dawn, fishing boats part waters hurriedly;	向曉漁帆分水急[43]
Following the tide, passenger boats carry clouds so light.	趁潮客舫載雲輕
I, too, know that in the eight seas, fish-dragons hide;	也知八海魚龍匿
Radiant moon and glittering waves, at ease, I understand. (Poem 8)	月朗波光自在明[44]

Mạc Thiên Tứ rejoices in the vastness of South Bay, whose clear waters extend to the shoreline where boats are moored. In meditating on the scene, he experiences a "familiar autumn feeling," a feeling of contentment in the

42. The EFEO manuscript records the third character of this line as 畢; CJH and the DH record it as 帶. The characters have contrary meanings; in the first, the rain concludes and in the second, it begins. I choose to retain the character from the EFEO manuscript because I understand this poem and the preceding one to be a pair; there, the rain had just concluded, and here it has also.

43. The EFEO manuscript records the third character of this line as 漁; the CJH and the DH manuscripts record it as 孤. Both work with the poem's prosody, and I see no reason to deviate from the EFEO manuscript.

44. There is a lacuna in the EFEO manuscript in the place occupied by the second character of this line; CJH and the DH record the character as 朗, which I adopt.

wake of the harvest and the completion of the year's work.[45] This poem describes a bay just after rainfall, when the rain has abated and a delicate mist forms, scattering the light in a colorful dispersion. The setting is reminiscent of the one that Mạc Thiên Tứ painted in "Moon's Reflection on East Lake," where the rain ceased long enough for the mist to dissipate. The surface of South Bay's waters, however, could hardly be more different from that of East Lake. Whereas the surface of the latter is unperturbed save for a few gentle ripples, South Bay's surface bustles with movement. Boats cruise along on the water, bringing fishermen out to sea and travelers in to land. Parted by the moving boats and subject to the rhythm of the tides, the waters are in constant motion.

In both poems, fish-dragons are conspicuously present by virtue of their absence. Fish-dragons have a habit of autumnal slumbers; taking autumn days as their long night, they submerge themselves in deep pools of water, where they rest for the season and consolidate their strength.[46] This helps explain why the fish-dragons in the previous poem, "Moon's Reflection on East Lake," are in a dream-like state and unable to break through the surface of the water; it also helps us understand why, in the autumnal landscape of "Clear Waves on South Bay," they remain in hiding. There are two possible interpretations of the latter poem's last couplet, particularly the last three characters. The first, as I have translated above, is that the author is at ease with his situation and content in the knowledge that fish-dragons exist in the eight seas, even though they remain hidden from him. The second, taking the final character to mean "to show" (another translation of 明), expresses the thought that fish-dragons will naturally reveal themselves at the proper time. These two interpretations are complementary, and the layered meanings help deliver the final couplet's message; the poet is at ease in his knowledge that when the right moment arrives, the hidden fish-dragons will finally surface. The poems about East Lake and South Bay show the poet's proclivity for vast expanses of water, under which the elusive fish-dragons

45.   Autumn could also be a time for dissolution and despair, because with autumn comes the destruction and death of nature. I believe it refers to contentment in this case because this feeling of contentment finds a corresponding sentiment at the conclusion of the poem, being "at ease."

46.   For the most comprehensive account of the commentarial tradition describing fish-dragons and their autumnal slumbers, see Ye Jiaying, *Du Fu qiuxing ba shou jishou*, 206–17.

remain concealed. However, the lake and the bay inspire different feelings. In the former poem, the poet remains steadfast even as he suffers isolation from the fish-dragons; in the latter, the poet is hopeful that his separation from them is but a passing phase as he awaits the moment of their imminent arrival. This difference can best be attributed to the sense of stillness in the former and the presence of movement in the latter.

In the final poem of his suite, "Mooring to Fish at Sea-Perch Creek," Mạc Thiên Tứ alternates between descriptions of the nearby creek and the distant sea, where stillness governs the former and movement characterizes the latter. He brings the reader from the background of the scene to its foreground, and in the contrasting visual perspectives, he draws out the gulf that separates the two.

Mooring to Fish at Sea-Perch Creek	鱸溪漁泊
At a distance, watchet billows suspend the dusky glow;	遠遠滄浪啣夕照
At Sea-Perch Creek, from within the mist, emerges a fishing lamp.	鱸溪烟裡出漁燈
Rippling waves, receding light, a small moored skiff;	橫波晻映泊船艇[47]
Moon descends, floating baskets and nets, bobbing up and down.	落月參差浮罩罾[48]
Draped merely in a rain cape—the frosty air presses in;	一領蓑衣霜氣迫
A few sounds of the bamboo oar, the water's glitter frozen still.	幾聲竹棹水光凝
Adrift, alone—I laugh—at the open sea beyond;	飄零自笑汪洋外[49]
I wish to be near to fish-dragons but still cannot.	欲附魚龍却未能
(Poem 10)	

47.   There is a lacuna in the EFEO manuscript where the fourth character of this line should be; CJH and the DH record it as 映; the LQD manuscript records it as 暎, a variant form of the same character. The EFEO manuscript records the sixth character of this line as 船; the CJH, the DH, and the LQD manuscripts record it as 孤. I retain the character from the base text.

48.   The EFEO manuscript records the second character of this line as 月; the others do the same, with the exception of the CJH manuscript, which records it as 日. The CJH manuscript retains 月 in parentheses beside the selected character, however, suggesting that Chen Jinghe might have thought 月 to be out of place and thus modified it to 日. I am sympathetic to Chen Jinghe, as time seems to pass too quickly in this poem, from sun set to the moon's descent; however, I retain 月 because it occurs in the other manuscripts and does not appear to be a result of scribal error.

49.   EFEO, CJH, and DH record the last three characters of this line as 汪洋外; LQD records them as 江湖客. I retain the characters from the base text.

The poem begins with a description of distant blue-gray waves rising up to meet the setting sun, where the frothy tips of the billows act as lips to suspend the glowing orb.[50] The second line moves the reader's perspective away from the distance and to the foreground, where out of the mist of Sea-Perch Creek another light emerges—not a star, but a humble fishing lamp. Its glow illuminates a small skiff and fishing paraphernalia—baskets and nets "bobbing up and down" on the water. We see a fisherman, wearing only a light raincoat, who feels the chill as the sun sets and night falls. The poem captures the stillness of the activity of fishing in a creek; a few sounds from the laps of the oar can be heard, but the light on the water seems "frozen still" on its surface. The fisherman is lightly draped, and the reader perceives that he shivers slightly in the cold night. In the concluding couplet, the reader looks out into the distance again—to the wide vista that is the open sea—through the eyes of someone "adrift" and "alone." We encounter a similar line in "Moon's Reflection on East Lake." There the solitary character did not resent the "sea so vast and cold"; here, the drifter laughs to himself, one imagines in a bittersweet manner, and gazes at the "open sea beyond." Fish-dragons are dispersed in the open sea, and the poet longs to be nearer to them.

"Mooring to Fish at Sea-Perch Creek" draws together the sensations and the sentiments of "Moon's Reflection on East Lake" and "Clear Waves on South Bay." The stillness of the former is captured in the person of the fisherman shivering on the creek and the movement of the latter in the vast waves rising to meet the descending sun. The open sea, depicted from the perspective of the poet on the shores of Hà Tiên, brings to mind Mạc Thiên Tứ's vision for his domain in a wider maritime world. Gazing outward, he longs to be integrated into an extended community, even as a gulf presently separates him from it.

50. The term *Canglang* 滄浪, taken here to indicate watchet blue billows, is also a literary reference to a river, sometimes associated with a portion of the Han River.

The Drifter and the Dragons

I have so far resisted the temptation to read the repeated motif of fish-dragons in Mạc Thiên Tứ's poetry in allegorical terms. The phrase "fish-dragon" (魚龍) might simply refer to a particular kind of dragon, one that dwells under the sea—a figure not infrequently met with in Chinese mythological lore. It might also be understood as a composite of its two components parts, fish and dragons, here deployed as a general term inclusive of various animals that live in the water. It is also possible to interpret the term as designating "rulers and their entourages"; construed in this manner, the image would constitute a self-reference, with Mạc Thiên Tứ as the dragon leader and the fishes as members of his retinue.[51] Certainly, a case can be made that Mạc Thiên Tứ gives more agency to fish-dragons than to other animals in his poems. The crane, crow, and rooster in "Dawn Bell at the Temple of Seclusion," for example, call out because they are part of the natural and domestic scenery. In another poem, "Rustic Dwellings at Deer Cape," the raven, ape, deer, and buffalo are similarly depicted as part of the peaceful and rustic landscape.

Rustic Dwellings at Deer Cape	鹿峙村居
Breezes blow by bamboo huts; dreams are beginning to awaken.	竹屋風過夢始醒
A raven cries outside the eaves, but one can barely hear it.	鴉啼簷外却難聽[52]
Inverted images of remnant rose clouds tint the shutters purple;	殘霞倒影沿窓紫[53]
Dense trees, bending low, touch the garden greens.	密樹低垂接圃青

51. Keith Taylor, for example, understands "fish and dragons" in this manner in his analysis of Mạc Thiên Tứ's seventh poem "Moon's Reflection on East Lake." See Taylor, "Surface Orientations in Vietnam," 968.

52. The EFEO, CJH, and DH manuscripts record the last character of this line as 聽; the LQD manuscript records it as 咱. Both characters work with the poem's prosody. I retain the character recorded in the base text.

53. There is a lacuna in the EFEO manuscript where the fourth character of this line is. CJH and the DH record it as 掛; LQD records it as 影. Both characters work with the poem's prosody. I adopt the character recorded in the CJH and the DH manuscripts because I have previously accepted their variant, which was similar to that in the base text.

My rustic nature intently desires the quietude of gibbon
  and deer;

My honest heart always longs for the fragrance of
  rice and millet.

If travelers should ask where to stop and lodge;

From the buffalo's back, just one more note,
  and the flute playing ceases.

(Poem 9)

野性偏同猿鹿靜[54]

清心每羨稻粱馨

行人若問住何處

牛背一聲吹笛停

On Deer Cape, the day is beginning, and its inhabitants stir after their night of slumber. The transition from sleep to wakefulness is depicted as slow and tranquil, and the people, barely awakened, can hardly hear the raven crying just outside their huts. The poem is composed in the style of farmstead poetry, which is typically about the spiritual fulfillment that political recluses enjoy after relocating from the capital to the countryside. It follows a standard four-part structure: the first couplet sets the scene with a depiction of a quiet countryside in the early morning, and the second couplet expands on it by focusing on the huts and the trees. The poet bestows a light touch of the spiritual realm onto Deer Cape in the form of the clouds that paint the shutters purple, which are reminiscent of the purple auroras (v: *tử hà*, p: *zixia* 紫霞) or mystical mists, associated with Daoist mysticism. The third couplet enacts a turn, shifting focus from the landscape to the poet's inner world, and the final couplet concludes with the unhurried gestures of a boy sitting on a buffalo's back, who, when asked a question, lingers on the flute with "just one more note" before responding.

In this poem, ostensible antitheses—dreaming and waking, above and below, human and animal—are merged and made indistinguishable, thereby conjuring the image of Deer Cape as a place where normal laws are suspended in favor of an idealized reality. Its enigmatic ending harks back to poems from the Tang dynasty such as "Qingming" 清明, attributed to Du Mu (v: Đỗ Mục 杜牧, 803–52), and "Zhongnan Mountain" 終南山 by Wang Wei (v: Vương Duy 王維, 699–759); in the former, a traveler asks a shepherd boy where a tavern, a place to lodge, might be found, and in the latter, the poet calls out to a woodcutter to ask where he might

---

54. The EFEO, the CJH, and the DH manuscripts record the fourth character of this line as 同; the LQD manuscript records it as 隨. Both characters work with the poem's prosody. I retain the character from the base text.

find lodging for the night.[55] Each inquiry is an interruption; the interruption, however, does not herald a transition from passivity to activity. In Du Mu's "Qingming," the shepherd boy points the traveler toward a place where time stands still (Apricot Blossom village, which evokes Peach Blossom spring). In Mạc Thiên Tứ's "Rustic Dwellings on Deer Cape," the boy on the buffalo's back does not jump to action but nonchalantly finishes his tune before offering a reply. The traveler's interruption, a request for directions to a place to lay down his head, represents a desire for rest, and the poem invites the reader to pause, come to Deer Cape, and linger.

In fact, the whole suite of poems can be read as an invitation to come and linger before the wondrous sites of Hà Tiên. When I first discussed "Golden Islet Blocking Waves," I described a scene where fish struggled to breach the rocky limits of the stream to find waters where they would turn into dragons: "Arriving in its waters, fish to dragons will transform; / Beside cliffs of trees and rocks, they naturally splash a-flitter" 得水魚龍隨變化 / 傍崖樹石自聯翩. There is another possible reading of this line, which is to reconstitute the fish and the dragon into fish-dragons: "Arriving in its waters, fish-dragons accordingly transform; / Beside cliffs

---

55.
Qingming 清明

At the time of the Qingming festival, a light rain drizzles on,	清明時節雨紛紛
A traveller on the road desires to escape from it all.	路上行人欲斷魂
He asks about a tavern where he might find a place to lodge,	借問酒家何處有
A shepherd boy points to the distance at Apricot Blossom village.	牧童遙指杏花村

The authorship of "Qingming" has been a subject of debate; for a discussion of the history of its attribution, see Wu Zaiqing (ed.), *Du Mu ji xinian jiaozhu, Jiwai shi* 集外詩 3.1432–33.

Zhongnan Mountain	終南山
Taiyi Peak approaches heaven's capital,	太乙近天都
The rolling mountains extend to the edge of the sea.	連山到海隅
White clouds, when I look back, converge,	白雲佪望合
The greenish haze, once I walk in to see it, disappears.	青靄入看無
The divided regions, when seen from the middle peak, change,	分野中峰變
Shaded or in the sun, the myriad valleys look different.	陰晴眾壑殊
To find a dwelling of man for the night,	欲投人處宿
Across the brook I call to a woodcutter.	隔水問樵夫

Quan Tang shi, 126.1277.

Translated by Cai Zong-qi. See Cai Zong-qi, "Recent-Style Shi Poetry," 177–79.

of trees and rocks, they naturally splash a-flitter." In line with this interpretation, fish-dragons, upon their arrival in the waters of Hà Tiên, find themselves truly in their element, full of life and splashing about merrily. These two readings, both noteworthy in and of themselves, are layered one upon the other and so magnify the significance of the motif of the fish-dragon. In "Moon's Reflection on East Lake," the fish-dragons sleep within the waters: "Fish-dragons, dreaming in slumber, start, but do not break through; / Now as always, loyal of heart, just as light reflects above and below" 魚龍夢覺衝難破 / 依舊冰心上下光. Likewise, they remain hidden in the autumnal scene of "Clear Waves on South Bay": "I, too, know that in the eight seas, fish-dragons hide; / Radiant moon and glittering waves, at ease, I understand" 也知八海魚龍匿 / 月朗波光自在明. Finally, in "Mooring to Fish at Sea-Perch Creek," they are dispersed in the open sea: "Adrift, alone—I laugh—at the open sea beyond; / I wish to be near to fish-dragons but still cannot" 飄零自笑汪洋外 / 欲附魚龍却未能.

If "fish-dragons" referred to a leader and his entourage, and Mạc Thiên Tứ were the dragon, then he could not possibly be the subject of the final couplet in "Mooring to Fish at Sea-Perch Creek." According to the tripartite structure of regulated verse, the first couplet sets the scene or topic of the poem, the second and third couplets elaborate on it, and the final couplet contains the poet's commentary. In the poem's two concluding lines, the reader can confidently interpret a sigh or a chuckle as belonging to the poet himself, and the translator has the authority to add a subject, in the form of an "I," into her translations.[56] In the case of "Mooring to Fish at Sea-Perch Creek," the "I-comment" would indicate that Mạc Thiên Tứ was the person "adrift, alone," and "fish-dragons" would necessarily refer to someone or something else to which he longed to be near. I maintain that "fish-dragons" refers in fact to the members of a larger network of dispersed Ming loyalists, of which Mạc Thiên Tứ considered himself an integral part. Of the poets who contributed to the *Ten Songs of Hà Tiên* project, several declared their Ming loyalist sentiments by adopting pen names identifying themselves as Minh Hương (p: Ming xiang 明香), literally the "Fragrance of the Ming." This society of poets, dispersed on the Vietnamese coast and in

56. Owen, *The Poetry of the Early Tang*, 378–79.

the southern Chinese coastal provinces of Fujian and Guangdong, communicated with one another through the ships that plied the coastal trading route. We know that Chen Zhikai, for one, accompanied Mạc Thiên Tứ on his tour of his domain's scenic sites and facilitated the distribution of his poetry to other poets in the network, but it is unclear if all members of this literary circle would have personally made their way to Hà Tiên, and it is unlikely that they ever gathered there at the same time. There was at least one other literary project, the *Four Scenes of Planting Virtue Pavilion* (v: Thụ Đức Hiên Tứ Cảnh, p: Shudexuan sijing 樹德軒四景), that was carried out in this same way. This project took for its subject the Planting Virtue Pavilion in the four seasons of spring, summer, autumn, and winter. Although most of this collection has been lost to posterity, Lê Quý Đôn recorded a small sample of the poems and the names of a different group of thirty-two poets who contributed to it. Incidentally, Chen Zhikai's name appears on this list of participants.[57]

For a dispersed community that continued to harbor loyalties to the defunct Ming dynasty rather than the ruling Qing dynasty, Hà Tiên was one of the new centers where ethnic Chinese of a different political leaning from those ruling the mainland could come together. In the first postface to the *Ten Songs of Hà Tiên*, Yu Xichun, who called himself the "old man from Lingnan," describes an excursion to a garden where he imagines the poems celebrating Hà Tiên were composed. He makes free use of imperial imagery such as "flying canopy" (v: *phi cái*, p: *feigai* 飛葢) to describe the palanquin that carried the party and waxes lyrical about the "gateway and rooflines of the palace" (v: *cung khuyết tha nga*, p: *gongque cuo'e* 宮闕嵯峨).[58] His descriptions of the palace and the royal excursion constitute a view of Hà Tiên as an overseas Chinese political center.

My argument that the "fish-dragons" in Mạc Thiên Tứ's poetry refer to Ming loyalists finds further support in the historical record. Forces loyal to the Ming dynasty grouped together in a few locations during the dynastic transition of Ming to Qing. The story of Zheng Chenggong (v: Trịnh

57. Lê Quý Đôn, *Kiến Văn Tiểu Lục*, 146a–146b; Đông Hồ, *Văn học Hà Tiên*, 108–9.
58. *An Nam Hà Tiên Thập Vịnh*, EFEO microfilm, 49a–49b.

Thành Công 鄭成功, 1624–62), or Koxinga, is well known. With his impressive naval forces, Zheng fought the Qing for many years until his final defeat in 1661, when he retreated across the Eastern Straits to Taiwan.[59] His was the most famous strand of anti-Qing resistance, but there were other resistance forces that deserve our attention. Outside of Zheng's Fujian base, the biggest base for Ming loyalist activity was Longmen (Dragon Gate) Island, the largest of a group of islands by that same name situated on the northern rim of the Gulf of Tonkin and to the west of the Leizhou Peninsula, which offered strategic access to Qinzhou.[60] In 1651, Ming loyalist forces belonging to Deng Yao (v: Đặng Diệu 鄧耀, d. 1661), an officer of the Southern Ming regime, occupied Longmen and maintained it as a base for eleven years. The Qing army finally defeated his forces at Longmen in 1661; Deng Yao fled but was captured and killed that year. In 1662, Yang Yandi (v: Dương Ngạn Địch 楊彥迪, d. 1688), another Ming loyalist, took control of Longmen, but his forces held the strategic island for only a year before abandoning it in 1663. Yang and his forces spent the next sixteen years hiding on the northern Vietnamese coast in the Gulf of Tonkin, appearing occasionally in the historical records when they engaged in skirmishes with Qing forces.[61] The *Đại Nam Thực Lục* records that:

> In the spring, the first month of the *jiwei* year [v: *kỷ miù*, 1679], the thirty-first year [of Nguyễn Phúc Tần 阮福瀕 (1620–87)], generals of the Ming dynasty, the Commander of Long Môn Dương Ngạn Địch [p: Yang Yandi] and his deputy Hoàng Tiến [p: Huang Jin], together with the Commander of the Cao, Lôi, and Liêm prefectures [in Guangdong province] Trần Thượng Xuyên [p: Chen Shangchuan] and his deputy Trần An Bình [p: Chen Anping], led more than 3,000 men and over 50 warships to the Tư Dung and Đà Nẵng seaports. They declared that they

59. For an overview of Zheng Chenggong's anti-Qing activities, see Struve, "The Southern Ming, 1644–1662."

60. On Longmen as a center for anti-Qing resistance, see Pan Dinggui, *Annan jiyou* 3–4; see also Robert Antony, "'Righteous Yang,'" 326–27; see also Niu Junkai and Li Qingxin, "Chinese 'Political Pirates,'" 134–36.

61. For more information about Deng Yao and his piracy in the Tongking Gulf, see Niu Junkai and Li Qingxin, "Chinese 'Political Pirates,'" 138–40. For an account of Yang Yandi's activities between 1656 and 1688, see Antony, "'Righteous Yang,'" 331–38; on the possibility of an epidemic decimating up to two thirds of Yang's forces in 1682, see Li Tana, "Epidemics, Trade, and Local Worship," 195–99.

were run-away subjects of the Ming who, out of propriety, refused to serve the Qing. Therefore, they came desiring to be [southern Vietnamese] subjects.[62]

己未三十一年春正月，故明將龍門總兵楊彥迪，副將黃進，高雷廉總兵陳上川，副將陳安平，率兵三千餘人戰船五十餘艘，投思容，沱㶞海口，自陳以明國逋臣義不事清，故來願爲臣僕。

Whereas Zheng Chenggong's forces took Taiwan as their base, the Longmen (v: Long Môn 龍門) arm of resistance appears to have sought a home with the southern Vietnamese regime after being routed by the Qing. Unlike the Lê-Trịnh regime in the northern Vietnamese polity, which shared a border with the Middle Kingdom, the Nguyễn lords in southern Vietnam were less embroiled in the politics of the Chinese mainland. It was probably for this reason that Yang Yandi's forces approached the southern Vietnamese regime rather than its northern counterpart. The Vietnamese chronicles record a discussion in the Nguyễn court over the sudden influx of Ming loyalists:

At this point, there was a deliberation [in the Vietnamese court, during which some advisors argued]: Their customs and language are different [from ours]. [This request] comes so suddenly, it is difficult for us to assign them positions and employment; but their dire situation has forced them to come here to seek refuge, and [we] could not be so cold hearted as to refuse them. In the Cambodian Kingdom's Đông Phố [the old name of Gia Định], there are thousands of miles of fertile fields and lands that the court has yet to have the leisure to manage. Nothing would be better than to use their labor to open up the lands in order [for them] to live there. In this way, one move would benefit us in three aspects.

The lord, having heard the discussion, thereupon ordered a feast to encourage and reward [the Ming loyalists], gave them each an official position, and ordered [them] to go to the land of Đông Phố and live there. Moreover, he announced an edict to the kingdom of Cambodia to show that he did not have any other intentions. Ngan Địch and the others went to the palace to thank the emperor for his grace and then left.[63]

62. *Đại Nam Thực Lục Tiền Biên*, 5.22. See note 6 in the introduction to this book, which discusses 1682 instead 1679 as the year of their arrival.
63. *Đại Nam Thực Lục Tiền Biên*, 5.22.

時議以彼異俗殊音。猝難任使，而窮逼來歸，不忍拒絶。眞臘國東浦（嘉定古別名）地方沃野千里，朝廷未暇經理。不如因彼之力使闢地以居，一舉而三得也。上從之乃命宴勞嘉奬，仍各授以官職，令往東浦居之。又告諭眞臘以示無外之意。彦迪等詣闕謝恩而行。

In response to the arrival of politicized Chinese troops in their capital, the Nguyễn court decided on a plan that would advance its own interests in three aspects: by relocating the Ming loyalists to lands located in the far south that were still not Vietnamese lands, the court succeeded in removing a large body of foreigners from the capital. The court was also able to use the Ming loyalists to secure the Cambodian lands for the Vietnamese kingdom, and it could rely on their labor to bring those lands into productive use.[64] One group of Ming loyalists was sent to Mỹ Tho and another was sent to Biên Hòa:

> Ngạn Địch and Hoàng Tiến steered their men and ships towards Lôi Lạp (which now belongs to Gia Định) seaport and stationed at Mỹ Tho (which now belongs to Định Tường). Thượng Xuyên and An Bình steered their men and ships towards Cần Giờ seaport and stationed at Bàn Lân (which now belongs to Biên Hòa). They opened up idle lands and constructed shophouses; merchant ships from the Qing and such lands as the Western Ocean, Japan, Java, and Sumatra gathered in great numbers. From this time on, Han influence permeated the land of Đông Phố.[65]

彦迪黃進兵船駛往雷巤（今屬嘉定）海口駐札于美湫（今屬定祥）。上川安平兵船駛往芹蓏海口駐札于盤鱗（今屬邊和）。闢閒地構舖舍。清人及西洋日本闍婆諸國商船湊集。由是漢風漸清于東浦矣。

The Cambodian provinces fell under the control of the southern Vietnamese kingdom through the labor of a particular camp of Ming loyalists: the Longmen faction. Vietnamese chronicles explicitly refer to Yang Yandi as the "commander of Longmen," or the "commander of Dragon

---

64. Trouble brews in the southern lands in 1688, when Yang Yandi's deputy, Huang Jin, assassinates Yang Yandi to promote himself. See entries for 1688 and 1689 in *Đại Nam Thực Lục Tiền Biên*, 6.5–14.

65. *Đại Nam Thực Lục Tiền Biên*, 5.22–23. The ports of Lôi Lạp and Cần Giờ appear in the Gia Định Gazetteer, which was compiled in the 1820s. See Trịnh Hoài Đức, *Gia Định Thành Thông Chí*, 42 and 62–64.

Gate," although he had only held Longmen for a year and had not had control of it for a decade and a half prior to his arrival in southern Vietnam. It was the "Longmen strand" of Ming resistance against the Qing that came to settle on the eastern part of the Mekong delta.

Mạc Cửu, Mạc Thiên Tứ's father, did not arrive in Vietnam with these Dragon Gate troops. He came from Guangdong almost a decade earlier, in 1671, and set up his own kingdom in the western part of the delta through Khmer and then Vietnamese patronage (see map 3). Although separate paths of migration led the two groups to settle on the different ends of the Mekong delta, as fellow Chinese migrants and Ming loyalists, Mạc Cửu and his family undoubtedly had contact with the Dragon Gate troops in the eastern regions.[66] In the late seventeenth and mid-eighteenth centuries, Hà Tiên housed a busy port that maintained connections with other ports of the Vietnamese and southern Chinese coast; in this regard, the port at Gia Định, established by the Dragon Gate faction, was their closest neighbor. It is therefore unsurprising that Mạc Thiên Tứ's poetry was filled with references to Dragon Gate and the myth of fish-dragons. In the southern Vietnamese regions, fish-dragons had come to be the symbol for Ming loyalists.

Through the *Ten Songs of Hà Tiên* project, Mạc Thiên Tứ was able to bring together this Chinese diasporic group and communicate his vision to them. His opening poem, in which he described fish struggling to reach the waters where they would transform into dragons, positions Hà Tiên as the new Dragon Gate, the new strategic stronghold for the remaining Ming loyalists. Rereading the poem with this message in mind reveals secrets encoded within its lines:

Golden Islet Blocking Waves 　　　　　　　　　　金嶼欄濤
An island of rocky peaks settles the emerald waters; 　一島崔嵬奠碧漣
Flowing waters by a wondrous beauty at mighty Hà Tiên. 橫流奇勝壯河僊

---

66. See Salmon, *Ming Loyalists in Southeast Asia*, 41–48, for a succinct discussion of the two distinct groups of Ming loyalists. In her discussion, Salmon associates the Dragon Gate troops with the Mekong delta, and she orients the Mạc family away from the Mekong delta and toward the Gulf of Siam. The two groups, however, had close ties with each other; on marriage relations between the leaders of the Dragon Gate troops and the Mạc clan, see Chen Jinghe, "Qingchu Zheng Chenggong canbu," part 2, 478–79.

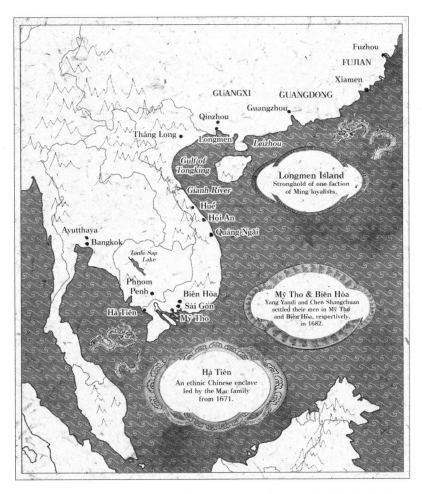

MAP 3: Ming loyalist settlements on the Mekong delta. Illustrated by Natalie Christian Tan, 2018.

Obstructing the power of waves and billows from the southeast seas;	波濤勢截東南海
Sun's and moon's radiance reflect from the sky and down below.	日月光迴上下天
Arriving in its waters, fish to dragons will transform;	得水魚龍隨變化
Beside cliffs of trees and rocks, they naturally splash a-flitter.	傍崖樹石自聯翩
Wind-sighs and wave-traces see it fit to linger long,	風聲浪跡應長據

In this landscape of shadow and light, an unusual　　　　濃淡山川異國懸
　　kingdom, distant.
(Poem 1)

The fourth line, "Sun's and moon's radiance reflect from the sky and down below" 日月光迴上下天, is visually significant because placing 日 and 月 together represents the character Ming 明. The two characters embellish the already forceful opening poem with a coded line that reads: "The radiance of the Ming reflects from the sky and down below." Sounded aloud in Cantonese, 下天 is homophonically similar to Hà Tiên, which would make the spoken sentence: "The radiance of the Ming reflects upon Hà Tiên."[67] In Hà Tiên the vestiges of the winds and the waves, themselves remnants like the Ming loyalists, choose to linger; they linger in a landscape of contrasting darkness and light, evoking the moon and the sun, guardians of night and day, again bringing to mind the character Ming 明. In addition, the last three characters of the poem that I translate as "an unusual kingdom, distant" (v: *dị quốc huyền*, p: *yiguo xuan* 異國懸) can also be understood as "distant from that heterodox kingdom," a reference to the Qing, the illegitimate Manchu dynasty. The final couplet would then read: "Wind-sighs and wave-traces see it fit to linger long; / In this landscape of shadow and light, distant from that heterodox kingdom."

Unlike the original Dragon Gate, this new strategic stronghold of the Ming loyalists was a site of potency with the power to endure. Even though it was situated outside of the Chinese mainland, Hà Tiên was a center of culture, where nature did not exist in a state of chaos but was regulated and patterned through poetic discourse. As the ruler of the new Dragon Gate, Mạc Thiên Tứ issued an invitation to his fellow Ming loyalists. At Hà Tiên, they could be in their element, and they could rest and consolidate their strength like fish-dragons in the autumn. He confided in them, in the closing couplet of "Clear Waves on South Bay," the steadfastness of his fealty: "I, too, know that in the eight seas, fish-dragons hide; / Radiant moon and glittering waves, at ease, I remain Ming" 也知八海魚龍匿 / 月朗波光自在明.[68] In the final couplet of his tenth poem, he

---

67. My thanks to Flora Cheung for pointing out the homophonic similarity.
68. My original translation of the line reads: "I, too, know that in the eight seas, fish-dragons hide; / Radiant moon and glittering waves, at ease, I understand."

remarked on their unfortunate dispersal across the seas; he felt keenly his physical distance from them and wished to draw them near.

Conclusion: A Different Kind of Frontier Poetry

Mạc Thiên Tứ's suite of landscape poems is not typical of poetry composed in far-flung peripheral regions. His work contrasts with those of Han Chinese officials sent to the northwestern frontier region of Xinjiang during the Qing dynasty, which constructed the image of a frontier region that "was not only part of China, but it was also becoming Chinese."[69] They are unlike those composed by the officials sent to Yunnan, a region in southwestern China where indigenous communities were at the receiving end of Qing territorial expansion. Lyrical descriptions of the scenic sites of Dongchuan in Yunnan "emphasized the successful civilizing project of transforming a wild peripheral landscape into a well-ordered Chinese landscape, while eliding the brutal military expansion."[70] Rather than conveying to the mainland Chinese capital that Hà Tiên was becoming a part of Qing-controlled China, Mạc Thiên Tứ's poetry sent the message to other Ming loyalists that Hà Tiên was a haven situated far away from the Qing Chinese mainland and was therefore a suitable home for Chinese peoples with alternative political loyalties. His mission was not to make Hà Tiên an acceptable peripheral region for a distant metropole but to inscribe Hà Tiên as the new Ming loyalist cultural and political center.

What, then, was ultimately the nature of Mạc Thiên Tứ's Ming loyalism? Our study uncovers no evidence that his call for a Ming renaissance included ambitions to restore a Ming descendant to the Chinese imperial throne; neither did he gather military forces to oppose the new dynasty. Rather than turn his back on the Qing, he maintained contact with Qing envoys and even sought the aid of the Qing in an attempt to defeat the advancing Tây Sơn army in the autumn of 1777.[71] His poetry,

69. Newby, "The Chinese Literary Conquest of Xinjiang," 467.
70. Fei Huang, "The Making of a Frontier Landscape," 67.
71. *Đại Nam Liệt Truyện Tiền Biên*, 6.10.

however, composed well into the rule of the Qing dynasty, conveys the depth of his self-identification as a Ming loyalist. His poems expressed not nostalgia for the fallen Ming but longing for unification with his scattered brethren. On the Chinese mainland, the landscape poetry of remnant Ming partisans focused on rhetorically constructing emblems of loyalism out of historically and culturally important sites.[72] In a similar fashion, Mạc Thiên Tứ literarily transformed Hà Tiên in accordance with his ambitions and desires. But unlike the literati of the Chinese mainland, who infused historically significant sites with new meanings, he sought to ennoble a domain that did not belong in the geographical confines of the empire. In so doing, he infused the new landscapes with symbolism relevant to the sojourning experience of a Ming loyalist in the eighteenth century, as he created a new home outside of the Middle Kingdom where he and others like him could participate in an ongoing cultural project that was, at once, novel and rooted in history.

72. In her study of the reconstruction of Yangzhou between 1645 and 1700, Tobie Meyer-Fong presents the case that the literati of Yangzhou reconstructed sites that facilitated their expression of nostalgia for the Ming. Rather than enlarge the political gulf between the literati that remained loyal to the Ming and those that sought office with the Qing, she argues that the commemoration strengthened what was common to both groups—their social and cultural class. See Meyer-Fong, *Building Culture in Early Qing Yangzhou.*

CHAPTER 5

Epistolary Expositions

Geopolitical Realities on
the Delta

The historical role that Mạc Thiên Tứ played on the Mekong delta was not confined to the domain of Ming loyalist politics. As a dependent of the southern Vietnamese polity of Đàng Trong, which lay to the east of Hà Tiên, and as an ally of the Khmer kingdom, which occupied the lands to the west, he developed a reputation as a shrewd political actor well versed in the forms and fashions of life on the Mekong delta. This same political acumen distinguished the undertakings of Nguyễn Cư Trinh, whose career with the Nguyễn court carried him deep into the delta lands from 1754 to 1765. As noted before, Nguyễn Cư Trinh was made governor of Quảng Ngãi province in 1750, but he did not stay there for many years. After his memorial detailing solutions to problems plaguing Quảng Ngãi received no response from Nguyễn Phúc Khoát, he resigned in protest from his position. He was thereupon summoned to return to the capital, and in 1753 he was appointed secretary of the Bố Chính Garrison. Whereas Quảng Ngãi bordered the upland territories, Bố Chính was Đàng Trong's northernmost province and shared a border with the Trịnh-controlled Đàng Ngoài; recognizing the precarity of its geographical location, Nguyễn Cư Trinh's first priority, on his arrival in Bố Chính, was to shore up its defensive structures and jealously guard its borders. Not long thereafter, there arose an occasion for him to be thankful for his earlier foresight and current vigilance. A letter arrived from the Trịnh, who were in pursuit of a Lê prince who had fled with his men into the Laotian mountains, requesting permission to pass through Nguyễn Cư Trinh's garrison en route to capture their quarry. Nguyễn Cư Trinh denied their request, confident of his defensive capabilities, and his official biography reported that the Trịnh army, aware of Nguyễn Cư Trinh's work in the province, knew better than to tresspass on Bố Chính's territory. His experience with the administration of Đàng Trong's border regions made him the best candidate for overseeing the expansion of Nguyễn control into its southernmost frontier, the Mekong delta. There, Nguyễn Cư Trinh's expanding geopolitical world ran up against Mạc Thiên Tứ's autonomously governed state.

Details of Mạc Thiên Tứ's and Nguyễn Cư Trinh's activities on the Mekong frontier can be pieced together from the *Đại Nam Thực Lục* and the *Đại Nam Liệt Truyện*, the premier sections of which were compiled by the Nguyễn Dynasty Historical Institute in the nineteenth century.[1] The Đại Nam chronicles are modeled on the dynastic records of the Middle Kingdom, which have a long and venerable heritage beginning with Sima Qian's *Records of the Historian*. In this genre of recording history, information lies scattered across different sections of the work, of which the most important for the present study are the basic annals (v: *bổn kỷ*, p: *benji* 本記) and the official biographies (v: *liệt truyện*, p: *liezhuan* 列傳).[2] Deliberately assigned rather than haphazardly distributed, historical anecdotes and events are carefully recounted either in the basic annals or in the biographies, and compilers bring order to the past by consigning the information they have about it to their proper place in the historical record. To form as complete a picture as possible of a year or an event, the interested reader has to look in the relevant chapter of the basic annals, which are organized according to the reigns

1. The premier sections of both the *Đại Nam Thực Lục* and the *Đại Nam Liệt Truyện* were composed during the reigns of Minh Mạng (p: Ming Ming 明命, r. 1820–41) and Thiệu Trị (p: Shao Zhi 紹治, r. 1841–47). The *Đại Nam Thực Lục tiền biên* was completed in 1844 and the *Đại Nam Liệt Truyện tiền biên* a year later, in 1845. For a survey of the various chronicles produced by the Nguyễn, see Langlet, *L'ancienne historiographie*. The sections in the veritable records relevant to this chapter are the entries for the years 1750–57. *Đại Nam Thực Lục Tiền Biên*, 10.16–30. Nguyễn Cư Trinh's and Mạc Thiên Tứ's biographies can be found in *Đại Nam Liệt Truyện Tiền Biên*, 5.5–11 and 6.3–14.

2. Sima Qian's *Shiji* comprises five sections: basic annals, tables, treatises, hereditary houses, and biographies. The structure that Sima Qian developed in the second century BCE proved to be remarkably resilient, and the History of the Ming (v: *Minh Sử*, p: *Mingshi* 明史), completed in 1739, comprises all but the section on the hereditary houses.

of kings and which register important events in each reign on a chronological basis; in the case of the Đại Nam chronicles, the "veritable records" (v: *thực lục*, p: *shilu* 寔錄) stand in for the basic annals.[3] Comple-
menting the basic annals are the official memoirs of court officials and
others of significance, which are found in the section of the work devoted to historical biographies. The narratives contained within the
basic annals and the official biographies conform to the prescriptions of
the respective sections; in general, basic annals illuminate the deeds and
decisions of the emperors, and biographies tell about the lives of their
subjects as related to official political history. Nguyễn Cư Trinh's and
Mạc Thiên Tứ's official biographies thus inform us about their political
activities as subjects of the Vietnamese court, although it should be noted
that the placement of Mạc Thiên Tứ's biography, grouped with that of
other Chinese settlers on the Mekong delta, suggests that nineteenth-
century scribes discerned a political distance between Mạc Thiên Tứ
and the Nguyễn. In reading the biographies of the two men against the
grain and in relation to each other, one is able to form a clearer picture of
mid-eighteenth-century politics on the Mekong delta.

Both Nguyễn Cư Trinh's and Mạc Thiên Tứ's official biographies tell
us that their respective subjects played important roles in managing the
conflict the Nguyễn had with the Cambodian prince, Chey Chétta IV,
known in the Vietnamese chronicles as Nặc Nguyên. Nguyễn Cư Trinh's
biography records that in the winter of 1753, Chey Chétta IV attacked the
Côn Man (p: Kun Man 崑蠻), possibly a reference to the Cham people, in
the Mekong delta.[4] Sensing an opportunity to extend his political reach,
Nguyễn Phúc Khoát sent Nguyễn Cư Trinh and another Đàng Trong
general, Thiện Chính (p: Shanzheng 善政), there to join in the fray.[5] They

3. In the dynastic chronicles of the Middle Kingdom, the veritable records are the
detailed accounts of important occurrences and significant decisions undertaken in an
emperor's reign; they serve as the source from which the official histories of a dynasty
are later compiled.

4. In fact, the *Đại Nam Thực Lục* dates Nặc Nguyên's attack on the Côn Man to
1750, while Nguyễn Cư Trinh was still in Quảng Ngãi. It was probably recorded as
1753 in his biography because that was the year he entered the scene of action.

5. The *Đại Nam Thực Lục* and Nguyễn Cư Trinh's official biography report that
Thiện Chính's surname is unknown. He does not have his own entry in the *Đại Nam
Liệt Truyện*.

advanced to Ngâu Chưa, formulated their strategies, and took their leave of each other in the summer of 1754 to advance on Chey Chétta IV separately.[6] Nguyễn Cư Trinh's route took him through Tần Lộ Bắc and Đại Giang, and then he rejoined Thiện Chính's troops in Lô Yêm. He experienced a successful streak in winning new provinces for the Nguyễn, and by the time he reached the Côn Man, the four Cambodian prefectures of Soi Rạp (Lôi Lạp), Tầm Bôn, Câu Nam, and Nam Vang he had passed through along the way had all surrendered to him. However, Nguyễn Cư Trinh fell out with Thiện Chính in spring 1755 when the latter allegedly abandoned the Côn Man to reprisals from Chey Chétta IV. Thiện Chính had been in charge of bringing the Côn Man to the Mỹ Tho camp, but the latter were attacked en route by the Cambodian army at Vô Tà Ân. Claiming to be hindered by the marshlands of the Mekong delta, Thiện Chính failed to come to their aid and left them to their own defenses. Incensed by this sorry excuse, Nguyễn Cư Trinh led his troops to rescue them, escorting more than 5,000 men and women back to the base of Bà Đanh Mountain. He then memorialized the throne to report Thiện Chính's negligence. In response, the king demoted the general and replaced him with Trương Phúc Du (p: Zhang Fuyou 張福猷). Nguyễn Cư Trinh and Trương Phúc Du, using the Côn Man as guides, pursued Chey Chétta IV and went on the attack at Câu Nam and Nam Vang. Recognizing his perilous position, Chey Chétta IV fled to Hà Tiên and imposed on Mạc Thiên Tứ to act as his intermediary; he asked to gift the lands of the two provinces of Tầm Bôn and Soi Rạp (Lôi Lạp) as compensation for the tribute that was owed to Đàng Trong three years earlier.

At this point, the episode of Chey Chétta IV's attack on the Côn Man enters the narrative arc of Mạc Thiên Tứ's biography. It states that this attack occurred in the spring of 1756, not the winter of 1753. The contradictory dating of the Cambodian prince's attack on the Côn Man—it is dated to 1753 in Nguyễn Cư Trinh's biography, 1756 in Mạc Thiên Tứ's, and 1750 in the basic annals—offers the student of the dynastic chronicles a glimpse into its creation, where narrative logic appears to be prized over factual accuracy, for each of those dates signifies the moment the subject of the biography (or the emperor for whom the basic annal is

6. A river by the name of Ngâu Chưa separates Biên Hòa and Gia Định. See the map of Gia Định in the *Bản Quốc dư Đồ*.

compiled) becomes personally involved in the event. In Mạc Thiên Tứ's biography, a single phrase, "The lord sent officers of five garrisons to suppress him" 上命五營將士討之, stands in for the elaborate account given in Nguyễn Cư Trinh's biography. The biographies concur that Chey Chétta IV fled to Hà Tiên and that Mạc Thiên Tứ petitioned on his behalf to the Nguyễn lord. Whereas Mạc Thiên Tứ's biography presents the request as unproblematic, Nguyễn Cư Trinh's biography states that the Nguyễn lord was initially reluctant to accede to the request. Although Nguyễn Cư Trinh's biography does not state explicitly that he worked with Mạc Thiên Tứ to resolve the issue, he did in fact memorialize the throne in support of Mạc Thiên Tứ's proposal, saying:

> From time immemorial, soldiers have been employed only to punish rebel leaders and expand territory. Today Nặc Nguyên regrets his disastrous mistake and offers us land in earnest. If we continue to pursue the matter of his duplicity, he will escape; from Gia Định to La Bích the way is far and remote, and it will be inconvenient to be in hot pursuit. If we desire to expand our territory, it is appropriate to first take these two provinces, so as to strengthen [our position] with two garrisons at the back. In previous years, to expand to Gia Định province, we had to first clear the lands of Hưng Phúc, then those of Lộc Dã; we had to populate the lands with soldiers and people before we could expand into Sài Gòn. This is the strategy of nibbling. Now even though the old territory from Hưng Phúc to Sài Gòn are merely two days apart [from each other], the settlements there are not yet stable and there are not enough soldiers to spread around. How much more so [will be the case for the lands] from Sài Gòn to Tâm Bôn, which are six days apart; [I] truly fear that [the number of soldiers posted there] will be insufficient [to fight off any attack]. I have seen the Côn Man fight very skillfully on foot, and the Cambodians, for their part, are now fearful [of our military might]. If we use these lands to settle [the Côn Man] and make them guard and defend [our frontier], we will be using barbarian to fight barbarian, which would be a suitable strategy. I request that you allow Cambodia to atone for their crime and accept [its offer of] the lands of the two provinces. Appoint me to carefully observe the terrain, establish ramparts and military systems, give soldiers and people estates, and redraw the boundaries [of the two provinces] to attach them to Định Viễn prefecture so as to absorb them completely.[7]

7. *Đại Nam Liệt Truyện Tiền Biên*, 5.8–9.

自古用兵不過欲誅渠魁開疆土。今匡原悔禍納地獻款。若窮其詐，彼將奔竄，
而自嘉定至羅壁途行遼遠，不便窮追。欲開拓疆土，宜先取此二府，以固二營背
後。昔年，拓嘉定府，必先開興福，次開鹿野，使軍民完聚而後拓柴棍。是乃蠶
食之計。今舊地自興福至柴棍僅二日程，民居尚未安集，守兵亦有未敷。況自柴
棍至尋奔六日程，戍兵駐防，誠恐不足。臣見崑蠻步戰長技，真臘亦已寒心。
如以此地處之，使爲制禦，以蠻攻蠻，亦爲得策。請許真臘贖罪，取二府之地。
委臣審觀形勢，設壘屯兵制，給軍民田產，申畫地界隸定遠州以收全幅。

Nguyễn Phúc Khoát gave his assent to the proposal in the memorial. It was only with Nguyễn Cư Trinh's intercession that Chey Chétta IV's offer of compensation, sent via Mạc Thiên Tứ, was accepted. This episode is revealing of the relative positions of the various political actors on the Mekong delta. The fact that the Cambodian prince sought refuge with Mạc Thiên Tứ was indicative of his standing among the various political players of the Mekong region, some two decades after he first inherited control of Hà Tiên from his father. The fact that the Nguyễn lord did not trust him enough to take his advice is suggestive of his political distance from the Nguyễn, although his official biography, composed by the Nguyễn dynasty, insists on his fealty. Nguyễn Cư Trinh's allegiances and alliances on the delta can also be discerned from this episode. Although he was on the delta as a representative of the Nguyễn court in Phú Xuân, he also had a relationship with Mạc Thiên Tứ and, at least in this instance, lent his voice in support of him.

After noting Nguyễn Cư Trinh's success in persuading the Nguyễn lord to accept the Cambodian provinces and cease his pursuit of Chey Chétta IV, his biography records that the Khmer king died shortly thereafter and the Nguyễn recognized Outeireachea III, referred to in the Vietnamese chronicles as Nặc Tôn, as the next king of Cambodia. It states, without explication, that Outeireachea III offered the Nguyễn the lands of Tầm Phong Long in return for their support. Nguyễn Cư Trinh's biography concludes its narration of this episode with a description of his work in establishing Nguyễn rule on the delta, both on the land and on the waterways. By all indications, Nguyễn Cư Trinh was responsible for drawing the eastern part of the Mekong delta closer to the Vietnamese court: after incorporating the Cambodian provinces, he pacified (with the strength of the soldiers of the Long Hồ garrison) the Tâm Bào region, established the Đông Khẩu circuit in Sa Đéc, the Tân Châu circuit in

Tiền Giang, and the Châu Đốc circuit in Hậu Giang.[8] In addition, to reduce opportunities for pirate ships, which had the habit of lying in wait in the myriad waterways of the delta to prey on merchant vessels, Nguyễn Cư Trinh mandated that every boat, regardless of size, had to display the name of its owner and the origin of its official registration prominently on its prow. His guardianship over the lands and seas of the Mekong delta brought order to the realm under his charge.

As for Mạc Thiên Tứ, his biography provides information on a succession crisis in the Cambodian kingdom that is only obliquely alluded to in Nguyễn Cư Trinh's biography, and which explains Outeireachea III's generosity toward the Nguyễn in return for their support. Chey Chétta IV died only a year after the surrender of the two provinces, after which his uncle, Nặc Nhuận, took over temporarily as regent. When the uncle's followers sought Nguyễn support to establish him as king, the Nguyễn pushed their political advantage and demanded the two Cambodian provinces of Trà Vinh and Ba Thắc in exchange for their backing. At this juncture, Nặc Nhuận died at the hand of his son-in-law Hình, who usurped the throne. Nặc Nhuận's son, Outeireachea III, fled to Hà Tiên, where once again, a Cambodian prince's request for Nguyễn support was made via the enclave's ruler. Mạc Thiên Tứ successfully negotiated Vietnamese backing for the Cambodian prince, and in exchange for their support, Outeireachea III offered the lands of Tầm Phong Long to the Nguyễn. In addition and as an expression of his thanks, Outeireachea III offered a further five provinces to Mạc Thiên Tứ, who astutely presented these lands in turn to the Nguyễn lord. Recognizing Hà Tiên as part of Vietnamese territory, the king allowed him to add them to its jurisdiction, significantly expanding its size. Mạc Thiên Tứ's official biography elaborates on his work in establishing circuits in the delta's west just as Nguyễn Cư Trinh had done in the east, the implication being that the expanded territory was added to Đàng Trong's territory rather than to Hà Tiên's. In presenting the acquisition of territory in this manner, the Nguyễn scribes attributed to Mạc Thiên

---

8.   A circuit is a jurisdiction or a subsection, named so because it was the path of an itinerant supervisory official. Nguyễn Cư Trinh inserts a "person on inspection tours" (v: *hành bộ nhân*, p: *xingbu ren* 行部人) in his eighth poem on Hà Tiên, "Clear Waves on South Bay," which I believe to be a self-referent.

Tứ the achievement of drawing the western regions of the Mekong delta into Nguyễn control.

Nguyễn Cư Trinh spent eleven years on the delta lands, from 1754 to 1765, and under his able administration, the Nguyễn progressively tightened their grip on the Mekong delta. During this time Mạc Thiên Tứ's domain, which he had hitherto run autonomously, increasingly came to be placed under Nguyễn Cư Trinh's watchful supervision. Just as their political lives became intertwined, so did their literary worlds. Sometime in the course of his lengthy career in the administration of Đàng Trong's southern frontier, Nguyễn Cư Trinh contributed ten response poems in praise of the ten scenic sites of Hà Tiên to match Mạc Thiên Tứ's poems composed in 1736.

Fortuitously, Nguyễn Cư Trinh's poems about Hà Tiên were deemed important enough for Lê Quý Đôn, the northern Vietnamese traveler from Đàng Ngoài who came to the southern Vietnamese kingdom in the tumultuous years of the 1770s, to record them in their entirety in his *Frontier Chronicles* (v: *Phủ Biên Tạp Lục*, p: *Fubian zalu* 撫邊雜錄).[9] Although he had never met either man, Lê Quý Đôn wrote about the elegance of Nguyễn Cư Trinh and Mạc Thiên Tứ's friendship, evident in their exchange of poems and letters.[10] Impressed with the scope of Mạc Thiên Tứ's *Ten Songs of Hà Tiên*, Lê Quý Đôn exclaimed, in a statement that betrayed his northern prejudices, that "it cannot be said that there is no literature in the far-flung regions!" 不可謂海外無文章也.[11] The idea that Mạc Thiên Tứ was a faithful official of the Đàng Trong court was perpetuated by Lê Quý Đôn, who praised his unwavering loyalty to the Nguyễn lords and lauded his selflessness in offering assistance to Nguyễn Phúc Thuần when the latter fled to Gia Định to escape

9. Nguyễn Cư Trinh's poems about Hà Tiên constitute the subject of the next chapter. A Chinese character manuscript is appended to the back of Giáo Dục Publishing House's translation of Lê Quý Đôn, *Phủ Biên Tạp Lục*. For Nguyễn Cư Trinh's poems in Chinese characters, see Lê Qúy Đôn, *Phủ Biên Tạp Lục*, 5.144a–46b.

10. Lê Quý Đôn, *Phủ Biên Tạp Lục*, 5.144a. Nguyễn Cư Trinh had died by the time Lê Quý Đôn arrived in Đàng Trong. Of Mạc Thiên Tứ's fate, Lê Quý Đôn wrote that in 1775, when the Nguyễn lord, Nguyễn Phúc Thuần, fled to Gia Định, Mạc Thiên Tứ at an age in excess of seventy years still aided the Nguyễn lord to fight the enemy. He marveled at his loyalty and stated simply that "at the present moment, no one knows where he is." Lê Quý Đôn, *Phủ Biên Tạp Lục*, 5.170b.

11. Lê Quý Đôn, *Phủ Biên Tạp Lục*, 5.170a.

the Tây Sơn.[12] Lê Quý Đôn's characterization has influenced later writings and colored scholars' readings of Mạc Thiên Tứ's landscape poems.[13] My earlier analysis of these poems, however, reveals that Mạc Thiên Tứ's political loyalties were oriented more toward his fellow Ming loyalists than to the Nguyễn court. This opens the way to reinterpreting his relationship with Nguyễn Cư Trinh, which has typically been depicted as one of intimate friendship between two like-minded men, both of whom were in the service of the Nguyễn court. However, if we understand Nguyễn Cư Trinh and Mạc Thiên Tứ as two educated gentlemen who sought solace in each other in the midst of the harsh realities of frontier living and yet hailed from different political realms with competing ambitions for the Mekong delta lands, Nguyễn Cư Trinh's response poems appear in new light.

In addition to his response poems, Lê Quý Đôn recorded two excerpts from Nguyễn Cư Trinh's personal letters, which were addressed to Mạc Thiên Tứ. These letters reveal more about the two men's relationship than can be found in Lê Quý Đôn's cursory notes. Since Mạc Thiên Tứ's letters are unfortunately no longer extant, our assessment of their relationship is limited by our reliance on one of the correspondents' vantage point. This skewed perspective is corrected in some measure by the inherently dialogical nature of correspondence. We have, in Nguyễn Cư Trinh's letters, only one side of the dialogue he carries out with Mạc Thiên Tứ, but this side is conditioned by its counterpart, and traces of the missing letters can be discerned through those of his interlocutor. Of the two letters Lê Quý Đôn records, one is significantly longer than the other, and the shorter one was probably appended to Nguyễn Cư Trinh's response poems about Hà Tiên, which he sent as a gift to Mạc Thiên Tứ. The letters disclose the extent to which the men defined themselves in relation to their work on the frontier lands, and they show us how closely intertwined their lives were with their cultural projects.

12.   Lê Quý Đôn, *Phủ Biên Tạp Lục*, 5.170b.

13.   The idea of Mạc Thiên Tứ as a loyal official of the Đàng Trong court can be found in his official biography, which was compiled in the first half of the nineteenth century by Nguyễn scribes. For ways this characterization of Mạc Thiên Tứ has influenced readings of his poetry, see Đông Hồ, *Văn học Hà Tiên*, and Kelley, "Thoughts on a Chinese Diaspora."

Letter One: On Gratefulness, Civility, and Shifting Position

The first letter is fairly lengthy, comprising 1,170 characters; it lacks a salutation and a signature, but otherwise it appears to be quite complete as its contents are framed by opening and closing sections that mirror each other. It begins with the word *nang* (v: *năng* 曩), translated as "previous[ly]"; this is one of several possible signal words indicating the start of the body of a letter, particularly when it is paired, as is the case here, with *jin* (v: *kim* 今), translated as "presently."[14] I translate the letter in full, but in my discussion of it, I have broken it up into three sections. The first section reads as follows:

> [I] am unworthy of your previous kindness in sending me a gracious message, charging me to express my thoughts in words and to show them to you if, in the course of my reading, I should gain ideas on matters of fundamental importance or great strategies. Presently you have asked this of me again. You have given me this charge so as to use it to instruct me. Your intention, so earnest and solicitous, fills me with gratefulness and embarrassment. I gathered together these thoughts: when eating of the freshness of the pond, one should consider the grace of the one who worked the net; when tasting the sweetness of the garden, one should consider the favor of the one who planted the trees. As a catch it may be small, but as profit it is great. What more for [matters as important as to require] relying on the tools of governance and regulation, and for [matters that require] maintaining equitabily using the aides of morality and justice, how could I forget from whence my profit comes? I think to myself: even if I could gather the jade of the world and amass the pearls of the ocean in a bottle to offer to you, it would still be too meager [a gift to adequately express my gratitude].
>
> How does one possess civility? I have heard this: when the ancients studied, they lifted up a mound of the Way as the meat they ate, they poured from the pool of virtue as the wine they drank, they wove together a hundred actions as their shelter, and they gathered ten thousand benevolent

---

14. Richter, *Letters and Epistolary Culture*, 93. Richter identifies *xi* (v: *tích* 昔) as the signal word, especially when it is supported by *jin*. The pairing of *nang* and *jin* here functions in a similar manner.

deeds as their clothing. They spoke what was permissible and when it was timely, and nothing was off-target. They acted as was permissible and when it was timely, and nothing was out of line. When they cultivated at home, they made their renown at the court; when they cultivated within the state, their influence extended even to distant lands. Should one be able to do this, he is considered to possess [civility].

As for me, that is not the case at all. I was selected from the least capable among the literary talents and placed on top of the clerks and the common people. Moreover, I was registered as the lowest ranking of hereditary positions and entrusted with overseeing the frontiers. What an honor it is for me, what an auspicious time! For if it were not I [who was chosen], then someone else would have done the work of ensuring that the inner and outer regions are indistinguishable. Zhao Meng [v: Triệu Mạnh] opened up the borders not less than a thousand *li*, and Gaozong [v: Cao Tông] captured enemy multitudes without even needing three years.[15] Yet I can only admire Huang Gong's [v: Hoàng Công] ability to extend his virtue, but I cannot add more to its extent; I can only praise Nan Zhong's [v: Nam Trọng] success in maintaining his troops without casualty, but I would not be able to surpass it. As for the strategy, "Three Models and Five Incentives," it is as murky to me as talking in a dream.[16] The teaching, "One Year and Three Years," is as remote as if I were gazing at it from across the ocean.[17] In my coming and my going [at court], I am a fumbling fool; in advancing and retreating [militarily], I merely make things worse. And yet you, my worthy lord, still single me out as someone who possesses [civility]?

In all cases, greatness within will be manifest without. When the greatness is applied to action, it will flow everywhere. As for me, I am but a

---

15. The name is recorded in the text as 高尊, but I believe it is 高宗. See discussion in text.

16. "Three Models and Five Incentives" is a Han dynasty defensive strategy in relation to the Xiongnu, formulated by the Western Han statesman, Jia Yi (v: Giả Nghị 賈 誼, c. 200–169 BCE); explicated in his treatise, *Xinshu* (v: Tân thư 新書; *New Writings*), Jia Yi recommended using good faith, kindness, and fondness as the three external manifestations (v: *tam biểu*, p: *sanbiao* 三表), and granting carriages, fine foods, singing girls, slaves, and intimacy as the five baits (v: *ngũ nhị*, p: wu'er 五餌) to pacify the Xiongnu; see Jia Yi, *Xinshu*, 4.2a–6a.

17. "One Year and Three Years" is a reference to *Lun yu*, 13.10. D. C. Lau translates the passage as "The Master said: If anyone were to employ me, in a year's time I would have brought things to a satisfactory state, and after three years I should have results to show for it" 子曰：苟有用我者，期月而已可也，三年有成. See Lau, *Confucius: The Analects*, 120.

person who reads books; when my capacity and my actions are compared
to the ideal, they are, in every instance, not worthy of my lord's attention.
If not for transmitted knowledge and distilled lessons, I would not know
the *wuxing*[18] and the *liuding*.[19] With this it is enough to see how untal-
ented I am; yet you, my worthy lord, still take me as one whose talent is
real and who possesses [civility]?[20]

曩者辱惠好音，責以開卷有得，或要務弘謀，一二必以文示。今茲又如是。是責
之者所以教之也。公之意氣懇懇懃斯，鄙也不覺感愧。交集彼：啖涔池之鮮亦
當思作網之恩；味園林之甜亦當思蓄樹之惠。其爲獲也小，其爲利也[大]21矣。況
假之以經緯之具，公之以道義之資，而忘其所以獲之之利之所自乎。靜言思之，
雖括群口之环，族眾潛之珠以供一瓶，亦斯爲薄矣。

夫何有於文。嘗聞之：古之爲學也，舉道丘以爲肉，傾德淵以爲酒；編百行而廬屋
之，集萬善而冠服之。言可言於可言之時，無不中；爲可爲於可爲之時，無不從。
修之於家而鳴之於王廷，修之於國而行之於絕域。其如是之，謂有得。鄙也則不
然。采於翰墨之微，而加之吏民之上。又錄於資陰之末，而責以邊疆之效。則何
等榮遇，何等辰節哉。苟不然鄙也，必能經權並行，內外無間。趙孟開疆何翅千
里，高[宗]獲醜何待三年，而鄙也徒摹黃公之廣德，其所以廣也弗克益；善南仲
之全師，其所以全也弗克濟。三表五餌之策，渾然說夢。期月三年之教，茫若望
洋。出入膠柱，進退觸藩，賢侯而獨以鄙也爲能有得乎。

夫中之閫也，必無外而弗肆。迹之行也，必無疏而弗至。鄙也，開卷人也，而乃
如之閫，如之行，皆賢侯之不足觀也。匪識垂識鑒，將不知五行，不識丁六，
亦駸見其無能也已。賢侯而又以鄙也爲能眞有得乎。

It is prudent, in the reading of letters, to bear in mind that a show of
humility was almost a formulaic requirement for the epistolic genre. Even
after taking the perfunctory aspects of his posturing into account,

18. *Wuxing* (v: *ngũ hành* 五行) refers to the five phases that correspond to the five
elements: wood, fire, earth, metal, water. The *Wuxing* theory was influential in all areas
of thought, including that pertaining to the military.

19. Recorded in the text as 丁六. *Liuding* (v: *lục đinh* 六丁) refers to the following
six heavenly stems: 丁丑、丁卯、丁巳、丁未、丁酉、丁亥. These stems are also the names of
deities associated with the *yin* element, and they complement the *Liujia* (v: *lục giáp* 六甲)
deities, associated with the *yang* element. The *Liuding* dieties are said to have specific
martial powers that make it suitable to employ them against demonic forces.

20. Nguyễn Cư Trinh's letter to Mạc Thiên Tứ can be found in Lê Quý Đôn,
Phủ Biên Tạp Lục, 5.149b–153a.

21. The character is recorded as 下. I believe this to be scribal error and that it should
be 大, which complements 小 in the previous line perfectly as its parallel counterpart.

however, it is clear that Nguyễn Cư Trinh adopts a tone of great respect toward Mạc Thiên Tứ. Addressing him as "my worthy lord" (v: *công*, p: *gong* 公), Nguyễn Cư Trinh referred to himself using the term *bi* (v: *bỉ* 鄙), which can be translated as "my boorish self."[22] It was appropriate for Nguyễn Cư Trinh to assume the subordinate position because he was Mạc Thiên Tứ's junior by eight years. The younger man makes clear to the elder that he is conscious of his inferior status as he opens the letter with an expression of gratitude to Mạc Thiên Tứ for his guidance; at the same time, he states the reason for his correspondence, which is to communicate his thoughts on matters of strategy and governance. The letter illustrates Nguyễn Cư Trinh's adroitness in executing a rhetorical dance, where he conveys lessons to the recipient but masks them so that it does not appear as if he is playing the part of the teacher. He keeps his forward motions discrete and couples them with overtly theatrical backward steps, thereby perfecting the performance of an activity as impudent as that of educating an older man.

The portion of the letter reproduced here alludes to a letter that Mạc Thiên Tứ had previously sent, in which he praised Nguyễn Cư Trinh as someone who possessed civility. Even without this letter, we can tell that the compliment related to Nguyễn Cư Trinh's accomplishments on the frontier for he now demurs, insisting that anyone else could have done the work. In the course of his protestation, during which he states all the ways he was inferior to those who came before him, he draws his reader's attention to four historical exemplars. The first of these is Zhao Meng (v: Triệu Mạnh 趙孟), a Zhao general of the Jin state who greatly expanded its territory.[23] The second figure is Gaozong of Shang, also

22.   One wonders if Nguyễn Cư Trinh might in fact have been a little tongue-in-cheek when he selected his self-referent; *bi* also refers to a far-off locale—such as a frontier region.

23.   There are three possible Zhao Mengs 趙孟 in the historical record: one is Zhao Wu (v: Triệu Vũ 趙武, d. 541 BCE) another is his grandson, Zhao Yang (v: Triệu Ưởng 趙鞅, d. 475 BCE), and the third is the son of Zhao Yang, Zhao Wuxu (v: Triệu Vô Tuất 趙毋卹, d. 425 BCE). The *Shiji* does not refer to any of these men as Zhao Meng, but the *Zuozhuan* uses the name on all three. Zhao Wu brought together the various vassal states of the Jin and eased tensions between them; even when the soldiers of the state of Chu hid body armor under their outer shirts to come to an assembly to discuss the cessation of war, he put on a show of good faith to facilitate peace. In this way, he strengthened the boundaries of the house of the Jin; see Yang Bojun, *Chunqiu Zuozhuan zhu*, Xiang 27,

known as King Wu Ding (v: Vũ Đinh 武丁, ca. 1250–1192 BCE), who successfully suppressed the "Guifang" (v: Quỷ Phương 鬼方; the [states of the] malevolent regions) in three years.[24] The third exemplar, Huang Gong, is a reference to Huang Shi Gong (v: Hoàng Thạch Công 黄石公), the titular strategist of the *Three Strategies of Huang Shi Gong* (v: *Hoàng Thạch Công Tam Lược*, p: *Hoang Shi Gong sanlue* 黄石公三略), one of the seven military classics (v: *Võ Kinh Thất Thư*, p: *Wujing qishu* 武經七書).[25] Finally, he cites the example of Nanzhong (v: Nam Trọng 南仲), a Zhou general renowned for incurring minimal casualties in the course of his military campaigns.[26] The historical figures are famous for four different

---

1129–32. Zhao Yang was implicated in an act of aggression against Wei, a vassal state of the Jin, in which he demanded that they render to him 500 households to populate territory he desired as his own; he failed in his bid, but he emerged unscathed from the incident; see Yang Bojun, *Chunqiu Zuozhuan zhu*, Ding 13, 1589–90. As a member of one of the three states that eventually partitioned the Jin, Zhao Yang's punitive actions on behalf of the Jin, in which he won territories for them, could also be conceived as actions taken for Zhao's benefit. Zhao Wuxu appears in the *Zuozhuan* when, while he was in mourning for his father, the Yue attacked the Wu, with whom the Jin had an alliance. Wuxu decided eventually not to break his mourning to come to the aid of Wu; see Yang Bojun, *Chunqiu Zuozhuan zhu*, Ai 20, 1716–17. See *Shiji*, 43.2141–42, 43.2142–49, and 43.2149–53 for biographies of Zhao Wu, Zhao Yang, and Zhao Wuxu, respectively.

24. The *Bamboo Annals* records that in the thirty-second year of his reign, Wu Ding attacked the Guifang, and in his thirty-fourth year, he subdued them, whereupon the Di (v: Đê 氐) and Qiang (v: Khương 羌) tribes submitted to him. *Zhushu jinian* 1A.16a. For an English translation of the passage, see Legge, *The Annals of the Bamboo Books*, 136; the *Shiji* notes several other events that happened during Wu Ding's reign, but it does not record this one. The *Classic of Changes* states, moreover, that Gaozong defeated the Guifang in three years. Refer to Hexagram 63: *jiji* (v: ký tế 既濟) in the *Yi jing*, 6.11a; for an English translation of this hexagram, see Lynn, *Classic of Changes*, 538–44; reference to specific line on the Guifang can be found on 540.

25. The authorship of the *Three Strategies of Huang Shi Gong* is contested, but it is typically dated to the first century CE and is popularly attributed to Jiang Ziya, a political strategist who aided King Wen, the first king of the Zhou. For more on Jiang Ziya, see note 2 in chapter 3. The text is associated, moreover, with the early Han general Zhang Liang's (v: Trương Lương 張良, d. 186 BCE) success in consolidating the power of the Han dynasty; for the story of its transmission to Zhang Liang, see *Shiji*, 55.1459; see Sawyer, *The Seven Military Classics of Ancient China*, 281–91 for a discussion of the authorship and content of the text and 292–306 for a translation of the *Three Strategies of Huang Shi Gong*.

26. Nan Zhong is traditionally placed in the period of King Xuan (v: Tuyên 宣, r. 827–782 BCE) of the Zhou dynasty. The *Bamboo Annals* state that in the third year of

types of frontier work: expanding the borders of the state, pacifying enemy peoples, developing military strategy, and ensuring the welfare of the troops. With these exemplars, Nguyễn Cư Trinh highlights four categories of practical work on the frontier that he considered to be of paramount importance. Even though he insists that he has fallen short of the standards set by these eminent men, he positions himself as someone following in their footsteps. The type of work that Nguyễn Cư Trinh emphasizes reveals to the contemporary reader that the most pressing concern of his day was the protection of the frontier from enemy incursions; his desire to secure Mạc Thiên Tứ's allegiance more firmly to the Vietnamese side is perhaps rooted in this anxiety.

Nguyễn Cư Trinh believed in the correspondence between a man's civility and his capacity to successfully transform the frontier. Disregarding any separation between the personal and the professional, he measured his life's success by his achievements on the frontier and finds that he falls short in that regard. He acknowledges that in spite of his failings, he has attained a rather high level of bureaucratic advancement, and he explains that accomplishment to his situation in contextual circumstances that enable rather than obstruct the manifestation of the Way. To that end, Nguyễn Cư Trinh conveys to Mạc Thiên Tứ his thoughts about one's "position" and its relationship to the Way:

> Although, a person cannot be detached from the Way and be a complete person, the Way, for its part, also cannot be far from people and become the Way. Are not all things fundamentally rooted in the Way? The Way is latent in all things, without a fixed name and without a fixed course. In

---

his reign, the king ordered the general Zhong to the western frontier to suppress the Rong (v: Nhung 戎) tribes. *Zhushu jinian*, 1B.9a; Legge, *The Annals of the Bamboo Books*, 155. Nan Zhong's victory in the Zhou campaigns over the Xianyun (v: Hiểm Duẩn 獫狁) tribes is celebrated in "Bringing Out the Carts" (v: Xuất xa, p: Chu che 出車; *Maoshi*, no. 168). See *Shijing* (*Maoshi zhengyi*), 9D.147–48; Waley, *The Book of Songs*, 141–42. His military prowess is also praised in "Always Mighty in War" (v: Thường vũ, p: Chang wu 常武). See *Shijing* (*Maoshi zhengyi*), 18E.308–309; Waley, *The Book of Songs*, 281–83. A person by the name of Nan Zhong appears, however, in the *Bamboo Annals* under the reign of King Yi 帝乙 (r. 1110–1101 BCE), who, in the third year of his reign, ordered Nan Zhong to the western frontier to repel the Kun (v: Côn 昆) and the Yi (v: Di 夷) tribes and build walls in Shuofang (v: Sóc Phương 朔方; the northern quarter). *Zhushu jinian* 1B.18b; Legge, *The Annals of the Bamboo Books*, 139.

terms of its form, when divided it is the Three Powers,[27] and when conjoined it is the Six Classics.[28] There are people who, in relation to the Way, are curbed and constrained by it, and others who are liberated and expanded by it; who is to say that either one is inappropriate? As can be observed from among the people, there are those who obtain the Way through normal means, and there are those who obtain it through unusual means, but there is no case where someone asks for it and does not obtain it, and no case where someone goes toward it and does not obtain it. The Way is the same, but it has different names according to the function of its position. In former times there were healers who were friends but their treatment methods diverged; one cured with herbs and the other cured with minerals. The one who cured with minerals asked of the other, saying: "If you would be so kind as to give me something with which I could use to help others, I will forever make good use of it!" The one who cured with herbs obliged and thus gave him some urine that he had collected. His friend's wife excoriated her husband and almost left him. But to healers, urine is nothing to be ashamed of. Collecting it and dispensing it, each has its position.

From the time when I came of age, owing to the books that my ancestors left me, I accumulated the dregs of the world; once I understood an idea I kept it in my bosom and allowed it to either give me free rein or to rein me in; that is to say, it advanced me on my course. By the time I entered official service, [I realized that] that which was taut has become lax and that which was lax has become taut; gradually they each became half of what they originally were, and they could hardly be used to regulate me anymore. For a person such as me, not yet fifty years of age, to have already been the *ji* star and the *bi* star; how can one say I have not been a servant of my "position"?[29]

雖然，人不能離道以成人，道亦不能遠人以爲道。事本無道乎。道藏於事，無定名，無定行。形分之而三才，合之而六籍。有人於此，或卷而約之，或舒而博之，夫誰曰不宜。自人觀之，固有正得，有奇得，有無求而不得，有無往而不得。道一也，名之不同，位之役也。昔有医焉，友善而攻岐，一藥者也，一石者也。石者囑

27. These are: heaven, earth, and man.

28. These are: *Book of Songs, Book of History, Book of Rites, Book of Music* (lost), *Book of Changes*, and *Spring and Autumn Annals.*

29. The *ji* (v: *cơ* 箕) constellation has the pattern of the Winnowing Basket and is also referred to as Heaven's Ford or Heaven's Cockerel. It is located in the eastern quadrant, and it has authority over wind. The *bi* (v: *tất* 畢) constellation takes the shape of a net and is the equivalent of Hyades; it is located in the western quadrant and has authority over rain.

之曰：苟能惠我以濟人者，吾其永矢之哉。藥者然之，遺之以所得溲勃。友之妻詬之，幾於離夫。溲勃之於医，非可詬也。收之舍之，各得其位也。

爰自弱冠，奉先人之遺編，竊累世之糟粕，一得意則厭之不已，又從而韋之，而絃之，曰進吾往也。既仕則絃者韋，韋者絃，漸而半矣，今不能以一二均之矣。是人也，曾未五十，既胡然而箕，又胡然而畢，謂非位之役而何？

What does "position" mean? In Nguyễn Cư Trinh's story of the two healers, it refers to urine's place in the medical tradition. When understood in the context of its "position" in the herbalist's trade, it is considered a treasure; taken out of context, it is deemed filth. In like manner, Nguyễn Cư Trinh attributes his success at the young age of "not yet fifty" not to his education—his inherent worth—but to his "position," by which he means his place in a particular historical and political moment. An object's (or a person's) significance is intimately related to its context; when it is removed from one context and placed in another in which it does not belong, it cannot help but lose its signification. Nguyễn Cư Trinh believes that if he were to be placed in a different context, and here I understand him to mean either the frontier at a different political moment or a different geographical location altogether, he would not attain the same level of bureaucratic success. In this vein, he implicitly urges Mạc Thiên Tứ to place himself in a historically and politically appropriate "position" to fully reap the benefits of being a conduit of the Way.

With regard to the relationship between a person and the Way, Nguyễn Cư Trinh puts forward a rather bold idea that the fundamental, universal Way is dependent on people for its manifestation. This circumscribed view of the Way ascribes a great degree of historical agency to humans. It is, then, not just for the sake of one's personal advantage that one should take up a "position" best suited to the times; not doing so would in effect constrain the Way's ultimate manifestation in the world. In this manner, Nguyễn Cư Trinh emphasizes the role of human action in moving history along its course; his view of the Way's dependence on people attributes importance to taking fitting action, where action is to be understood as actively locating one's contextually appropriate "position." It is perhaps unsurprising, then, that he transitions from a discussion of his own situation to that of Mạc Thiên Tứ's, and here begins his attempt to "position" his interlocutor as an official of the Vietnamese king:

I have heard that you, my worthy lord, do not boast about the land that has been conferred upon you, burn bonds of contract for the sake of friendship, forgive past wrongs and uphold promises, hold back on giving orders until absolutely necessary, are regulated by the example of Xiao Bo's [v: Tiểu Bạch] uprightness toward the Zhou [v: Chu], diligently examine military personnel to confer rewards and punishments, and esteem Baozhen's [v: Bảo Chân] loyalty toward the Tang [v: Đường]. If your wisdom were a compass, everyone would be made round by it; if your propriety were a carpenter's square, everyone would be made angular by it. Just one word [from you] and a hundred consent, one gesture and a hundred follow suit; you are neither cowed by others nor do you impede them. Even so, you are not self-satisfied, and you do not cease to undertake study; to you, encountering a virtue makes you as happy as climbing the Spring Terrace. In contrast, I could never be that man. Not only could I not be like you, even if I could attain to the height of your ability, I would never be as thoroughly influential, and even if I could be as thoroughly influential, it would never be to the same extent. And why is this so? Because I pay attention to sound but am deaf to thunder, examine hairs but am blind to form. With regard to [the story of] the person who cured with herbs and the one who cured with minerals, I would not have been able to discern [the urine's] position. As such, I am beholden to my worthy lord's perceptive wisdom, but I am not worthy of your recognition. If you insist on sowing grain in a field of stones, it would really still be empty; if you insist on offering wine in a leaking goblet, it would be like not having offered any at all. I'm afraid that there are many things that will trip me up, and yet a gentleman like you esteems me! When the top is too heavy then the foundation will be shaky, when too much is withheld on the inside then the outside is deprived; perhaps it is for this reason that you have been so earnest and insistent, and that is why I said earlier that this charge you have given me was intended to instruct me. Today I have heeded your directive. This bird on the wing, for its part, may be hit, but it is not anxious about the moment of capture. I keep constant watch, tentatively, for I have laid bare the inner feelings of my heart.

側聞賢侯謙茅土之封，履焚券之誼，遺過失，重然諾。廉後命而咫尺。律小白之正於周，勤都試而賞罰，慕抱真之忠於唐。智欲為規，誰使圓之。義欲為矩，誰使方之。繞一言而百諾，一行而百從，則不膚撓，不掣肘。既而不自滿足，不停服讀，一善之來，如登春臺。則非鄙也之可能得也。不惟不可能，況能之而不周，周之而不及。焉者也。何則注於响者聾於霆，察於毫者蔽於形。則於藥者石者見之，思不出其位之謂也。此則賢侯之識鑒又不足知者矣。顧乃責穡於石田而竄若虛，責献於漏卮而有若無。得非恐鄙也之困於多也，君子多乎哉。末重則本搖，內聚而外匱，而有是言之，諄諄勤勤，故曰責之者所以教之也。鄙也今聞命矣。飛虫亦弋，無慮辰獲。望風依依，敢佈腹心。

Nguyễn Cư Trinh made a careful account of Mạc Thiên Tứ's many virtues, which were well chosen to represent his talent in managing frontier lands and people. Importantly, he presented these virtues as relational, thereby situating Mạc Thiên Tứ in a web of relationships with others; he identified the older man's propensity to forgive debts "for the sake of friendship" as a virtue, and he lauded him for his restraint in issuing commands to his followers and subordinates, doing so only when absolutely necessary. Of particular significance are the instances in which Mạc Thiên Tứ is discursively compelled to occupy the position of a subject. In writing that Mạc Thiên Tứ does not boast about the land that has been conferred on him, Nguyễn Cư Trinh reminds him of his indebtedness to the Nguyễn. He further notes that Mạc Thiên Tứ is "regulated by the example of Xiao Bo toward the Zhou," an allusion to Duke Huan of Qi (v: Tề Hoàn Công 齊桓公, d. 634 BCE), who, as hegemon among the feudal lords of the house of the Zhou, assumed responsibility for protecting the royal house and carried out punitive campaigns on its behalf. The duke particularly excelled in his expeditions against the non-Zhou peoples and in keeping order among the Zhou vassals. In 663 BCE he came to the aid of the state of Yan 燕, a Zhou vassal, after the Mountain Rong (v: Sơn Nhung, p: Shanrong 山戎) people had attacked it, and in 656 BCE, he attacked the state of Chu 楚 for its failure to present tribute to the Zhou.[30] Nguyễn Cư Trinh remarks, moreover, that Mạc Thiên Tứ "esteem[s] Bao Zhen's loyalty toward the Tang," which is a reference to Li Baozhen (v: Lý Bảo Chân 李抱眞, 733–94), a general of the Tang dynasty, who during the reign of Emperor Dezong (r. 799–805), distinguished himself in his counterattacks against the four military governors who rebelled against the Tang. Li Baozhen persuaded them to renounce their

30. Duke Huan of Qi was greatly aided by Guan Zhong (v: Quản Trọng 管仲, 720–645 BCE), whom Sima Qian presents as exceeding Duke Huan in righteousness and propriety; the historian suggests that the duke was in fact covetous of the Mandate of Heaven, but Guan Zhong kept him in check. *Shiji*, 32.1796–97. For an account of his activities undertaken on behalf of the Zhou, see *Shiji*, 32.1791–1801; see also Nienhauser, *The Grand Scribe's Records*, 5(1):56–81.

independent titles and return to the Tang; in the process of gaining their trust, he even risked his own safety to demonstrate his sincerity.[31] The last two historical exemplars call to mind the political role that Mạc Thiên Tứ played in the Mekong delta region, where he carried out military campaigns and smoothed tense relations among the various regional actors. However, Nguyễn Cư Trinh's comparisons also downplay Mạc Thiên Tứ's political independence and position him as an able political administrator of the frontier, managing it on behalf of a distant lord.

The fact that Nguyễn Cư Trinh had to spell out this alternative role for Mạc Thiên Tứ indicates to the reader that the latter had yet to fully inhabit that position. After this instructional moment, Nguyễn Cư Trinh quickly reassumes the posture of the inferior. He enumerates his failings, which prevent him from achieving greatness, and this self-deprecation doubles as an exhortation to the letter's recipient. Nguyễn Cư Trinh confesses that he has a tendency to fixate on detail to such an extent that he fails to perceive that which is of greater significance ("I pay attention to sound but am deaf to thunder, examine hairs but am blind to form"), and he claims to lack the mental agility to transcend what is immediately before him ("I would not have been able to discern [the urine's] position"). He compares Mạc Thiên Tứ's attentiveness to him to "sowing grain in a field of stones" and "offering wine in a leaking goblet," two futile and fruitless actions. In this statement, we find the writer's appeal to the recipient to reconsider his political ambitions for his domain, which, if left unchanged, will yield barren results.

Nguyễn Cư Trinh was not unaware of the potential prickliness of the contents of his letter. As the letter reaches its conclusion, he notes with humility that in writing as he has done, he has upset the proper order of things; however, he reminds Mạc Thiên Tứ that it was he who had first

---

31. In 782, Zhu Tao (v: Chu Thao 朱韜, d. 785), Tian Yue (v: Điền Duyệt 田悦, 751–84), Wang Wujun (v: Vương Vũ Tuấn 王武俊, 735–801), and Li Na (v: Lý Nạp 李納, 758–92), previously military governors of the Tang, declared themselves the princes of Ji (v: Kí 冀), Wei (v: Nguy 魏), Zhao (v: Triệu 趙), and Qi (v: Tề 齊), respectively; see *Zizhi tongjian* 227.7335–36. Li Baozhen sought to win them back to the Tang. In one incident, though he had already formed an alliance with Wang Wujun, their two armies remained suspicious of each other, and, to allay their fears and to demonstrate his sincerity, Li Baozhen went to Wang Wujun's camp with only a few men and even spent the night there. Thereafter, Wang declared that he would die for Li; see *Zizhi tongjian* 230.7426–27.

charged him to do so. The letter concludes with an allusion to a bird in flight, which is at risk of being hit and yet is unafraid. Animals, especially carp or birds, are often used as metaphors for letters, and the "bird on the wing" in this case is a reference to the very letter Nguyễn Cư Trinh was in the process of writing. The allusion can be traced to stanza 14 of "Tender Mulberry Leaves," found under the category of Major Odes in the *Book of Songs*.[32] James Legge's translation of the stanza is as follows:

Sangrou: Ah! my friends,
            Is it in ignorance that I make [this ode]?
            [But it may happen] as in the case of a bird on the wing,
            Which sometimes is hit and caught.
            I go to do you good,
            But you become the more incensed against me.[33]

桑柔: 嗟爾朋友、予豈不知而作。
            如彼飛蟲、時亦弋獲。
            既之陰女、反予來赫。

With this reference, Nguyễn Cư Trinh points to the fact that he is aware his good intentions may be met with indignation rather than understanding. He remained unafraid, however, and hopes that Mạc Thiên Tứ would nonetheless appreciate his affection.

Lê Quý Đôn's writings and the official Nguyễn biographies, composed by nineteenth-century court scribes, present Mạc Thiên Tứ as a loyal subject of the Nguyễn lords, but this letter suggests that he had to be persuaded to fully embrace that role. A careful reading of his official biography in the Vietnamese chronicles reveals that Mạc Thiên Tứ had, for decades, been an important but independent political player on the Mekong delta; recognizing further subordination to the Nguyễn lords would severely circumscribe the range of his political influence. The

32. "Tender Mulberry Leaves" (v: Tang nhu, p: Sangrou 桑柔; *Maoshi*, no. 257). *Shijing* (*Maoshi zhengyi*), 18B.290–93.

33. Legge, *The She King, or Book of Poetry*, 519–27. Stanza 14 can be found on 526. For another translation of the poem, see "The Mulberry's Tender Leaves" in Waley, *The Book of Songs*, 266–69. Stanza 14 reads: "Oh, you, my colleagues, / How do I not know what you do! / Like those flying pests, / You will be caught too. / I go quietly to your aid, / But you turn on me in rage" (translated by Joseph R. Allen).

letter captures Nguyễn Cư Trinh's attempt to persuade his friend to accept the impending political change on the delta and fully submit to the Nguyễn; this sentiment is more fully expressed in his poems to Mạc Thiên Tứ, which we examine in the following chapter. Nguyễn Cư Trinh's double position—as Mạc Thiên Tứ's personal friend and as a high-ranking member of the Vietnamese bureaucracy—is readily apparent in his letter. Also apparent is his finesse in negotiating the two positions to the best of his advantage, in both his personal and his political dealings with the older man.

Letter Two: An Exposition of Poetry

Nguyễn Cư Trinh's intention to shape Mạc Thiên Tứ's "position" is revealed in the other epistolic excerpt that Lê Quý Đôn recorded. This short piece consists of only 201 characters; like the longer letter, it lacks an addressee and a signature. Whereas the first letter is neatly framed by its opening and closing sections, this shorter one begins abruptly; it is impossible to tell if it is a part of a longer correspondence or if it constitutes a short note in itself. The excerpt contains Nguyễn Cư Trinh's exposition of the nature of poetry and its relationship to the poet's intent. In its last lines, he remarks that it was written to accompany some poems that he was sending to Mạc Thiên Tứ at the latter's behest; given what we know of Lê Quý Đôn's interest in the poetic exchange between the men, it is highly plausible that he recorded the note that accompanied Nguyễn Cư Trinh's response poems on Hà Tiên. I thus read this letter as a preface to Nguyễn Cư Trinh's version of the *Ten Songs of Hà Tiên*, which was completed at least two decades after Mạc Thiên Tứ first initiated his literary project. The excerpt of Nguyễn Cư Trinh's letter that Lê Quý Đôn recorded begins thus:

> Anything that is kept within the heart-mind [v: *tâm*, p: *xin*] constitutes intent [v: *chí*, p: *zhi*], [and that which] resides intently on the mind [v: chí, p: *zhi*] constitutes poetry.[34]
>
> 夫存心爲志・寓志爲詩。

34. This letter can be found in Lê Quý Đôn, *Phủ Biên Tạp Lục*, 5.153a–153b.

The first line is a rephrasing of what is regarded as the canonical defini-tion of poetry found in the "Great Preface" of the *Book of Songs*, where it is written that: "The poem is where that which is intently on the mind goes. In the heart-mind, it constitutes intent; coming out in language, it constitutes a poem" 詩者，志之所之也。在心爲志，發言爲詩.[35] This defini-tion of poetry is, in turn, an adaptation of the definition given in the *Book of History* (v: *Kinh Thư*, p: *Shujing* 書經), which states that "the poem articulates what is intently on the mind" (v: *thi ngôn chí*, p: *shi yan zhi* 詩言志).[36] In both definitions, "speech" (v: *ngôn*, p: *yan* 言) is inte-gral to the formation of poetry. Interestingly, Nguyễn Cư Trinh does not explicitly refer to speech in his exposition; instead, he substitutes "coming out in language" (v: *phát ngôn*, p: *fayan* 發言) with "[that which] resides intently on the mind" (v: *ngụ chí*, p: *yuzhi* 寓志). In his conceptualization of poetry, Nguyễn Cư Trinh stresses the realm of the internal, which is hidden, rather than the realm of the external, which is one of verbal articulation. This interest in what is not explicitly stated leads to the topic of opacity, which he elaborates on in the next two lines of his letter:

> Of people, there are those who are profound and those who are shallow, and that is why in poetry there are differences in the way in which some are subtle while others make explicit, and some are learned and others limited. Of times, there are ascendants and descendants, and that is why in poetry there is the differentiation among the early, high, mid, and late. All poetry takes loyalty as its foundation, subtlety as its propriety, and simple plainness as its artistry; embellishments that beautify and burnishes that enchant are the outer verses of the six principles[37] and the resultant affairs of the five periods.[38]

35. *Shijing (Maoshi zhengyi)*, 1A.1.

36. Refer to Stephen Owen, "The 'Great Preface,'" in *Anthology of Chinese Litera-ture*, 37–56. Translations of passages in the *Book of Songs* and the *Book of History* in this passage are adapted from Owen's.

37. The six principles are airs (v: *phong*, p: *feng* 風), exposition (v: *phú*, p: *fu* 賦), comparison (v: *bỉ*, p: *bi* 比), affective image (v: *hứng*, p: *xing* 興), odes (v: *nhã*, p: *ya* 雅), and hymns (v: *tụng*, p: *song* 頌). See Owen, "The 'Great Preface,'" 45–46.

38. The five periods are *mao* (v: *mão* 卯), *you* (v: *dậu* 酉), *wu* (v: *ngọ* 午), *xu* (v: *tuất* 戌), and *hai* (v: *hợi* 亥). Yi Feng (v: Dực Phụng 翼奉, fl. 48 BCE), a scholar of the Qi school of poetry, asserts that these five periods are contained within the *Book of Songs*. The idea is that whenever these chronological periods happen to converge with the

人有深淺，故詩有隱顯博約之不同。辰有[升]降，故詩有初盛中晚之或異。[39]
總之不外乎忠厚爲本，含畜爲義，平淡爲工，而文之以綺麗，鍜之以奇巧，特六
義之外篇，五際之餘事者也。

In the chapter on "Style and Nature" in his work *The Literary Mind and the Carving of Dragons* (v: Văn Tâm Điêu Long, p: *Wenxin diaolong* 文心雕龍), Liu Xie (v: Lưu Hiệp 劉勰, ca. 465–ca. 522) explores how differences in people's talent (v: *tài*, p: *cai* 才), physical vitality (v: *khí*, p: *qi* 氣), learning (v: *học*, p: *xue* 學), and manner (v: *tập*, p: *xi* 習) result in different styles of poetry.[40] Like Liu Xie, Nguyễn Cư Trinh identifies a correspondence between the nature of poets and the poems they produced. He differs from Liu Xie, however, in that he does not dwell on the various resulting genres; instead, he focuses his attention on two very specific topics: the degree of opacity in poetry and the timing of its success. Given that Mạc Thiên Tứ's poetry contained hidden codes intended for his Ming loyalist counterparts, Nguyễn Cư Trinh's ruminations on poetry's penetrability are especially pertinent. They suggest to the letter's recipient that he was aware of the political messages in the initial poems, and they prime Mạc Thiên Tứ to expect not only lyrical but also political responses to his poetry. The second topic that Nguyễn Cư Trinh takes up is that of the correspondence between political times and the poetry they engender. The four phases of time he notes in his letter are a reference to the classification system within Tang poetry, which divides works into the four stages of early, high, mid, and late Tang. Each age, and each distinctive tone, achieves a peak before yielding to the next. As we shall see in the next chapter, Nguyễn Cư Trinh's poems about Hà Tiên contain a different political vision from the one found in Mạc Thiên Tứ's poems. His statement here can be understood as a gesture of acknowledgment that Mạc Thiên Tứ's poetry had found earlier political resonance, but it also serves notice that that particular star has since passed its zenith; the

---

beginning and end of the *yin* and *yang*, opposing forces that govern the physical world, there will be correspondingly major events in the realm of man, such as affairs of governance. See Yi Feng's biography in *Han Shu*, 75.3167–78.

39. The character 升 in this passage is absent in the text. To preserve the parallelism with the previous line, I inserted the character 升, an antonym of 降.

40. Liu Xie, *Wenxin diaolong*, 27.535; Shih, *The Literary Mind and the Carving of Dragons*, 210–11.

time has come for the poetry of another age, namely, the present one made manifest in Nguyễn Cư Trinh's poems, to replace Mạc Thiên Tứ's.

Notwithstanding the various forms that poetry assumes in the different ages, its principal purpose is to be found in its service to the state. In making this claim, Nguyễn Cư Trinh espouses a utilitarian view of poetry, which is certainly not unique to him. The "Great Preface" of the *Book of Songs* asserts that poetry has a regulatory function; it influences those above and harmonizes the affairs of the state.[41] In accordance with the dictates of propriety, Nguyễn Cư Trinh notes that admonishments have to be made tactfully, not obtrusively; furthermore, a poem's artistry, manifest in its ornamentation, should bolster the peace and stability of the state. This letter, clearly addressed to an official of the state, exhorts him to take loyalty to constitute the foundations of his poetry. This statement provides insight into the letter writer's implicit formulation of yet another function of poetry. In his "Exegesis on Poetry" in *The Literary Mind and Carving of Dragons*, Liu Xie asserts that "poetry means discipline, disciplined human emotion. The single idea that runs through the three hundred poems in the *Book of Poetry* is freedom from undisciplined thought."[42] Nguyễn Cư Trinh's exposition of what poetry should be also throws into sharp relief poetry's role as a vehicle for disciplining the poet's emotions. Poetry should serve to bring the thought and intent of the poet in line with what is expected of him; in this case, it means to cultivate that which is appropriate to an official of the state.

In the remainder of Nguyễn Cư Trinh's letter to Mạc Thiên Tứ, he describes his own relationship to poetry in modest terms. As is expected in the genre of letter writing, he exalts the person he is addressing by humbling himself:

The heart-mind [v: *tâm*, p: *xin*] is difficult to fathom; its outpouring is poetry. To make poetry, it sometimes takes three years to get a word just right; yet it will take a thousand sacrifices [years] before someone will truly understand it. This [i.e., coming up with the right word] is where I apply myself the hardest. Moreover, when I was young, I was unable to

41. Owen, "The 'Great Preface,'" 43–45.

42. Liu Xie, *Wenxin diaolong*, 6.83; Shih, *The Literary Mind and the Carving of Dragons*, 40.

fully grasp the classics. Growing into manhood, I was lazy and had an acute aversion to literary fame. For these reasons, of all my compositions there are few that are fine. Moreover, out here in the golden rivers and jade frontiers, [I am] situated at a great distance and occupied with the duties of the three armies;[43] in such circumstances, how can one find enough leisure to wax poetic? Even if I have composed one or two verses, it was done at others' insistence; it was not because the inspiration arose from within me. I did not observe the rules of prosody all that strictly; truly, they make me embarrassed. I am obliged to your kindness for wanting to collect them, but they are really not good enough to talk to others [about them].

心者，難測之。物泄之爲詩。而成乎爲詩，要於一字，至有三年而後得，千祀而弗解。余是用艱之。況存少涉獵，未能窮思於經論。長頗疎慵，切戒希名於文字。以故平生佳作者鮮，矧乃金河玉塞，萬里之情，三軍之務，其能暇及乎。縱有吟咏一二亦黽勉由人，初非盡出己興，律之不苟，良亦多懟。善爲我藏之，不足與人道也。

Nguyễn Cư Trinh reiterated the difficulty in apprehending a person's heart-mind, which is the fount of poetry. Because poetry is sited in the heart-mind, the words that compose it are difficult to comprehend even if their meaning is intelligible when they stand alone as words. Even though he claims to have written his response poems only at Mạc Thiên Tứ's insistence, he makes it clear that he has put a lot of thought into their composition. Nguyễn Cư Trinh's letter to Mạc Thiên Tứ reveals the circumscribed character of his poetic contribution. Unlike Mạc Thiên Tứ's landscape poems, which were written for multiple poets scattered across the oceans, Nguyễn Cư Trinh composed his *Ten Songs of Hà Tiên* for Mạc Thiên Tứ alone; even so, he recognized that the recipient intended to "collect" his poetry, which suggests that the poet might have composed them with the intention of leaving his thoughts to posterity. In truth, he might, of his own accord, have circulated his poetic works, and it is possible that they were distributed without Mạc Thiên Tứ's. On their own, they add to the "airs and odes" of Hà Tiên, but they remain primarily responses to Mạc Thiên Tứ's political vision for his domain. As for the personal letters he sent, Nguyễn Cư Trinh adhered to

43. These are the armies of the right, center, and left.

decorum and framed his interaction with Mạc Thiên Tứ as that of a junior toward his senior. At the same time, he attempted bring Mạc Thiên Tứ's political position into alignment with his own. The letters reflect the changing political scene on the Mekong delta in 1750s and 1760s, when Mạc Thiên Tứ's autonomous enclave increasingly came to be subjected to Đàng Trong's expanding influence.

CHAPTER 6

A Vietnamese Reimagining of a Chinese Enclave

Nguyễn Cư Trinh spent eleven long years on the delta lands, where he won provinces that had previously belonged to the Cambodian kingdom for the southern Vietnamese court. Buoyed by the winds of political change, he sought to bind Mạc Thiên Tứ ever more securely to the Vietnamese side. His ten poems on Hà Tiên's scenic sites, which were composed sometime during his tenure on the Mekong frontier, were a pointed response to Mạc Thiên Tứ's original ones, written some two decades earlier. Nguyễn Cư Trinh's letters suggest that it was the older man who first pressed the younger one to compose the verses, although the poems show that the latter made full use of the opportunity to reshape the recipient's "intent" (v: *chí*, p: *zhi* 志). Compared with the epistolic genre, which demanded overt expressions of humility from the writer, the poetic genre, though pithier and subject to strict rules of versification and prosody, allowed Nguyễn Cư Trinh more freedom to express views that diverged from those of Mạc Thiên Tứ. Perhaps, after having noted in his accompanying letter the relationship between poetry and the age in which it arises, he felt at liberty to resituate Hà Tiên in what he considered to be its proper geopolitical place within the Đàng Trong political realm. His respect for his fellow custodian of the delta, however, was always present, and Nguyễn Cư Trinh's attempt to shape his friend's mode of comportment, an endeavor that might be construed as overbearing, was tempered with a gentle tone of persuasion.

Nguyễn Cư Trinh's landscape poems of Hà Tiên have hitherto been treated in isolation from the ones to which they were responding, but without this context the meaning of particular utterances is lost. More important still, ignoring the responsive character of his poetry necessarily results in a failure to grasp his motivation in undertaking this project—and only by being clear about this motivation are we able to discern the underlying unity that holds his poems together and lends them coherence.[1] His poetic compositions regularly include personal messages for Mạc Thiên Tứ, which are typically found in the poem's final couplet. In these poems, the "I-comments" are frequently directed at the recipient. In some, the poet imagines his interlocutor as a part of Hà Tiên's landscape; in others, he addresses him directly. Occasionally, the implicit "I" disappears completely, replaced by an implied "you." In substituting you-comments for I-comments, the poet reveals not so much the feelings that are aroused in him on account of the scene but his reflection on his interlocutor's position within that landscape. Although it is possible to find expressions of Nguyễn Cư Trinh's emotional state concealed in the lines of his poems, it is important to recognize that his primary aim was to align two subjects, Mạc Thiên Tứ and Hà Tiên, with his own political vision for the frontier domain.

We earlier examined Nguyễn Cư Trinh's correspondence with Mạc Thiên Tứ without the benefit of any of the latter's letters. For the landscape poems of Hà Tiên, we have the original poems and the responses to them. This enables us to study Nguyễn Cư Trinh's poems with greater contextual specificity. Whereas Mạc Thiên Tứ was free to determine the direction of his literary project, Nguyễn Cư Trinh was conditioned and

---

1. As part of the project of translating all of Lê Quý Đôn's works, including the *Frontier Chronicles*, from Chinese characters into *quốc ngữ*, Nguyễn Khắc Thuần has provided modern Vietnamese translations of Nguyễn Cư Trinh's poems. See Lê Quý Đôn, *Phủ Biên Tạp Lục*, 71–87. (The text in Chinese characters can be found on 5.144a–46b). Phan Hứa Thụy has similarly published a translation of all ten poems as part of his project focusing on Nguyễn Cư Trinh's literary works. See Phan Hứa Thụy, *Thơ văn Nguyễn Cư Trinh*, 104–19. In none of the cases above were Nguyễn Cư Trinh's poems studied with an adequate appreciation of the context of their original composition, namely, as responses to Mạc Thiên Tứ's poems. Unfortunately, Phan Hứa Thụy does not reproduce the poems in the original Chinese characters, which prevents me from using them as a point of comparison with the variant contained in the *Phủ Biên Tạp Lục*.

constrained by the poems of his interlocutor. But far from passively re-flecting the earlier poet's vision, Nguyễn Cư Trinh's poems contest it and reimagine a different world. Examining the two suites of poetry in succession offers a window through which we catch a glimpse of the po-litical transformation of the Mekong delta in the middle decades of the eighteenth century. Mạc Thiên Tứ's poems reveal that his ambitions for Hà Tiên were shaped by Ming loyalist politics; Nguyễn Cư Trinh's po-ems bear witness to a historical moment in which Đàng Trong had grown so much that it threatened to eclipse and subsume the autonomously gov-erned diasporic Chinese enclave. Just as the expanding Vietnamese state undermined the independence of Hà Tiên, Nguyễn Cư Trinh's poems subverted Mạc Thiên Tứ's political vision and replaced it with one better suited to the delta's changed political scene.

New Patterns and Changed Positions

The cultural patterns that Mạc Thiên Tứ brought to his poetry infused Hà Tiên's scenic sites with politically charged symbolism. Perhaps the most important of these patterns was that of the mythical Dragon Gate, which he fashioned onto the island of rocky peaks at Hà Tiên's coastal entrance in "Golden Islet Blocking Waves." In so doing, he positioned Hà Tiên as the new Ming loyalist capital. Tellingly, Nguyễn Cư Trinh's response ignored the weighty significance of Dragon Gate and instead inscribed a different design onto Golden Islet.

Golden Islet Blocking Waves	金嶼攔濤
The Thearch, angry with Wave Spirit for repeatedly attacking the shores,	帝怒陽侯數犯邊
Decreed to move a mountain peak to secure the riverfront.	勑移山岳鎮前川
Drenching waves no longer reached the face of the long ramparts;	波霄不拭長城面
Crashing waters thereupon knew the power of the majestic rock.	水猛方知砥柱權
The *jingwei* bird partially dispels her stone-carrying resentment;	精衛半消啣石恨

The black dragon holds securely a pearl while he is   驪龍全穩抱珠眠
fast asleep.
I know that you, gentleman, are likewise   知君亦是擎天物
a sky-bearing pillar,
Now as before, in the rolling waves of time, you stand 今古滔滔獨儼然
alone, loftily.
(Nguyễn Cư Trinh, Poem 1)

Nguyễn Cư Trinh devises an origin story that explains how Golden Islet's rocky peak found its way to Hà Tiên's coastal entrance. To protect
Hà Tiên from the destructive Wave Spirit, who rolled willy-nilly onto its
shores, the Thearch strategically placed a mountain to better "secure" the
land.[2] The poet's use of the verb *to secure* (v: *trấn*, p: *zhen* 鎮) is instruc-
tive because it indicates actions of both fixing in place what would otherwise float away and quelling what is unsettled; using the word *zhen*
here effectively makes Golden Islet a "fixatrice" mountain, which denotes
a sacred peak that has the ability to fix a nearby landmass in its place and
control the stormy seas. The most famous of such mountains is Mount
Luofu (v: La Phù Sơn 羅浮山), a familiar feature in landscape poetry
about Guangdong, which quiets the Southern Sea and prevents the
province from floating away.[3] In Nguyễn Cư Trinh's reconceptualization
of the landscape of Hà Tiên, Golden Islet bears a marked resemblance in
form and function to Mount Luofu, and from its coastal situation it
hinders the Wave Spirit and keeps Hà Tiên from drifting away with the
Southeast Sea.

　　Golden Islet's competence at keeping in check the misbehaving Wave
Spirit has a calming effect on the behavior of creatures of the air and the

　　2. The Wave Spirit, or Wave God, refers to the Marquis of Yang (v: Dương Hầu,
p: Yanghou 陽侯), who is believed to have drowned in the Yellow River and whose spirit
could cause destructive waves. Scholars have been unable to identify definitively whom
the Marquis of Yang refers to. For some of the earliest known associations of the
Marquis of Yang with great waves, see *Zhanguo ce*, 27.3a and *Huainanzi*, 6.1b. For
a translation of this passage from the *Zhanguo ce*, see Crump, *Chan-kuo Ts'e*, 440. For a
translation, with commentary, of this chapter of the *Huainanzi*, see Le Blanc, *Huainanzi*;
the specific reference to the Marquis of Yang is found on 104.
　　3. For Mount Luofu's place in Guangdong poetry, see Honey, *The Southern Garden Poetry Society*, 9. For more information about "fixatrice" mountains, see Michel
Soymie, "Le Lo-Feou Chan," 74–77.

sea, most notably the *jingwei* bird and the black dragon. The *jingwei* is a mythical bird believed to be the reincarnation of Nüwa (v: Nữ Oa 女娃), the legendary Thearch Yan's (v: Viêm Đế, p: Yandi 炎帝) daughter, who drowned in the Eastern Sea. Reborn as the *jingwei* bird, she harbored such hatred for the sea that she carried stones in her beak to drop them one by one into the water so as to fill it up and destroy it.[4] In her pursuit of this unrealizable Sisyphean task, the *jingwei* symbolizes despair over labor spent in vain; here, however, Golden Islet has the sea so firmly under its control that even the *jingwei*'s anger is somewhat assuaged. This well-behaved sea also exercises its power over the black dragon (v: *ly long*, p: *lilong* 驪龍), which is known for its jealous guardianship of a precious pearl.[5] Yet in the quieted waters around Golden Islet, the ever-vigilant black dragon is so lulled by the sea's tranquility that it has nodded off while holding its treasure.

In the poem's final couplet, the poet likens Mạc Thiên Tứ, the "gentleman," to a "sky-bearing pillar," one of eight mountains that acts as a supporting column holding up the sky.[6] The simile in the final couplet finds a correspondence with the imagery of Golden Islet as a fixatrice mountain contained in the first couplet, and the two images bring out the resonance between man and nature. As a sky-bearing pillar, Mạc Thiên Tứ holds Hà Tiên in place and orders its natural world, just as Golden Islet stabilizes the land and settles the sea. Here, Nguyễn Cư Trinh writes Mạc Thiên Tứ directly into the landscape of Hà Tiên, and in so doing makes him a natural part of it. In this manner, Nguyễn Cư

4. The earliest known source that records this mythical bird is the *Classic of Mountains and Seas*, in which it is described as a bird with a patterned head, white beak, and red feet. The passage also identifies it as the reincarnation of Nüwa. See *Shanhai jing jianshu*, 3.16b–17a. For an English translation of this passage, see Strassberg, *A Chinese Bestiary*, 132.

5. One of the earliest references to the black dragon appears in the *Zhuangzi*, in which a fishing family's son brings home a costly pearl only to have his father demand that he destroy it since he could only have taken it from the black dragon while it was asleep. Zhuangzi uses this story as a rebuttal against an unnamed man who had come bragging to him of his gift of ten carriages from the king of Song. See Wang Shumin, *Zhuangzi*, 32.1284–85. For English translations of this passage, see Mair, *Wandering on the Way*, 331 and Watson, *The Complete Works of Chuang Tzu*, 360.

6. The earliest reference to the eight sky-breaing pillars is in the *Songs of Chu* (v: Sở Từ, p: *Chuci* 楚辞); see *Chuci buzhu*, 3.87.

Trinh lent form to Mạc Thiên Tứ's pattern (*wen*). Given that patterns are the manifestation of Heaven's Way, Mạc Thiên Tứ's pattern as an anchor for Hà Tiên's natural world must also be understood as a manifestation of the Way, one with a cosmic significance. The pattern of Golden Islet as a fixatrice mountain supplants Mạc Thiên Tứ's vision of Hà Tiên as the mythical Dragon Gate. And the image of fish "splash[ing] a-flitter," the harbinger of the fish-dragons that inhabit Mạc Thiên Tứ's poems, is nowhere to be found. Whereas Mạc Thiên Tứ's poem was suffused with movement and mutability, as humble carp leap into the air fueled by the ambition to transform into mighty dragons, Nguyễn Cư Trinh's is a picture of stillness and stability. And so the vision of hope and possibility yields to one of responsibility and reality.

Nguyễn Cư Trinh's second poem, "Verdant Folds of Screen Mountain," solidifies Hà Tiên's position in the Vietnamese political hierarchy. This poem is a response to Mạc Thiên Tứ's poem by the same title, in which he depicts Screen Mountain as a site of vitality and a fitting abode for his fellow Ming loyalists. I place the two poems one after the other to facilitate comparison and analysis.

Verdant Folds of Screen Mountain   屏山疊翠
Luxuriant vegetation grows naturally on this lofty peak;   龍葱草木自岧嶢
Folded ridges, fanning open, in graceful purple
    and verdant.   疊嶺屏開紫翠嬌
A cloud-filled sky, encircling light, the mountain
    presses up-close;   雲靄匝光山勢近
Just after rain, crisp and pleasant, fauna and flora aplenty.   雨餘爽麗物華饒
Maturing together with heaven and earth, amassing
    potency through the ages;   老同天地鐘靈久
Sharing in the splendor of mist and rosy clouds,
    extending as far as the eye sees.   榮共烟霞屬望遙
I dare say that in Hà Tiên, the scenery is unusual;   敢道河僊風景異
Swelling vapors swirl and trees swish and rustle.   嵐堆鬱鬱樹蕭蕭
(Mạc Thiên Tứ, Poem 2)

Verdant Folds of Screen Mountain   屏山疊翠
Center stage amid rustic villages, stands a lofty peak;   中分村落立岧嶢
Light and dark hues, vibrants and pastels,
    form a picturesque scene.   淡墨濃青作意描

To know if the earth's pulse is weak or robust,　　　地脉衰靈觀樹石
　　just observe its trees and rocks;
Whether people's moods are anxious or happy,　　　民情愁樂問蒭蕘
　　just ask about hay and fodder.
Spring opens up a brocade screen to welcome the　　春開錦幕邀戎府
　　martial governor;
Autumn raises up a golden palisade to greet the　　秋起金城拱聖朝
　　sagely court.
In such delights, a Guangzhou man derives his pleasure!　此味廣州人樂得
Plants and flowers will never, because of their　　　草花不爲陸沉凋
　　obscurity, wither.
(Nguyễn Cư Trinh, Poem 2)

Nguyễn Cư Trinh responds to Mạc Thiên Tứ's pronouncement about Screen Mountain's inherent potency with his own observations on its generative powers, evident in the density of the trees and rocks and the abundance of hay and fodder. His careful pairing of the words that make up the two lines of the third couplet, in which characters in similar sequential positions parallel each other, is revealing of his reimagining of Hà Tiên's position in the world. In it, spring "opens up" an embroidered screen, a reference to Screen Mountain enveloped in variegated blossoms, to "welcome the martial governor," and autumn "raises up" a "golden palisade," a reference to the same mountain covered in the opulent colors of fall, to "greet the sagely court." The pairing of "martial" (v: *nhung*, p: *rong* 戎) and "sagely" (v: *thánh*, p: *sheng* 聖) implies harmony between the two component aspects of governance, which are in fine balance with one another. I understand the "great governor" as designating Mạc Thiên Tứ, the governor of Hà Tiên to whom the poem is addressed; to what its counterpart, the "sagely court," refers is more difficult to determine. One possibility is that it denotes Mạc Thiên Tứ's civil governance of Hà Tiên; but "court" (v: *triều*, p: *chao* 朝) is elevated above "prefecture" (v: *phủ*, p: *fu* 府; in the poem personified as "governor"), and the pairing establishes a political hierarchy. Taking this into account, it is more likely that the "sagely court" refers to the Nguyễn court, which Nguyễn Cư Trinh serves, and Mạc Thiên Tứ its "martial governor" out on the frontier. Lending weight to this interpretation are the poet's choice of the verbs, "opens up" (v: *khai*; p: *kai* 開) and "raises up" (v: *khỉ*; p: *qi* 起).

They have an enlivening effect on the couplet and make nature an active participant in Hà Tiên's political activities; they also hint at expansion and establishment, particularly of something new, thereby solidifying Hà Tiên's newfound place in the expanding Vietnamese state. Notably, these characters in Nguyễn Cư Trinh's poem occur in the same locations Mạc Thiên Tứ had used the words "together with" (v: *đồng*, p: *tong* 同) and "sharing in" (v: *cùng*, p: *gong* 共); this discursive act of substitution mirrors the project of replacing one political vision with another.

In investing spring and autumn with agency, Nguyễn Cư Trinh signals that it is Hà Tiên's *natural* predisposition to orient itself toward the Vietnamese realm—it is nature that determines the direction to which Hà Tiên looks. Given that in his poem Mạc Thiên Tứ bound his personal fate with that of Hà Tiên's natural state, it is cunning of Nguyễn Cư Trinh to invoke nature to reposition his friend's political orientation. Nguyễn Cư Trinh concludes his poem with the assertion that Mạc Thiên Tứ—the Guangzhou man—would surely find pleasure in the sites that Hà Tiên has to offer. Mạc Thiên Tứ's family was originally from Leizhou rather than Guangzhou, but as the capital Guangzhou represents the apex of cultural refinement in the Guangdong province. In asserting that a man from the capital ought to delight in the scenery of this frontier land, Nguyễn Cư Trinh is not suggesting that the exoticism of Hà Tiên should gratify him; on the contrary, it is the resemblances with his ancestral place of origin that the Guangzhou man finds so agreeable and that assuages his sense of displacement. The displaced sojourner here encounters happy reminders of the cultured province his ancestors were forced to leave behind. The last couplet needs to be read, then, as a direct response to Mạc Thiên Tứ's own, in which he describes Hà Tiên as an "unusual" place; challenging the portrayal of the enclave as foreign and mysterious, Nguyễn Cư Trinh counters that he ought find it pleasantly familiar. With subtle cajoling, he instructs his friend to feel at home in his domain and be content with his present circumstances—a seemingly banal lesson that carries profound political consequences.

The fourth poem in the series, "Night Drum on River Wall," addresses the issue of Hà Tiên's physical situation on the outermost periphery of the Vietnamese domain. In his original poem, Mạc Thiên Tứ placed himself on a fortress wall on the enclave's western extremity to keep watch over Hà Tiên; Nguyễn Cư Trinh's response expands the scope of River Wall's guardianship. The pair of poems is as follows:

Night Drum at River Wall   江城夜鼓

Heavenly winds swirl round and around the icy clouds up high;   天風迴繞凍雲高

Fettered and locked upon the long river, its martial air resplendent.   鎖鑰長江將氣豪

A vast stretch of armored ships chills the waters under the moon;   一片樓船寒水月

Drum and horn at night's third watch steady waves and billows.   三更鼓角定波濤

A sojourner remains throughout the night melded with his coat of mail;   客仍竟夜銷金甲

A man presently on the fortress wall is wrapped in brocade robes.   人正干城擁錦袍

Military strategy received from old: a brilliant ruler pays attention;   武略深承英主眷

The whole realm of Rinan, thankfully, is stable and secure.   日南境宇頼安牢

(Mạc Thiên Tứ, Poem 4)

Night Drum at River Wall   江城夜鼓

Impregnable ramparts stand erect on the emerald river's bank;   金城峙立碧江阜

Crouching and still, a drum tower howls at the moon.   僵臥譙樓對月號

Fine mist, so dense, the sound is all but muffled;   細雨有權聲欲遜

Crashing waves, so unrhythmic, resound much more gaily.   狂波無韻響偏豪

Afar, a cawing magpie circles the trees, indecisive about where to roost;   遙呵鵲樹依難定

Nearby, a lamia churns in a pool, its dream has dissipated.   近蕩蛟潭夢亦消

Who is aware of the sound of military strategy at the end of the earth;   誰念天涯鳴武略

In the capital, because of this, pillows are filled high.   京華從此枕彌高

(Nguyễn Cư Trinh, Poem 4)

As in Mạc Thiên Tứ's poem, the beat of a drum marks the start of the third watch. Whereas the drumbeat in the former poem serves to quiet the waters around River Wall, the sound in the latter carries the reader toward a place located at a distance from it. One imagines that this location is Hà Tiên's center, the heart of the realm over which the fortress wall stands guard, and from which one can barely hear the drum beat. The poem's middle couplets effect the transition from the periphery to the center through a play on aural perspectives, where the muted sounds emanating from River Wall (the "all but muffled" drumbeat and the faraway magpie's caw) are contrasted with the raucous noises produced nearby ("crashing waves" and the lamia's splashing). The poem's depictions of a quiet periphery and a noisy center corresponds to the physical situation of Hà Tiên, whose periphery lies on the riverine inland and whose town center lies on the coast, from which the sound of waves can be heard. The last couplet broadens the scope of the poem from the immediate vicinity of Hà Tiên to the entire span of Đàng Trong's political realm. There, the reader is firmly ensconced in "the capital," which I understand to be a dual-layered reference indicating both Hà Tiên's center and Đàng Trong's political center in Phú Xuân. From the capital, the sound of the night drum is faint; yet Nguyễn Cư Trinh notes that it is because of it that people sleep soundly. Just as the fortifications at the distant River Wall protect Hà Tiên, Hà Tiên serves as a distant province protecting Đàng Trong.

Because fish-dragons and their habit of autumnal slumbers were of such symbolic significance in Mạc Thiên Tứ's poems, the reader cannot help but pause at line 6, where a lamia (v: *giao*, p: *jiao* 蛟), freshly awoken from its nourishing sleep, tosses about in its watery abode.[7] The opening line statement of the *Book of Changes*'s first hexagram, *qian* (v: *càn* 乾), reads: "a submerged dragon does not act" (v: *tiềm long vật dụng*, p: *qian-long wuyong* 潛龍勿用); there is a right and wrong time to act, and the sagacious man, represented by the dragon, knows to wait for the right moment before taking action.[8] The image of a dragon whose "dream

7. The lamia, either simply as *jiao* or as the compound of two characters *jiaolong* (v: *giao long* 蛟龍; jiao-dragon), appears in many classical works and historical documents, such as the *Shanhai jing*, the *Chuci*, and the *Han shu*. The texts are in agreement that it is an aquatic dragon, and their descriptions of the *jiao* include characteristics such as its small head, its narrow neck, and its white scales; moreover, it lays eggs, is hornless, occasionally eats people, and sometimes is itself eaten. *Yiwen leiju*, 96. 1664.

8. *Yi jing*, 1.1a; Lynn, *The Classic of Changes*, 132.

has dissipated" tempts the reader to understand it to mean that the time for action has come. The lamia's pairing with the magpie (v: *thước*, p: *que* 鵲) in the fifth line lends weight to this interpretation. The image of a magpie circling the trees comes from the fourth stanza of Cao Cao's "Short Song" (v: Đoản Ca Hành, p: Duan'ge xing 短歌行), where magpies represent displaced men of talent seeking a ruler or a patron.[9] Taken together, the figures of the magpie and the lamia signal that Hà Tiên at that precise moment is where Mạc Thiên Tứ should roost and where his talent will be appreciated. But the Hà Tiên that Nguyễn Cư Trinh depicts in his poem is different from what Mạc Thiên Tứ originally envisions. In this poem, Hà Tiên is Đàng Trong's outpost on the frontier. Here and in the poems to come, Nguyễn Cư Trinh avoids using the term "fish-dragon" altogether, even though he invokes aquatic dragons and dragons awakening from sleep. I consider these to be cases of substitution, in which the politically significant fish-dragon is replaced with other aquatic creatures to effect a symbolic manipulation whereby the Ming loyalists are erased from Hà Tiên's political landscape and supplanted with worthy men faithful to the Vietnamese state.

The distance that the reader travels in the course of the poem from River Wall to the center of Hà Tiên simulates the distance from Hà Tiên to the capital. For half a century, the enclave had served as Đàng Trong's stronghold in the western regions of the Mekong delta, due in large part to the Mạc family's alliance with the Vietnamese state. "Verdant Folds of Screen Mountain" and "Night Drum at River Wall," however, accord new significance to its geopolitical location and bind it even more closely to Đàng Trong. Moreover, the poems depict the leader as a pillar of the newly defined order of things and a defender of the entire southern Vietnamese realm. Notwithstanding the loftiness of this depiction, the role Nguyễn Cư Trinh's poems attribute to Mạc Thiên Tứ was at variance with what the older man had defined for himself in his original poems. The younger

9. The moon is bright, the stars are few, 月明星稀
   The magpies are all flying south. 烏鵲南飛
   They circle thrice around the trees, 繞樹三匝
   Wondering upon which branch to roost. 何枝可依

Cao Cao, "Duan'ge xing" in *Wen xuan*, 27.18.

man sought to persuade his friend of the need to adapt to the changing
political realities on the delta and allow himself to be coopted to his cause.

Power and Persuasion

From the poems already discussed, it is evident that Nguyễn Cư Trinh
was highly self-conscious of how language patterns and shapes the world.
His fifth poem, "Stone Grotto Swallows Clouds," acknowledges Mạc
Thiên Tứ's literary accomplishments, which were integral to the success
of his cultural project. But before looking at this poem, let us first revisit
Mạc Thiên Tứ's poem by the same name to understand the tone of
Nguyễn Cư Trinh's response.

Stone Grotto Swallows Clouds	石洞吞雲
The mountain peak thrusts its verdant crest into the river of stars;	山峰聳翠砥星河
A grotto hides its latticework chambers beneath green jade stones.	洞室玲瓏蘊碧珂
Uninhibited, mists and clouds come and go as they please;	不意烟雲由去住
Unconstrained, grasses and plants dance carelessly together.	無垠草木共婆娑
Wind and Frost, since ages recurring, patterns a-changing;	風霜久歷文章異
Crow and Rabbit, repeatedly swapping, sights aplenty.	烏兔頻移氣色多
At the utmost, the quintessence, heights where few men reach;	最是精華高絕處
I breathe according to the wind, from the lofty peak.	隨風呼吸自嵯峨
(Mạc Thiên Tứ, Poem 5)	

This poem, among Mạc Thiên Tứ's most playful, testifies to his expert
use of language to bring out the natural patterns in Hà Tiên's landscape.
Here, two elements of nature, Wind and Frost, function as metaphors for
the seasonal passage of time, and two small animals, Crow and Rabbit,
serve as symbols for the sun and moon, respectively. What he describes as
the "changing" (v: *di*, p: *yi* 異) seasonal "patterns" (v: *văn chương*, p: *wen-zhang* 文章) of Wind and Frost is simultaneously his commentary on the

"unusual" (another meaning of 異) ability of "literature" (another meaning of 文章) to take on multiple meanings. Mạc Thiên Tứ ascribes "luster" (v: *khí sắc*, p: *qise* 氣色) to the two animals that are in constant motion. In repeatedly exchanging their positions, these two figures—at once animal and celestial—cast light on Hà Tiên's beautiful "sights," another meaning of *qise*. Nguyễn Cư Trinh seizes on the wordplay in Mạc Thiên Tứ's poem to craft a response that puts on display some of his own.

Stone Grotto Swallows Clouds	石洞吞雲
One mountain breaks apart into two yawning cliffside caves;	一山開破兩岩阿
Gulping down the passing clouds, it lets none escape.	吞下浮雲不放過
Coiling looper and extending dragon are enveloped and swallowed;	蠖屈龍伸歸嗽納
Soaring simurgh and flying phoenix are encompassed and entrapped.	鸞翔鳳翥入包羅
In a bottle gourd, fire is wet and mist is dense;	葫蘆火濕烟凝重
In the stone chamber, man is cold and purple hues are intense.	石室人寒紫積多
Emerging from the peak, about to demonstrate its capacity for brilliant colors;	出岫待教能五彩
The mighty sun brings order to mountains and rivers.	光扶神武定山河
(Nguyễn Cư Trinh, Poem 5)	

The "coiling looper," "extending dragon," "soaring simurgh," and "flying phoenix" are descriptions of clouds in their wide variety of shapes, which are "swallowed" and "entrapped" by Stone Grotto. The phrase "coiling looper and extending dragon" is an inversion of the more typically used "extending dragon and coiling looper" (v: *long thân oách khuất*, p: *longshen huoqu* 龍伸蠖屈); used in this poem in a manner that accords better with the rhyme scheme, the idiom refers to fine penmanship and beautiful flourishes in writing, as does "soaring simurgh and flying phoenix" (v: *loan tường phụng chử*, p: *luanxiang fengzhu* 鸞翔鳳翥).[10] By deploying

10. For an example of this usage of "extending dragon and coiling looper," see *Yutai xinyong*, preface, 2a. For an example of this usage of "soaring simurgh and flying phoenix," see the essay "White Jade Toad" (v: Bạch Ngọc Thiềm, p: Baiyu chan 白玉蟾) in Zhu Guozhen, *Yongzhuang xiaopin*, 29.676. The phrase "extending dragon and coiling

these figures, Nguyễn Cư Trinh complements Mạc Thiên Tứ's "wind and frost" and "crow and rabbit" and pays a compliment to the fine writing of his fellow poet, which I interpret as a nod of respect toward Mạc Thiên Tứ's cultural project for Hà Tiên.

The third couplet gives the poem on a surprising twist. The pairing of "bottle gourd" (v: *hồ lô*, p: *hulu* 葫蘆) and "stone chamber" (v: *thạch thất*, p: *shishi* 石室) calls to mind the myth of Pan Hu (v: Bàn Hoạch 盘瓠), the "brilliant-colored" (v: *ngũ thải*, p: *wucai* 五彩) dog who began life in a bottle gourd and ended up living in a stone chamber in the Southern Mountain with a princess, with whom he had twelve children. In the myth of Pan Hu, set in the southern extremities of the Middle Kingdom, his offspring are the Man barbarians who are considered the enemies of the Hoa people.[11] By drawing on this myth, Nguyễn Cư Trinh portrays Hà Tiên as a peripheral and uncivilized region; the bottle gourd and the stone chamber represent miasmic environments, and the association with the Man tribes is a further indication of the unruly nature of the southern lands. It is surprising that Nguyễn Cư Trinh would paint such an unflattering picture of Stone Grotto given that he had earlier contested Mạc Thiên Tứ's depiction of Hà Tiên as mysterious and foreign. But such an image allows the poet to accentuate the clarifying effects of the sun, which emerges from behind the mountain and obliterates the

---

looper," moreover, contains the idea of withdrawing as a form of awaiting a more opportune moment before extending oneself. However, in this poem, it appears that the dragons, coiled or extended, are just clouds and nothing more.

11. In the myth, set in the time of the Three Sovereigns and Five Thearchs, an old woman in the palace of King Ku (v: Khốc 嚳) cured herself of an illness by extracting a worm from her head. Not sure what to do with the offending worm, she placed it in a hollowed-out gourd and covered the opening of the gourd with a plate; while inside, the worm transformed into a "brilliant-colored" dog. The dog was named Pan Hu (literally "platter gourd") on account of its origins. When King Ku was attacked by the Quanrong (v: Khuyển Nhung 犬戎), who had a general he could not defeat, he declared that he would marry his daughter off to anyone who could bring him the head of the general. Instead of a man, however, it was Pan Hu who succeeded, and the dog carried his prize off to a stone chamber in the Southern Mountain. Pan Hu and the princess had six sons and six daughters, and they became the ancestors of the Man people on the southern border. See Shafer, *The Vermilion Bird*, 107–8. The story of Pan Hu opens the "Treatise on the Southern Man and Southwestern Yi" 南蠻西南夷 in the *Hou Han shu*, 86.2829–30.

miasma with its rays of "brilliant colors." The last couplet is all the more powerful when juxtaposed with the finale of Mạc Thiên Tứ's poem, where he places himself at the top of the mountain, "at the utmost, the quintessence, heights where few men reach." Putting the final couplets of these poems beside each other, it becomes clear that Nguyễn Cư Trinh's "mighty sun" is none other than Mạc Thiên Tứ himself, who has illuminated the dark wilderness with his brilliant colors. Through his clever manipulation of classical allusions, Nguyễn Cư Trinh draws attention to Mạc Thiên Tứ's role in the cultural transformation of Hà Tiên.

In this particular instance, Nguyễn Cư Trinh's agenda dovetailed with Mạc Thiên Tứ's, and his poem is an affirmation of the role the latter carved out for himself. In other poems, however, he expresses his opposition to Mạc Thiên Tứ's ambitions for Hà Tiên, particularly in regard to its role as the new Dragon Gate. "An Egret Descends from Pearl Cliff" is the only poem where Nguyễn Cư Trinh touched on the myth of Dragon Gate. Remarkably, this single reference appears in response to a poem in which Mạc Thiên Tứ made no mention of the motif. Such an unexpected location for a direct rebuttal of Mạc Thiên Tứ's political vision evinces the tactfulness and subtlety of Nguyễn Cư Trinh's poetic subversions.

An Egret Descends from Pearl Cliff	珠崖落鷺
Green foliage and dusky clouds mix with the rosy sunset;	綠陰幽雲綴暮霞
Flying out of the enchanted cliff, a white bird emerges, aslant.	靈崖飛出白禽斜
At night, arrayed in heavenly formation, fragrant trees spread out;	晚排天陣羅芳樹
At day, falling off the edge of the cliff, jade flowers spill forth.	晴落平崖瀉玉花
A waterfall and its shadow, together tumbling, under moonlight on the peak;	瀑影共翻明月岫
Clouds and lights, encircling evenly, dusk's glow thrown on the sand.	雲光齊匝夕陽沙
Brash sentiments about the course of events, ready to act on plans;	狂情世路將施計
In the midst of rushing, I pause, on this rocky shore. (Mạc Thiên Tứ, Poem 6)	碌碌棲遲水石涯

An Egret Descends from Pearl Cliff 　　　　　　珠巖落鷺

The mountain doused with the sea appears like 　　山涵海色碧無瑕
flawless jade;

Who gifted these little frosty flakes to make the 　　誰送霜兒到作花
tiny flowers?

Traveling alongside cresting waves, fish neglect 　　行傍浪頭魚失計[12]
their plans;

Standing amid dense pine needles, swans forget 　　立當松髮鵠忘家
their way home.

Dusk and dawn tides rise and fall, naturally cresting 　汐潮興替自巍業
and peaking;

Ducks and cranes, the short and the long-legged, simply 　鳧鶴短長空嗢啞
quack and caw.

You had wanted to be a guest in the halls of Black 　　爲想烏衣堂上客
Robe Lane;

In the end, in the midst of bustling, you chuckle from 　還將碌碌笑天涯
the end of the earth.

(Nguyễn Cư Trinh, Poem 6)

Nguyễn Cư Trinh depicts a scene of exquisite beauty at Pearl Cliff, transforming the rocky crag, where coursing waters mark its lines out as veins, into unblemished jade. The combination of water and rock at the site of Pearl Cliff is reminiscent of Dragon Gate. But unlike Mạc Thiên Tứ's "Golden Islet Blocking Waves," where fish leap out of the water to transform into dragons, in this poem the fish are so mesmerized by the splendor of the landscape that they "neglect their plans." The enthralled fish are paired with swans, likewise captivated by the magnificence of the cliff, who "forget their way home." Instead of planning a transformation, a move away from the present state, the animals at Pearl Cliff rejoice in the condition in which they find themselves. Just as waves crest of their own accord, and short-legged ducks and long-legged cranes would not appreciate having their legs either stretched long or cut short, the animals

---

12. Lê Quý Đôn records the first character in this line as 花. The translator of the *Frontier Chronicles*, Nguyễn Khắc Thuần, suggests that it should be 行, which forms a good pairing with its counterpart in the second half of the couplet, 立. Phan Hứa Thuy does not include chinese characters in his book about Nguyễn Cưu Trinh's literary compositions, but he transcribed the chracter as *hành*, the vietnamese pronunciation of 行. 花 is clearly a mistake, and I adopt Nguyễn Khắc Thuần's suggestion in my reading of this poem.

embrace their natural state and do not seek change, even if the change is perceived as a betterment.[13] The feeling that the poem inspires is not wistfulness at a lofty plan now abandoned, but delight in one's in-born nature and disdain for unnatural alternatives.

This sole parry to Mạc Thiên Tứ's ever-present politically charged motif is tucked away inconspicuously in the second couplet of the poem. In the final couplet, he compares Mạc Thiên Tứ's Ming loyalist plans, on which the latter had been "ready to act," to a desire to be a guest at Black Robe Lane (v: Ô Y Hạng, p: Wuyi Xiang 烏衣巷), an allusion to the second of five poems about Jiankang (v: Kiến Khang 建康; present-day Nanjing) composed by Tang poet Liu Yuxi (v: Lưu Vũ Tích 劉禹錫, 772–842).[14] In Liu Yuxi's account, Black Robe Lane appears as a street where all the elites once lived, but which has since undergone decline; having lost its former glory, its only guests now are the swallows that fly inside, where they find, in place of the great halls of old, only the residences of commoners. Comparing Mạc Thiên Tứ's Ming loyalist plans to a desire to be a guest in Black Robe Lane is to insinuate that his dreams belong to a bygone age. In his poem, Mạc Thiên Tứ pauses on the rocky shore just as he is about to embark on his plans. Nguyễn Cư Trinh places Mạc Thiên Tứ in a similar position "at the end of the earth," but he extends his pause to an eternity. His plans are no longer relevant, and he

13. The reference to short-legged ducks and long-legged cranes alludes to a passage in the *Zhuangzi*, which states that it would be wrong to correct natural deformities, such as webbed toes and sixth fingers in men; likewise, the duck's short legs should not be stretched and the crane's long legs should not be shortened. The chapter goes on to argue that the struggle to attain benevolence and virtue could similarly constitute a form of violence to man's inborn nature. Wang Shumin, *Zhuangzi jiaoquan*, 8.313–14. For an Enlish translation of the chapter, see Mair, *Wandering on the Way*, 75–79; see also Watson, *The Complete Works of Chuang Tzu*, 98–103.

14. The locus classicus of this allusion is the Tang poet Liu Yuxi's "Black Robe Lane," the second of five poems collected under the title "Five Topics on Jinling" (v: *Kim Lăng ngũ đề*, p: *Jinling Wuti* 金陵五題):

By the Crimson Bird Bridge, wild flowers and weeds grow;	朱雀橋邊野草花
At the Black Robe Lane, the setting sun shines.	烏衣巷口夕陽斜
Swallows, which used to stay by the hall of Wang's and Xie's,	舊時王謝堂前燕
Now, they fly into the homes of the common folks.	飛入尋常百姓家

Quan Tang shi, 365.4117. Translated by Ye Yang in Luo Yuming, *A Concise History of Chinese Literature*, 1:357.

remains on the shore in perpetuity; he experiences no regret, however, and simply chuckles to himself about his obsolete plans.

Whereas Nguyễn Cư Trinh undermines Mạc Thiên Tứ's political ambitions in "An Egret Descends from Pearl Cliff," he crafts a new role for him in "Clear Waves on South Bay." The original poem takes as its subject the limpid waters of the bay; I argued previously that Mạc Thiên Tứ's focus on the sea was revealing of his political orientation, which was directed outward and toward the dispersed Ming loyalists.

Clear Waves on South Bay	南浦澄波
A stretch of vastness, a stretch so pure;	一片蒼茫一片清
Clarity extending to the mooring bay; familiar autumn feeling!	澄連夾浦老秋情
The heavenly river concludes its rain, radiant mists form;	天河畢雨烟光結
A watery region without any winds, where wave-froth is calm.	澤國無風浪沫平
Approaching dawn, fishing boats part waters hurriedly;	向曉漁帆分水急
Following the tide, passenger boats carry clouds so light.	趁潮客舫載雲輕
I, too, know that in the eight seas, fish-dragons hide;	也知八海魚龍匿
Radiant moon and glittering waves, at ease, I understand.	月朗波光自在明
(Mạc Thiên Tứ, Poem 8)	

Clear Waves on South Bay	南浦澄波
Waves overflow into the marshlands, pouring out when it's almost dawn;	盈窪波浪幾辰傾
Turning the bankside glassy, arrayed on the ground so gleaming.	還把玻瓈列地明
With *ji* and *bi* stars sharing in defense, heavenly affairs are few;	箕畢分閑天事少
Jing and *ni* whales have lost their strength, the heart of the sea is calm.	鯨鯢權失海心平
The sojourner on the fortress wall has ascended the watch tower;	干城客有乘桴思
The governor on an inspection tour has no questions about sword sounds.	行部人無問劍聲
An aged rustic and a seagull share a place on the mat;	野老與鷗分席罷
From Chang'an they laugh and point toward this sage born.	長安笑指聖人生
(Nguyễn Cư Trinh, Poem 8)	

Nguyễn Cư Trinh's response shifts the focus from the sea to the land. He begins with a depiction of the effect of the tides on Hà Tiên's waterlogged delta lands, whose inlets are filled and drained in accordance to its rhythm; the watery inlets reflect the moonlight and create a display of luminescence on the ground. The description of the marshlands directs the reader's attention inland, and this shift in focus guides Mạc Thiên Tứ's reorientation from the sea-bound Ming loyalists to land-based Đàng Trong.

In Mạc Thiên Tứ's original poem, the poet sees himself as being alone because his fellow Ming loyalists remain hidden in the eight seas. Nguyễn Cư Trinh presents four pairings of close companions to steer Mạc Thiên Tứ's thoughts away from solitude and toward companionship. The first is the pairing of the *ji* and *bi* stars, whose shared guardianship over the bay ensures untroubled skies.[15] The second is the pairing of the *jing* (v: *kình* 鯨) and *ni* (v: *nghê* 鯢) whales, whose restfulness within the waters results in a calm surface; I consider this to be another case of the poet's strategy of substitution, in which he replaces the politically charged fish-dragons with other large sea creatures.[16] Of particular importance are the third and fourth pairings. The "sojourner on the fortress wall" in the first half of the third couplet alludes to a passage in Mạc Thiên Tứ's poem, "Night Drum at River Wall"; there, Mạc Thiên Tứ positioned himself on the fortress wall as he kept watch over Hà Tiên in the cold night. Here, Mạc Thiên Tứ is still standing on the watchtower, but he is no longer alone because he is paired with a "governor on an inspection tour." Inspection tours, in which the governor reviewed his troops, were typically carried out in the eighth month. The time of the year corresponds to the season (autumn) in which Mạc Thiên Tứ set his poem. I suggest that the governor in the poem refers to Nguyễn Cư Trinh himself, the official in charge of Đàng Trong's southern frontier. Nguyễn Cư Trinh thus inserts himself into the landscape of Hà Tiên as part of a pairing with Mạc Thiên Tứ, where he provides companionship and shares the duties of governorship over Hà Tiên with his friend. In so doing, Nguyễn Cư Trinh presents Mạc Thiên Tứ's administration of Hà Tiên as one that coexists easily with his own.

15. The *ji* and *bi* constellations were also featured in Nguyễn Cư Trinh's letter to Mạc Thiên Tứ. The *ji* governs the winds and the *bi*, the rains.

16. The *jing* is a large whale or a leviathan, presumably male, while the *ni* is a female whale.

The fourth pairing, present in the final couplet, brings together "an aged rustic" and a seagull. The source of this allusion is "Written after Prolonged Rain at Wang River Estate," by Tang poet Wang Wei.

Written After Prolonged Rain at Wang River Estate	積雨輞川莊作
A prolonged rain in the empty woods: cookfire smoke rises slowly,	積雨空林煙火遲
As we steam pigweed and stew millet to feed those on the eastern fields.	蒸藜炊黍餉東菑
Over vast and boundless paddies fly the white herons;	漠漠水田飛白鷺
In dense, dark summer trees warble yellow orioles.	陰陰夏木囀黃鸝
Within the mountains practicing peace I watch the morning hibiscus.	山中習靜觀朝槿
Beneath the pines in a cleansing fast I cut off a dewy sunflower.	松下清齋折露葵
The rustic old man has done with the struggle to win a place on the mat;	野老與人爭席罷
Seagull, for what reason are you still suspicious of me?[17]	海鷗何事更相疑

In Wang Wei's poem, the rustic old man who wins a place on the mat alludes to the story of Yang Zhu in the *Liezi* (v: Liệt Tử 列子). In it, Laozi criticizes Yang Zhu for his arrogance, and Yang Zhu modifies his behavior so much that he has to fight for a place on the mat at the inn where he was previously given it. The suspicious seagull in the last line is a reference to a different story in the *Liezi*, where a man who is asked to catch a seagull finds that the gulls who were once comfortable with him now eye him suspiciously. Pauline Yu understands the last couplet of Wang Wei's poem to mean that Wang Wei has doubts about the sincerity of his withdrawal from the courtly world; the couplet can also be interpreted as Wang Wei's question to those who remained at court, asking them why they should be suspicious of his intentions to retire.[18] In Nguyễn Cư Trinh's poem, the seagull is not suspicious of the aged rustic and understands that he has truly embraced his newfound position. Given that Nguyễn Cư Trinh has just assigned Mạc Thiên Tứ, the aged

17. *Quan Tang shi*, 128.1298. Translated by Pauline Yu. See Yu, *The Poetry of Wang Wei*, 194.
18. Yu, *The Poetry of Wang Wei*, 162.

rustic, a role as his companion in governing Hà Tiên, this image must be understood as a portrayal of the older man's withdrawal from the Ming loyalist politics of the Chinese diaspora and his wholehearted participation in southern Vietnamese politics. In the third and fourth couplets, Nguyễn Cư Trinh effects the transition for him through a narrative reframing. In this reimagining, Mạc Thiên Tứ has abandoned his Ming loyalist ambitions to become Nguyễn Cư Trinh's own companion in governing Hà Tiên on behalf of the Nguyễn lords.

Political Stability and the Transience of the World

Nguyễn Cư Trinh's poems draw attention to the changing political world of the Mekong delta. In emphasizing moments of transition—as captured in periods of dawn and dusk, for instance—he expressed his conviction in the naturalness and inevitability of change. But his emphasis on transience, far from participating in the old trope of *sic transit gloria mundi*, was coupled with a faith that it was possible to preserve and even attain new glory in the midst of a changing world. The condition of such success was at least in part an attentiveness to the changes occurring in one's midst and the appropriate conforming of one's actions to them. The four poems discussed next help the reader understand Nguyễn Cư Trinh's offer to Mạc Thiên Tứ to participate in something noble and great under the leadership of the Nguyễn court.

"Dawn Bell at the Temple of Seclusion" presents Nguyễn Cư Trinh with an excellent opportunity to meditate on the nature of transition.

Dawn Bell at the Temple of Seclusion	蕭寺曉鍾
Remnant stars, the residual few, toward the heavens are cast;	殘星寥落向天抛
At the fifth watch, a bell tolls, resounding far from the temple.	戊夜鯨音遠寺敲
Purified region and human destiny awaken to the world;	淨境人緣醒世界
A singular sound, clear and distinct, goes out to the river and beyond.	孤聲清越出江郊
Suddenly startled, a crane calls out, soaring on wind around the trees;	忽驚鶴唳绕風樹

Also jolted, a crow caws from a branch that dangled
the moon.

又促烏啼倚月梢

At once roused, the thousand households push their
pillows back;

頓覺千家欹枕後

Roosters spread the news of dawn, calling out
cock-a-doodle-doo.

雞傳曉信亦嘐嘐

(Mạc Thiên Tứ, Poem 3)

Dawn Bell at the Temple of Seclusion

蕭寺曉鐘

Dawn breezes shake and scatter, dewdrops are flung
from flowers;

晨風搖落露花抛

Traveling afar, a lone sound passes high above
the treetops.

迢遞孤聲過樹梢

Metal Beast roars at the lingering stars over the sea's bank;

金獸哮殘星海渚

Wooden Whale beats the descending moon into its
earthly crater.

木鯨打落月村坳

The myriad households awaken from dreams, Buddha
faces the entrance;

萬家醒夢佛朝關

The Eight Rivers break open their countenance,
a monk descends from his lodge.

八水開顏僧下巢

Just before knocking—you pause—out of the pity you
feel for the monk;

待扣堪怜禪亦有

Yet whether or not you knock, the sun will substitute
[the moon].

不鳴鳴得太陽交

(Nguyễn Cư Trinh, Poem 3)

To match Mạc Thiên Tứ's poem, which was filled with animals, Nguyễn
Cư Trinh incorporates two strange creatures—the Metal Beast and the
Wooden Whale. The curious creatures are references to the hour of dawn.
Time, marked using night watches and day divisions, was partitioned
into twelve intervals; each interval came to be associated with an animal
of the zodiac, starting with the rat to symbolize the third watch. The
fifth watch, the end of which marks the hour of dawn, is the time of the
tiger.[19] Besides being the third animal of the zodiac, the tiger is one of
the five directional beasts: the White Tiger. According to the Five-Phase

19.   For an explanation of the watch hours, see Wilkinson, *Chinese History*, 532–43.
See especially 537–38 for the association of animals and time intervals.

theory correspondences, the White Tiger comes under the metal element.[20] The Metal Beast in Nguyễn Cư Trinh's poem is thus a reference to the fifth watch, and it "roars" at the remaining stars as it heralds the break of dawn. The key to identifying the Wooden Whale lies in understanding the workings of the night watches. Each night watch is separated into five subdivisions; drumbeats mark the changing of the watch and the ringing of clappers or bells signals the passing of each division.[21] The Wooden Whale refers to the large, barrel-shaped drum found in many temples; at dawn, this drum sounds to mark the end of the fifth watch. Like the Metal Beast, who roars to hurry the stars along, the boom of the Wooden Whale chases the moon into its crater. The zoomorphism of time and the temple drum complements the animals of Mạc Thiên Tứ's poem. In both poems, the animals—animate and inanimate—make the sounds that accompany the moment of dawn.

The logic of cause and effect lies at the foundations of Mạc Thiên Tứ's original poem; Nguyễn Cư Trinh's work likewise captures the illuminating effect of dawn as a function of cause and effect. With the coming of daylight, scenes that are otherwise cloaked in darkness now come to light. The statue of the Buddha, typically outward facing and placed in the center of the hall, aligned with the temple's main doors, appears framed in the temple's doorway as dawn illuminates the land, just as the "Eight Rivers," a reference to the delta's inlets and tributaries, become visible with the breaking light. In the concluding couplet of the poem, Nguyễn Cư Trinh places Mạc Thiên Tứ at the Temple of Seclusion's gate with his fist raised in preparation to knock on its doors; he catches himself just before knocking, however, and waits a moment before awakening the monk. At this point, the poem's thematic focus on cause and effect falters. In pausing, Mạc Thiên Tứ attempts to delay the dawning of the day, but the poem concludes with the assertion that the sun will rise regardless of his actions. Nothing that a person does can alter the natural course of things, which belongs to a higher order. With this

20. The others directional beasts are Green Dragon, Scarlet Bird, Yellow Dragon, and Black Tortoise; the other elements are water, wood, fire, and earth. See Wilkinson, *Chinese History*, 468.

21. Wilkinson, *Chinese History*, 536.

in mind, Nguyễn Cư Trinh persuades his reader that accepting the inevitable was both wise and prudent. Confident that the Nguyễn would gain control of all the lands on the Mekong delta, he felt the time had come for the older man to recognize the impossibility of preventing this outcome. He thus urged Mạc Thiên Tứ to cease lingering over his Ming loyalist dreams and exhorted his friend to work with him to secure the delta lands for Đàng Trong.

Nguyễn Cư Trinh's certainty regarding the inevitability of change, articulated confidently in "Dawn Bell at the Temple of Seclusion," was accompanied, rather paradoxically, by an assurance in the ultimate triumph of reality over appearance in "Moon's Reflection on East Lake." Mạc Thiên Tứ's original poem took an unconventional approach to a conventional poetic theme of the moon and its reflection. Instead of reflecting on which was true and which false, Mạc Thiên Tứ turned the constancy of the moon's reflection on the undisturbed waters of East Lake into a symbol of his perpetual loyalty to the Ming. Conversely, Nguyễn Cư Trinh responded to the original poem with a meditation on appearance and reality.

Moon's Reflection on East Lake	東湖印月
The rain has cleared, mist dissipates into a boundless expanse;	雨霽烟鎖共渺茫
Alongside the water's bend, scenery becomes primeval chaos.	一灣風景接鴻荒
Clear sky and pellucid waves suspend a pair of images;	晴空浪淨懸雙影
Cyan Net awash with limpid clouds, purifies the myriad directions.	碧落雲澄洗萬方
All-encompassing waters suspend a reflection, like a gently rippling sky;	湛潤應涵天蕩漾
Adrift, alone, I do not resent, the sea so vast and cold.	漂零不恨海滄凉
Fish-dragons, dreaming in slumber, start, but do not break through;	魚龍夢覺衝難破
Now as always, loyal of heart, just as light reflects above and below.	依舊冰心上下光
(Mạc Thiên Tứ, Poem 7)	
Moon's Reflection on East Lake	東湖印月
Night has come—who has polished these two circles of light?	夜來誰琢兩圓光

One in tribute to its heavenly abode, the other to its
    watery home.   一貢天家一水鄉

The water calls it a silver plate, which the sky
    has mimicked to cast.   水謂銀盤天學鑄

The sky is doubtful of that jade mirror, which the water
    considers its true adornment.   天疑玉鏡水真粧

Should lamias and wyverns heave and let fall their
    mighty forms;   蛟螭若漏遁形勢

If gulls and cranes should spread and expand their
    paired wings?   鷗鶴如添博翼方

Think about Tao Zhu, after affairs have passed;   概想陶朱成事後

With Heaven with Earth, he'll sing and pour wine,
    right at the center.   乾坤歌酌最中央

(Nguyễn Cư Trinh, Poem 7)

Nguyễn Cư Trinh's poem follows a typical four-part structure. The first couplet offers a description of two moons—one in the sky and one on East Lake—that appear with nightfall. The second couplet expands on this opening description with the water boasting that its orb of light constitutes the genuine version, believing that the one in the sky is a mere imitation of it. The sky is doubtful but offers no rebuttal. The first two couplets dwell on the visual appearance of the landscape; the third couplet, however, effects a turn toward reality. The truth of the rightful owner of the moon will be revealed when lamias and wyverns splash about with their undulating bodies disrupting the water's smooth surface, or when the birds of the air spread out their wings, preventing the moon from casting its reflection on the water.[22] This change from appearance to reality informs the final couplet of the poem, in which Nguyễn Cư Trinh directs Mạc Thiên Tứ to consider the example of Zhu Gong of

22. I identify this as another case of substitution, where the poet employs lamias and wyverns, two types of aquatic dragons, to replace the fish-dragons of Mạc Thiên Tứ's poem. Here, lamias and wyverns disrupt the smooth surface of the water, which, in Mạc Thiên Tứ's poem, had been calm because fish-dragons slumbered beneath it. Because the second half of the poem focuses on reality rather than on appearance, I interpret the gulls, cranes, lamias, and wyverns literally rather than figuratively. It is meaningful, however, that in this poem the fish-dragon substitutes disrupt the constancy of the moon and its reflection on the water, which Mạc Thiên Tứ had taken to be a symbol of his loyalty to the Ming.

Tao (v: Đào Chu Công 陶朱公), whose story is recorded in Sima Qian's *Records of the Historian* as part of the memoir devoted to moneymakers. Zhu Gong, after helping the king of Yue take revenge on the state of Wu, sought to better his own financial situation and traveled to Tao in the middle of the empire; owing to its central location, it was a busy trading center through which many feudal lords passed. Zhu Gong decided to build his business there, profiting from fluctuating prices to buy and sell goods. He grew wealthy, and even though he was very generous with friends and relations, he eventually left a fortune to his heirs when he died. Zhu Gong is an example of someone who is attentive to circumstances and able to take advantage of the times for personal triumph.[23]

The invocation of Zhu Gong of Tao suggests that Nguyễn Cư Trinh wishes for his friend to profit from his situation; to do that, he first has to acknowledge the reality of the times. In his discourse on the moneymakers, Sima Qian begins the memoir devoted to them with a note on how they were able to make money without interfering with the government or hindering the activities of the people.[24] Likewise, Nguyễn Cư Trinh wants for his friend to seek advantage without obstructing the political activities of the Vietnamese state. In demonstrating the impermanence of the moon's reflection, Nguyễn Cư Trinh rhetorically undermines the wisdom of Mạc Thiên Tứ's professed loyalty to the Ming. The moon's reflection on East Lake is no longer a symbol of loyalty to the Ming cause but a reminder of the irrefutable truth undergirding reality.

In Mạc Thiên Tứ's penultimate poem, "Rustic Dwellings at Deer Cape," the poem's enigmatic ending invites the reader to pause in Hà Tiên and discover a utopia. Nguyễn Cư Trinh's last two poems depict two visions of utopia, one built on the land and the other on the sea; in these poems, the poet shines a spotlight on the people of Hà Tiên and their social and political situation. I consider Nguyễn Cư Trinh's ninth and tenth poems in turn, paired with their counterparts from Mạc Thiên Tứ's

23.   Zhu Gong of Tao, also known as Fan Li (v: Phạm Lãi 范蠡), was active during the Spring and Autumn period of Chinese history. His story is recorded in the *Shiji*'s penultimate biography, which was devoted to moneymakers. See *Shiji*, 129.3924–26; see also Burton Watson (trans.), "Shih chi 129: The Biographies of the Money Makers" in *Records of the Historian*, 336–39.

24.   *Shiji*, 129.3922; Watson, *Records of the Historian*, 333.

suite. In "Rustic Dwellings at Deer Cape," Mạc Thiên Tứ portrays Deer Cape as a site of his political reclusion. Nguyễn Cư Trinh's response focuses not on a single person's inner world but on the rustic utopia in which all of Deer Cape's inhabitants live.

Rustic Dwellings at Deer Cape	鹿峙村居
Breezes blow by bamboo huts; dreams are beginning to awaken.	竹屋風過夢始醒
A raven cries outside the eaves, but one can barely hear it.	雅啼簷外却難聽
Inverted images of remnant rose clouds tint the shutters purple;	殘霞倒影沿窗紫
Dense trees, bending low, touch the garden greens.	密樹低垂接圃青
My rustic nature intently desires the quietude of gibbon and deer;	野性偏同猿鹿靜
My honest heart always longs for the fragrance of rice and millet.	清心每羨稻梁馨
If travelers should ask where to stop and lodge;	行人若問住何處
From the buffalo's back, just one more note, and the flute playing ceases.	牛背一聲吹笛停
(Mạc Thiên Tứ, Poem 9)	

Rustic Dwellings at Deer Cape	鹿峙村居
A rustic region of austere dwellings, where silence can be heard;	僻壤窮居可寂聽
There is no worry that children and grandchildren are robbed of thatched roofs.	子孫無患奪茅亭
Dried deer jerky to entertain a guest, washed down with dark coarse tea;	鹿脩留客野茶黑
Suckling pig's trotter to welcome a wife, accompanied by garden fruit green.	豚足迎妻園果青
Well-fed and warm, yet they are unacquainted with the efficacy of the Son of Heaven;	飽煖不知天子力
Reaping bumper harvests, they believe only in the wonder of the God of the Seas.	豐登惟信海神靈
Unburdened with rents and taxes and blessed with utter leisure;	更無租稅又閒事
More than half of the people boast of living close to a hundred years.	太半人稱近百齡
(Nguyễn Cư Trinh, Poem 9)	

Nguyễn Cư Trinh adopts an easy-going, folksy tone in this poem. The first half depicts Deer Cape as a simple village, which contains everything its inhabitants need and remains insulated from the world around it. The third couplet enacts a turn from a description of village life to a portrayal of the villagers' political and spiritual beliefs. It juxtaposes two sources of good fortune, the Son of Heaven and the God of the Seas; whereas the former occupies the apex of a political system, the latter is associated with the spiritual realm. The God of the Seas, in whom the villagers place their faith, is possibly a reference to Mazu, the sea goddess believed to guide sailors on their journeys; in any case, the seaward orientation of the land-based villagers' beliefs brings their diasporic Chinese heritage into sharp relief. The concept of utopia in the Han world is typically bucolic; it is envisioned as a self-contained pastoral realm, where the people live off the fruit of the land and the harvests from light farming. Most important, it is a place where the villagers are free to exist outside of the power structures of chaotic or oppressive dynastic systems.[25] The breeziness in the poem's tone mirrors the simplicity of the people's lives in utopia.

In this simple poem, with its vision of untroubled village life, Nguyễn Cư Trinh conveys his envy of the blissful inhabitants of Deer Cape. Put in the context of the rough life he lived on other parts of the delta, Hà Tiên, helmed by the highly cultured Mạc Thiên Tứ, must have seemed like a haven to the battle-weary man. It is perhaps for this reason that he writes himself into Hà Tiên's landscape in "Clear Waves on South Bay." Yet in painting such an idyllic picture, the poet implicitly asks the leader of the enclave why he would consider politicizing his utopian realm. This poem is best studied in conjunction with the final poem of the series, "Mooring to Fish at Sea-Perch Creek." Nguyễn Cư Trinh continues his depiction of Hà Tiên as idyllic and isolated, but here he brings to Mạc Thiên Tứ's attention the potentially disastrous consequences of leading his domain in a wrong political direction.

Mạc Thiên Tứ's original poem was a musing on the experience of a man fishing on a creek at night. It showed him alone, gazing at the horizon, wishing he could be nearer to the Ming loyalists who live far away.

---

25. The most famous of such utopias is Peach Blossom Spring. See my reading of Nguyễn Cư Trinh's tenth poem, "Mooring to Fish at Sea-Perch Creek," for a discussion of it.

Mooring to Fish at Sea-Perch Creek 鱸溪漁泊

At a distance, watchet billows suspend the dusky glow; 遠遠滄浪啣夕照

At Sea-Perch Creek, from within the mist, emerges
   a fishing lamp. 鱸溪烟裡出漁燈

Rippling waves, receding light, a small moored skiff; 橫波晻晻泊船艇

Moon descends, floating baskets and nets, bobbing
   up and down. 落月參差浮罩罾

Draped merely in a rain cape—the frosty air presses in; 一領蓑衣霜氣迫

A few sounds of the bamboo oar, the water's glitter
   frozen still. 幾聲竹棹水光凝

Adrift, alone—I laugh—at the open sea beyond; 飄零自笑汪洋外

I wish to be near to fish-dragons but still cannot. 欲附魚龍却未能

(Mạc Thiên Tứ, Poem 10)

Mooring to Fish at Sea-Perch Creek 鱸溪漁泊

A flotilla of fishing boats float in orderly rows under
   the moonlight; 漁家營隊月層層

Escaping from among the dense reeds, a few small spots
   of light. 漏出籔芦幾点燈

Village elders have never heard of the court of Han; 父老空聞朝號漢

Womenfolk and children only know of a guest
   named Ling. 妻兒偏慣客名陵

Punting along the Yangtze and Han rivers, pulling
   two wooden oars; 撐扶江漢雙枝棹

Gathering and collecting of Heaven and Earth,
   with one casting net. 收拾乾坤一把罾

I heard that the white lamia is now stretching once again, 聞道白蛟今又長

Awakening from sleep, assessing movements, testing
   its abilities. 睡來行擬試餘能

(Nguyễn Cư Trinh, Poem 10)

Nguyễn Cư Trinh takes the reader on a journey where he discovers, beyond the dense reeds, an entire floating village illuminated by the moonlight. This encounter calls to mind the fifth-century story of Peach Blossom Spring (v: *Đào Hoa Nguyên Ký*, p: *Taohua Yuan ji* 桃花源記) by Tao Yuanming (v: Đào Uyên Minh 陶淵明, 365–427 CE), in which a fisherman wanders down a river flanked by peach trees. At the end of the river he espies a grotto, and, sailing through it, finds himself among a community of people who have been isolated from the world since the time of unrest in the Qin dynasty. They have escaped the period of chaos and are unaware of the dynastic transition from the Qin to the Han. With its carefree and well-fed people, Peach Blossom Spring shows us a utopian vision in which all the necessities of life are easily obtained and the inhabitants are untroubled by the vicissitudes of politics. After briefly enjoying an idyllic existence in this secret paradise, the fisherman departs, never able to find his way back again.[26]

Like the people of Peach Blossom Spring, the people of Hà Tiên came to settle there in a time of political unrest; living an isolated life, they seem to be unaware of the power transition and know loyalty only to the previous rulers. Whereas the dynastic transition of which the inhabitants of Peach Blossom Spring were unaware was that of the Qin to the Han, the people of Hà Tiên know of the transition from the Ming to the Qing but seem to be unaware of Hà Tiên's transition from an autonomous diasporic Chinese settlement to a province of the southern Vietnamese kingdom. This poem restates his earlier observation about Hà Tiên's seclusion; here, he points out their ignorance of the political change that has taken place on the Mekong delta.

The conclusion of the poem is rather enigmatic. A white lamia, just awakening, is stretching out tentatively, but the poet does not observe the aquatic dragon's movements, which remain hidden from his sight; he merely hears rumors that it is testing its strength. As a conclusion to a poem depicting a utopian vision, the dragon's awakening is ambiguous at best. It may symbolize a great man rising, but the context of the dragon's stirring gives us reason for caution. The last line statement of the *Book of Changes*'s first hexagram, *qian*, reads: "a dragon that overreaches should have cause for regret" (v: *kháng long hữu hối*, p: *kanglong youhui* 亢龍有悔); this statement counsels against excessive ambition that leads to depletion and warns us not to perform actions that are at odds with the moment.[27] Whereas the image of a freshly awoken lamia in "Night Drum at River Wall" tempts us to read it as a foretelling of a favorable

26. Tao Yuanming's Peach Blossom Spring comprises two parts, the first in prose and the other in verse. See Lu Qinli (ed. and comm.), *Tao Yuanming ji*, 165–68. For a translation of and commentary on this composition, see Hightower, *The Poetry of T'ao Ch'ien*, 254–58; see also Davis, *T'ao Yüan-ming*, 1:195–201, for additional notes, see 2:139–43.

27. *Yi jing*, 1.1b; Lynn, *The Classic of Changes*, 138.

moment, the image of a stretching white lamia in Nguyễn Cư Trinh's final poem portends the potential disruption of Ðeer Creek. It is not unreasonable to read this image as a response to the concluding couplet of Mạc Thiên Tứ's poem, where the poet laments his distance from his fellow fish-dragons. The white lamia in Nguyễn Cư Trinh's poem could be a reference to Mạc Thiên Tứ, who, in deciding whether to be nearer to fish-dragons, is contemplating leaving the creek. But like the guest at Peach Blossom Spring, leaving would mean squandering his chance at life in a utopia. Moreover, the stretching of the white lamia, a mighty dragon, places the world built above its watery home at risk, and its inopportune emergence from the watery depths threatens to destroy the peaceful floating village. In the final couplet of his tenth poem, Nguyễn Cư Trinh lays out the possibilities to Mạc Thiên Tứ; as the white lamia testing his abilities, he risks losing everything he has worked so hard to build.

The change that Nguyễn Cư Trinh asks Mạc Thiên Tứ to accept is not a disruption but a guarantee of the continued prosperity, and perhaps even autonomy, of his domain. His opening and concluding poems of the suite suggest the potential devastation that Mạc Thiên Tứ can bring to Hà Tiên. In "Golden Islet Blocking Waves," Mạc Thiên Tứ is a sky-bearing pillar; as an anchor for the sky above and the land below, he functions as a keeper of the natural order in Hà Tiên. "Mooring to Fish at Sea-Perch Creek" warns of the destruction that a person in such a position, where he acts as a lynchpin that holds everything in place, will cause, should his leadership direct the enclave on the wrong political path. As his landscape poetry attests, Nguyễn Cư Trinh's vision for Hà Tiên was at loggerheads with Mạc Thiên Tứ's ambition in multiple respects. The two men represented two different political realms on the Mekong delta, and their poems reflect the difference. Written two decades after the *Ten Songs of Hà Tiên* project was completed, Nguyễn Cư Trinh's responses constitute a reinscription of Hà Tiên's landscape at a time when Hà Tiên was being drawn increasingly deeper into the Vietnamese political orbit. Perhaps because Nguyễn Cư Trinh, as Ðàng Trong's representative, was considered the more important political actor on the southern Vietnamese frontier, in the 1770s Lê Qúy Ðôn recorded all ten of Nguyễn Cư Trinh's poems in their entirety while he copied only two of Mạc Thiên Tứ's. The woodblock-printed copies of Mạc Thiên Tứ's *Ten Songs of Hà Tiên* project have not survived, and only a hand-copied version of poor quality remains, a withered testament to Mạc Thiên Tứ's ambitious political vision. Conversely, Nguyễn Cư Trinh's poems, as they were captured in Lê Qúy Đôn's *Frontier Chronicles*, survive in excellent condition. Nguyễn Cư Trinh's literary reinscriptions of Hà Tiên remain etched more deeply in the historical record than Mạc Thiên Tứ's original inscriptions, a fact that mirrors the fates of their competing cultural projects.

Deaths of Authors, Lives of Texts

Nguyễn Cư Trinh died in 1767, two years after he left the Mekong frontier to return to the capital. The Nguyễn lord under whom he had served for most of his life in officialdom, Nguyễn Phúc Khoát, died in 1765.[1] Upon Nguyễn Phúc Khoát's death, Trương Phúc Loan (p: Zhang Fuluan 張福巒), a rogue viceroy infamous for the alleged role he played in causing the Tây Sơn uprising in the 1770s, schemed to place Nguyễn Phúc Khoát's sixteenth son, a twelve-year-old boy, in the seat of power.[2] Trương Phúc Loan was well connected and came from one of the most powerful families in Đàng Trong. With the young boy nominally in charge, he made himself regent and attempted to rule over Đàng Trong. The *Đại Nam Thực Lục* records that he was afraid the powerful Nguyễn Cư Trinh would interfere with his consolidation of power from his position on the frontier, thus he persuaded the young Nguyễn lord to call him back to the capital to keep an eye on him.[3] Nguyễn Cư Trinh did not give Trương Phúc Loan an easy time while he was in the capital. His biography records a story in which Trương Phúc Loan, in a show of strength, summoned the officials of Đàng Trong to his private residence to deliberate on affairs of the court. Nguyễn Cư Trinh expressed his

---

1. Born in 1714, he was the eighth Nguyễn lord of Đàng Trong. He ruled from 1739 to the year he died, 1765.
2. For more information about Trương Phúc Loan, see Li Tana, *Nguyễn Cochin-china*, and Dutton, *The Tây Sơn Uprising.*
3. *Đại Nam Thực Lục Tiền Biên*, 11.4.

disapproval, saying: "Discussing official affairs [openly] in the imperial
court is a long-established system. How dare Phúc Loan defy ritual in
this way? Does the general desire to arrogate power? This must be the
man who will bring chaos to all under heaven" 居貞正色曰:公朝議事自有
定制。福巒何敢如此無禮?將欲擅權乎? 亂天下者必此人也. As a result of
these scathing words, the officials did not dare present themselves at the
regent's home. Although furious, Trương Phúc Loan was fearfully re-
spectful of Nguyễn Cư Trinh and chose not to risk defying him.
Nguyễn Cư Trinh died in the fifth month of 1767, during the summer,
within two years of returning to the capital. The reasons for his death are
not recorded; he was fifty-one years old.[4]

In the mid-eighteenth century Đàng Trong was undergoing rapid
decline. It had successfully maneuvered for control over the lands of Gia
Định and Biên Hòa in the closing decades of the seventeenth century,
when it settled Chinese Ming loyalists on lands that had hitherto belonged to Cambodia. In 1708, the leader of Hà Tiên, Mạc Cửu, chose
Nguyễn suzerainty over the tepid and ineffective protection of his Khmer
overlords. With the fall of these two key territories in the Mekong delta to
the Nguyễn, the rest of the delta swiftly followed suit.[5] Along with the
delta came the prize of rice, which began to be cultivated in excess of sub-
sistence production on its fertile lands. From the 1720s, the Nguyễn started
to systematically export rice from the delta to feed populations in other
parts of Đàng Trong. However, the Nguyễn administrative system failed
to keep pace with their gains in territory. The heavy labor demands for the
transportation of vast amounts of rice fell on the shoulders of the people
the Nguyễn could control—namely, the people of the south-central Quy
Nhơn–Bình Thuận region.[6] In addition, the Nguyễn increased taxes
to make up for the deficits from the declining overseas trade. The situation spun out of control when Trương Phúc Loan seized power in 1765.

Nineteenth-century Vietnamese chroniclers place the blame for
Đàng Trong's decline on the shoulders of this one corrupt official, but

4. *Đại Nam Liệt Truyện Tiền Biên*, 5.10.
5. Hán Nguyên, "Hà Tiên." Hán Nguyên depicted Hà Tiên as the other half of the
"pincer" that captured the Mekong delta for the Nguyễn.
6. Li Tana, *Nguyễn Cochinchina*, 141–48.

it appears that structural problems, including bureaucratic bloat, had plagued the south-central regions of Đàng Trong decades before Trương Phúc Loan came on the scene. The lower ranks of the Nguyễn bureaucracy were open to anyone capable of forwarding the required amount of money to the Nguyễn, and their extraction of taxes from the population base was carried out in the absence of regulation or oversight.[7] As taxation and labor demands steadily increased, an uprising, later known as the Tây Sơn uprising, broke out in Quy Nhơn in the early years of the 1770s. Three brothers—Nhạc, Huệ, and Lữ—seized control of the region of Quy Nhơn and started a thirty-year war that overturned the balance of power between the Trịnh and the Nguyễn families that had been in place in Vietnam for more than 200 years. The young Nguyễn lord, together with an uncle, organized troops to resist the Tây Sơn forces, but in 1777 both of them were killed, along with most of the Nguyễn family members. One who survived was Nguyễn Phúc Ánh, who fled southward and sought refuge in the wilderness of the Mekong delta. After several unsuccessful battles and a period of exile in Siam, Nguyễn Phúc Ánh finally gained control of the territories in Đàng Trong and in Đàng Ngoài. In 1802, Nguyễn Phúc Ánh declared himself Emperor Gia Long of the Nguyễn dynasty.[8]

With his death in 1767, Nguyễn Cư Trinh was perhaps the lucky one. He avoided the turmoil of the 1770s, while Mạc Thiên Tứ was left to face the chaos that ensued. Hà Tiên was pillaged and destroyed by Siamese troops in 1771, and Mạc Thiên Tứ's sons and daughters were captured and taken to Siam in 1772. At the time of writing his *Frontier Chronicles*, Lê Quý Đôn remarked that Mạc Thiên Tứ's whereabouts were unknown.[9] In fact he had taken refuge in Trấn Giang on the Mekong delta; according to his biography, he sought opportunities to help the Nguyễn lords whenever he could. In 1777 he joined his forces with

7. Hardy and Nguyễn Tiến Đông, "Đá Vách."

8. For more information about the Tây Sơn uprising, see Dutton, *The Tây Sơn Uprising*; for more information about the nature of Nguyễn Phúc Ánh's regime that was based in Gia Định, see Choi, *Southern Vietnam under the Reign of Minh Mạng*, 24–30.

9. Lê Quý Đôn, *Phủ Biên Tạp Lục*, part 2, 5.170b.

the imperial troops in Cần Thơ and successfully repelled the Tây Sơn for a brief interlude. Later that year, while awaiting a ship that was to bring a Nguyễn petition for help to the Qing government in China, he received news that the Nguyễn lord had been captured. He is said to have wept and cried out to the heavens, exclaiming, "From now onwards, my eyes will never see my lord again!" He fled to Phu Quốc, whereupon the king of Thonburi, Taksin, sent a boat to meet him. Mạc Thiên Tứ spent the next few years in the Siamese capital, but a false accusation was lodged against him in 1780. He is reported to have committed suicide in the same year, thus bringing to an end the luminous life that was forged on the Mekong plains.[10]

The *Sãi Vãi* is recorded in the *Đại Nam Thực Lục* and the *Đại Nam Liệt Truyện* as one of Nguyễn Cư Trinh's most masterful literary works. It was composed in 1750 as part of his strategy of pacifying the frontier, and Nguyễn dynasty chroniclers cited it as evidence of its author's literary and military genius. The copy of the *Sãi Vãi* that I found in the Bibliothèque Interuniversitaire des Langues Orientales in Paris is a beautifully preserved woodblock print publication dating to 1874 (see figure 1). Interestingly, nowhere on this text does it bear Nguyễn Cư Trinh's name.[11] Lê Ngọc Trụ and Phạm Văn Luật, the two scholars who undertook the job of synthesizing six *quốc ngữ* transliterations of the *Sãi Vãi* into one master transliteration in 1951, observed that half of the transliterations into the romanized Vietnamese script did not state Nguyễn Cư Trinh's name. They believed the transliterators of those texts were in fact unaware of its original authorship.[12] Even as the text lived on, the name of its author was forgotten.

The cover information of the 1874 woodblock print notes instead that it was edited in Gia Định by someone called Duy Minh Thị (p: Weiming Shi 惟明氏), a man from the "Uniquely Ming Clan," a pen name with

---

10.   *Đại Nam Liệt Truyện Tiền Biên*, 6.9–11. Taksin repelled the Burmese from Ayutthaya in 1767 and established the Thonburi kingdom, which lasted until 1782. See Wyatt, *Thailand: A Short History*, 140–45.

11.   This text, which I used as the basis of my translation, was probably also used by Chéon in his 1886 translation of the *Sãi Vãi* into French. See Chéon (trans.), "Bonze et Bonzesse." Chéon's translation of the *Sãi Vãi* does not indicate that he had any knowledge of who the author was.

12.   See Lê Ngọc Trụ and Phạm Văn Luật, *Nguyễn Cư Trinh với quyển Sãi Vãi*, 58.

甲戌秋刊刻

仕娌書集

嘉定城惟明氏訂正 在提岸廣盛南發客

粵東省佛山鎮金玉樓藏板

FIGURE 1: Title page of the Golden Jade Publishing House's 1874 printing of the *Sāi Vāi*.

Ming loyalist overtones. The woodblock itself was carved and stored by the Golden Jade House (v: Kim Ngọc Lâu, p: Jinyu lou 金玉樓), in the city of Foshan in the southern Chinese province of Guangdong. The printed books were distributed by a bookstore in the ethnic Chinese enclave of Chợ Lớn for a southern Vietnamese readership. One of several dozens of *chữ Nôm* texts published and distributed in this manner in the 1870s, the *Sãi Vãi* is now dependent on the Chinese diasporic community for its publication and circulation. These *chữ Nôm* publications direct our attention to the domestic politics of the various Chinese communities living in Vietnam. In the nineteenth century, the Chinese in Vietnam were divided into two categories: Minh hương (p: Mingxiang 明香) and Thanh nhân (p: Qingren 青人). The Thanh nhân moved to Vietnam in the eighteenth and nineteenth centuries, arriving long after the Ming loyalists had settled in Vietnam as Minh hương. Ironically, the Minh hương, who escaped the rule of the Manchu dynasty to retain their purity as Han Chinese, joined Vietnamese society in speech and dress, and some featured prominently in the Vietnamese governing hierarchy.[13] The Thanh nhân, conversely, wore Manchu-styled clothing and hairstyles. Unlike the Minh hương, they did not assimilate into Vietnamese society and made little effort to learn the language.[14] The Minh hương publication of *chữ Nôm* books exemplifies the divergence between the Minh hương and the Thanh nhân communities, as the former had the ability to read the vernacular Vietnamese books. The Minh hương of nineteenth-century Vietnam appear anxious to distinguish themselves from what they considered to be the less pure Chinese immigrants. Less concerned with demonstrating their former allegiance to the Ming and more with preserving their social position in Vietnamese society, the Minh hương sought to separate themselves from the Qing newcomers. The *chữ Nôm* books were symbols of their contribution to traditional Vietnamese literary culture, whose publishing was undertaken at a time when printing in the Romanized Vietnamese script, *quốc ngữ*, was just taking off.[15]

13. Noteworthy members of the Minh hương community include Trịnh Hoài Đức, author of the gazetteer of Gia Định. See Choi Byung Wook, *Southern Vietnam under the Reign of Minh Mạng*, 38–41.

14. Choi, *Southern Vietnam under the Reign of Minh Mạng*, 41.

15. The earliest publication in *quốc ngữ* was the *Gia Định Báo*, first published in 1865.

More than a century and a half after their composition, Mạc Thiên Tứ's poems resurfaced in a modified form in Vietnam. In 1926, Vietnamese literary scholar Đông Hồ (Lâm Trắc Chi) publicized his discovery of *chữ Nôm* versions of Mạc Thiên Tứ's ten poems about Hà Tiên, composed in the 7/7/6/8 rhyme pattern.[16] Trịnh Hoài Đức, the nineteenth-century compiler of the Gia Định gazetteer who found and reprinted the *Ten Songs of Hà Tiên*, made no mention of accompanying poems composed in vernacular Vietnamese; neither did Lê Quý Đôn, who recorded all of Nguyễn Cư Trinh's poems on Hà Tiên and several of Mạc Thiên Tứ's, make any mention of the *chữ Nôm* poems. Some scholars in Vietnam have questioned the authenticity of these poems, while others have vouched for them.[17] Instead of participating in a discussion of whether the poems are authentic or apocryphal, I believe it is worthwhile to consider them as "Mạc Thiên Tứ–style" poetry. Mạc Thiên Tứ has come to be so closely associated with the literature of Hà Tiên, particularly poems about its scenic sites, that any literary project based on the same sites invariably bears his name. In the twentieth century, these ten Mạc Thiên Tứ–style *chữ Nôm* poems about Hà Tiên served to draw Mạc Thiên Tứ and Hà Tiên into the larger Vietnamese political and literary realm. As landscape poems, they contribute to the "airs and odes" of Vietnam in general, not just those of Hà Tiên in particular. As in the case of the Minh hương appropriation of the *Sãi Vãi*, Mạc Thiên Tứ's landscape poems have come to serve the politics of a different group of people. The two texts, which their authors conceived as cultural projects for particular frontier regions, were released from the confines of their native places and, gifted with new life after their authors' deaths, came to inspire the divergent projects of others.

16. The poems were published in *Nam Phong* 107 (July 1926), 31–47.

17. On the occasion of the 300th-year commemoration of Hà Tiên's incorporation into the southern region of Vietnam, Vietnamese scholar Trương Minh Đạt published an essay listing the times during which suspicions over the authenticity of the vernacular Vietnamese poems have been raised and his refutation of those claims. See Trương Minh Đạt, *Nghiên cứu Hà Tiên*, 113–30.

APPENDIX

Translation of Nguyen Cu Trinh's Sãi Vãi
(A Monk and a Nun), 1750

Sãi rằng:

1   Mới tụng kinh rồi vừa xuống, nghe tiếng khánh gióng lên.

2   Ngỡ là chuông vua Hạ Vũ chiêu hiền; ngỡ là đức Trọng Ni đạc giáo.

3   Sãi yêu vì đạo, Sãi dấu vì duyên.

4   Thấy mụ vãi ví nhan sắc có hơn; Sãi theo với tu hành kẻo thiệt.

5   Khoan khoan! Chưa biết Vãi ở chùa nào?

6   Thanh tân mi liễu má đào; đẹp đẽ mắt sao da tuyết.

7   Lòng người dầu thiết, thời đạo cũng gần.

8   Qua Tây Phương còn cách trở non thần; sau phương trượng sẵn sàng bàn Phật.

9   Ngoài che sáo nhặt, trong rủ màn thưa.

10   Lạnh thì có gấm bát tơ; nực thì có quạt lá phủ.

11   Chiếu du trơn như mỡ; thuốc lá ướp hoa ngâu.

12   Rượu hồng cúc ngàu ngàu; trà tiên thơm phức phức.

13   Sẵn đồ, sẵn đạc; sẵn vãi, sẵn thầy;

14   Liễu sau cũng gần đây; vào cùng Sãi tu hoài tu huỷ.

The Sãi Vãi *was originally composed in* chữ Nôm. *The demotic-character woodblock print, on which this translation is based, was edited by Duy Minh Thị, printed by the Golden Jade House* 金玉樓 *in Foshan, Guangdong, and distributed for sale in Chợ Lớn, Vietnam, in 1874. In my study of it, I divide the play into eight sections, which I have represented here; the original play was published without section breaks.*

[Section 1] The monk says:

1   I had just recited sutras and was descending,
     When I heard the sound of a stone gong beating.
2   I mistook it for Hạ Vũ's bell summoning the sages;
     Thought it was Confucius's clapper announcing his teaching.
3   I love the Way;
     I also love beauty.
4   Seeing that this nun has beauty beyond measure,
     I'll follow after and cultivate with her, lest I lose out.
5   Wait up! I do not yet know
     Which temple you are residing in.
6   Pure and fresh are your willowy eyelashes and peachy cheeks;
     How beautiful are your starry eyes and snowy skin!
7   The human heart might be desirous,
     But the time for the Way is also near.
     The passage to Western Paradise remains blocked by
8   sprite-filled mountains;
     But behind, in the monk's room, a Buddhist altar stands at the ready.
9   Outside, thick blinds conceal us;
     Inside, thin curtains hang low.
10   If it is cold, there is brocade of eight silks;
     If it is hot, I have a fan of reed leaves.
11   A sleeping mat glossy and smooth as grease;
     Tobacco scented with aromatic *ngâu* blossoms.
12   Wine the color of red chrysanthemum, oh so red;
     Tea of everlasting perfume, oh so fragrant!
13   There are things, there are fittings;
     There is you, there is me.
14   The small back room is so near here;
     Enter with me to cultivate to depletion, cultivate to destruction.

Vãi rằng:

15   Lời sao nói ngụy, chẳng phải tính chân.

16   Tu làm sao mà lo thiệt lo hơn? Tu làm sao mà tham tài tham sắc?

17   Ấy chẳng là bồi đức. Chớ tu những điều gì!

Sãi rằng:

18   Sãi cũng muốn tu trì, khốn thiếu đồ khí dụng.

19   Thiếu chuông thiếu trống; thiếu kệ thiếu kinh.

20   Thiếu sứa thiếu sinh; thiếu tiêu thiếu bạt;

21   Thiếu bình thiếu bát; thiếu đậu thiếu tương;

22   Thiếu lục bình lư hương; thiếu quần bàn lá phủ;

23   Thiếu hài thiếu mũ; thiếu hậu thiếu y;

24   Thiếu tiền đường sơ ly; thiếu hoa đường liễn đối;

25   Thiếu bê son bình sái; thiếu tích trượng cà sa;

26   Thiếu hương thiếu hoa; thiếu kinh thiếu mõ.

27   Thiếu đồ vặt dụng, Sãi hãy sắm sau.

28   Thứ nào làm đầu, Sãi phải sắm trước.

29   Nhiễu Thượng Hải, Sãi sắm một cái quần cho tốt; bố cát căn, Sãi sắm một cái áo cho xuê.

30   Nón cảnh hàn, Sãi sắm một cái xinh xuê; quạt ban trúc, Sãi sắm một cây cho báu thiết.

[Section 2] The nun says:

15   Why do you speak such falsehoods;
     You must not be true in character.

16   Why is your cultivation concerned with loss and gain?
     Why is your cultivation greedy for worldly riches and sensual pleasure?

17   That certainly does not foster virtue;
     Do no cultivate those things!

The monk says:

18   I, too, would like to cultivate properly;
     Unfortunately, I lack the necessary implements.

19   I lack a bell and lack a drum;
     I lack prayer books and lack the sutras.

20   I lack castanets and lack clackers;
     I lack a flute and lack cymbals.

21   I lack a jar and lack a bowl;
     I lack beans and lack soy sauce.

22   I lack earthenware for an incense burner;
     I lack a tablecloth of lotus leaf.

23   I lack shoes and lack a hat;
     I lack a tunic and lack a robe.

24   I lack a front hall enclosed within a bamboo fence;
     I lack an ornamental hall decorated with parallel scrolls.

25   I lack a vermilion stick and sprinkling vase;
     I lack a sounding staff and a Buddhist cassock.

26   I lack incense and lack flowers;
     I lack the sutras and a wooden fish.

27   These practical odds and ends that I lack,
     I shall acquire them later.

28   There are things that are of greater importance,
     That I must buy first.

29   Shanghai fabric! I will buy a pair of trousers for good occasion;
     Ko-hemp cloth! I will buy a shirt to look nice and pretty.

30   A hat adorned with wintry landscapes! I will buy one to look good and handsome;
     A fan bearing images of spotted bamboo! I will buy one to treasure and display.

31 Giầy hồng, sắm để mà đạp gót; bích khăn, sắm để mà bịt đầu.

32 Sãi lại sắm một thằng đạo nhỏ nhỏ, để cấp ống điếu cho mầu.

33 Chợ nào nhiều bạn hàng các ả, xóm nào đông bổn đạo các dì,

34 Sãi một tu lại tu đi, Sãi một tu lên tu xuống.

35 Sãi lại sắm một cái phương trượng, để sau liêu vắng vẻ một mình,

36 Trên mặt thì rộng thanh; dưới chân cho kín mít.

37 Đang khi ăn cơm thịt, thấy bổn đạo vừa lên;

38 Nghe tiểu đồng nó tằng hắng lên, mấy đĩa thịt Sãi quăng vào đó.

39 Sãi lại sắm một cái vườn nhỏ nhỏ, ở cho cách xóm xa xa.

40 Phòng khi bổn đạo chửa nghén ra, dễ khiến Sãi khoanh tay mà ngồi vậy.

41 Sãi lại sắm một hai bình thuốc tráng, năm bảy đạo bùa mê;

42 Sắm một thằng tiểu đồng cho hay tin lại tin qua; sắm một dì vãi cho hay nói ngon nói ngọt;

43 Phải ni gái tốt, mà lại nhiều tiền;

44 Nó chẳng đến chùa chiền, chớ khiến Sãi làm thinh mà giả điếc.

45 Việc Sãi thì Sãi biết, việc Vãi thì Vãi hay;

46 Ghé cho khỏi cánh tay, kẻo mà tuồng nhằm vế.

Vãi rằng:

47 Lời sao nói quấy, tai chẳng muốn nghe.

48 Lời nói chẳng kiêng gì, tu sao cho nên Phật.

31   A pair of red shoes! I will buy to tread on;
An emerald headwrap! I will buy to cover my head.

32   I will also train a young novice, quite small,
to carry my pipe under his arm, oh marvelous!

33   Whichever market has many damsel customers;
Whichever hamlet is crowded with maiden laypersons;

34   I'll definitely cultivate here and there;
I'll certainly cultivate up and down!

35   I will, on the one hand, prepare a monk's room,
So I have a deserted back room for myself.

36   On the face of it, it is open and reputable,
But underfoot, there is a secret space.

37   For when I am enjoying a meal of meat,
And see a layperson about to arrive,

38   I'll hear that small child calling softly,
And the plates of meat I'll toss in there.

39   I will, on the other hand, prepare a villa, quite small,
That is situated away from the hamlet, quite far,

40   As shelter for when a layperson becomes pregnant,
Then it shall be easy for me to fold my arms, sitting thus.

41   I will moreover prepare one or two jars of medicines for male strength,
Five or seven spells of love charms.

42   Train a small child to bring messages back and forth,
Train a young nun to say sweet and sugary things.

43   She must be a beautiful girl,
Who also has a lot of money,

44   Who does not attend temples,
And never causes me to keep quiet and act deaf.

45   As for the affairs of a monk, I know them;
As for the affairs of a nun, you know them.

46   Keep away to avoid my arms,
Or I might inadvertently touch your thigh.

[Section 3] The nun says:

47   Why do you speak in this joking manner;
My ears do not want to listen to you!

48   If in your speech, you abstain from nothing,
How do you cultivate to become a Buddha?

49   Tuy là mật thất, nào phải đạo tu!

50   Trời xa xa xem tỏ mà chẳng mù; lưới lồng lộng bủa thưa mà
      chẳng lọt.

51   Một lời lỗi luật, muôn kiếp khôn đền.

52   Nơi Thiên Đường, ông hối chưa lên; chốn Địa Ngục, ông toan
      kíp xuống.

      Sãi rằng:

53   Hễ là quân tử, thì đức thắng tài.

54   Thờ vua, hết ngay; thờ cha, hết thảo.

55   Một lời nói phải nhân phải đạo, ấy là tu ngôn; Một việc làm chẳng hại
      chẳng tham, ấy là tu hạnh.

56   Lấy nhân mà tu tính, lấy đức mà tu thân.

57   Tu minh đức để mà tân dân; tu tề gia để mà trị quốc.

58   Ấy là trang hiền đức, người tu phải đạo tu.

59   Ngoài thì tu ôn dụ khoan nhu; trong thì tu hoà bình trung chính.

60   Tu cung, tu kính; tu tín, tu thành.

61   Nếu phải đạo tu hành, thì càng đầy phúc lý.

62   Tự nhiên đắc lộc, đắc vị; đắc thọ, đắc danh.

63   Đắc phú quý vinh hoa; ấy Thiên Đường là đó.

64   Hễ những trang hiền ngõ, thì tu lên Thiên Đường.

49 Although you remain hidden in your chamber,
You are not making a way of cultivation!

50 The distant heaven sees clearly and is not blind;
The vast [heavenly] net is sparsely woven but nothing falls
through.

51 For one word that falls short of the law,
Ten thousand lifetimes cannot compensate for it.

52 To the heavenly places, you, sir, alas have yet to ascend;
To the hellish places, you, sir, are about to quickly descend.

The monk says:

53 Whoever is a gentleman,
His virtue exceeds his talent.

54 When venerating his king, he is completely upright;
When venerating his father, he is completely filial.

55 A single word spoken for humaneness and for the Way, that is
cultivating speech.
A single deed done that is not harmful or greedy, that is cultivating
action.

56 Taking up humaneness, he cultivates his personality;
Taking up virtue, he cultivates his physical self.

57 He cultivates luminous virtue so as to renew the common people;
Cultivates running a household so as to govern a country.

58 That is a worthy and virtuous person;
A person who correctly cultivates techniques of cultivation.

59 Externally, he cultivates gentleness and generosity;
Internally, he cultivates peacefulness and uprightness.

60 He cultivates reverence, cultivates respectfulness;
Cultivates trustworthiness, cultivates sincerity.

61 If he masters the techniques of cultivating his actions,
He will increasingly embody good fortune and fine form.

62 Arising from this, he will get official status, get position;
Get a long life, get a reputation.

63 Get wealth and honor and glory and splendor;
That is heaven indeed.

64 Whoever is a worthy man,
He cultivates ascending to heaven.

65   Còn những kẻ tiểu nhân, thì tu vào Địa Ngục.

66   Tiểu nhân thói tục, tu những tính phàm.

67   Tu những lòng bạc ác gian tham; tu những dạ ngoan hung tàn bạo.

68   Nuôi cho lớn mà tu lòng bất hiếu; ăn cho no mà tu dạ bất trung.

69   Sắc tu lành để mà a ý khúc tùng; lời tu khéo để mà sức phi văn quá.

70   Người hiền ngỗ, ghét ghen ngăn trở đón; kẻ lỗi lầm, tìm kiếm mà đon ren.

71   Tu uốn lưỡi mà lấy của mới đành lòng; tu mưu độc hại người cho đã giận.

72   Đứa tiểu nhân như rận; nó tu rút máu người.

73   Tu càng dày càng nhục ông cha; tu càng dày càng hại con hại cháu.

74   Tu vơ tu váo, tu chạ tu càn.

75   Hễ là đứa tiểu nhân, tu những đường bất ngãi.

76   Vậy cho nên: Âm vi quỷ thần sở hại, dương vi vương pháp sở tru.

77   Ấy là đứa tiểu nhân chi tu, thì tu vào Địa Ngục.

78   Tu mà thoát tục, hãy còn có kẻ thượng trí chi tu.

79   Nhớ thuở Đường Ngu, thánh xưng Nhị Đế;

80   Nhị Đế người tu kỷ, mà thiên hạ đều an.

81   Tam Vương người tu nhân, mà muôn dân đều trị.

65 And as for petty men,
They cultivate entering hell.

66 Petty men's vulgar manners,
Cultivate worldly natures.

67 They cultivate hearts that are ungrateful, cruel, treacherous, and greedy;
Cultivate minds that are stubborn, ferocious, tyrannical, and wicked.

68 Having been nurtured to adulthood, they yet cultivate hearts that are unfilial;
Having eaten to fullness, they yet cultivate stomachs that are disloyal.

69 They cultivate attractive looks to flatter others and ingratiate themselves;
They cultivate clever speech to gloss over wrongdoings and faults.

70 Of worthy men, they are jealous and hold back their welcome;
But guilty men, they seek out ever so eagerly.

71 They cultivate slick tongues to take property and gratify their desire;
Cultivate wicked schemes to harm people and satisfy their anger.

72 Petty men are like lice,
They cultivate sucking the blood of people.

73 The more they cultivate the more they humiliate their grandfathers and
fathers;
The more they cultivate the more they harm their children and grandchildren.

74 They cultivate recklessness and thoughtlessness,
Cultivate promiscuity and wantonness.

75 Whoever is a petty man,
He cultivates unrighteous paths.

76 In this way, in darkness he is one whom sprites and ghosts harm,
In daylight he is one whom the king's laws punish.

77 That is the cultivation of a petty man,
And so he cultivates entering hell.

[Section 4]

78 As for cultivation that is free from the mundane;
There remain those with the cultivation of superior wisdom.

79 Recall the ancient times of Đường and Ngu,
When sages were proclaimed the Two Thearchs.

80 The Two Thearchs were people who cultivated themselves;
Consequently all under heaven was stable.

81 The Three Sovereigns were people who cultivated humaneness;
Consequently the entire population was in order.

82　　Dầu những Hán, Đường dật kế, Minh, Tống tương truyền.

83　　Có tu đức, thì thiên hạ mới trị an; có tu nhân, thì cơ đồ mới sáng tạo.

84　　Tu văn tu võ, người cũng tùy thời mà tu.

85　　Những thuở thái bình, yển võ tu văn; cơn bát loạn, yển văn tu võ.

86　　Thì một người tu đủ, mà thiên hạ thăng bình.

87　　Hây hây cõi thọ đường xuân; tu làm vậy chẳng là thượng trí?

88　　Hãy còn kẻ trung trí chi tu.

89　　Mặc Địch, Dương Chu, tu một sự vị nhân, vị kỷ.

90　　Nhổ một mảy lông làm lợi trung thiên hạ, thì Dương Chu một sự chẳng vui.

91　　Mài hết tráng mà lợi có một người, thì Mặc Địch một lòng chẳng ngại.

92　　Dầu những Thích Ca tu lại, Đạt Ma tu qua.

93　　Tu cho tinh chuyên là Cưu Ma Thập Ha; tu cho khổ não là Văn Thù Bồ Tát.

94　　Số là người ngoại quốc, luận theo thói Trung Hoa.

95　　Chê việc đời phú quý vinh hoa; muốn vui thú thanh nhàn dật lạc.

96　　Mình tên là Phật, "chữ phất chữ nhân";

97　　Như luận lý chí chân thì phất tri nhân sự.

98　　Vậy cho nên: Ai dữ thì mặc dữ, ai lành thì mặc lành.

82 Be it in the rise and fall of the Hán and the Đường dynasties,
Or the successions and transitions of the Minh and the Tống dynasties,
83 [It holds true that] when there was the cultivation of virtue,
then all under heaven was stable;
When there was the cultivation of humaneness,
then foundations were created.

84 As for cultivating civil administration and cultivating military might,
People cultivated these according to the times.
In times of great peace, they abandoned the military to cultivate civil
85 administration;
In times of rebellion and suppressing chaos, they abandoned civil
administration to cultivate military might.

86 When just one person cultivated himself sufficiently,
Then all under heaven was victorious and peaceful.
87 Hale and hearty in the region of longevity and the palace of springtime;
To cultivate in this way, is it not the cultivation of superior wisdom?

88 There are still those with the cultivation of middling wisdom.
89 [Such were] Mạc Địch and Dương Chu;
Who cultivated either for the people or for the self.

90 Even if by plucking one tiny hair he could benefit all of humanity,
Dương Chu would not be happy to do it.
91 To exhaust all of his strength to benefit just one person,
Mạc Địch would wholeheartedly give and not flinch.

92 As for those who cultivate like *Thích Ca* on the one hand,
Đạt Ma on the other;
93 Kumarajiva cultivated assiduously,
Manjusri cultivated with agonizing effort.

94 This is how it all started, foreigners came
Discoursing according to the customs of the Central Hoa civilization.
95 Spurning wealth, honor, glory, and splendor,
Seeking pleasure in quietness, idleness, reclusivity, and happiness.

96 Calling themselves by the name of Buddha,
[Written with] the characters "not" and "human";
97 Just as their logic in the truest form
Is to be unconcerned with human affairs.

98 And so it goes: whoever suffers infelicity is left to his adversity,
Whoever meets serendipity is left to his good fortune.

99   Nhà hưng vong, phụ tử cũng chẳng bênh; nước trị loạn, quân thần cũng
       không đoái.

100   Vậy mà thuyết nhân thuyết ngãi; thuyết tính thuyết tình.

101   Người thế gian tham Thiên Đường thì phải làm lành; sợ Địa Ngục nên
       chừa thói dữ.

102   Muôn đời phụng tự; ấy là trung trí chi tu.

103   Tu mà rất ngu, hãy nhiều trang hạ trí.

104   Kìa như Hán Võ Đế; đã nên đứng cao minh;

105   Nọ như Tần Thủy Hoàng; đã nên trang hung bạo.

106   Tham lam tu đạo, lặn lội tu tiên.

107   Mỏi sức người, thiên hạ chịu lao phiền; hao của nước, muôn dân kêu đồ khổ.

108   Trăm chước tu hành thì có, mảy lông thiện niệm thì không.

109   Đất Luân Đài phải Hán chẳng hối ngộ tấm lòng; ải Hàm Cốc thì Tần đã
       rắp ranh làm phản.

110   Hối nhiều như Hán, chẳng phải như Tần.

111   Đời nào tu cho kịp Tống Đạo Quân; đời nào trọng cho bằng Lương Võ Đế.

112   Vậy mà vị sao chẳng tiên ra cứu cấp; đói Đài Thành sao chẳng thể Phật
       trợ nạn.

113   Tiếc cơ đồ công gầy dựng giang sơn: hoài sự nghiệp đức tổ tông sáng tạo.

114   Chu Sư đã vang dậy tên pháo, sao Tề Nguyên nương án mà giảng đạo
       hoài hoài.

99   Then households may prosper or die out: fathers and sons need not
          defend them!
      Countries may be in order or in chaos: lords and officials need not care!

100   Nevertheless, they speak of humaneness and speak of propriety,
      Speak of human nature and speak of human affections.

101   A worldly person who is greedy for Heaven will do good;
      If he is afraid of Hell he gets rid of bad habits.

102   Ten thousand generations making offerings;
      That is the cultivation of middling wisdom.

103   As for cultivation that is very stupid,
      There are many people of inferior wisdom.

104   Yonder like Hán Võ Ðế,
      Who was a highly illustrious man;

105   Here like Tần Thủy Hoàng,
      Who was a ferocious and cruel fellow.

106   One was greedy to cultivate the Way,
      The other dived and forded to cultivate immortality.
      They exhausted the strength of the people—all under heaven suffered

107   worry and cares;
      They spent the resources of a country—ten thousand peoples cried out
          in hardship.

108   A hundred strategies for religious cultivation, there were,
      But even a tiny hair of benevolence or sympathy, there was not.

109   In the land of Luân Ðài, did Hán not have to repent his heart?
      [Only when the enemy was] at Hàm Cốc pass did Tần realize
      there were rebellious intentions.

110   Alas! Many resemble Hán;
      Many are unreasonable like Tần!

111   In what age has anyone cultivated to keep up with Tống Ðạo Quân,
      In what age is anyone esteemed to be the equal of Lương Võ Ðế?

112   Nevertheless, why did immortals not appear to give [Tống] urgent assistance?
      [When Lương] starved in Ðài Thành, why did Buddha himself not avert
          the disaster?

113   A pity about the foundational labors of establishing rivers and mountains;
      They destroyed the work that their virtuous ancestors created.

114   The army of Chu had let loose their arrows and cannons;
      Why did the ruler of Tề rely on preaching the Way endlessly?

115   Khiết Đơn đã vây phủ trong ngoài, sao Vương Khâm còn đóng cửa mà tu.

116   Hư thời đã phải, thác chẳng ai thương.

117   Hễ đạo làm đế làm vương, thì phải tu nhân tu chính;

118   Tu quyền, tu bính; tu kỷ, tu cương.

119   Trên, thì tu Nghiêu, Thuấn, Võ, Thang; dưới, thì tu kinh luân thao lược.

120   Có đâu bắt chước thầy sãi mà tu.

121   Luận việc tu cho luyện đặng phép mầu, suy trị đạo ích chi trong nước.

122   Mấy ai cho đặng phúc, hay toàn những mang tai.

123   Hãy còn mê đạo hoài hoài, tu làm sao cho phải đạo tu?

Vãi rằng:

124   Ngỡ là ông Sãi, biết một đạo tu.

125   Ai giả dè đứa ngu, mới hay là bợm lịch.

126   Khôn ngoan trong sạch, chữ nghĩa từ hoà.

127   Hẳn vàng nọ chưa pha; thiệt ngọc kia còn ẩn

128   Chẳng kiêu, chẳng lận; biết kính, biết nhường.

129   Biết tiểu nhân cỏ rác thì dẫy dùng, biết quân tử ngọc vàng mà yêu chuộng;

130   Biết khinh, biết trọng; biết của, biết người.

131   Chẳng hay ông có biết chuyện đời, nói nghe chơi cũng khá.

115 The Khitan had already encircled them inside and outside;
Why did Vương Khâm still advocate closing the door to cultivate?

116 [Dynasties] decayed: their time was up;
[Leaders] died: nobody mourned them.

117 As for the way to be an emperor or a king,
Cultivate humaneness and cultivate administration;

118 Cultivate power and cultivate influence,
Cultivate laws and cultivate principles.

119 First cultivate to be like Nghiêu and Thuấn and Vũ and Thang;
Then cultivate the classic books, moral laws, tactics, and strategy.

120 Where does anyone imitate masters and monks in order to cultivate?

121 Consider the matter of cultivation to hone magic and obtain miracles;
Ponder that way of governing, what benefit has it for the country?

122 How many people have really received blessings?
Know that all [those ways] brought disaster.

123 Always mesmerized with the way endlessly;
How is that practicing correct techniques of cultivation?

[Section 5] The nun says:

124 I had mistakenly thought that you, sir,
Knew to cultivate in only one way.

125 Who could have known that this foolish fellow
Was really a smart and polite person.

126 You are sagacious and uncontaminated,
You care about knowledge and love harmony.

127 Certainly, there is gold there that is not yet alloyed;
Truly, there is jade there that is still hidden.

128 You are not arrogant and not deceitful;
You know reverence and know deference.

129 You know that a petty man is like weed or rubbish so you throw
him out;
You know that a gentleman is like jade and gold so you cherish him.

130 You know what to despise and what to respect;
You know what is one's own and what belongs to others.

131 If, by chance, you know stories of the times,
Speak and I will listen, it is enjoyable and also good.

Sãi rằng:

132   Vãi nầy cũng lạ, chớ nói mà sầu.

133   Uổng năm dây đàn gẩy tai trâu; hoài muôn hộc nước xao đầu vịt.

134   Sãi không có biết, Sãi chẳng có hay.

135   Ghé cho khỏi cánh tay, kẻo mà xuông nhằm vú.

Vãi rằng:

136   Ông nầy thất lễ, vả lại bạc tình.

137   Ông thấy Vãi đi tu hành, ông tưởng Vãi chẳng thông thời sự.

138   Đã hay rằng nam tử, thì có chí kinh luân;

139   Song le đấng phụ nhân, cũng ghe tài tế thế.

140   Kìa như Chu Thái Tự, kinh còn khen đức rạng khuê môn.

141   Nọ như Tống Tuyên Nhân, sử còn ngợi nữ trúng Nghiêu, Thuấn.

142   Gái như Tạ Đạo Uẩn, gái mà hay vịnh tuyết nên thơ;

143   Gái như Thái Văn Cơ, gái mà biết ngâm cầm nên khúc.

144   Mưu cứu chúa khỏi nơi dật dục, chẳng là Đường Huệ thứ phi.

145   Sách cứu cha khỏi chốn nạn nguy, chẳng là Hán Đề Oanh thiếu nữ.

146   Nam tử nhiều trang nam tử; phụ nhân ghe đấng phụ nhân.

147   Thuyền bách trôi ngàn dặm hãy có có; sách Hán để muôn năm còn vặc vặc.

The monk says:

132 This nun is somewhat strange;
Don't speak, you make me miserable.

133 To waste a five-stringed instrument on the ear of a buffalo;
To waste ten thousand measures of water washing the head of a duck.

134 I know nothing, I discern nothing.

135 Lean in, but avoid my arm,
Or else I might inadvertently touch your breasts.

The nun says:

136 This mister lacks manners,
And moreover is unfeeling.

137 You see that I have chosen a religious life,
And you think that I do not understand the affairs of the times.

138 We already know that men
Have the ambition for administration.

139 However, illustrious women
Also have many talents to assist the world.

140 Yonder like Chu Thái Tự,
Whom the classics still praise for her virtue that shone beyond the women's
quarters.

141 There like Tống Tuyên Nhân,
Whom history still praises as a woman who attained the level of Nghiêu
and Thuấn.

142 A woman like Tạ Đạo Uẩn,
A woman who could chant about snow to make poetry.

143 A woman like Thái Văn Cơ,
A woman who could sing with her lute to make airs.

144 As for the scheme to help her lord abandon idleness and desire,
It is attributed to no one but Đường Huệ, the second-rank consort.

145 As for the plan to help her father escape danger,
It is attributed to no one but Hán Đề Oánh, the young girl.

146 Among men, there are many who are heroic men;
Among women, there are many who are heroic women.

147 A cypress boat drifts for a thousand miles and still goes on;
Hán books left aside for ten thousand years still remain bright.

148   Gái mà có tài có sắc; gái mà có đức có công.

149   Thuyền quyên đâu kém anh hùng; ông Sãi nỡ phụ chi mụ Vãi.

Sãi rằng:

150   Thậm phải! Thậm phải! Mừng thay, mừng thay!

151   Khát hạn nọ trông mây; ôm cầm đã gặp khách.

152   Chẳng cây cứng sao hay búa sắc; biết ngựa hay vì bời đường dài.

153   Vậy thì vén mây mù, rẽ chông gai, cho Vãi thấy trời xanh, tìm đường cả.

154   Hiếm chi chuyện lạ; hết mấy điều kỳ.

155   Kề tai lại mà nghe, ghé vú ra kẻo đụng.

156   Sãi muốn nói một chuyện xa xa cho gẫm, trong Kinh biên đã có xe;

157   Sãi muốn nói một chuyện gần gần mà nghe, trong truyện chép để nên chất.

158   Truyện Hán, truyện Đường, truyện Tống; truyện Thương, truyện Hạ, truyện Chu.

159   Chuyện phụ tử làm đầu; chuyện quân thần rất hệ.

160   Sãi muốn nói một chuyện: "Quân sử thần dĩ lễ," Sãi lại e Tần, Hán phiền lòng;

161   Sãi muốn nói một chuyện: "Thần sự quân dĩ trung," Sãi lại sợ Mãng, Tào sinh oán.

162   Sãi muốn nói một chuyện: "Vi phụ chỉ ư từ" cho Vãi ngó, Sãi lại e ông Cổ Tẩu dức rằng nghê;

163   Sãi muốn nói một chuyện: "Vi tử chỉ ư hiếu" cho Vãi hay, Sãi lại e Tùy Dương chê rằng ngô.

164   Sãi muốn nói một chuyện: "Vi nhân bất phú," Sãi lại e ông Nhan Tử mắng rằng: ai mở miệng mà tiến ơn.

148   There are women who have talent and who have beauty,
       Women who have virtue and who have merit.

149   Beautiful women are not inferior to heroic men;
       How could you, Mr. Monk, have the heart to bully me, a nun!

[Section 6] The monk says:

150   Very true, very true!
       How wonderful, how wonderful!

151   It's like seeing clouds when one is thirsty in a drought;
       Or like meeting an audience while one is holding a lute!

152   If the tree is not hard, how does one know the axe is sharp?
       One knows a good horse by means of a long road.

153   Therefore I will roll away the clouds and fog, clear away the spikes and thorns;
       So that you can see a blue sky and find the main road.

154   I do not lack strange tales,
       All the unusual things.

155   Bring your ear close so as to listen,
       But do move your breasts apart in case I bump against them.

156   I want to tell a story from a long time ago for you to ponder;
       That is in the recorded classics and already transmitted.

157   I want to speak of a recent story for you to listen to;
       That is in jotted-down tales to make up a stack.

158   Tales of Hán, tales of Đường, tales of Tống,
       Tales of Thương, tales of Hạ, tales of Chu.

159   Stories in which the relationship between fathers and sons is of first priority;
       Stories in which the relationship between lords and officials is of utmost
          importance.

160   I want to tell a story: "The lord employs his officials according to rituals";
       But I am afraid that Tần and Hán would be irritated.

161   I want to tell a story: "An official devotes himself to his lord with loyalty";
       But I am afraid that Mãng and Tào would be resentful.

162   I want to tell a story: "To be a father is to be compassionate" so you learn;
       But I am afraid that Mr. Cổ Tẩu would decry this idea as naive.

163   I want to tell a story: "To be a son is to have filial piety" so you know;
       But I am afraid that Tùy Dương would criticize it as doltish.

164   I want to tell a story: "To be humane is to be without wealth";
       But I am afraid that Mr. Nhan Tử would scold, saying:
       "Anyone who opens his mouth is just currying favor."

165 Sãi lại muốn nói một chuyện: "Vi phú bất nhân," Sãi lại e Thạch Sùng thêm mắng: khéo thổi lông mà tìm vết.

166 Sãi muốn nói một chuyện: "Tài tụ tắc dân tán" cho Vãi biết, thì Thương làm sao cho nên mất mà phải bày;

167 Sãi muốn nói một chuyện: "Tài tán tắc dân tụ" cho Vãi hay, thì Chu làm sao nên hưng mà lại thuyết.

168 Việc Vãi thì Vãi biết, việc Sãi thì Sãi hay;

169 Gắng công phu tu luyện cho lâu ngày, khi thanh vắng Sãi nói cùng một chuyện.

Vãi rằng:

170 Ông nầy tu luyện, có chí anh hùng;

171 Độc sử kinh chứa để đã đầy lòng; mang y bát chân truyền đã phải mặt.

172 Dầu chẳng "vạn gia sinh Phật", cũng là "nhất Lộ phúc tinh".

173 Thời chưa nên, sao ông còn chờ đợi công danh; vận chưa gặp, sao ông hãy khoe khoang thanh giá.

Sãi rằng:

174 Chứ phụ nhân nan hoá, mụ vãi biết là đâu?

175 Câu bên sông, Lữ còn chờ đợi công hầu; cày dưới nội, Doãn hãy mơ màng Nghiêu Thuấn;

176 Bất tri nhi bất uẩn, hữu đức tất hữu lân.

177 Sớm Cam La cũng đội đầu cân; muộn Khương Tử ghe phen cầu tướng.

178 Nhân vì Sãi hay nói quanh, Sãi mang một bịnh thất tình.

165   I want to tell a story: "To be wealthy is to lack human-heartedness";
But I am afraid that Thạch Sùng would heap reproach, saying:
   "Why be so clever at splitting hairs to find fault?"

166   I want to tell a story: "When wealth accumulates, the population scatters"
   for you to know;
Then the reason the Thương dynasty was lost must be revealed.

167   I want to tell a story: "When wealth scatters, the population gathers"
   for you to grasp;
Then the reason the Chu dynasty arose must be declared.

168   As for the affairs of a nun, you know them;
As for the affairs of a monk, I know them.

169   Let's labor and practice for a very long time;
And when it is quiet and deserted, I will finish telling you a story.

[Section 7] The nun says:

170   You, mister, cultivate and train;
You have the ambition to be a hero!
As a reader of history and classics, you retain them until your heart is
171   filled;
As a bearer of the robe and bowl, the true transmission has surely surfaced.

172   If you are not to be "The living Buddha of the ten thousand households,"
Then surely you will be the "One in Lộ who seeks the fortune star."

173   Your fate is yet to be realized; why are you just waiting around for a title?
Your destiny is yet to be fulfilled; why are you still boasting of your fame?

The monk says:

174   It has been written, "Women are hard to teach";
What, oh nun, do you really know?

175   With a hook beside the river, Lã waited for the nobles;
Plowing in the plains, Doãn dreamt of Nghiêu and Thuấn.

176   I may not be known, but I'm not indignant;
For those with virtue will surely have neighbors.

177   In youth, Cam La wore an official's headwrap;
Late in life, Khương Tử time and again sought generalship.

178   Because I am skilled at talking in a round-about fashion,
I carry an illness of seven emotions.

179 Thành ư trung vị đắc hòa bình, hình tại ngoại bất năng trung tiết.

180 Tu dầu lòng chí thiết, Sãi có bịnh hay vui.

181 Sãi vui dưới đất dài, Sãi vui trên trời rộng.

182 Vui nước biếc non xanh lộng lộng; vui trăng thanh rạng rõ ngời ngời.

183 Trong ba ngàn, Sãi chứa để một bầu; ngoài sáu đạo, Sãi trải thông tam giới.

184 Non Bồng Lai bước tới, Sãi vui với Bát Tiên;

185 Cảnh Sơn Nhạc tìm lên, Sãi vui cùng Tứ Hạo.

186 Vui nhân vui đạo, vui thánh vui hiền.

187 Vui tiếng chuông giục khách lui thuyền; vui chiếc dép buồm trương nương gió.

188 Ngăn thói tục, Sãi vui dòng Bát Nhã; rửa màu trần, Sãi vui nước Ma Ha.

189 Đạo thương người, Sãi vui giáo Thích Ca; nhân cứu chúng, Sãi vui lòng Bồ Tát.

190 Vui một bình, một bát; vui một đạo, một hề.

191 Luận sự vui cho ngỏa cho nguê, chi bằng Sãi vui cùng mụ Vãi?

192 Sãi lại có một bịnh hay thương.

193 Sãi thương thuở Tam Hoàng; Sãi thương đời Ngũ Đế.

194 Thương vì nhân vì nghĩa; thương vì đức vì tài.

195 Thương vua Nghiêu áo bả quần gai; thương vua Thuấn cày mây cuốc nguyệt.

179 When true feelings within are not yet tempered and calm,
   Its manifestation without cannot be centered and moderate.

180 Though I cultivate with an ardent heart,
   I have the illness of excessive happiness.

181 I am happy because, below, there is the broad ground;
   I am happy because, above, there are the expansive heavens.

182 Happy with the blue waters and green mountains, splendid, splendid;
   Happy with the clear and radiant moon, dazzling, dazzling.

183 Internally, [as for the] three thousand, I keep them in a gourd;
   Externally, [as for the] six ways, I penetrate and understand the three worlds.

184 Toward Bồng Lai Mountain, I step forward;
   I am happy together with the eight immortals.

185 For the scenery of Sơn Nhạc, I go up in search;
   I am happy together with the four hoary heads.

186 Happy with humaneness and with the way;
   Happy with sages, happy with worthies.

187 Happy with the bell's ringing, urging pilgrims as they depart in their boats;
   Happy with the sandal, spreading out its sail against the wind.

188 For blocking out vulgar customs, I am happy with the course of Prajña;
   For washing away the dust, I am happy with the waters of Ma Ha.

189 For its way of compassion for people, I am happy with the teachings of
   the Buddha;
   For his humaneness to save mankind, I am happy to call on the Bodhisattva.

190 I am happy with one bottle and one bowl;
   I am happy with one Way and one servant.

191 Discussing happy matters for a splendid time;
   Why don't I be happy together with you?

192 I, moreover, have an illness of frequent compassion.

193 I have compassion for the period of the Three Sovereigns;
   I have compassion for the age of the Five Rulers.

194 I have compassion for humaneness and for righteousness,
   Compassion for virtue and for talent.

195 I have compassion for King Nghiêu, who wore a coarse shirt and
   hemp trousers;
   I have compassion for King Thuấn, who plowed in the clouds and hoed
   by moonlight.

196   Ăn cơm hẩm hút, thương vua Võ, thương càng chí thiết; chịu lao tù, Sãi thương một vua Văn, thương rất xót xa.

197   Thương cho ông Chu Công, trung đã nên trung mà mắc tiếng gièm pha; thương đức Phu Tử, thánh đà nên thánh hãy ghe phen hoạn nạn.

198   Thương mấy kẻ mưu thần nhà Hán, vô sự mà thác oan; thương mấy người văn học đời Tần, vô can mà chôn sống.

199   Thương Gia Cát đã nên tôi lương đống, gặp chúa chẳng phải thời;

200   Thương Nhạc Phi đã nên tướng ân oai, lâm nguy mà bị hại.

201   Thương đi thương lại, thương chẳng hay cùng.

202   Ngồi đêm đông, thì thương người nằm giá khóc măng; lên ải Bắc, thì thương kẻ chăn dê uống tuyết.

203   Thương càng chí thiết, thương rất nỗi thương.

204   Thương cho khắp bốn phương, rồi lại thương mụ Vãi.

205   Sãi lại có một bịnh hay ghét.

206   Sãi ghét Kiệt, ghét Trụ; Sãi hay ghét Lệ, ghét U.

207   Sãi ghét nhân chính chẳng tu, khiến nước nhà đều mất.

208   Suy lộng ghét cho quá rất, thì Sãi ghét đứa bội phụ, bội quân.

209   Sãi hay ghét cho quá mười phần, thì Sãi ghét đứa đại gian đại ác.

210   Ghét ngang ghét ngược; ghét lạ ghét lùng.

196   For eating mean fare, I have compassion for King Võ—my compassion is
        increasingly intense;
      For suffering imprisonment, I have utmost compassion for King Văn—
        my compassion is burningly painful.

197   I have compassion for the Duke of Chu, whose loyalty was the ideal of
        loyalty yet was trapped by slanderous talk;
      I have compassion for Confucius, a sage who had already become a sage,
        yet time and again faced adversity.

198   Compassion for the strategizing advisers of Hán, who, for no good reason,
        died unjustly;
      Compassion for the scholars of Tần, who did nothing wrong but
        were buried alive.

199   I have compassion for Gia Cát, who was a pillar of the state
      but met his lord at an inopportune time.

200   I have compassion for Nhạc Phi, who was an imposing general
      but was imperiled and suffered harm.

201   I have compassion here and compassion there;
      My compassion knows no end.

202   Because he sat out in the winter night, I have compassion for the person
        who lay on the ice and cried for bamboo;
      For being on the northern pass, I have compassion for the fellow who herded
        rams and drank snow.

203   My compassion is increasingly intense;
      My compassion is very sentimental.

204   I have compassion for all the four quarters;
      And I have compassion for you.

205   I, furthermore, have an illness of knowing hate.
206   I hate King Kiệt and King Trụ;
      I really hate King Lệ and King U.

207   I hate when humane governance is not practiced,
      Causing all dynasties to perish.

208   Pushing my hatred to its extreme—
      I hate a fellow who betrays his father, betrays his lord.

209   I frequently hate in excess of ten parts;
      I hate those who are very wicked and very cruel.

210   I hate the crude and hate the oppressive;
      I hate the peculiar and hate the odd.

211 Đọc Ngu trong, thì Sãi ghét đảng Tứ hung; xem Tống Sử, thì Sãi ghét bầy Ngũ quỷ.

212 Ghét hoài, ghét huỷ; ghét ngọt, ghét ngon.

213 Ghét đứa gian cầu mị mà giết con, ghét đảng nịnh tham giàu mà hại vợ.

214 Uốn lưỡi vạy, Sãi ghét người nước Sở; dạ tham lương, Sãi ghét kẻ nước Tề.

215 Ghét đứa gian nương cậy thế cậy thời, ghét đứa dữ hại nhà khuấy nước.

216 Sãi ghét đứa thấy lợi mà chạy xuôi chạy ngược; ghét thấy nghĩa mà lo thiệt lo hơn.

217 Sãi ghét người ích kỷ hại nhân; Sãi ghét đứa gian phu dâm phụ.

218 Ghét đứa hay co hay cú; ghét người chẳng thật chẳng thà.

219 Ấy là ghét người ta; sau lại ghét mụ Vãi, sao có vô tình cùng Sãi?

220 Sãi lại có bịnh hay yêu.

221 Sãi chẳng yêu tà; Sãi hay yêu chính.

222 Luận trong thiên tính, chi bằng yêu thân?

223 Như luận lẽ chí chân, chót sau thì yêu vật.

224 Yêu chí thiết, yêu người hiền ngỗ; yêu mặn nồng, yêu kẻ trung thành.

225 Yêu trượng phu mở lượng rộng thanh thanh; yêu quân tử trống lòng không bối rối.

226 Yêu gan nặng, mài mà chẳng mỏng; yêu lòng son, nhuộm mà chẳng đen.

227 Yêu lỗ tai, lời trung chính nghe quen; yêu con mắt, sự cổ kim soi tỏ.

211 Reading about Ngu, I hate the four brutish clans;
     Perusing Tống histories, I hate the band of five devils.

212 I hate carnage and hate destruction;
     I hate the cloying and the saccharine.

213 I hate the wicked fellow so ready to fawn he killed his son,
     Hate the flatterer so greedy for wealth he harmed his wife.

214 For curled tongues bent crooked, I hate the people of the state of Sở;
     For stomachs greedy to be filled, I hate the people of the state of Tề.

215 I hate a dishonest fellow who presumes upon power and opportunity;
     I hate a violent fellow who harms his household and stirs up his country.

216 I hate a fellow who, seeing [a chance for] benefit, races upstream and
     downstream;
     I hate a fellow who sees [a chance for] righteousness but worries about loss
     and gain.

217 I hate people who are selfish and harm others;
     I hate adulterers and adulteresses;

218 I hate fellows who are querulous and quarrelsome;
     I hate people who are untruthful and dishonest.

219 That is to hate everyone,
     and then furthermore to hate you, that you should have no feelings
     for me.

220 I, moreover, have an illness of excessive love.

221 I do not love the wicked;
     I love to love the upright.

222 In considering one's heaven-given disposition,
     What is equal to loving one's family?

223 Taking [Buddhist] logic in its truest form,
     The last priority is to love physical substance.

224 I love profoundly—love the person who is wise and worthy;
     I love intensely—love the fellow who is loyal and steadfast.

225 I love the man who is expansively open and generous,
     Love the gentleman whose disinterested heart is never troubled.

226 I love strong courage that is not worn down when ground,
     Love a vermilion heart that does not turn black when dyed.

227 I love ears that are familiar with hearing loyal and upright words,
     Love eyes that see clearly the affairs of past and present times.

228 Năm lạnh lẽo, thì Sãi yêu bách tòng đồ sộ; dặm xa xuôi, thì Sãi yêu kì kí sỏi sành.

229 Con thảo cha, thì Sãi yêu bằng ngọc bằng vàng; tôi ngay chúa, Sãi yêu bằng châu bằng báu.

230 Luận như yêu đạo, thì Sãi yêu đạo trung dung; luận như yêu lòng, thì Sãi yêu lòng nhân nghĩa.

231 Yêu mà nhà lợi, nước lợi, thiên hạ lợi, chi bằng yêu hiền?

232 Yêu mà tài nên, đức nên, phú quý nên, chi bằng yêu sĩ?

233 Yêu người trí tuệ, yêu kẻ tài năng.

234 Như yêu sự lăng quăng, chi bằng yêu mụ Vãi?

235 Sãi lại có một bịnh hay giận.

236 Sãi hay giận thật, Sãi chẳng giận dối.

237 Sãi giận Sãi nhiều lầm nhiều lỗi; khi lỗi lầm, Sãi một giận hoài.

238 Sãi giận Sãi ít đức ít tài; tưởng tài đức, Sãi càng giận kiệt.

239 Sãi giận Sãi kinh luân chẳng biết; Sãi giận Sãi thao lược không hay.

240 Sãi giận Sãi xa quân vương uổng tấm lòng ngay; Sãi giận Sãi nghĩa cha mẹ không đền đạo thảo.

241 Tưởng trong nhân đạo; Sãi một giận căm;

242 Như suy lý cổ kim, Sãi càng thêm giận lắm.

243 Thấy Đổng Trác lung lăng trong nhà Hán, Sãi giận ngươi Hà Tiến vô mưu.

244 Thấy Khuyển Nhung phá phách trong nhà Chu, Sãi lại giận Thân Hầu thất kế.

245 Máu sục sục sôi dòng Vị Thủy, xương chan chan lấp nội Trường Thành.

228   In the wintry years, I love the imposing cypresses and pines;
      From a great distance, I love the experienced *kì* and *kí* horses.

229   If a son is devoted to his father, I love him like jade or gold;
      If a subject is upright with his lord, I love him like pearls or treasures.

230   When it comes to loving the Way—I love the doctrine of the mean;
      When it comes to loving the heart—I love a heart that is humane and proper.

231   As for love that benefits the household, country, and entire realm,
      What can compare with loving the sages?

232   As for love that brings talent, virtue, riches, and honor,
      What can compare with loving an official?

233   I love people of wisdom and intelligence,
      Love fellows of talent and ability.

234   As for loving the various things,
      What is equal to loving you?

235   I, moreover, have an illness of frequent anger.

236   I know true anger; I do not know false anger.

237   I am angry that I am often wrong and make many mistakes;
      When wrong and mistaken, I have destructive anger.

238   I am angry that I have little virtue and little talent;
      In thinking about talent and virtue, my anger increases to its utmost.

239   I am angry that I do not know about administration;
      I am angry that I do not know about military strategy;
      I am angry that I am far from my lord and king and waste a loyal

240   heart;
      I am angry that in honoring my parents I do not illuminate the way of
         filial piety.

241   In thinking about the humane way,
      I have a bitter anger.

242   When considering the past and present,
      I am increasingly angry.

243   Seeing Đổng Trác ravage the Hán dynasty,
      I am angry that Hà Tiến did not anticipate it.

244   Seeing Khuyển Nhung plunder the Chu dynasty,
      I am angry that the Marquis of Thân erred in his scheming.

245   Blood is boiling—bubbling down the waters of Vị;
      Bones are overflowing—filling up the city of Trường.

246   Giận Thương Quân hà chính mà chẳng lành, giận Bạch Khởi vô mưu rất dữ.

247   Hán dầu nghèo, sao Lữ toan ngắm nghía; Đường dầu suy, sao Võ dám lăng loàn.

248   Nếu vậy thì, Võ với Đường tội đã xấp xỉ tày Sơn; Lữ với Hán lỗi cùng rập rình tày Mãng.

249   Giận nhiều điều chướng, giận chẳng cùng.

250   Thấy Sãi già mà Vãi bỏ Vãi đi, chứ trách Sãi sao mà hay giận.

Vãi rằng:

251   Nghe qua các chuyện, ngẫm lại hữu tình.

252   Khen cho Sãi thuộc sử thuộc kinh; khen cho Sãi có tài có trí.

253   Lời ăn nói thánh hiền đạo vị; màu khoe khoang nghĩa lý tinh thông.

254   Đã tốt hành tốt ngôn, lại có thanh có sắc.

255   Lôi Âm Tự có công thì nên Phật; tới Thiên Thai tốt phúc thì thành tiên.

256   Biết đường nào thấu thấu Tây Thiên; xin chỉ bảo tu cùng khuya sớm.

Sãi rằng:

257   Vừa vừa nói bợm, bớt bớt yêu tinh.

258   Cõi Thiên Đường, còn cách trở minh minh; chốn Phạn sát, hãy xa chừng vọi vọi.

259   Tây phương không đường tới; Bắc phương khó nẻo qua.

260   Đường Nam phương thì đó chẳng xa, thì những sợ nhiều quân Đá Vách.

261   Nói thì lạc phách, nghĩ lại kinh hồn.

262   Nọ chém người như chém chuối; nọ đốn chúng cũng thường.

246   I am angry that Thương Quân was tyrannical and not gentle;
      I am angry that Bạch Khởi was incompetent and very cruel.

247   Hán was imperiled, why did [Empress] Lữ plot and covet?
      Đường was weakened, how dare [Empress] Võ be saucy!

248   In this case, [Empress] Võ's crime against Đường resounds like that of Sơn.
      [Empress] Lữ's guilt toward Hán reverberates like that of Mãng.

249   I am angry at the many offensive matters;
      My anger knows no end.

250   Seeing that I am old, you abandon me and go;
      Don't blame me for being frequently angry.

[Section 8] The nun says:

251   Having listened to the stories,
      I now think that they are charming.

252   Commendations to you for knowing the histories and classics by heart;
      Commendations to you for having talent and knowledge.

253   Your speech has the flavor of the moral truth of gentle sages;
      Your appearance shows off your proficiency in the principles of righteousness.

254   Already exceptional in action and speech,
      You moreover have fame and beauty.

255   At Thunderclap Temple, if one has merit one becomes a Buddha;
      On reaching Thiên Thai, if one is fortunate one becomes an immortal.

256   If you know of any road to penetrate the Western Heaven,
      Please instruct me and cultivate with me all night and day.

The monk says:

257   Moderate the crazy talk;
      Diminish this monster within!

258   The heavenly region is still so far beyond—it's very dim;
      The sacred temple is yet so far away—so very distant.

259   As for the western direction, there is no road to reach it;
      As for the northern direction, the way is very hard;

260   As for the southern direction, it is not very far;
      It's nothing but for the fear of the many bands of Đá Vách.

261   If I speak of them, I lose my soul;
      When I think of them, my spirit is terrified.

262   They cut down people like they do bananas;
      They ambush us with impunity.

263   Đến đâu thì tảo tận; nọ bắt giết tươi.

264   Đã vào làng cướp của hại người; lại xuống nội đuổi trâu bắt ngựa.

265   Hãy tu đây cho rớ; chớ qua đó làm gì?

266   Đừng đi quàng mà bắt Vãi đi, lại bỏ Sãi mồ côi mồ cút.

       Vãi rằng:
267   Trong kinh có thuyết: "Nhung Địch thị ưng."

268   Ai chịu quyền, ủy ký một mệnh.

269   Xin dẹp đảng loài hung kẻo tệ.

270   Nay thơ.

263   Everywhere they go they sweep through thoroughly;
       They capture and kill instantly.
264   They enter villages to loot property and harm people,
       Then descend into fields to chase after buffalos and capture horses.

265   For now let's cultivate here to the point of exhaustion;
       Why should we cross over there?
266   Do not go wandering off or they will capture and take you away,
       Then I'll be left alone, like an orphan.

       The nun says:

267   In the classics there is a saying:
       "Smite the barbarians."
268   Whoever is willing to respond,
       I'll entrust my life to him.

269   Please repress this ferocious band,
       Or else we'll be abused!
270   Here is poetry.

Works Cited

Primary Sources

An Nam Hà Tiên thập vinh (Ten Songs of Hà Tiên in An Nam). Comp. Mạc Thiên Tứ. École Française d'Extrême-Orient (EFEO) microfilm A.441, no. 661, n.d., 47a–49b. Echols Collection, Cornell University.

Ca văn thi phú thư truyện tạp biên 歌文詩賦書傳雜編 (A Diverse Compilation of Songs, Literature, Poems, Verses, Letters, and Stories). Viện Hán Nôm shelf no. VNv.520, n.d.

Cen Shen ji jiaozhu 岑參集校注 (Collected Works of Cen Shen, with Commentary). Ed. Chen Tiemin 陳鐵民 and Hou Zhongyi 侯忠義. Shanghai: Shanghai guji chubanshe, 2004.

Chuci buzhu 楚辭補注 (Supplementary Commentary to the *Chuci*). 17 *juan*. Hong Xingzu 洪興祖 (1070–1135). Ed. and comm. Bai Huawen 白化文 et al. coll. and punc. Beijing: Zhonghua shuju, 1983.

Đại Nam Liệt Truyện Tiền Biên 大南列傳前編 (Biographies of the Great South, Premier Period). Comp. Quốc Sử Quán Triều Nguyễn (Nguyễn Dynasty Historical Institute). Tokyo: Keio Institute of Linguistic Studies, Mita, Siba, Minato-ku, 1961.

Đại Nam Thực Lục Tiền Biên 大南寔錄前編 (Veritable Records of the Great South). Comp. Quốc Sử Quán Triều Nguyễn (Nguyễn Dynasty Historical Institute). Tokyo: Keio Institute of Linguistic Studies, Mita, Siba, Minato-ku, 1961.

Dijian tushuo 帝鑒圖説 (The Emperor's Mirror, Illustrated and Discussed). Comp. Zhang Juzheng 張居正 (1525–1582). In *Siku quanshu cunmu congshu* 四庫全書存目叢書. Jinan: Qi Lu shushe chubanshe, 1996.

Guanzi 管子 (Master Guan). Comm. Fang Xuan Ling 房玄齡 (579–648). In *Sibu beiyao*. Reprint, Taipei: Zhonghua shuju, 1981.

Han Feizi 韓非子 (Master Han Fei). In *Sibu beiyao*. Reprint, Taipei: Zhonghua shuju, 1981.

Han shu 漢書 (History of the Former Han). Comp. Ban Gu 班固 (32–92 CE). Reprint, Beijing: Zhonghua Shuju, 1964.

Hou Han shu 後漢書 (History of the Later Han). Comp. Fan Ye 范曄 (398–446). Reprint, Beijing: Zhonghua shuju, 1973.

Huainanzi 淮南子 (The Masters of Huainan). Comm. Gao You 高誘 (fl. 205–212). In *Sibu beiyao*. Reprint, Taipei: Zhonghua shuju, 1981.

Jia Yi 賈誼 (ca. 200–169 BCE). *Xinshu* 新書 (New Writings). In *Sibu beiyao*. Reprint, Taipei: Zhonghua shuju, 1981.

Jin shu 晉書 (History of the Jin). Comp. Fang Xuanling 房玄齡 (579–648) et al. Beijing: Zhonghua shuju, 1974.

Jiu Tang shu 舊唐書 (Old Book of Tang). Comp. Liu Xu 劉昫 (888–947) et al. Beijing: Zhonghua shuju, 1975.

Laozi Dao De jing 老子道德經. Comm. Wang Bi 王弼 (226–249). In *Sibu beiyao*. Reprint, Taipei: Zhonghua shuju, 1981.

Lê Quý Đôn. *Kiến Văn Tiểu Lục* (A Small Record of Things Seen and Heard). Trans. (into modern Vietnamese) Nguyễn Khắc Thuần. Hà Nội: Giáo Dục, 2009.

———. *Phủ Biên Tạp Lục* (Frontier Chronicles), parts 1 and 2. Trans. (into modern Vietnamese) Nguyễn Khắc Thuần. Hà Nội: Giáo Dục, 2008.

Liji 禮記 (Book of Rites). Comm. Zheng Xuan 鄭玄 (127–200). In *Sibu beiyao*. Reprint, Taipei: Zhonghua shuju, 1981.

Lienü zhuan 列女傳 (Biographies of Exemplary Women). Comp. Liu Xiang 劉向 (77–6 BCE). In *Sibu beiyao*. Reprint, Taipei: Zhonghua shuju, 1981.

Liu Xie 劉勰 (ca. 465–ca. 522). *Wenxin diaolong* 文心雕龍. Ed. and comm. Zhou Zhenfu 周振甫. *Wenxin diaolong zhushi* 文心雕龍注釋. Taipei: Liren shuju, 1984.

Lu Qinli 逯欽立. Ed. and comm. *Tao Yuanming ji* 陶淵明集 (Collected Works of Tao Yuanming). Beijing: Zhonghua shuju, 1983.

Lun yu 論語. Ed. and comm. He Yan 何晏 (d. 249). In *Sibu beiyao*. Reprint, Taipei: Zhonghua shuju, 1981.

Mengzi 孟子趙注 (Mencius). Comm. Zhao Qi 趙岐 (d. 201). In *Sibu beiyao*. Reprint, Taipei: Zhonghua shuju, 1981.

Mingru xue'an 明儒學案 (Record of Ming Confucians). Comp. Huang Zongxi 黃宗羲. In *Sibu beiyao*. Reprint, Taipei: Zhonghua shuju, 1981.

Pan Dinggui 潘鼎珪. *Annan jiyou* 安南記遊 (Travel Record of Annan). *Congshu jicheng xinbian* 叢書集成新編 ed. Taipei: Xinwenfeng chuban gongsi, 1984.

Qingchao wenxian tongkao 清朝文獻通考 (Comprehensive Investigations of the Documents of the Qing Dynasty). Hangzhou: Zhejiang guji chubanshe, 2000.

Quan Song ci 全宋詞 (Complete *Ci* Poetry of the Song). Ed. and comp. Tang Guizhang 唐圭璋 (1901–1990). Reprint, Beijing: Zhonghua shuju, 1992.

Quan Tang shi 全唐詩 (Complete *Shi* Poetry of the Tang). Comp. and ed. Peng Dingqiu 彭定求 (1645–1719) et al. Reprint, Beijing: Zhonghua shuju, 1960.

Quốc văn tùng kí 國文叢記 (Collected Recordings of National Literature). Comp. Hải Châu Tử. Viện Hán Nôm shelf no. AB.383, n.d.

Sāi Vāi thư tập (A Monk and a Nun). Ed. Duy Minh Thị 惟明氏. Guangdong: Jinyu lou, 1874.

Sanguo zhi 三國志 (Records of the Three Kingdoms). Comp. Chen Shou 陳壽 (233–297), with official commentary by Pei Songzhi 裴松之 (372–451). Beijing: Zhonghua shuju, 1959.

Shangshu 尚書 (Book of Documents). In *Sibu beiyao*. Reprint, Taipei: Zhonghua shuju, 1981.

Shanhai jing jianshu 山海經箋疏 (Guideways through Mountains and Seas with Supplmentary Commentary). Comm. Guo Pu 郭璞 (276–324). Ed. Hao Yixing 郝懿行 (1757–1825). In *Sibu beiyao*. Reprint, Taipei: Zhonghua shuju, 1981.

Shiji 史記 (Records of the Historian). Comp. Sima Qian 司馬遷 (145–ca. 86 BCE). Reprint, Beijing: Zhonghua shuju, 2013.

Shiji jijie 史記集解 (Collected Explanations of the *Shiji*). Comp. Pei Yin 裴駰 (Song dynasty?). *Jingyin Wenyuan ge siku quanshu* 景印文淵閣四庫全书 ed. Taipei: Taiwan shangwu yinshuguan, 1983.

Shijing 詩經 (Book of Songs). *Maoshi zhengyi* 毛詩正義 (Correct Meanings of the Mao Text of the Book of Songs). Comm. Kong Yida 孔穎達 (574–648). In *Shisanjing zhushu* 十三經注疏 (Commentary on the Thirteen Classics). Ed. Ruan Yuan 阮元 (1764–1849). Reprint, Beijing: Zhonghua shuju, 1980.

Shui jing zhu 水經注 (Commentary on the Water Classic). Ed. Li Daoyuan 酈道元 (d. 527). Reprint, Shanghai: Shangwu yinshuguan, 1936.

Sibu beiyao 四部備要 (Essentials of the Four Branches of Literature). Reprint, Taipei: Zhonghua shuju, 1981.

Song shi 宋史 (History of Song). Comp. Toqto'a (Chinese transcription 脱脱, 1314–56) et al. Beijing: Zhonghua shuju, 1977.

Trịnh Hoài Đức. *Gia Định Thành Thông Chí* (Gia Định Gazetteer). Trans. (into modern Vietnamese) Lý Việt Dũng and Huỳnh Văn Tới. Ho Chi Minh City: Tổng Hợp Đồng Nai, 2006.

Wang Shumin 王叔岷, ed. and comm. *Zhuangzi jiaoquan* 莊子校詮 (A Collated Commentary on *Zhuangzi*). Reprint, Taipei: Zhongyang yanjiuyuan lishi yuyuan yanjiusuo, 1999.

Wei shu 魏書 (History of the Wei). Comp. Wei Shou 魏收 (505–572) et al. Beijing: Zhonghua shuju, 1974.

Wen xuan 文選 (Selections of Literature). Comp. Xiao Tong 蕭統 (501–531). Comm. Li Shan 李善 (d. 689). Beijing: Zhonghua shuju, 2005.

Wu Cheng'en 吳承恩. *Xiyou ji* 西遊記 (Journey to the West). Comm. Li Zhuowu 李卓吾. Shanghai: Shanghai guji chubanshe, 1994,

Wu Zaiqing 吳在慶, ed. *Du Mu ji xinian jiaozhu* 杜牧集繫年校注 (Collected Works of Du Mu, Chronologically Arranged with Commentary). 4 vols. Reprint, Beijing: Zhonghua shuju, 2008

Xin Tang shu 新唐書 (New Book of Tang). Comp. Ouyang Xiu 歐陽修 (1007–1072) and Song Qi 宋祁 (998–1061) et al. Beijing: Zhonghua shuju, 1975.

Yang Bojun 楊伯峻. *Chunqiu Zuozhuan zhu* 春秋左傳注 (Zuo Tradition of the Spring and Autumn Annals, with Annotations). 4 vols. Reprint, Beijing: Zhonghua shuju, 1983.

Yi jing 易經 (Book of Changes). *Zhou yi* 周易. Comm. Wang Bi 王弼 (226–249). In *Sibu beiyao*. Reprint, Taipei: Zhonghua shuju, 1981.

Yiwen leiju 藝文類聚 (Anthology of Literary Excerpts Arranged by Categories). Comp. Ouyang Xun 歐陽詢 (557–641). Reprint, Shanghai: Shanghai guji chubanshe, 1982.

Yutai xinyong 玉台新咏 (New Songs from the Jade Terrace). Comp. Xu Ling 徐陵 (507–583). Commentary by Wu Zhaoyi 吴兆宜 (fl. 1672). In *Sibu beiyao*. Reprint, Taipei: Zhonghua shuju, 1981.

Zhanguo ce 戰國策 (Intrigues of the Warring States). Comm. Gao You 高诱. In *Sibu beiyao*. Reprint, Taipei: Zhonghua shuju, 1981.

Zhu Guozhen 朱國 (1557–1632), *Yongzhuang xiaopin* 湧幢小品 (An Unworthy Work from Yongzhuang). Beijing: Zhonghua shuju, 1959.

Zizhi tongjian 資治通鑑 (Comprehensive Mirror in Aid of Governance). 10 vols. Comp. Sima Guang 司馬光 (1019–1086 CE) et al. Reprint, Beijing: Zhonghua shuju, 2005.

Secondary Sources and Translations

Allen, Sarah. "The Identities of Taigong Wang in Zhou and Han Literature." *Monumenta Serica* 30 (1972–73): 57–99.

Ang, Claudine. "Regionalism in Southern Narratives of Vietnamese History: The Case of the 'Southern Advance' (*Nam tiến*)." *Journal of Vietnamese Studies* 8, no. 3 (Summer 2013): 1–26.

Antony, Robert. "'Righteous Yang': Pirate, Rebel, and Hero on the Sino-Vietnamese Water Frontier, 1644–1684." *Cross-Currents: East Asian History and Culture Review* 3, no. 2 (November 2014): 319–48.

Baldanza, Kathlene. *Ming China and Vietnam: Negotiating Borders in Early Modern Asia.* Cambridge: Cambridge University Press, 2017.

Bản Quốc du Đồ 本國與图 (Our Country through Maps). S.I.: s.n., 1800. Microfilm of the original in the École Française d'Extrême-Orient. Sài Gòn: [Refilmed by] Viện Khảo Cổ, 1973.

Beckwith, Christopher. *Empires of the Silk Road: A History of Central Eurasia from the Bronze Age to the Present.* Princeton, NJ: Princeton University Press, 2009.

Berkowitz, Alan. *Patterns of Disengagement: The Practice and Portrayal of Reclusion in Early Medieval China.* Stanford, CA: Stanford University Press, 2000.

Bokenkamp, Stephen. "Taoism and Literature: The *Pi-lo* Question." *Taoist Resources* 3, no. 1 (1991): 57–72.

Borri, Christoforo. *An Account of Cochin-China.* In *Views of Seventeenth-Century Vietnam: Christoforo Borri on Cochinchina and Samuel Baron on Tonkin*, ed. Olga Dror and Keith Taylor. Ithaca, NY: Cornell University Southeast Asia Program Publications, 2006.

Boudet, Paul. "La conquete de la Cochinchine par les Nguyễn et les role des emigres chinois." *Bulletin de l'Ecole française d'Extrême-Orient* 42 (1942): 115–32.

Bourotte, Bernard. "Essai d'histoire des populations montagnardes du sud-indochinois jusqu'à 1945." *Bulletin de la Société des Etudes Indochinoises*, n.s., 30, no. 3 (1955): 215–328.

Brandon, James R. *The Cambridge Guide to Asian Theatre.* Cambridge: Cambridge University Press, 1993.

Brokaw, Cynthia. "Reading the Best-Sellers of the Nineteenth Century: Commerical Publishing in Sibao." In *Printing and Book Culture in Late Imperial China*, ed. Cynthia Brokaw and Kai-Wing Chow, 184–231. Berkeley: University of California Press, 2005.

Cadière, Léopold. "Le changement de costume sous Vo-Vuong, ou une crise religieuse à Huế au XVIIIᵉ siècle." *Bulletin des Amis du Vieux Hué* 4 (October–December 1915): 417–24.

Cai Zong-qi. "Recent-Style Shi Poetry: Pentasyllabic Verse." In *How to Read Chinese Poetry*, ed. Cai Zong-qi, 161–80. New York: Columbia University Press, 2008.

Cao Hải Đễ, trans. *Sãi Vãi.* Sài Gòn: Imprimerie Jh. Nguyễn Văn Viết, 1923.

Chan Hok-Lam. "Chinese Refugees in Annam and Champa at the End of the Sung Dynasty." *Journal of Southeast Asian History* 7, no. 2 (September 1996): 1–10.

Chen Jinghe. "Kasen Tei shi no bungaku katsudō, tokuni Kasen jūei ni tsuite" 河仙鄭氏の文学活動・特に河仙十詠に就て (On the Literary Works of the Mạc, Governor of Hà Tiên, with Special Reference to the Hà Tiên Thập Vinh). *Shigaku* 史學 (Historical Science) 40, nos. 2–3 (1967): 149–211.

———. "Mac Thien Tu and Phrayataksin: A Survey on their Political Stand, Conflicts, and Background." In *Proceedings of the Seventh IAHA Conference*, 1534–75. Bangkok: Chulalongkorn University Press, 1977.

———. "Qingchu Zheng Chenggong canbu zhi yizhi nanqi" 清初鄭成功殘部之移殖南圻 (The Migration of Zheng Partisans to South Vietnam), parts 1 and 2. *Xinya xuebao* 新亞學報 (New Asia Journal) 5, no. 1 (1960): 433–59 and 8, no. 2 (1968): 413–85.

Chéon, A., trans. "Bonze et Bonzesse: Dialogue Annamite." *Excursions et Reconnaissances* (Sài Gòn, Imprimerie Coloniale) 11, no. 25 (1886): 45–98.

Chin, James Kong. "Junk Trade between South China and Nguyen Vietnam." In *Water Frontier: Commerce and the Chinese in the Lower Mekong Region, 1750–1880*, ed. Nola Cooke and Li Tana, 53–66. Singapore: Singapore University Press and Lanham, MD: Rowman and Littlefield, 2004.

Choi Byung Wook. *Southern Vietnam under the Reign of Minh Mạng (1820–1841): Central Policies and Local Response.* Ithaca, NY: Cornell University Southeast Asia Program Publications, 2004.

Cooke, Nola. "Later-Seventeenth-Century Cham-Viet Interactions: New Light from French Missionary Sources." In *Annalen der Hamburger Vietnamistik* 4–5 (2010): 13–52

———. "Regionalism and the Nature of Nguyen Rule in Seventeenth-Century Dang Trong (Cochinchina)." *Journal of Southeast Asian Studies* 29, no. 1 (March 1998): 122–61.

———. "Strange Brew: Global, Regional, and Local Factors behind the 1690 Prohibition of Christian Practice in Nguyễn Cochinchina." *Journal of Southeast Asian Studies* 39, no. 3 (September 2008): 383–409.

Cooke, Nola, and Li Tana, eds. *Water Frontier: Commerce and the Chinese in the Lower Mekong Region, 1750–1880*. Singapore: Singapore University Press and Lanham, MD: Rowman and Littlefield, 2004.

Cooke, Nola, Li Tana, and James A. Anderson, eds. *The Tongking Gulf through History*. Philadelphia: University of Pennsylvania Press, 2011.

Crossley, Pamela Kyle, Helen F. Siu, and Donald S. Sutton, eds. *Empire at the Margins: Culture, Ethnicity, and the Frontier in Early Modern China*. Berkeley: University of California Press, 2006.

Crump, J. I. *Chan-kuo Ts'e*. Ann Arbor: Center for Chinese Studies, University of Michigan, 1996.

Davis, Albert Richard. *T'ao Yüan-ming (AD 365–427): His Works and Their Meaning*. 2 vols. Cambridge: Cambridge University Press, 1983.

Davis, Bradley C. *Imperial Bandits: Outlaws and Rebels in the China–Vietnam Borderlands*. Seattle: University of Washington Press, 2017.

de Bary, William Theodore. *Sources of East Asian Tradition: Premodern Asia*, vol. 1. New York: Columbia University Press, 2008.

de Crespigny, Rafe. *A Biographical Dictionary of Later Han to the Three Kingdoms, 23–220 A.D.* Leiden: Brill, 2006.

———. *Imperial Warlord: A Biography of Cao Cao 155–220 AD*. Boston: Brill, 2010.

Deng Zhiyuan 邓志瑗 and Deng Gang 邓刚译注. *Youxue qionglin* 幼學瓊林. Jiangnan: Jiangnan renmin chubanshe, 1996.

Di St. Thecla, Adriano. *Opusculum de Sectis apud Sinenses et Tunkinenses (A Small Treatise on the Sects among the Chinese and the Tonkinese): A Study of Religion in China and North Vietnam in the Eighteenth Century*. Trans. and annot. Olga Dror. Ithaca, NY: Cornell University Southeast Asia Program Publications, 2002.

Đông Hồ. *Văn học Hà Tiên* (The Literature of Hà Tiên). Reprint, Ho Chi Minh City: Văn Nghệ, 1999.

Dror, Olga, and Keith Taylor. Introduction. In *Views of Seventeenth-Century Vietnam: Christoforo Borri on Cochinchina and Samuel Baron on Tonkin*. Ithaca, NY: Cornell University Southeast Asia Program Publications, 2006.

Durrant, Stephen W. *The Cloudy Mirror: Tension and Conflict in the Writings of Sima Qian*. Albany: State University of New York Press, 1995.

Dutton, George. *The Tây Sơn Uprising: Society and Rebellion in Eighteenth-Century Vietnam*. Honolulu: University of Hawai'i Press, 2006.

Duyvendak, J. J. L. *The Book of Lord Shang: A Classic of the Chinese School of Law*. London: Arthur Probsthain, 1928.

Ebrey, Patricia. *Emperor Huizong*. Cambridge, MA: Harvard University Press, 2014.

Fei Huang, "The Making of a Frontier Landscape: The 'Ten Views of Dongchuan' in Eighteenth-Century Southwest China." *Late Imperial China* 35, no. 2 (December 2014): 56–88.

Gaspardone, Émile. "Un chinois des mers d u sud, le fondateur de Hà Tiên." *Journal Asiatique* 240, no. 3 (1952): 363–85.

Goodrich, Chauncey S. "The Reign of Wang Mang: Hsin or New?" *Oriens* 10, no. 1 (1957): 114–18.

——. "Ssu-Ma Ch'ien's Biography of Wu Ch'i." *Monumenta Serica* 35 (1981–83): 197–233.

Hãn Nguyên. "Hà Tiên, chìa khóa nam tiến của dân tộc Việt Nam xuống đồng bằng sông Cửu Long" (Hà Tiên, the Key to the Southern Advance of Vietnam into the Mekong Delta). *Sử Địa* 19–20 (July–December 1970): 259–83.

Handler-Spitz, Rivi. *Symptoms of an Unruly Age: Li Zhi and Cultures of Early Modernity.* Seattle: University of Washington Press, 2017.

Hardy, Andrew, and Nguyễn Tiến Đông. "Đá Vách: Nguyễn Cochinchina's Eighteenth-Century Political Crisis and the Origins of Conflict in Quảng Ngãi." Paper presented at "Nguyễn Vietnam: 1558–1885: Domestic Issues," Harvard University Asia Center, May 11–12, 2013.

Harrell, Stevan, ed. *Cultural Encounters on China's Ethnic Frontiers.* Seattle: University of Washington Press, 1995.

He Yuming. *Home and the World: Editing the "Glorious Ming" in Woodblock-Printed Books of the Sixteenth and Seventeenth Centuries.* Cambridge, MA: Harvard University Asia Center, 2013.

Hegel, Robert E., ed. *Idle Talk under the Bean Arbor: A Seventeenth-Century Chinese Story Collection, compiled by Aina the Layman with commentary by Ziran the Eccentric Wanderer.* Seattle: University of Washington Press, 2017.

Hickey, Gerald. *Sons of the Mountains: Ethnohistory of the Vietnamese Central Highlands to 1954.* New Haven, CT: Yale University Press, 1982.

Hightower, James Robert. *The Poetry of T'ao Ch'ien.* Oxford: Claredon Press, 1970.

——. "The Wen Hsüan and Genre Theory." *Harvard Journal of Asiatic Studies* 20, nos. 3–4 (December 1957): 512–33.

Hoàng Xuân Hãn. *Chinh Phụ Ngâm bị khảo.* Paris: Minh Tân, 1953.

Honey, David B. *The Southern Garden Poetry Society: Literary Culture and Social Memory in Guangdong.* Hong Kong: Chinese University Press, 2013.

Hostetler, Laura. *Qing Colonial Enterprise: Ethnography and Cartography in Early Modern China.* Chicago: University of Chicago Press, 2001.

Hsiao Kung-chuan. *A History of Chinese Political Thought.* Trans. F. W. Mote. Princeton, NJ: Princeton University Press, 1979.

Huang Tsung-hsi. *The Records of Ming Scholars: A Selected Translation,* ed. Julia Ching. Honolulu: University of Hawai'i Press, 1987.

Huguet, H. "Les provinces d'Annam—les mois de la région de Quang-Ngai." *Revue Indochinoise,* n.s. 2, 2, no. 19 (October 15, 1905): 1419–29.

Hulsewe, A. F. P. *China in Central Asia: The Early Stage: 125 BC–AD 23; an Annotated Translation of Chapters 61 and 96 of the History of the Former Han Dynasty.* Leiden: Brill, 1979.

Huỳnh Khắc Dụng. *Hát bội, théâtre traditionnel du Việt Nam.* Saigon: Kim Lai Ấn Quán, 1970.

Huỳnh Sanh Thông. *The Song of a Soldier's Wife.* New Haven, CT: Yale Southeast Asian Studies, 1986.

Idema, Wilt L., and Stephen H. West. *Battles, Betrayals, and Brotherhood: Early Chinese Plays on the Three Kingdoms*. Indianapolis, IN: Hackett, 2012.

Kelley, Liam. *Beyond the Bronze Pillars: Envoy Poetry and the Sino-Vietnamese Relationship*. Honolulu: University of Hawai'i Press, 2005.

———. "Thoughts on a Chinese Diaspora: The Case of the Mạcs of Hà Tiên." *Crossroads: An Interdisciplinary Journal of Southeast Asian Studies* 14, no. 1 (2000): 71–98.

——— "Vietnam as a 'Domain of Manifest Civility' (*Văn Hiến chi Bang*)." *Journal of Southeast Asian Studies* 34, no. 1 (February 2003): 63–76.

Knapp, Keith Nathaniel. *Selfless Offspring: Filial Children and Social Order in Medieval China*. Honolulu: University of Hawai'i Press, 2005.

Knechtges, David R., ed. and trans. *Wen xuan, or Selections of Refined Literature*, vol. 1: *Rhapsodies on Metropolises and Capitals*, Xiao Tong (501–531). Princeton, NJ: Princeton University Press, 1982.

———. *Wen xuan, or Selections of Refined Literature*, vol. 2: *Rhapsodies on Sacrifices, Hunting, Travel, Sightseeing, Palaces and Halls, Rivers and Seas*, Xiao Tong (501–531). Princeton, NJ: Princeton University Press, 1987.

Koffler, Jean. "Description historique de la Cochinchine." Trans. V. Barbier. *Revue Indochinoise* 15, no. 5 (May 1911): 448–62; 15, no. 6 (June 1911): 565–75; 16, no. 9 (September 1911): 273–85; and 16, no. 12 (December 1911): 582–607.

Kroll, Paul. "The Life and Writings of Xu Hui (627–650), Worthy Consort, at the Early Tang Court." *Asia Major* 3rd ser., 22, no. 2 (2009): 35–64.

Kuhn, Philip A. *Chinese among Others: Emigration in Modern Times*. Lanham: Rowman and Littlefield, 2009.

Kutcher, Norman. *Mourning in Late Imperial China: Filial Piety and the State*. New York: Cambridge University Press, 1999.

Langlet, Philipe. *L'ancienne historiographie d'Etat au Vietnam*. Paris: Ecole française d'Extrême-Orient, 1985.

Lau, D. C. *Confucius: The Analects*. Harmondsworth: Penguin Books, 1979.

———. *Mencius*. Harmondsworth: Penguin Books, 1970.

Le Blanc, Charles. *Huainanzi: Philosophical Synthesis in Early Han Thought*. Hong Kong: Hong Kong University Press, 1985.

Lê Duy Thiện, trans. *Sãi Vãi luận đàm*. Sài Gòn: Lưu Đức Phương, 1929.

Lê Ngọc Trụ and Phạm Văn Luật. *Truyện Nhị Độ Mai & Nguyễn Cư Trinh với quyển Sãi Vãi*. Paris: Institut de l'Asie du Sud-Est, 1984.

Lê Phước Thành. *Sãi Vãi Luận Đàm*. Sài Gòn: Dực Lưu Phương, 1929.

Lechesne, P. "Les mois du centre Indochinois." *Revue Indochinoise* n.s. 2, 2, nos. 9–10 (September–October 1924): 165–81; 2, nos. 11–12 (November–December 1924): 365–79; 1, nos. 1–2 (January–February 1925): 37–62.

Legge, James. *The Shoo King, or the Book of Historical Documents* [including *The Annals of the Bamboo Books*]. In *The Chinese Classics: With a Translation, Critical and Exegetical Notes, Prolegomena and Copious Indexes*, vol. 3, part 1. London: Trubner, 1865.

———. *The She King, or Book of Poetry*. In *The Chinese Classics: With a Translation, Critical and Exegetical Notes, Prolegomena and Copious Indexes*, vol. 4. London: Trubner, 1871.

"Les mois de la Cochinchine et du Sud-Annam." *Revue Indochinoise Illustrée* ser. 1, 2, no. 4 (November 1893): 42–51.

"Les mois de Ta-my (Région de la cannelle)." *Revue Indochinoise Illustrée* ser. 1, 4, no. 11 (June 1894): 82–113.

Li Tana. "Epidemics, Trade, and Local Worship in Vietnam, Leizhou Peninsula, and Hainan Island." In *Imperial China and its Southern Southern Neighbors*, ed. Victor Mair and Liam Kelley, 194–213. Singapore: Institute of Southeast Asian Studies, 2015.

———. "Jiaochi (Giao Chi) in the Han Period Tongking Gulf." In *The Tongking Gulf through History*, ed. Nola Cooke, Li Tana, and James A. Anderson, 39–52. Philadelphia: University of Pennsylvania Press, 2011.

———. *Nguyễn Cochinchina: Southern Vietnam in the Seventeenth and Eighteenth Centuries*. Ithaca, NY: Cornell University Southeast Asia Program Publications, 1998.

Li Tana and Anthony Reid, eds. *Southern Vietnam under the Nguyễn: Documents on the Economic History of Cochinchina (Đàng Trong), 1602–1777*. Singapore: Institute of Southeast Asian Studies, 1993.

Lin Shuen-fu. "Ci-Poetry: Long Song Lyrics." In *How to Read Chinese Poetry*, ed. Cai Zong-qi New York: Columbia University Press, 2008.

Liu, James C. "Yueh Fei and China's Heritage of Loyalty." *Journal of Asian Studies* 31, no. 2 (February 1972): 291–97.

Luo Yuming. *A Concise History of Chinese Literature*, vol. 1. Trans. Ye Yang. Leiden: Brill, 2011.

Lynn, Richard John. *The Classic of Changes: A New Translation of the I Ching as interpreted by Wang Bi*. New York: Columbia University Press, 1994.

Mair, Victor. *Wandering on the Way: Early Taoist Tales and Parables of Chuang Tzu*. Honolulu: University of Hawai'i Press, 1998.

Mann, Susan. *Precious Records: Women in China's Long Eighteenth Century*. Stanford, CA: Stanford University Press, 1997.

Maybon, Charles. "Jean Koffler, auteur de Historica Cochinchinae Descriptio." *Revue Indochinoise* 17 (June 1912): 539–53.

McKeown, Adam. *Chinese Migrant Networks and Cultural Change: Peru, Chicago, Hawaii, 1900–1936*. Chicago: University of Chicago Press, 2001.

Meyer-Fong, Tobie. *Building Culture in Early Qing Yangzhou*. Stanford CA: Stanford University Press, 2003.

Mote, Frederick. "Confucian Eremitism in the Yüan Period." In *The Confucian Persuasion*, ed. Arthur Wright, 202–40. Stanford, CA: Stanford University Press, 1960.

———. *Imperial China, 900–1800*. Cambridge, MA: Harvard University Press, 1999.

Murray, Dian H. *Pirates of the South China Coast, 1790–1810*. Stanford CA: Stanford University Press, 1987.

Murray, Julia K. "Didactic Illustration in Printed Books." In *Printing and Book Culture in Late Imperial China*, ed. Cynthia J. Brokaw and Kai-wing Chow, 417–50. Berkeley: University of California Press, 2005.

———. "From Textbook to Testimonial: The Emperor's Mirror, an Illustrated Discussion (Di jian tu shuo/Teikan Zusetsu) in China and Japan." *Ars Orientalis* 31 (2001): 65–101.

Neininger, Ulrich. "Burying the Scholars Alive: On the Origin of a Confucian Martyrs' Legend." In *East Asian Civilizations: New Attempts at Understanding Traditions*, ed. Wolfram Eberhard et al., 2:121–36. Munich: Simon and Magiera, 1983.

Newby, L. J. "The Chinese Literary Conquest of Xinjiang." *Modern China* 25, no. 4 (October 1999): 451–74.

Nguyễn Cư Trinh. *Câu chuyện Sãi Vãi*. Trans. Dương Mạnh Huy. Sài Gòn: Tín Đức Thư Xã, 1929.

Nguyễn Gia Thiều. *Cung oán ngâm khúc* (Elegy of Resentment in the Palace, 宮怨吟曲). Hà Nội: Văn Học, 1994.

Nguyễn Lộc. *Từ Điển Nghệ Thuật Hát Bội Việt Nam*. Hanoi: Khoa Học Xã Hội, 1998.

Nguyễn Tài Thư, chief ed., Hoàng Thị Thơ, assistant ed., Dinh Minh Chi, Ly Kim Hoa, Ha Thuc Minh, and Ha Van Tan. *The History of Buddhism in Vietnam*. Washington, DC: Council for Research in Values and Philosophy, Vietnamese Academy of Social Sciences, 2008.

Nguyễn Tô Lan. *Khảo luận về tuồng Quần Phương Tập Khánh*. Hanoi: Thế Giới, 2014.

Nguyen Tu Cuong. *Zen in Medieval Vietnam: A Study and Translation of the "Thiền Uyển Tập Anh."* Honolulu: University of Hawai'i Press, 1997.

Nguyễn Văn Sâm. *Văn học Nam Hà: Văn học Đường Trong thời phân tranh* (Literature of the Southern Region: Literature of Đàng Trong in the Period of Separation). Sài Gòn: Phong Phú, 1974.

Nienhauser, William, Jr., ed. *The Grand Scribe's Records*. Multiple volumes. Bloomington: Indiana University Press, 1995–2016.

Niu Junkai and Li Qingxin. "Chinese 'Political Pirates' in the Seventeenth-Century Tongking Gulf." In *The Tongking Gulf through History*, ed. Nola Cooke, Li Tana, and James A. Anderson, 133–42. Philadelphia: University of Pennsylvania Press, 2011.

Owen, Stephen. *An Anthology of Chinese Literature: Beginnings to 1911*. New York: Norton, 1996.

———. *The Great Age of Chinese Poetry: The High Tang*, rev. ed. Basel: Quirin Press, 2013.

———. *The Poetry of the Early Tang*, rev. ed. Basel: Quirin Press, 2012.

———. "Reading the Landscape." In *The End of the Chinese 'Middle Ages': Essays in Mid-Tang Literary Culture*, 34–54. Stanford, CA: Stanford University Press, 1996.

Phan Hứa Thụy. *Thơ văn Nguyễn Cư Trinh* (Poetic Literature of Nguyễn Cư Trinh). Huế: Thuận Hóa, 1989.

Pulleyblank, E. G. *The Background of the Rebellion of An Lushan*. Oxford: Oxford University Press, 1955.

Richter, Antje. *Letters and Epistolary Culture in Early Medieval China*. Seattle: University of Washington Press, 2013.

Rickett, Allyn. *Guanzi: Political, Economic, and Philosophical Essays from Early China: A Study and Translation*, 2 vols. Princeton, NJ: Princeton University Press, 1998.

Robson, James. *Power of Place: The Religious Landscape of the Southern Sacred Peak (Nanyue 南嶽) in Medieval China*. Cambridge, MA: Harvard University Asia Center, 2009.

Sakurai, Yumio. "Eighteenth-Century Chinese Pioneers on the Water Frontier of Indochina." In *Water Frontier: Commerce and the Chinese in the Lower Mekong Region, 1750–1880*, ed. Nola Cooke and Li Tana, 35–52. Singapore: Singapore University Press and Lanham, MD: Rowman and Littlefield, 2004.

Salmon, Claudine. *Ming Loyalists in Southeast Asia as Perceived through Various Asian and European Records*. Wiesbaden: Harrassowitz, 2014.

Sargent, Clyde Bailey. *Wang Mang: A Translation of the Official Account of His Rise to Power as Given in the History of the Former Han Dynasty*. Shanghai: Graphic Art Book Company, 1947.

Sawyer, Ralph D. *The Seven Military Classics of Ancient China*. New York: Basic Books, 2007.

Scott, James C. *The Art of Not Being Governed: An Anarchist History of Upland Southeast Asia*. New Haven, CT: Yale University Press, 2009.

Shafer, Edward. *The Vermilion Bird: T'ang Images of the South*. Berkeley: University of California Press, 1967.

Shih, Vincent Yu-chung. *The Literary Mind and the Carving of Dragons*, rev. ed. Hong Kong: Chinese University of Hong Kong Press, 2015.

Shin, Leo. *The Making of the Chinese State: Ethnicity and Expansion on the Ming Borderlands*. Cambridge: Cambridge University Press, 2006.

Soymie, Michel. "Le Lo-Feou Chan: Etude de Geographie Religieus." *Bulletin de l'École française d'Extrême-Orient* 48, no. 1 (1956): 1–139.

Stein, Rolf A. *The World in Miniature: Container Gardens and Dwellings in Far Eastern Religious Thought*. Trans. Phyllis Brooks. Stanford, CA: Stanford University Press, 1990.

Sterckx, Roel. *Food, Sacrifice, and Sagehood in Early China*. New York: Cambridge University Press, 2011.

Strange, Mark. "Representations of the Liang Emperor Wu as a Buddhist Ruler in Sixth- and Seventh-Century Texts." *Asia Major* 24, no. 2 (2011): 53–112.

Strassberg, Richard E. *A Chinese Bestiary: Strange Creatures from the Guideways through Mountains and Seas*. Berkeley: University of California Press, 2002.

———. *Inscribed Landscapes: Travel Writing from Imperial China*. Berkeley: Universty of California Press, 1994.

Struve, Lynn A. "The Southern Ming, 1644–1662." In *The Cambridge History of China, vol. 7, The Ming Dynasty, 1368–1644, Part 1*, ed. Frederick W. Mote and Denis Twitchett, 710–25. Cambridge: Cambridge University Press, 1988.

Taberd, J. L. *Dictonarium Anamtico-Latinum*. Reprint, Hà Nội: Văn Học, 2004.

Taylor, Keith W. *A History of the Vietnamese*. Cambridge: Cambridge University Press, 2013.

———. "Nguyễn Hoàng and the Beginning of Việt Nam's Southward Expansion." In *Southeast Asia in the Early Modern Era*, ed. Anthony Reid, 42–85. Ithaca, NY: Cornell University Press, 1993.

———. "Surface Orientations in Vietnam: Beyond Histories of Nation and Region." *Journal of Asian Studies* 57, no. 4 (November 1998): 949–78.

Teng, Emma Jinhua. *Taiwan's Imagined Geography: Chinese Colonial Travel Writing, 1683–1895*. Cambridge, MA: Harvard University Asia Center, 2004.

Thich Thien-An. *Buddhism and Zen in Vietnam in Relation to the Development of Buddhism in Asia.* Ed. Carol Smith. Los Angeles: College of Oriental Studies, Graduate School, 1975.

Tran Tuyet Nhung. *Familial Properties: Gender, State, and Society in Early Modern Vietnam, 1463–1778.* Honolulu: University of Hawai'i Press, 2018.

Trương Minh Đạt. *Nghiên cứu Hà Tiên* (Research on Hà Tiên). Ho Chi Minh City: Trẻ, 2008.

Từ điển Phật học Hán Việt (Han-Việt Buddhist Dictionary), 2 vols. Hà Nội: Nông Nghiệp, 1992.

Waley, Arthur. *The Book of Songs: The Ancient Chinese Classic of Poetry*, rev. ed. Ed. Joseph R. Allen. New York: Grove Press, 1996.

———. *Yuan Mei.* London: George Allen and Unwin, 1956.

Warner, Ding Xiang. "The Two Voices of *Wangchuan Ji*: Poetic Exchange between Wang Wei and Pei Di." *Early Medieval China* 10–11, no. 2 (2005): 57–72.

Watson, Burton. *The Complete Works of Chuang Tzu.* New York: Columbia University Press, 1968.

———. *Courtier and Commoner in Ancient China: Selections from the History of the Former Han by Pan Ku.* New York: Columbia University Press, 1974.

———. *Records of the Historian: Chapters from the Shih chi of Ssu-ma Ch'ien.* New York: Columbia University Press, 1969.

———. *Records of the Grand Historian: Qin Dynasty.* New York: Columbia University Press, 1993.

West, Stephen, and Wilt Idema. *Monks, Bandits, Lovers, and Immortals.* Indianapolis, IN: Hackett, 2010.

Wheeler, Charles. "Buddhism in the Re-ordering of an Early Modern World: Chinese Missions to Cochinchina in the Seventeenth Century." *Journal of Global History* 2, no. 3 (November 2007): 303–24.

Wilhelm, Hellmut. "From Myth to Myth: The Case of Yue Fei's Biography." In *Confucian Personalities*, ed. Arthur F. Wright and Denis C. Twitchett, 146–61. Stanford, CA: Stanford University Press, 1962.

———. "Shih Ch'ung and His Chin-Ku-Yüan." *Monumenta Serica* 18 (1959): 314–27.

Wilkinson, Endymion. *Chinese History: A New Manual.* Cambridge, MA: Harvard University Asia Center, 2012.

Wolters, O. W. "Assertions of Cultural Well-Being in Fourteenth-Century Vietnam," parts 1 and 2. *Journal of Southeast Asian Studies* 10, no. 2 (September 1979): 435–50 and 11, no. 1 (March 1980): 74–90.

Woodside, Alexander. "Central Vietnam's Trading World in the Eighteenth Century as Seen in Lê Quý Đôn's 'Frontier Chronicles.'" In *Essays into Vietnamese Pasts*, ed. Keith W. Taylor and John K. Whitmore, 157–72. Ithaca, NY: Cornell University Southeast Asia Program Press, 1995.

———. "Conceptions of Change and of Human Responsibility for Change in Late Traditional Vietnam." In *Moral Order and the Question of Change: Essays on Southeast Asian Thought*, ed. David K. Wyatt and Alexander Woodside, 104–50. New Haven, CT: Yale University Southeast Asia Studies, 1982.

Wu Fusheng. "Sao Poetry: The Lyrics of Chu." In *How to Read Chinese Poetry: A Guided Anthology*, ed. Cai Zong-qi, 36–56. New York: Columbia University Press, 2008.

Wyatt, David. *Thailand: A Short History*. Reprint, Bangkok: Silkworm Books, 2002.

Xiong, Victor Cunrui. *Emperor Yang of Sui: His Life, Times, and Legacy*. Albany: State University of New York Press, 2006.

Yang Jun 杨君. *Ershisi xiao tushuo* 二十四孝圖説 (Twenty-four Filial Exemplars, an Illustrated Discussion). Shanghai: Shanghai daxue chubanshe, 2006.

Ye Jiaying 葉嘉瑩. *Du Fu qiuxing ba shou jishuo* 杜甫秋興八首集説 (Du Fu's Eight "Autumn Meditations," a Discussion). Reprint, Shijiazhuangshi: Hebei jiaoyu chubanshe, 1998.

Yu Insun. "Lê Văn Hưu and Ngô Sĩ Liên: A Comparison of Their Perception of Vietnamese History." In *Việt Nam: Borderless Histories*, ed. Nhung Tuyet Tran and Anthony Reid, 45–71. Madison: University of Wisconsin Press, 2005.

Yu, Pauline. *The Poetry of Wang Wei*. Bloomington: Indiana University Press, 1980.

Index

Page numbers for maps and figures are in italics.

Guangdong province, 13, 121–22, 156, 159, 198; coastal trading system and, 127, 155; Foshan, 228; Golden Jade House publisher, 228; landscape poetry of, 194

Guanzi, 99

Gugong Danfu (v: Cổ Công Đản Phủ), 80

"Guifang" (v: Quỷ Phương) states, 177

Gulf of Siam, 1, 159n66

Gu Sou (v: Cổ Tẩu), 74, 77, 81

Han dynasty, 54, 55, 60, 94, 177n25; battle of Red Cliff, 134; Emperor Gaozu, 96; founder of, 92, 104; officials of, 75, 95; transition from Qin, 220

Han shu (*History of the Han dynasty*), 67n21, 70n26, 76n40, 92n14

Han Tiying (v: Hán Đề Oánh), 68, 70, 71

Han tradition/world, 51, 52, 83; universal status of, 53; vernacular Vietnamese alongside, 82; Vietnamese literati in, 52

Han Wudi (v: Võ Đế), 59, 60, 61, 75

Han Xin (v: Hàn Tín), 96, 104n44

hát bội ("Vietnamese opera"), 26–27, 32–33

Hà Tiên, *xvi*, 2, 121, 164, 209, 211; Chinese settlement at, 6, 123; depicted as mysterious and foreign, 198, 204; depicted as uncivilized, 204; fortress wall of, 136; incorporation into expanding Vietnamese state, 13n31, 198; Khmer kings' flight to, 167, 168, 170; landscape of, 3, 123, 124, 126, 143; Mạc Thiên Tứ in, 12–15; Mạc Thiên Tứ's administration of, 121, 123, 197, 209; Ming loyalists in, 155, 159, *160*, 161, 162, 193; as ostensible land of barbarism, 17; as periphery of Chinese cultural civilization, 131, 139; pillaged by Siamese troops, 225; place in cultured discourse, 19; as stronghold of Đàng Trong, 201; trading networks of,

13, 14, 127, 137, 144, 155. See also *Ten Songs of Hà Tiên*

heart-mind (v: *tâm*, p: *xin*), 185, 186, 188–89

He Jin (v: Hà Tiến), 102, 103

Hou Jing (v: Hầu Cảnh), 62

Hrê people, 109, 116

Huang Gong (v: Hoàng Công), 174, 177

Huang Jin (v: Hoàng Tiến), 156, 158

Huan of Qi, Duke (v: Tề Hoàn Công), 182

Huan Xuan (v: Hoàn Huyền), 69

Huizong (v: Tống Huy Tông), Emperor, 61

"human heartedness" (v: *nhân*, p: *ren*), 74, 78

humor: in public entertainment, 23–25, 32; in the *Sãi Vãi*, 29, 33, 35, 41

hyperbole, 31, 42, 51

Japan, 6, 14n33

Jesuits, 23–25

Ji, Viscount of (v: Cơ Tử), 80

Jiang Ziya (v: Khương Tử Nha), 87n2, 88, 177n25

Jia Yi (v: Giả Nghi), 174n16

Jie (v: Kiệt), King, 96, 98

Jin dynasty, 31, 32, 69, 176

jingwei bird, 193, 195

Journey to the West (v: *Tây Du Ký*, p: *Xiyou ji*), 106n47

Jurchens, 61

Khitan Liao, 60, 63

Khmer kings, 2, 127, 164

Khmer language and people, 1, 13, 14n33

Koffler, Jean, 26, 27

Kou Zhun (v: Khấu Chuẩ), 63n18

Ku (v: Khốc), King, 204n11

Kumarajiva, 57, 58

language: cultural projects and, 15–20; world shaped and patterned by, 202

Laozi, 210

Harvard East Asian Monographs
(most recent titles)